2004

PEACE IN THE MIDST OF WARS

STUDIES IN INTERNATIONAL RELATIONS
Charles W. Kegley, Jr., and Donald J. Puchala, Series Editors

PEACE
IN THE
MIDST
OF WARS

Preventing
and Managing
International
Ethnic Conflicts

edited by
David Carment and Patrick James

UNIVERSITY OF SOUTH CAROLINA PRESS

Library of Congress Cataloging-in-Publication Data

The international politics of ethnic conflict : prevention and
peacekeeping / edited by David Carment and Patrick James.
    p. cm. — (Studies in international relations)
  Includes bibliographical references and index.
  ISBN 1570032173
  1. Ethnic relations—Political aspects. 2. Culture conflict. 3.
Political violence. 4. International relations. 5. Conflict
management. I. Carment, David, 1959– II. James, Patrick, 1957– III.
Series: Studies in international relations (Columbia, S.C.)
  GN496 .I594 1998
  303.48'2—ddc218910   98-8910

Dedications

Dedicated to Carolyn James,
and Madeleine, Martine, Eleanor, and Bill

CONTENTS

SERIES EDITORS' PREFACE

The pace of global change has accelerated greatly in the last decades of the twentieth century, and new problems occurring under novel conditions are challenging the academic study of international relations. There is today a renaissance in scholarship directed toward enhancing our understanding of world politics, global economics, and foreign policy. In examining the changing structure of the international system and the expanded agenda of global affairs, researchers are introducing new concepts, theories, and analytic models. Knowledge is expanding rapidly.

Our goal in this series of books is to record the findings of recent innovative research and theorizing in international relations and to make them readily available to a broader readership of professionals and students. Contributors to the series are leading scholars who are experts in subfields of the discipline of international relations. Their contributions represent the most recent work located at the discipline's research frontiers. Topics, subjects, approaches, methods, and analytical techniques vary from one volume to the next in the series, as each book is intended as an original contribution in the broadest sense. Common to all volumes, however, are careful research and the excitement of new discovery.

Peace in the Midst of Wars: Preventing and Managing International Ethnic Conflicts is a welcome addition to Studies in International Relations. It speaks directly to our goal of publishing innovative and conceptually rich writings in international relations which deal with the most timely topics on the emerging global agenda. David Carment and Patrick James have produced a very insightful anthology of original and provocative interpretations of theories bearing on the control of ethnic conflict, and as a result the book well serves the scholarly mission of our series.

Although broad in scope and comprehensive in coverage, *Peace in the Midst of Wars: Preventing and Managing International Ethnic Conflicts* is integrated in content and focused in purpose. The volume successfully pursues three goals: to identify the conditions most likely to lead to an outbreak of violent ethnic conflict, to assess third-party interventionary strategies for the containment and reduction of ethnic strife, and to identify the circumstances under which active peacekeeping operations are most likely to be effective. Hence, the anthology provides a context to facilitate the study of violent ethnic conflicts and the available methods for managing them, in order to broaden our understanding of alternative peacekeeping and conflict-prevention policies and improve their chances of success.

We are confident that the contributors' essays break new ground in achieving these ambitious objectives. Students of international relations are certain to find much in the collection of essays that enlightens and provokes. In the context of ongoing theoretical debates in our discipline, Carment and James and their colleagues challenge many contending approaches currently being proposed about peacekeeping and humanitarian intervention, and also raise important questions about the most efficacious methods for managing the epidemic of ethnic conflicts that has erupted throughout the world since the end of the Cold War. While these creative analyses collectively integrate existing works into their treatment, the contributors go beyond criticism of orthodoxy and detached analysis by also generating imaginative policy prescriptions. Throughout, the treatments rest on firm empirical evidence, and the new insights exert pressure for rethinking an area of international relations that promises to expand in the future, if only because the problem of ethnic conflict shows no evidence of diminishing as a key concern in world affairs. This book is likely to become the seminal starting point for new research. We are proud to publish it in our series.

Charles W. Kegley, Jr.
Donald J. Puchala

ACKNOWLEDGMENTS

The editors are grateful to several organizations and people who helped to bring the volume to completion. We would like to thank the Co-operative Security Programme of the Department of Foreign Affairs and International Trade (Canada) for a very generous grant that permitted us to hold two conferences. At these gatherings, six months apart from each other, drafts of the respective chapters were developed, and all those in attendance benefited from a lively exchange of ideas. We are grateful to McGill University and Florida State University for hosting those conferences.

The authors also would like to thank the excellent scholars who read and supplied valuable commentaries on various chapters in this volume: Mark Brawley, Michael Brecher, Dave Davis, Andre Donneur, David Goetze, Ted Robert Gurr, Fen Hampson, Athanasios Hristoulas, Keith Jaggers, David Lake, Douglas Lemke, David Long, Zeev Maoz, Monty Marshall, Pierre Martin, Manus Midlarsky, Will Moore, T. V. Paul, James Lee Ray, Dale Smith, John Stack, Jonathan Wilkenfeld, and Franke Wilmer.

We are also grateful to Suzannah Baum, Mike Elliot, Michael Penner, Troy Joseph, Scott Jenkins, and Ryan Larson for excellent service as research assistants. David Carment also wishes to thank the Security and Defence Forum of the Department of National Defence (Canada), the Social Sciences and Humanities Research Council of Canada, the Fonds de Chercheurs et l'Aide à la Recherche, NATO, and the Hoover Institution (Stanford University) for their support in this research.

I

Ethnic Conflict at the International Level

Causation, Prevention, and Peacekeeping

David Carment and Patrick James

The most stubborn facts are those of the spirit not those of the physical world and one of the most stubborn facts of the spirit remains nationalist feeling....
Quoted in Knight (1984: 520) (Gottman 1951)

The government is best which pays least attention to ethnicity.
Van den Berghe (1987: 353–54).

INTRODUCTION

Given the basic truth contained in the first quotation, it is unlikely that governments will be able to take the advice of the second at any point in the near future. Governments and international organizations alike face a rapidly changing matrix of ethnic nationalisms that coexist with quasi-sovereign states. For those living in such a period, the desire for greater stability is overwhelming. This is becoming almost as true for worried spectators in calm and prosperous locations as it is for those unfortunate enough to be caught in the middle of simmering or openly violent conflict.[1]

As Michael Ignatieff argued in 1993, "huge sections of the world's population have won the right of self determination on the cruelest possible terms: they have been simply left to fend for themselves. Not surprisingly, their nation-states are collapsing" (8). Robert Kaplan's highly influential 1994 *Atlantic Monthly* article on the "The Coming Anarchy" offered a more bleak assessment of state failure in Africa. In this pessimistic assessment the world is plagued by increasing conflict and crises generated by ethnic strife and weakening state capacity to regulate conflict where it is most needed.[2]

Ethnic conflict presents a sustained and serious challenge to theories and policies on prevention, management, and resolution. Pervasive ethnic struggle, the defining characteristic of the post-Cold War era, reflects the inability of whole systems to confront and solve this state-level problem. The record of ethnic strife indicates that while awareness of danger is more acute, the international community is slow to close the gap between conflict formation on the one hand and mediation or resolution on the other.[3] Intervention in the form of missions or mediation often comes too late—only after violence and hostility are widespread. The ability to anticipate, understand, and mediate conflicts before they become violent needs to be upgraded (Diehl, Reifschneider, and Hensel 1996).[4]

CAUSATION

Three objectives motivate this volume. The first is to identify domestic and international conditions associated with the onset of violent ethnic strife. A second task is to relate this knowledge to preventive strategies for third-party intervention that promote early and rapid de-escalation of tensions. Third, and perhaps most challenging, is the search for conditions under which proactive, conventional, and aggravated peacekeeping operations are likely to succeed. With respect to policy, the volume's approach is to provide a practical context for study of the potential for violent ethnic conflicts and existing mechanisms to deal with them; evaluate regional and international instruments for conflict prevention; and suggest a set of measures for the improvement of peacekeeping and conflict prevention policies. The rest of this chapter consists of an outline that links the forthcoming chapters to the three major objectives.

Factors that generate conflict may differ from those that produce escalation to violence. Indeed, the label "ethnic conflict" itself reveals very little about what underlies intercommunal tensions. In the abstract these problems may be about human rights, participation, and justice, while concrete manifestations become ethnic because that is the basis for exclusion or repression. Furthermore, the positive attributes of conflict itself should not be overlooked.

The term properly refers to a situation of discord between two or more parties, which either can be resolved peacefully or through aggression. Conflict means a perceived divergence of interest or a belief that the current aspirations of the antagonists cannot be achieved simultaneously.

Unlike most conflicts, which are not zero-sum, ethnic strife unfolds against a backdrop of fear that it will be resolved through destruction or assimilation of a group. Vital interests are likely to be perceived and threatened in the context of incompatible and incontrovertible demands. For elites who play on these fears, the benefits are obvious. Conflict serves a functional, potentially positive role for the elite and its followers. When group cohesion is relatively low, performance expectations may be the only way to ensure mobilization, cohesion, and stronger support—conflict is transformed or escalated. New issues become salient, the conflict spreads, and a pernicious cycle begins. Ethnic conflicts are eruptions of intense, direct, physical violence, but they may also refer to organized or unorganized resistance to the dominant group's discrimination, exploitation, and other kinds of felt oppression (Kriesberg). Most, if not all, serious ethnic conflicts arise because the parties concerned believe there to be incompatible interests between them. These may be about the constitutional status of the groups, the degree of autonomy groups are to enjoy, the future destiny of particular regions, or the sense of injustice that can arise when there is not deemed to be a fair allocation of resources.

Stavenhagen makes a similar point when he argues that ethnic conflicts "generally involve a clash of interests or a struggle over rights: rights to land, education, the use of language, political representation, freedom of religion, the preservation of ethnic identity, autonomy, or self-determination, etc." (1990: 77). When choices are far-ranging, finding a compromise on specific issues such as minority language rights is almost impossible. More than one observer has noted that, at the outset, ethnic conflict (either in perception or reality) normally approximates a zero-sum game for one or both sides. Initial military and political gains often define the entitlements that an ethnic group will enjoy for decades to come. Thus, armed struggle frequently becomes the defining characteristic of an ethnic group; it is the result of a movement's quest for identity, positive distinctiveness, and cohesion.[5]

Various theories provide important clues about the motivation behind demands for a distinct national identity and some form of political, social, or territorial separation based on common ethnocultural features. For primordialists, the motivation comes from subjective, psychological forces internal to the individual and related to the basic human need for communal organization and survival (Geertz 1973; Isaacs 1975). Individuals are bound to an ethnic group "in great part by virtue of some unaccountable absolute import attributed to the very tie itself" (Geertz 1973: 259).

Although shared historical experiences and cultural traits may strengthen ethnic identities, the pressure such forces exert on individuals and groups is variable. Explanations for this variability have underscored the prominent role played by ethnic elites in the mobilization process. These "instrumentalists" posit that ethnicity is a resource that becomes politicized by ethnic elites in the competition for power, prestige, and authority (Rothschild 1981). In fact, ethnicity enhances the ability of group leaders to mobilize support by "facilitating identification of potential supporters," thereby making it easier to detect and sanction free riders (Mason 1994: 9).

Others conceptualize the mobilization of ethnicity in the language of pluralism and the competition over scarce economic and political resources (Furnivall 1948; Gellner 1964; Smith 1965; Hechter 1975; Despres 1976; Horowitz 1985). Where culturally divergent groups inhabit a common society, there is a "structural imperative" in which one group becomes subordinate to another (Smith 1965: 62). This is especially common when ethnic cleavages are reinforced by differences in class and status (Hechter 1975) or when labor markets are divided along ethnic lines (Smith 1981, 1986).

Ethnonationalism also has been interpreted as a defense against the forces of modernization—i.e., contemporary conditions of rapid social and technological change, intrusive state institutions, impersonal bureaucracies, an absence of political consensus, etc.—that tend to create a sense of "anomie" and a "loss of identity." Under these conditions, people may rediscover their ethnicity as a way of establishing the emotional security that comes from communal association.

Crighton and MacIver (1991) have shown that ethnic conflict often requires at least three necessary and sufficient conditions: a threat to the identity and/or existence of the ethnic group; elites with the political skills and resources to play on those fears; and third-party military, political, and economic support for the cause. Van Evera (1994) also addressed the interdependence of causal factors in his study of nationalism and war, which measured the relative importance of structural (geographic and demographic), political/environmental (institutions), and perceptual (nationalist self-image) variables to determine when and under what conditions nationalist sentiments are more or less likely to lead to violence.

Repression of minorities and ethnic conflict go hand in hand. Between 1945 and 1980 there was a gradual increase in ethnic rebellion and nonviolent protest among ethnic groups. As new institutionally weak and divided states emerged on the geopolitical map in the 1960s the upward trend in violent ethnic conflict began. The trend is most closely associated with decolonization and contention for state power in Africa and Asia. However, the collapse of the Soviet Union and all other European communist states has since provided the basis for ethnic rebellions in these transitional states. As a consequence, overall levels of ethnic violence in the international system reached a peak in the 1990s.[6]

By 1993 there were at least forty-eight existing or potentially violent ethnic conflicts in progress, including those in Romania, Mauritania, Rwanda-Burundi, Senegal, Togo, Nigeria, Kenya, Papua New Guinea, Algeria, Fiji, Egypt, China, Bhutan, Brazil, Mexico, India, Kosovo, Albania, Greece, Bulgaria, East Timor, the Republic of Macedonia, and Tajikistan.

By 1996, the total number of ongoing serious conflicts (those with one thousand or more battlefield fatalities) had declined either because of military defeat, government concessions, or some form of concerted third-party intervention. Some long-standing conflicts were either settled or at least brought to a truce during which the ethnic cleansing and bombing campaigns were interrupted. Among the most notable settlements were those in Bosnia, Northern Ireland, and the Philippines. These successes contrast with failed attempts of governments to end internal wars in the Sudan, Burma, India, Iraq, and Sri Lanka.

There are still a number of evolving conflicts about which we can be far less certain. These are cases not easily understood from a conventional security perspective. Even in developed societies fragmented along ethnic lines, genuine attempts at liberalization or democratization can lead to ethnic chauvinism, interelite struggles for power, and the shattering of fragile states.

Extreme cases usually involve a combination of refugee flows, political assassinations, military intervention, and state collapse. Most, but not all, are concentrated in Sub-Saharan Africa and involve states that were functionally weak prior to the end of the Cold War. Liberia, Rwanda, and Zaire are notable examples.

While studied primarily at the domestic level, ethnic conflict also creates interstate spillover effects. Strife in Bosnia, Rwanda, and elsewhere opens a range of interstate possibilities that is difficult to comprehend. The line that separates internal from external processes is especially easy to cross because of several interlocking factors: the increasing importance of global diasporas, large-scale refugee flows, transnational media networks, the worldwide market for small arms, and expanding global support for human rights. On the other hand, protracted regional conflicts and intervention in civil wars represent better-understood connections between the domestic and international levels.

The literature on the relationship between security and ethnic conflict suggests that ethnic conflict carries serious risks of contagion and diffusion through horizontal escalation. Most diffusion is sustained through ethnic diasporas which provide material and nonmaterial support for politically mobilized ethnic groups in the following ways:

> the mobilization of political and ideological support from kindred groups in third countries, foreign governments, and international or nongovernmental organizations; the establishment of sanctuaries in neighboring countries, particularly common where insurgent minorities are dispersed over two or more contiguous states (for example, the Kurds in Turkey, Iran, and Iraq); the spillover of violence into neighboring countries (Rwanda/Zaire, Sri Lanka/India, and Afghanistan/Pakistan, among other examples); the spillover of terrorist violence into countries that are geographically distant from the initial locus of conflict (Irish terrorist operations on the European continent, Sikh terrorist operations in Europe and North America); flights of refugees now numbering in the tens of millions, the vast majority of whom are displaced by ethnic conflicts.

Rwanda is a telling case. In the spring of 1996, nineteen United Nations member countries released a report entitled *The Interna-*

tional Response to Conflict and Genocide (Joint Evaluation of Emergency Assistance to Rwanda, 1996). The report assessed the failure of the UN Assistance Mission in Rwanda (UNAMIR) to prevent the massacre of approximately five hundred thousand to eight hundred thousand Tutsi and moderate Hutu citizens of Rwanda. The UN formally designated the mass murders as genocide. Between April and July 1994 an estimated eight thousand people were systematically killed *per day* by extremist Hutus bent on finding a "final solution" to the long and sordid history of ethnic killing in Rwanda. In the fall of 1996 Hutu "warrior refugees" as well as moderate Hutus scattered across the Zaire-Rwanda border were caught in crises involving the armies of Rwanda and Zaire and paramilitary Tutsi ethnic militias. The on-again, off-again conflict continues to threaten to engulf all of Central Africa.

According to the report, errors in interpreting the crisis and the reluctance of Security Council members to commit money or troops to the conflict in a small country of no strategic importance explains the United Nations' failure to prevent genocide in Rwanda.[7] The report concludes that the UN needs to develop a more effective early warning system. More specifically, the UN General Assembly should develop criteria for proclaiming a "genocide emergency" as well as a new type of mandate for UN interventions that would fall somewhere between traditional peacekeeping and full-scale Chapter VII operations.

PHASES

Ethnic conflicts cannot be resolved without the consent and cooperation of the adversaries. While it is difficult to identify all the parties to conflicts within states (and often impossible for states to agree on their status), the failure to acknowledge movements with popular support may undermine moderates, accelerate militancy, and lead to escalating violence. Conflicts become intractable when discussion of issues gives way to symbols, polarized communities begin to vilify each other as scapegoats, and control of territory by a community becomes nonnegotiable. A major priority, therefore, is to gain support from the parties to a conflict before they learn through bitter experience the need to deal constructively with their differences.

Table 1.1 identifies this downward spiral into violence and the chapters in this volume that focus on the respective phases of conflict prevention. The phase concept builds on the work of Kriesberg and Ryan (chapters 2 and 6, respectively). The table is intended to explicate relationships among phases, appropriate international actions, and ultimate goals. No effort is made at this stage to link specific actions with a given phase—that task is carried out in subsequent chapters. The table is laid out in a step-level fashion to emphasize the time-dependent relationship between phases and desired goals. It should be noted that few conflicts follow a truly linear path to resolution (Kriesberg).[8] In particular, ethnic conflict resolution, the ultimate goal, rarely is approximated.

Table 1.1

Conflict Prevention: Phases, Actions, and Goals

Phases	Condition	Actions	Goals
Conflict formulations (2)	Latent Conflict/ Unstable Relations	Preventive Diplomacy/ Preventive Deployment (3, 4, 7)	Mitigate/Stabilize
Conflict Escalation (2)	Sporadic Violence/ High Tensions	Crisis Management/ Crisis Intervention (3, 4, 5, 8, 10)	De-escalate/Reduce Violence
Conflict Endurance	Intense Armed Violence	Mediation/Peacekeeping/ Peace Enforcement (4–8)	Control/Contain Violence
Conflict Termination	Conflict Termination	Negotiation/ Peacekeeping (2, 3, 6, 9, 10)	Prevent Recurrence
Conflict Resolution	Conflict Resolution	New Institutions and Projects/Peacebuilding (10)	Address Underlying Sources of Conflict

Note: chapters covering the respective topics are notated in parentheses.

Chapter 2, by Kriesberg, examines the causes and context of ethnic strife with a view to specifying political and historical conditions associated with conflict escalation and diffusion. Kriesberg introduces evidence into the debate on why ethnic conflict emerges in some societies and not in others and why some conflicts become violent while others do not. On the one hand, it is believed widely that the collapse of ethnically divided states signals the rebirth of ancient and irrational tribal hatreds. When states are confronted with the simultaneous tasks of political and economic liberalization, antagonisms grow and take on numerous political, economic, and international patterns. Instrumental in this process of disintegration are nationalist ideology and party pluralism. Popular appeals to long-held and dormant ethnic grievances result in a self-destructive escalation of conflict, diffusion, and violence. On the other hand, compelling theoretical reasons suggest that individuals within ethnic groups act on rational impulses even when pursuing violent strategies. Interaction effects between leaders and the groups who support them are significant; collective action results from either historical struggles for autonomy and self-determination or outgrowths of current political processes.

Kriesberg's chapter provides a pertinent introduction to the sources and phases of ethnic conflict and seeks an answer to a basic question: what proactive measures are appropriate within respective phases of an ethnic conflict? More specifically, what domestic and international policies can prevent communal conflict from deteriorating into destructive behavior? The findings are based in part on the seminal work of the research program on the analysis and resolution of conflicts undertaken at Syracuse University under Kriesberg's direction. This chapter performs an essential introductory task in the study of ethnic strife and is relevant to practitioners of conflict resolution techniques as well as members of the policy-making community.

Kriesberg suggests that many conflict resolution techniques can be identified and most of them have been used effectively. Noting successes, not just failures, he identifies key conditions for conflict reduction and resolution at different phases of a conflict's life cycle. Some of these conditions may embolden a variety of actors to attempt early and even effective preventive action. More specifically, several kinds of ethnic conflicts and conditions affecting their resolution are identified. Four conditions are specified as sources of deteriorating ethnic strife: increasing power; economic and status inequalities; a deteriorating economy; and lessening of communal interaction and communication and dissolving of shared institutions and identities. On the basis of evidence from South Africa, Yugoslavia, and Canada, long-term policies have the greatest chance of success. This means that multitrack strategies should be planned.

PREVENTION

Broadening the conflict management spectrum is vital in an era when "conventional" interstate strife is declining, at least in relative terms (Wallensteen and Sollenberg 1996). A fundamental challenge faced by regional organizations and the UN is their basis in state sovereignty and institutional relationship to states. International organizations represent the interests of states, not nations.[9] They therefore have difficulty in relating to substate actors who lack any legal standing and serve as the engines of war and peace in many intrastate disputes, ethnic conflicts, and civil wars.

Strategies of third-party intervention and mediation, with a specific focus on institutions, are examined by Ryan, Haglund and Pentland, and Fortmann, Martin, and Roussel in chapters 3, 4, and 5, respectively. These authors examine actions taken early in the life cycle of a conflict to prevent disputes from escalating or problems from worsening. Preventive action encompasses a range of techniques, including preventive diplomacy by representatives of regional organizations (Haglund and Pentland; Fortmann, Martin and Roussel) and long-range approaches targeted at structural inequalities (Ryan).[10] Table 1.2 identifies these concepts and draws on *An Agenda for Peace* as well as NATO interpretations.

Table 1.2

Peacekeeping and Related Topics

	Agenda for Peace	NATO
Preventive Diplomacy	Action to prevent disputes from arising between parties, to prevent disputes from escalating into conflicts, and to limit the spread of the latter when they occur.	
Peacemaking	Action to bring parties to an agreement, essentially through such peaceful means as those foreseen in Chapter VI of the United Nations Charter.	Diplomatic actions conducted after the commencement of conflict, with the aim of establishing a peaceful settlement. They can include the provision of good offices, mediation, conciliation, and such efforts as diplomatic isolation and sanctions.
Peacekeeping	Deployment of a UN presence in the field, hitherto with the consent of all parties concerned, normally involving UN military and/or police personnel and frequently involving civilians as well. Peacekeeping is a technique that expands the possibilities for both the prevention of conflict and the making of peace.	Containment, moderation, and/or termination of hostilities between or within states, through the medium of an impartial third-party intervention, organized and directed internationally; using military forces and civilians to complement the political process of conflict resolution and to restore and maintain peace.
Peacebuilding	Action to identify and support structures that will tend to strengthen and solidify peace and order so as to avoid a relapse into conflict.	Postconflict action to identify support structures that will tend to strengthen and solidify a political settlement in order to avoid a return to conflict.

Sources: Boutros-Ghali (1991, 1995) and NATO (1994)

The basic logic of conflict prevention is to reduce the need for more coercive (and even harmful) third-party measures and enhance the prospects for a lasting peace (Lund 1996). The corollary also is politic; while early action is not guaranteed to be successful, prospects for intervention get worse with time (Jentleson 1996). In general, conflict prevention involves perception of the opportunity and need to act in order to reduce risks. Fact-finding, theory building, and development of models are emphasized as essential to accumulation of timely and accurate knowledge. According to Lund:

> Preventive diplomacy, or conflict prevention, consists of governmental or non-governmental actions, policies and institutions that are taken deliberately to keep particular states or organized groups within them from threatening or using organized violence, armed force, or related forms of coercion, such as repression, as the means to settle interstate or national political disputes, especially in situations where the existing means cannot peacefully manage the destabilizing effects of economic, social, political and international change. (1996: 11)

Conflict prevention, in its most robust form, includes a full range of political, diplomatic, and military instruments (Kaufman, Lund 1996). Primary goals should be (a) to act prior to outbreak of armed violence; (b) to encourage alignments based on interests other than ethnicity; (c) to reduce disparities between groups; and (d) to deter regional adventurism, which can result in interstate crisis.

What are the limits to conflict prevention? With a focus on structural dimensions as constraints on prevention of ethnic conflict, Ryan seeks an answer to that question in chapter 3. He asserts that some peacekeeping missions are consistent with the goals laid out by Boutros-Ghali in *An Agenda for Peace* while others are not. Ryan develops the concept of preventive peacekeeping (a topic covered by Kaufman in a later chapter) to highlight these differences:

> [Preventive peacekeeping entails] action that is taken to stop destructive conflict developing, not action that is taken after the destructive conflict is underway. Therefore we can distinguish between preventive peacekeeping and "traditional" peacekeeping because the former tries to stop destructive conflict occurring, while the latter responds after destructive violence is underway. It is,

therefore, not the tasks of conflict prevention that distinguishes the two types of peacekeeping, but the timing of intervention in the conflict.

If its objective is to take action to discourage or reduce conflicts with the potential for recurrent destruction and violence, then the mission represents preventive peacekeeping. Examples include the UN operation in Cyprus and OSCE-mandated peacekeeping missions in Russia's "near-abroad."

According to Ryan it is a much broader set of objectives that Boutros-Ghali had in mind when the word "preventive" was applied to peacekeeping: "It recognizes that police and civilians (e.g., human rights monitors, election supervisors), as well as soldiers, can play an important role in peacekeeping. If peacekeeping is to be more than border patrols, it is likely that international forces will find themselves in complex and difficult situations with which military personnel are not always equipped to deal. The way that UN peacekeeping is evolving in practice means that forces have to engage in a large number of military and non-military tasks." Thus Ryan (and later Kaufman) points out that preventive peacekeeping is related, but not equivalent, to the more narrowly defined preemptive operation known as preventive deployment, in which a few troops are inserted strictly as a trip wire to deter the outbreak of violence. An example of preventive deployment is the UN Preventive Deployment operation in Macedonia (UNPREDEP), which included fifteen hundred US troops and support staff.

While underdeveloped in terms of both practice and theory, especially when applied to ethnic conflict, observed instances of peacekeeping as a conflict-prevention mechanism and an expanding bibliography reveal growing interest. Optimism about the "New World Order" between 1989 and 1992 drew attention to the conflict prevention role of the UN, culminating in Boutros-Ghali's *An Agenda for Peace*. (Since then, the OSCE, OAU, and OAS also have developed mechanisms for conflict prevention.) The UN's long-term role in international politics, however, is regarded pessimistically because of apparent failures in the former Yugoslavia, Somalia, and Angola. Shashi Tharoor, special assistant to the undersecretary general for peacekeeping operations at the UN, sums up the organization's difficulties in one major region: The UN's experience at peacekeeping in Europe "has thrown into question the existing principles and practices relating to United Nations control, financing, and composition of peacekeeping operations; to the traditional requirement for the consent and cooperation of the parties; and for United Nations impartiality between them; and to the non-use of force to achieve the ends established by the mandate" (1995: 127).

One basic reason for the unimpressive performance of the UN is that it lacks effective leverage relative to most adversaries and is poorly equipped to act as an interface between states and nonstate actors. The latter point highlights the main weakness of current thinking at the UN (and OSCE); prevention is regarded as a "technical" issue that encompasses early warning, arms control, preventive deployment of peacekeepers, fact-finding, and related matters. This very superficial approach, however, does not deal with the structural causes of ethnic conflict (such as cultural differences, which can undermine efforts to create stable and democratic multiethnic societies).

Structural factors create several problems that contribute to violent ethnic conflict: reconciling multicultural reality with the principle of national self-determination; pursuit of a stable, democratic society in a turbulent regional or international system; uneven economic development; and coping with fundamental changes brought about by the outbreak of violent conflict. Greater understanding of these deeper problems will be needed before effective ethnic conflict prevention becomes a possibility. Three strategies seem to be especially important: (1) creating a civil society that is sensitive to cultural differences by establishing and implementing norms of minority rights and protection—progress in this area is symbolized by the UN's Declaration on the Rights of Persons Belonging to National or Ethnic, Religious or Linguistic Minorities (1992) and OSCE's monitoring missions to various parts of Central and Eastern Europe; (2) dealing with the international dimensions of insecurity that affect interethnic relations; and (3) implementing development strategies that are sensitive to ethnic differences and inequality.

Chapters 4 and 5 assess the limitations of preventive diplomacy by regional organizations, with a special focus on the recent and destructive Balkans war. In chapter 4, Haglund and Pentland determine the extent to which Yugoslavia is a precedent for, or a prototype of, conflicts likely to appear elsewhere in post-Cold War Europe. They ask a multifaceted and disturbing question: why was the EC unable to prevent the Balkans war, and what are the implications of this perceived failure for conflicts elsewhere? General acquiescence by governments and public opinion across Europe (and elsewhere) in the proposition that Yugoslavia is a test-case, foreshadowing issues soon to crowd into Europe's security agenda from other quarters of the continent, would have at least two serious implications. First, it would affect the force and confidence with which ethnic claims are advanced and borders challenged in the latent conflicts of Central and Eastern Europe. Secondly, if Yugoslavia is widely accepted as a fair—and failed—test of how European institutions are likely to perform as preventive mechanisms, damage to their credibility may be beyond repair, with serious long-term consequences for regional security.

Each of the two preceding arguments is assessed in four ways. First, the way in which European strategists have attempted to isolate the Yugoslav case conceptually and immunize it institutionally is reviewed. Arguments about the character of the Yugoslav conflict are appraised; elements that make it *sui generis* and threaten its status as a precedent or a prototype are underlined. Second, institutional response to the conflict, with a focus on the pivotal and illustrative role of the European Community, is assessed. Third, NATO's prospects for assuming the central role in managing future ethnic conflicts are evaluated. Fourth, and finally, the transatlantic fabric of the alliance as it seeks to position itself with respect to (and possibly in response to) the kind of conflict it is likely to confront in the coming years (especially in Central and Eastern Europe) is explored. NATO helps preclude violent conflict between its members, and the North Atlantic Cooperation Council (NACC) and Partnership for Peace (PFP) initiatives attempt to project that internal stability eastward. A June 1992 ministerial decision placed NATO resources at the disposal of the OSCE and UN, reflecting the organization's decision to support but not initiate peacekeeping operations.

Conflict prevention and third party mediation in the former Yugoslavia also provide the focus for chapter 5, by Fortmann, Martin, and Roussel. However, Fortmann et al. argue that the Balkan crisis challenged a fragile regional system still in the early stages of reconstruction, so the failure to prevent war is not surprising. What, then, are the implications of the Yugoslav conflict for European security and conflict mediation structures? As early as 1991, commentators deplored the inability of Western Europe to intervene and mediate in a situation that was degenerating into a major European civil war. The new architecture of security rested on the shaky foundations of a divided Europe and an indifferent United States. In response to this bleak assessment, Fortmann et al. suggest that pessimism obscures the positive aspects of Western Europe's reactions. Passions unleashed by the war create the unrealistic expectation of a rapid solution to a deeply rooted conflict. The role of regional organizations, however, cannot extend much further than encouraging adversaries to engage in dialogue. They cannot bring peace without consent from the warring parties.

Efforts by the international community to help build the foundations for a settlement amid the horrors of war are documented effectively by Fortmann et al. Have the efforts of the OSCE, the UN, and NATO been sufficient? In light of potential conflicts elsewhere in Eastern Europe, the record seems adequate.

DIMENSIONS OF PEACEKEEPING

Chapters 6–9 focus on the military and operational dimensions of peacekeeping, including conventional Chapter VI operations (James), preventive peacekeeping (Kaufman and Morrison), and peace enforcement or Chapter VII operations (Harvey). Weiner pointed out—more than two decades ago—the difficulty of resolving ethnic disputes "without the active involvement of third parties prepared to exercise their power to enforce a settlement" (1971: 682). Today debate focuses on intervention in internal conflict and the kinds of measures required in these situations. The UN remains the principal organization with responsibility for international peacekeeping. The organization's thinking about contemporary peacekeeping is expressed in a number of documents, most notably in Boutros-Ghali's *An Agenda for Peace* and its January 1995 supplement. In the original version from January 1992, the secretary-general set out four categories of activities: preventive diplomacy; peacemaking; peacekeeping; and peacebuilding. The secretary-general's report to the General Assembly in March 1994 on "Improving the Capacity of the UN for Peacekeeping" added a fifth category: "Peace Enforcement." More recently, in the supplement, the secretary-general outlined six instruments for peace and security. Three of these reflect the categorization from 1992, now represented as diplomatic and related activity aimed at preventing conflict, peacekeeping, and peacebuilding.[11]

Cold War diplomatic tools such as the UN had been intended primarily for use by the superpowers and their clients. Since the end of the Cold War, however, the military dimensions of peacekeeping have been broadened significantly. Two main tasks are containment and stability. The UNPROFOR peacekeeping operation in Bosnia illustrates the former. NATO operations such as Sharp Guard and Deliberate Force, along with the Implementation Force (IFOR) and UNPREDEP, provide examples of conflict containment in the service of specific UN resolutions. Conflict containment requires a more active role for regional organizations and a greater level of cooperation and coordination among the great powers. Peacekeepers also must establish a stable and secure internal environment to create the conditions necessary for a negotiated settlement and lasting peace. The tasks include guarantee and denial of movement (which requires large and well-protected forces, ground and air cargo craft, increased use of armor, and substantial offshore facilities); protection of humanitarian relief through military operations; forceful separation of ethnic groups; and counterinsurgency activities.

During the Cold War an ad hoc, "law and order" approach emerged. By and large, humanitarian concerns took a backseat to maintaining international stability. Few states questioned the de facto status of peacekeeping operations as a kind of crisis management technique.[12] However, practitioners and policy makers alike erroneously assumed that with removal of the structural impediments imposed on the UN during the Cold War conflict management would not be much different than in the past. Old rules would apply to new situations.

Peacekeeping is an improvised technique with no legal basis in the UN Charter and is consequently not addressed as such. The rules surrounding peacekeeping have been built by practice over the years, much like common law. The legal basis for operations is the mandate of each separate mission. The UN Security Council has, by its actions, established a broad body of de facto principles for traditional peacekeeping, but no measures exist specifically for *intrastate* conflict. In general, Security Council resolutions and agreements between the UN and individual states are the legal basis for initiation and implementation of peacekeeping operations. A coalition of forces may have the effective right to intervene once the

Security Council labels events as aggression (although that term is not clearly defined in the charter), and any state that has ratified the charter agrees to its interpretation by the Security Council.[13]

Consider a situation in which interstate violence has broken out and escalation is imminent. The conventional wisdom holds that external influence, a combination of "dictatorial" interference, coercion, and international law, is sufficient to manage a crisis. Translating this into a regional conflict such as the Gulf War, tradition would suggest that the optimal choice is to use overwhelming force against a single aggressor in a well-defined operation and terminate the engagement as soon as its objectives have been fulfilled. While this strategy might work in a dyadic interstate war, it clearly is not applicable in situations like Bosnia, where discriminating and proportional force is deemed necessary, there are zones of both peace and war, consent is not easily obtained, and exit strategies are impractical and undesirable.[14] The ad hoc nature of peacekeeping operations engenders a great deal of resistance from regime leaders, self-appointed warlords, demagogues, and insurgents, all of whom may perceive multilateral involvement as proto-imperialism or at least an infringement on their authority. In principle, state sovereignty does not permit outside intervention; peacekeepers found committing an offense against local law (assuming they are enforceable) may be arrested, despite the high status of "experts on mission." However, sovereignty only confers a primary competence upon a nation; it is not, and never was, exclusive. This primary competence presumably would include whatever is essentially domestic, as opposed to what might affect another state. The latter entails situations in which states lose their ability to regulate a conflict due to events that occur outside their control (like famine brought on by environmental change) or through spillover effects (such as refugee flows)(Roberts 1996).

On one side of the debate are James (chapter 6) and Kaufman (chapter 7). James argues in chapter 6 that while peacekeeping may contribute to the amelioration or resolution of ethnic conflict, it would be a mistake to assume that it often can have a substantial input. What, then, are the conditions for a successful Chapter VI operation? James is skeptical about the idea that peacekeeping will be more valuable if it goes beyond a traditional, cooperative basis into assertiveness vis-à-vis one or more of the parties. The basic reasons are the depth of the conflict and associated urgency of the need to come out on top. Thus peacekeepers are likely to be viewed instrumentally rather than as independent actors worthy of respect.

James suggests that assertive peacekeeping is a very risky strategy with a low likelihood of success because ethnic group leaders can be expected to promote violence for their own ends, especially when the UN risks its neutral status (i.e., making the transition from peacekeeping to peacemaking). Peacekeepers may become targets rather than intermediaries when at least one antagonist becomes convinced that favoritism is at work. In fact, a viable peacekeeping mission may require territorial demarcation and some minimal agreement between enemies.

Circumstances in which peacekeeping is likely to be more or less effective are placed in contrast. Two key elements are a territorial demarcation between distrustful ethnicities and an agreement (even if only interim) between them. Of these two components, the first is more important. Thus the most and least propitious contexts for peacekeeping are those in which both elements are present or absent, respectively. Peacekeepers are more likely to make a useful contribution when there is territorial demarcation and an agreement rather than vice versa. This reflects the fragility of agreements between deeply distrustful ethnicities. Furthermore, assertive peacekeeping will tend to turn the peacekeepers, in the eyes of the adversaries, into participants. The parties will treat them accordingly, despite the best efforts of the peacekeepers to behave impartially.

These assertions are examined in light of the UN's experience with peacekeeping in relation to ethnic conflict throughout the fifty years of its existence. Numerous cases are noted under the rubric of traditional peacekeeping, and James identifies three as assertive: the Congo (1960–64), Somalia (1992–94), and Bosnia-Herzegovina (1993–95), each of which confirms the preceding analysis.

Impartiality and consent are the guiding principles for any Chapter VI peacekeeping mission. Chapter 7 by Kaufman argues that peacekeepers can place their mission at considerable risk when these principles are compromised. Like James, Kaufman asserts that peacekeeping works best when peacekeepers act as impartial referees who keep the peace primarily through negotiations, persuasion, and reassurance. Can peacekeepers, however, play an effective role in conflict prevention? Kaufman finds that the evidence is mixed. Given the nature of their task, peacekeepers can succeed only if all major parties agree on the mission and cooperate in carrying it out.

The task of the international community is to provide skilled peace-keepers and support—material and diplomatic—for their operation. These requirements are individually necessary and collectively sufficient for successful preventive peacekeeping in ethnic conflicts.

Numerous factors can affect these conditions. Governments typically agree to the deployment of peacekeeping troops on their territory primarily to stop intervention by another international actor whom they fear more, as in the cases of the Congo (1960), Cyprus (1964) and Lebanon (1978). Ethnic peacekeeping is easiest when communities exist in clearly separated territories, but it also can work when groups live mixed together, as the United Nations operation on Cyprus from 1964 to 1974 shows. When key actors change policy and withdraw cooperation (as Turkey did on Cyprus in 1974 and the Israelis did in southern Lebanon in 1982), peacekeepers can do nothing further to prevent war.

Peacekeepers rarely succeed if they must use force. The UN Congo operation in the early 1960s is a rare example of effective forceful action by peacekeepers; it succeeded only because of a weak, isolated opponent. The multinational force in Beirut in 1982–1983 illustrates the more common fate of peacekeepers who try to use force: they are perceived as belligerent and become targets of the side they appear to oppose.

The 1991–1992 war in Croatia is a case in which preventive peacekeeping could not have succeeded. By 1991, Serbian president Slobodan Milosevic and Croatian president Franjo Tudjman were willing to fight for control of the Krajina region of Croatia; neither was prepared to cede such control either to the other or to peacekeepers. Furthermore, the Yugoslav People's Army—not wholly controlled by any government—in all likelihood would have opposed by force the deployment of preventive peacekeepers even if the politicians had agreed to it. International pressure probably could not have changed these preferences, so peacekeeping would have been futile.

The UN Preventive Deployment Force (UNPREDEP) force in Macedonia is an example of how preventive peacekeeping works. If fighting erupted in Kosovo (or possibly Albania), for example, peacekeepers might (if heavily reinforced) be able to prevent the spread of fighting to Macedonia. By patrolling the Macedonia-Kosovo border, they could neutralize Macedonia by dissuading Albanian fighters from crossing into Kosovo and Serbian troops from penetrating into Macedonia. And by handling assistance for Albanian refugees from Kosovo, they could minimize friction between those refugees and potentially hostile Macedonian security forces. In this situation, peacekeeping would offer a safe haven to the Albanians, protection from foreign enemies for the Macedonians, and a pacified border for the Serbs; thus all might be willing to cooperate. Alternatively, if large-scale violence between Macedonians and Albanians became imminent inside Macedonia, the peacekeepers could act as a buffer between the two groups, as the UN did on Cyprus before 1974. Such action would preserve Macedonian territorial integrity while providing de facto autonomy to the Albanians, so both sides would have reason to cooperate.

Chapter 8 by Harvey, which looks at ethnic conflict in the former Yugoslavia through the prism of deterrence theory, represents the other side of the debate. Harvey sets out to determine the implications of the Bosnian conflict for theories of international relations. In sum, could forceful measures have resulted in a shorter war?

Harvey argues that scholarship on Yugoslavia continues to theorize strictly in terms of ethnic conflict, ethnonationalism, and ethnic mobilization. While these aspects offer very important clues about the root causes of the conflict, they are not sufficient to explain the onset (i.e., timing), escalation, and/or duration of the violence. Evidence shows that, in almost every major encounter with the Bosnian Serbs between April 1993 and April 1994, US and European (NATO) officials failed to satisfy even the most basic strategic requirements of deterrence. These conditions include definition of unacceptable behavior, clear communication of a commitment to punish transgressors, and demonstration of intent to carry out retaliation. The external powers either diluted or intentionally qualified most of the retaliatory threats: "Instead of taking a firm stand, the West chose to emphasize conciliation mixed with humanitarianism. Inadequate military and humanitarian action, combined with sanctions and a negotiating charade, thus constituted a powerful diversion" (Weiss 1994: 20). As failures mounted, the adversaries simply ignored subsequent efforts to control hostilities. In contrast, satisfaction of the prerequisites for effective deterrence ultimately reestablished credibility. This process enabled NATO to control fighting and obtain cooperation in response to demands. Not only does deterrence offer a useful framework within which to describe and explain events in Yugoslavia; it also provides a set of specific policy guidelines with the potential to control hostilities and create an environment conducive to lasting peace.

Previous literature reveals that existing theories are limited in explanatory and predictive power, especially within the context of crisis and war. A more complete explanation for the ongoing conflict, which can be derived from deterrence theory, is desirable. A series of thirteen exchanges between US/NATO officials and Bosnian-Serb leaders from April 1993 to April 1994 can be conceived of as an instance of immediate deterrence. This evidence makes it possible to assess the extent to which external powers met the requirements for a successful containment strategy.

Both domestic and international forces continue as obstacles to a more forceful US/NATO position, which in turn creates the need for policy recommendations. The case of Bosnia points to the enduring relevance of realist theories like deterrence to the study of international relations and even ethnic conflict. Deterrence, a relatively abstract theory derived from analysis of states in an anarchical world, can make an invaluable contribution to the study of conflict and development of foreign policy in the post-Cold War world. Prospects for effective peacekeeping are enhanced by use of the logic of deterrence in the context of interstate ethnic conflict.

Morrison suggests in chapter 9 that while it is important to focus on the doctrinal aspects of peacekeeping, coordination and training are equally important. How can peacekeeping be broadened in order to address the multidimensionality of internal ethnic strife? Peacekeeping, Morrison argues, should be seen less as a means of ethnic conflict resolution and more as a way of stabilizing deeply divided societies through coordinated international action. He proposes a holistic approach, derived from the Canadian experience, that is broad in nature and interpretation: actions designed to enhance international peace, security, and stability that are authorized by competent national and international organizations and are undertaken cooperatively by military, humanitarian, and civilian policy and other interested agencies and groups.

This definition provides a unifying conceptual basis for the New Peacekeeping Partnership (NPP), which is composed of the military, departments of foreign affairs, governmental development agencies, humanitarian aid agencies, other nongovernmental organizations, good governance officials, and concerned citizens. The members of the NPP are dedicated to ensuring the widest, most inclusive response possible to the challenges and opportunities of the post-Cold War era, striving to balance their needs with sensitivity to those of local populations in distress. In other words, the NPP's participants are determined to cooperate to ensure that international stabilizing operations are as effective as possible. Given the desire to improve the NPP, the Canadian approach to peacekeeping research, education, and training is assessed in detail. This produces a series of policy applications for future peacekeeping operations.

As demonstrated by recent operations in Haiti, Somalia, and the former Yugoslavia, some military component will remain essential to all peacekeeping operations. It is recognized that general purpose, combat-capable troops still make the best peacekeepers. However, it also is clear that to succeed—success defined as the cessation of violence and the initiation of a process whereby parties to a conflict can address the underlying sources of their hostility—they must work in concert with nonmilitary actors. For policymakers this will mean a radical rethinking of the way governments prepare and deploy their troops for peacekeeping missions. It also will require a reevaluation of how best to (a) balance national interest with the overriding purpose of contributing to global peace; and (b) handle the competing needs for general combat capability and mission-specific training. Perhaps the most difficult task of all will be translating the NPP and its role in the post-Cold War environment to domestic constituencies.

Self-interested activities of nongovernmental organizations (NGOs), which may already be present in a conflict zone, need coordination. It takes strong and unified direction from outside actors to help the parties realize their mutual desire for peace. Competition for influence between and within institutions is a reality of any humanitarian intervention. The implication is that justification for a significant policy shift and subsequent debate over means must be pitched in a way that has broad cross-appeal to constituencies, interest groups, and policy-makers. For the UN, the convergence of needs and actors within the NPP requires that the organization's infrastructure "catches up" with global expectations and pronouncements of the secretary-general. Any effort to promote and sustain a closer working relationship among UN actors, agencies, and member states will be of little consequence without addressing the UN's acute financial problems.

CONCLUSION

Chapter 10 by Carment and James summarizes the contributions of the preceding chapters to conflict prevention and peacekeeping as related to international ethnic conflict. Practical insights are derived for at least three major areas.

First, academics can play an important role in identifying lessons and strategies that are overlooked by hard-pressed practitioners. Early identification and involvement to prevent escalation of internal conflicts is desirable, but states and institutions have only limited opportunity and willingness to do so (Most and Starr 1989). This increases the importance of nongovernmental initiatives in the early stages of internal conflicts.

Second, there *are* specific instances when a situation is ripe for effective coercive diplomacy—complex intrastate disputes often are equated with failed states. State failure is most closely associated with politicide, genocide, and power transitions. The most extreme example is when an armed group operates outside the control of recognized political authorities and resists peacekeeping efforts.

Third, constraints on implementing preventive measures also must be addressed. Existing decision-making regimes do not favor a coherent and timely military response to disaster. Decisions by third parties to intervene militarily are characterized by two patterns of behavior. They often are described as major policy shifts in which ground forces are inserted only after all other options are assumed to have failed. Such decisional shifts exhibit considerable institutional pulling and hauling within not only the UN organization but also each states' bureaucracy.

Progress is possible only if an approach is nested in a broader set of policies and strategies that include preventive peacekeeping, early warning, and denationalization of the institutions of newly emergent states. More specifically, sanctions, mediation, and international condemnation may be necessary—but not sufficient—conditions for the management of ethnic strife. It may be essential to augment these traditional approaches with those suited to the particularities of ethnic strife as delineated in the preceding chapters.

De-escalation of violent conflict may evolve as a result of exhaustion, creating conditions for settlement. External intervention to de-escalate a protracted conflict demands close coordination of military, diplomatic, and nongovernmental assets; a coordinated campaign plan and considerable resources to foster development;

and communal interdependence and attitude change over a long time—perhaps generations.

One central area for future debate is the extent to which minority or dissident groups should be recognized at the expense of traditional states and limits imposed on states' attempts to sustain sovereignty and domestic order. Objective criteria for early recognition of a movement pertain to its extent of popular support, government use of repression, and anticipated impact of recognition. Recognition by different outside parties may have different effects on the conflict.

NOTES

1. This volume constitutes the second phase of research on ethnic conflict. It builds on the findings of a related volume, *Wars in the Midst of Peace: The International Politics of Ethnic Conflict* (Carment and James 1997), a collection of essays, case studies, and empirical analysis which achieved two goals: it (a) surveyed and improved upon existing theoretical, empirical, and country-based literature; and (b) produced insights about historical and contemporary instances of international ethnic conflict, including specific examples and aggregate data. The central findings of that volume drew attention to both the importance and limited understanding of the prevention and management of ethnic strife.

2. For example, the United Nations Genocide Convention was created to address crimes with the intent to destroy in whole or in part a national ethnic or racial group. Despite growing evidence that genocides have been a recurring phenomena, since 1945 the convention has rarely been enforced. The lack of enforcement was most clearly played out in 1994 with the failure of the UN Assistance Mission in Rwanda (UNAMIR) to prevent the massacre of Tutsi and moderate Hutu citizens of Rwanda. The UN has formally termed the mass murders as genocide.

3. For example, the Human Rights Subcommission on the Prevention of Discrimination and Protection of Minorities has failed to live up to its billing (Ryan 1988). Occasionally this and other UN declarations of self-determination are cited in support of a minority's claims about historical injustice or threats to identity.

4. Ryan notes that when the UN came into being there was genuine concern among members that recognition of minority rights might weaken new states. Support for minority self-determination might legitimize minority claims and freeze the situation to create and strengthen animosities between groups that were essentially latent. In response, various fora within the UN structure were introduced as platforms for raising substate grievances, thereby raising the salience of ethnic interests as a basis for political mobilization. A few conflicts, most involving nonethnic issues, were

handled through carefully orchestrated state-creating enterprises (Namibia, Cambodia), while others were left off the agenda (Eritrea, Somaliland, East Timor).

5. We are indebted to Frank Harvey, Louis Kriesberg, Stuart Kaufman, and Stephen Ryan for these interpretations of the causes of ethnic conflict.

6. Source: "Minorities Report (1) Ethnopolitical Conflict in the 1990s: Patterns and Trends," by Ted Robert Gurr, Department of Government and Politics, University of Maryland, and Michael Haxton, Minorities at Risk, Project Center for International Development and Conflict Management, April 1996.

7. The report also notes that a relatively small contingent of soldiers with the right equipment and mandate could have been effective in stopping the killing.

8. References that exclude the year of publication refer to other chapters in this volume.

9. In general, the UN response to ethnic conflict has been diverse if not always successful. For example, in his assessment of the pre-1989 record, Esman (1994) defines UN intervention in ethnic conflict to include good offices, mediation, peacemaking, peacekeeping, protection of human rights, humanitarian assistance, and stigmatization of regimes.

10. See Bauwens and Reychler, eds., *The Art of Conflict Prevention,* for an institutional perspective on conflict prevention; Lund, *Preventing Violent Conflict*; Jentleson, "Preventive Diplomacy and Ethnic Conflict"; Bercovitch, "Understanding Mediation's Role in Preventive Diplomacy"; Stedman, "Alchemy for a New World Disorder"; Chigas, "Preventive Diplomacy and the Organization for Security and Cooperation in Europe"; and Sklelsbaek and Fermann, "The UN Secretary-General and the Mediation of International Disputes."

11. The remaining three instruments—disarmament, sanctions, and enforcement—are tools developed in the new multifunctional peacekeeping, basically as a result of experience in UNOSOM II in Somalia and UNPROFOR in the former Yugoslavia. These are not grouped in, or identified as, any particular category in the *Supplement,* but are identified as new "coercive" elements in peacekeeping. The question of peace enforcement as a category per se is left open. The UN once again acknowledges, this time in the *Supplement,* that it is not capable of directing peace enforcement operations (i.e., of the Gulf type), but does now see the need for specific and appropriate enforcement actions under particular circumstances within certain UN-controlled and -directed operations.

12. The principles that guided UN Charter Chapter VI operations during the Cold War included impartiality, consent, and the use of force only for self-defense. Application of these standards is most effective in

the management of disputes between member states of the international system, in which peacekeeping is essentially observation, belligerents are safely separated, and the peacekeepers themselves are not vulnerable to attack. This type of peacekeeping most often occurs after a cease-fire is obtained and when force and interposition are deemed unnecessary (i.e., no need for armed troops or buffer).

13. Six criteria apply: Whether (a) the continuation of a situation is likely to endanger or constitute a threat to international peace and security; (b) regional or subregional organizations and arrangements exist and are ready and able to assist in resolving the situation; (c) a cease-fire exists and the parties have committed themselves to a peace process intended to reach a political settlement; (d) a clear political goal exists and can be reflected in the mandate; (e) a precise mandate for a United Nations operation can be formulated; and (f) the safety and security of United Nations personnel can be reasonably ensured, including reasonable guarantees from the principal parties or factions.

14. Article 2(7) of the charter states that the UN should not intervene in matters that are essentially within the domestic jurisdiction of any state; but there is an out: "the Charter shall not prejudice the application of enforcement measures under Chapter VII." If a domestic conflict is construed as a threat to international peace and security, then the Security Council may sanction a mandate to intervene. Article 42 of the UN Charter is relevant to coercive measures taken by the UN in terms of the use of force, and article 51 authorizes states to use unilateral collective force in self-defense.

REFERENCES

Anderson, Benedict. 1991. *Imagined Communities: Reflections on the Origins and Spread of Nationalism.* Revised edition. London: Verso.

Atlantic Council of the United States. 1995. *Ethnic Conflicts: Old Challenges, New Dimensions.* Washington, D.C.: Atlantic Council of the United States.

Azar, Edward, and John Burton, eds. 1986. *International Conflict Resolution.* Boulder, Colo.: Lynne Rienner.

Bauwens, W., and L. Reychler, eds. 1994. *The Art of Conflict Prevention.* London: Brassey's.

Bercovitch, J. 1996. "Understanding Mediation's Role in Preventive Diplomacy." *Negotiation Journal* 12, no. 3: 241–58.

Betts, Richard. 1996. "The Delusion of Impartial Intervention." In *Managing Global Chaos,* edited by C. Crocker, C. Hampson, and P. Aaal. Washington, D.C.: United States Institute of Peace Press: 333–41.

Bloom, William. 1990. *Personal Identity, National Identity, and International Relations.* Cambridge: Cambridge University Press.

Boutros-Ghali, Boutros. 1992. *An Agenda for Peace: Preventive Diplomacy, Peacemaking and Peace-keeping.* New York: United Nations.
———. 1995. *An Agenda for Peace: An Addendum.* New York: DPI Press.

Brown, Michael, ed. 1996. *The International Dimensions of Internal Conflicts.* Cambridge: MIT Press.

Carment, David, and Patrick James. 1997. *Wars in the Midst of Peace: The International Politics of Ethnic Conflict.* Pittsburgh: University of Pittsburgh Press.

Chazan, Naomi, ed. 1991. *Irredentism and International Politics.* Boulder, Colo.: Lynne Rienner.

Chigas, D. 1996. "Preventive Diplomacy and the Organization for Security and Cooperation in Europe: Creating Incentives for Dialogue and Cooperation." In *Preventing Conflict in the Post-Communist World,* edited by A. Chayes and A. H. Chayes. Washington, D.C.: Brookings, 1996: 25–97.

Crighton, Elizabeth, and Martha Abele MacIver. 1991. "The Evolution of Protracted Ethnic Conflict." *Comparative Politics* 23: 127–42.

Diehl, Paul F. 1993. *International Peacekeeping.* Baltimore: John Hopkins University Press.

Diehl, J. Reifschneider, and Paul R. Hensel. 1996. "United Nations Intervention and Recurring Conflict." *International Organization* 50, no. 4: 683–700.

Despres, L. A., ed. 1976. *Ethnicity and Resource Competition in Plural Societies.* Paris: Mouton.

Durch, William J. 1993. *The Evolution of UN Peacekeeping: Case Studies and Comparative Analysis,* New York: St. Martin's.

Esman, Milton, and Shibley Telhami, eds. 1994. *International Organizations and Ethnic Conflict.* Ithaca, N.Y.: Cornell University Press. 21–47.

Furnivall, J. S. 1948. *Colonial Policy and Practice.* London: Cambridge University Press.

Geertz, Clifford. 1973. *The Interpretation of Culture: Selected Essays.* New York: Basic Books.

Gellner, Ernest. 1983. *Nations and Nationalism.* Ithaca, N.Y.: Cornell University Press.

Gurr, Ted Robert. 1994. "Peoples against States: Ethnopolitical Conflict and the Changing World System." *International Studies Quarterly* 38: 347–77.

Gurr and Michael Haxton. 1996. "Minorities Report 1: Ethnopolitical Conflict in the 1990s: Patterns and Trends." College Park: Department of Government and Politics, University of Maryland, and Minorities at Risk Project Center for International Development and Conflict Management.

Hardin, Russell. 1995. *One for All: The Logic of Group Conflict.* Princeton: Princeton University Press.

Hechter, Michael. 1995. "Explaining Nationalist Violence." *Nations and Nationalism* 1: 53–68.

———. 1975. *Internal Colonialism.* London: Routledge and Kegan Paul.

Horowitz, Donald. 1985. *Ethnic Groups in Conflict.* Berkeley: University of California Press.

Heraclides, Alexis. 1991. *The Self-Determination of Minorities in International Politics.* Portland, Ore.: Frank Cass.

———. 1990. "Secessionist Minorities and External Involvement." *International Organization* 44: 341–78.

Ignatieff, Michael. 1993. *Blood and Belonging.* Toronto: Viking Press.

Isaacs, Harold. 1975. *Idols of the Tribe: Group Identity and Political Change.* New York: Harper and Row. 39–45.

Jackson, Robert H. 1990. *Quasi-States: Sovereignty, International Relations and the Third World.* Cambridge: Cambridge University Press.

Jentleson, B. 1996. "Preventive Diplomacy and Ethnic Conflict: Possible, Difficult, Necessary." IGCC Policy Paper, May.

Joint Evaluation of Emergency Assistance to Rwanda. 1996. *The International Response to Conflict and Genocide: Lessons from the Rwanda Experience.* Bergen, Norway: Chr. Michelson Institute.

Kaplan, R. 1994. "The Coming Anarchy." *Atlantic Monthly* (February): 44–76.

Kipp, Jacob, and Timothy Thomas. 1992. *Ethnic Conflict: Scourge of the 1990s?* Fort Leavenworth, Kans.: Foreign Military Studies Office.

Knight, David B. 1984. "Identity and Territory: Geographical Perspectives on Nationalism and Regionalism." *Annals of the Association of American Geographers* 72: 514–31.

Lake, David, and Donald Rothchild, eds. 1997. *Ethnic Fears and Global Engagement: The International Spread and Management of Ethnic Conflict.* Princeton, N.J.: Princeton University Press.

Lund, M. S. 1996. "Early Warning and Preventive Diplomacy." In *Managing Global Chaos,* edited by F. Hampson, C. Crocker, and P. Aaal. Washington, D.C.: U.S. Institute of Peace Press, 1996, 379–403.

———. 1996. *Preventing Violent Conflict: A Strategy for Preventive Diplomacy.* Washington D.C.: United States Institute of Peace Press.

Mason, David T. 1994. "The Ethnic Dimension of Civil Violence in the Post-Cold War Era: Structural Configurations and Rational Choices." Paper presented at the annual meeting of the American Political Science Association, New York, 1994.

Roberts, A. 1996. "The Crisis in UN Peacekeeping." Edited by

F. Hampson, C. Crocker, and P. Aall. C. *Managing Global Chaos.*
Washington, D.C. Usip Press.

Rosenau, James, ed. 1964. *International Aspects of Civil Strife.*
Princeton, N.J.: Princeton University Press.

Rothman, Jay. 1992. *From Confrontation to Cooperation: Resolving
Ethnic and Regional Conflict.* Newbury Park, Cal.: Sage.

Rothschild, Joseph. 1981. *Ethnopolitics: A Conceptual Framework.*
New York: Columbia University Press.

Ryan, Stephen. 1990. "Ethnic Conflict and the United Nations." *Ethnic
and Racial Studies* 13, no. 1: 25–49.

Sklelsbaek, K., and G. Fermann. 1996. "The UN Secretary-General and
the Mediation of International Disputes." In *Resolving International
Conflicts,* edited by J. Bercovitch. Boulder, Colo.: Lynne Rienner.

Smith, Anthony. 1986. *The Ethnic Origins of Nations.* Oxford:
Blackwell.

———. 1993. "The Ethnic Sources of Nationalism." *Survival* 35, no. 1:
48–62.

———. 1991. *National Identity.* New York: Penguin.

Smith, M.G. 1965. *The Plural Societies in the British West Indies.*
Berkeley: University of California Press.

Snyder, Jack. 1993. "Nationalism and the Crisis of the Post-Soviet
State." *Survival* 35, no. 1: 1–26.

Stavenhagen, Rudolfo. 1990. *The Ethnic Question.* Tokyo: United
Nations University.

Stedman, S. J. 1995. "Alchemy for a New World Disorder: Overselling
Preventive Diplomacy." *Foreign Affairs* (May/June): 14–20.

Suhrke, Astri, and Lela Garner Noble, eds. 1977. *Ethnic Conflict and
International Relations.* New York: Praeger.

Van den Berghe, Pierre. 1987. *The Ethnic Phenomenon.* New York:
Praeger.

Van Evera, Stephen. 1994. "Hypotheses on Nationalism and War."
International Security 18: 5–39.

Väyrynen, R. 1996. "Toward Effective Conflict Prevention: Comparison of the Usability and Impact of Different Instruments." In *Preventive and Inventive Action in Intrastate Crises,* by Väyrynen, J. De
Leatherman, W. Mars, and P. Gaffney. Draft manuscript under
review. New York: United Nations Office of Information and Press.

Part 1

Sources and
Phases of
Ethnic Conflict

2

The Phases of Destructive Conflicts

Communal Conflicts and Proactive Solutions

Louis Kriesberg

INTRODUCTION

Attention to conflicts associated with differences among ethnic, religious, linguistic, and other communal identities is understandably great. Some of these conflicts are waged with great destructiveness and become seemingly intractable; furthermore, they often have a profound impact on peoples not themselves engaged in the conflicts. Consequently, governmental and nongovernmental policy-makers, academic analysts, and many other concerned persons are searching for ways that might forestall such conflicts from arising and stop them from persisting destructively.

Knowing that conflicts may escalate disastrously is not enough. Even knowing that this is very likely to happen does not ensure early and effective action to avert such developments, for at least three reasons. First, it is difficult to mobilize support for costly action unless the consequences of inaction are obviously appalling. Second, often it is not evident what early action would be effective. Third, it is likely that little credit would be gained even if effective action was undertaken, since the claims of success probably would not be recognized.

To help overcome these difficulties, I discuss a variety of proactive policies which may prevent communal conflicts from deteriorating, many of which have been effectively used.[1] Noting successes, not just failures, may embolden a variety of actors to attempt early action and to do so effectively. Success does not mean achieving utopian perfection but averting or limiting what might otherwise be highly destructive and intractable struggles.

Communal conflicts based on ethnic, religious, linguistic, and regional differences are examined here. The term *communal* is used to refer to identities shared by people who believe themselves to be or are treated by others as if they are members of a nationality, ethnicity, religious community, or even locality.[2] These identities are often acquired at birth, *ascribed* by others and not to be denied. Some identities, however, are *achieved* by choice and actions later in life. Furthermore, there are possible discrepancies between self-identity and the identities others try to impose. Consequently, identities are generally negotiated between individuals and collectivities, and among persons who do and do not share them. These communal identities, even ethnic ones, do not have a fixed primordial character.[3] It is true that growing up in a family, each person is socialized to form some communal identity; but that identity is socially constructed. Moreover, everyone is socialized into several identities, including membership in a family, a kinship group or clan, a particular linguistic group, a religious group, a social class, as well as citizenship of a specific country and locality. These multiple identities, insofar as they do not coincide, inhibit conflict escalation and foster reconciliation when the fighting ends.

As used here, the term *communal conflict* is not limited to contending communal groups within a single country. Since the existence of a particular state may be one of the issues in contention, the term includes conflicts both between states representing to a significant degree different communal identities and also conflicts between a state and a communally based social-movement organization struggling to become a state or striving for greater autonomy.

Mass media, official, and academic attention are most frequently given to conflicts when they erupt in violence. Relatively little attention is given to relationships which are peaceful or nonviolently contentious. Attention, however, should be given to such cases in order to learn what prevents them from becoming bloody and protracted struggles and to offer them as models of what humans can and do achieve.

Even now, looking around the world, there are many candidates for large-scale violent struggles that are quiescent, are being managed, or are in the process of settlement and perhaps resolution. Although their circumstances are not wholly satisfactory to all parties, they are better than the continuing violence and horrors of some communal conflicts. I cite several current and recent historical cases of not-so-bad achievements: (1) The Franco-German enmity went on for generations, but the policies instituted at the end of World War II resulted in a level of integration that makes war between Germany and France virtually unthinkable. (2) The Russian and Ukrainian republics, despite fundamental issues about borders and the control of the elements of the Red Fleet stationed in the Crimean Sea, are generally cooperative. (3) In Spain, the people of Catalonia have reached a mutually acceptable accommodation with the central government. (4) In Belgium, the peoples in the French-speaking (Wallonia) and Flemish-speaking regions have developed a mutually acceptable process of accommodation. (5) In South Africa, despite dire predictions for decades of large-scale fighting between blacks and whites, a fundamental and largely nonviolent transition to majority rule was accomplished. (6) In Canada, despite some violence years ago and the failure so far to reach a widely shared mutual accommodation between French-speaking Quebec and the rest of Canada, the disputants continue to seek a solution through the existing political system. (7) Czechoslovakia peacefully separated into the Czech and Slovak republics. (8) In many countries, even with significant communal differences, conflicts are much more significantly grounded on class, ideology, or ties to particular leaders.

Since the term *conflict* refers to a wide range of phenomena, prevention and other proactive actions also encompass a wide range of efforts. Typically, communal conflicts are seen as eruptions of intense, direct physical violence, but they may also represent organized or unorganized resistance to a dominant group's discrimination, exploitation, or indoctrination, as well as other kinds of felt oppression. Proactive policies, then, may mean avoiding an eruption of violence or may mean limiting it and stopping its escalation; but the term may also refer to efforts at reaching a settlement of the conflict or remedying the conditions underlying the possible eruption of violence.

Avoiding violence, however, is not the only goal that officials or citizens seek. For example, they often strive for justice or freedom for their own people. If avoidance of violence was the only goal, it could be achieved at any time by one party's surrender or acquiescence to its oppression. Many conflicts are ended and fighting stopped by the unilateral imposition of a settlement by one side or even the annihilation or expulsion of a people. Consequently, the kind of relationship to which conflict de-escalation contributes also must be considered.

In order to examine the issues raised in these introductory observations, this chapter is organized around four topics. First, I discuss the kinds of relations that communal groups have with each other. Second, I outline other conditions that affect the likelihood that one or another means of averting destructive conflict escalation will be effective. Third, I map out possible policies to prevent destructive conflicts. Finally, I examine several cases.

KINDS OF COMMUNAL RELATIONS

During any given period, communal groups live together in a relationship that is the result of past struggles and accommodations. Those relationships may be relatively stable but more often are in contention and transition. For the purposes of this paper, we focus on two dimensions of the relationship: the degree of interdependence of the communal groups and the degree to which the form of the relationship is imposed by one of the groups.[4] This focus will help provide a basis for discussing the circumstances from which communal conflicts emerge and the conditions for their settlement, at least for a while.

Communal relations vary in the degree to which communities are interdependent; interdependence may become so great that one of the parties is assimilated into the other or they merge together; or interdependence may be so minimal and indirect that one party is excluded by expulsion or by genocide. Furthermore, some relationships are largely imposed by one party and some are facilitated or even imposed by external powers, while others are varyingly the result of mutual accommodation and acceptance.

Table 2.1 maps out kinds of communal relations in terms of their degree of interdependence and degree of unilateral imposition. Although lines are drawn within the table to help in reading it, in actuality no clear boundaries between different kinds of relationships exist. The distinctions between the categories are not rigid, and many gradations exist—partly because communal groups are not monolithic and members pursue various strategies. Moreover, how the relations are seen to be shaped varies with the perspective taken, since relations exist in various settings. For example, more than two peoples may be living in the same territory and that territory may be governed or dominated by still another people, as is the case with colonial rule or in empires. The dominant group may establish an overall structure, accepting or modifying the ranking among the subordinated groups who had previously contended with each other. From the perspective of the ruling people, the relationship among the subordinated peoples may be regarded as of the subordinates' own making. From the perspective of the dominated groups, the structure of the relationship among them may seem externally imposed.

Table 2.1
Intercommunal Relationships

Actions Shaping Interdependence	Degree of Interdependence		
	Integration	Coexistence	Separation
Unilateral Imposition	forced assimilation	slavery; settlement; reservations apartheid; segregation; discrimination	genocide; expulsion; secession; population transfer
Unilateral Direction	encouraged assimilation	empire and indirect rule; autonomy; federation; discrimination	encouraged migration
External Imposition	imperial rules	protection of minority	population transfer
External Facilitation	desegregation	protection of human rights; power sharing	border shift
Mutual Accommodation	voluntary assimilation; pluralism, mosaic	power sharing; egalitarian federation; self-segregation	agreed-upon self-determination

We give most attention in this chapter to ways of avoiding or mitigating destructive conflicts that also promote relatively integrated relations among the communal groups. That is, integration resulting from mutual accommodation is emphasized. These kinds of relations are shown in the bottom left sections of table 2.1. Imposed separations, in the upper right of table 2.1, are understandably often viewed as immoral, accompanied as they often are by large-scale atrocities. Furthermore, they provide the basis for later efforts to redeem losses and often to extract revenge.

The high frequency of unilaterally imposed outcomes must be recognized.[5] Members of one community often have enforced their claims on another, denying the others' claims. This frequently has been done brutally, most notably in attempts at genocide, in settling one community on land occupied by another people, or by the forced removal of members of communities from where they lived. For example, between 1939 and 1945 the Nazi German government transferred hundreds of thousands of Germans to areas incorporated into the expanded German Reich from areas of Eastern Europe where they had been living; it also moved Hungarians from Yugoslavia to Hungary and Serbs from Croatia to Serbia within Yugoslavia. After World War II, immense numbers of many ethnic groups fled or were removed; for example, ethnic Germans were moved by the millions into the reduced territory that was now Germany. The Soviet government during Stalin's rule harshly transported many peoples from one region to others within the Soviet Union, while Russians moved into the areas from which they had been removed. The brutal treatment of ethnic groups related to these expulsions contributed to the recent dissolution of the former Soviet Union and to the communal violence among and within some of the states arising from their ruins.

Such forced migrations have sometimes produced a separation of communal groups into discrete territories and have also produced forced integration, as when one community moves into territory long held by others and thereafter dominates them politically, economically, and socially through systems of discrimination. For example, this occurred within states dominated by settlers who had moved into the area, as in southern Africa.

Several communal groups have frequently coexisted in the same political, social, and economic system under the dominating rule of another community or ruling group. In many of these systems the rule has been indirect, allowing considerable autonomy or even local political leadership to survive as long as taxes were paid and obedience was shown to the ruling emperor or king. This was the case, for example in the Ottoman and British empires.

Relations among the several subordinated communal groups within such systems can be hierarchical or involve discriminating against some communities and favoring others. Ruling groups often have been viewed as playing one community against the other to maintain their rule; sometimes they give particular opportunities in the military or educational system to a minority group, which is then greatly dependent on the rulers of the empire. When colonial rule ended, the minorities became vulnerable and sometimes subjected to repression by the majority people.

Various members of a subordinated community often respond in different ways to their position. Thus, some members of a religious community may seek assimilation within the dominant group while others seek collective autonomy elsewhere or attempt to transform the system so that communal differences become irrelevant, and still others individually seek to escape by emigrating out of the territory. For example, during the last century of czarist rule of the Russian Empire, many Jews took each of these routes to counter the anti-Semitism they suffered: some strove to assimilate and be Russian; some became Zionists and strove to establish a national homeland in Palestine; others joined socialist and communist parties dedicated to changing the Russian system; and still others emigrated to the United States or other countries of refuge.

External actors often try to intervene and establish new arrangements that structure intercommunal relations. This was done massively after World War I, when the victors established new borders in Europe. To some extent, the borders were drawn along ethnic territorial lines as the Austrian-Hungarian, Ottoman, and Russian empires were broken up or reduced. But ethnic lines could not be clearly drawn. In some cases large-scale population transfers were executed to bring ethnicity into more correspondence with the newly drawn state borders, for example, between Greece and Turkey. In other cases, new multiethnic states were created, as was the case with Yugoslavia and Czechoslovakia.

Finally, communal groups themselves sometimes reach an agreement about their relationship which reflects their acceptance of each other. These arrangements may involve separation into independent states, as for example with the independence of Norway from Sweden in 1905 or following the dissolution of the Soviet Union. Or the arrangements may entail cooperation for particular purposes, as with Franco-German relations in the European Coal and Steel Community. They may also take the form of amalgamated political unions but with institutionalized power sharing among the communal groups in the polity, as in Malaysia. Other arrangements include communal cantonization or egalitarian federation with considerable regional autonomy (for example, as in Switzerland, Belgium, and Spain). Mutual understandings may be less formally structured and allow for a high degree of integration, characterized by mutual acceptance of communal differences without discrimination; this is generally true of European ethnics in the United States.

CONDITIONS AFFECTING RESOLUTIONS

Specific conditions set the parameters for establishing one kind of communal relationship rather than another. In order to determine which policies might be employed to reach desired outcomes, we must recognize the basic conditions which shape the course and outcomes of communal conflicts. Three sets of conditions merit notice: those pertaining to features of each communal group; those pertaining to the relationship between communal groups; and those pertaining to the context in which they are related.

Internal Features of Communal Groups

An important feature of a communal group that affects its relations with others is the extent to which membership in the group tends to be ambiguous and open or is clearly bounded and ascriptively closed.[6] That is, some groups allow or even welcome entry, for example by assimilation, conversion, or other achievable characteristics. Other groups set up firm, impervious categories; membership in them is determined unalterably at birth. Such membership is ascriptive, as with kinship, and to varying degrees ethnicity and "race." Of course, the ascribed groups are social constructs, including racial groups. In many societies, people select some genetically related characteristics to distinguish one "race" from another. But all individuals cannot be unambiguously placed in one or another "racial" category. Social. cultural, and other features are used to help locate people, and the categories vary from culture to culture and over time.[7] For example, in the United States a clear social distinction is made between whites (mostly of European origin) and blacks (anyone with some African origin who was raised in the United States). However, in many other countries, clear dichotomous lines are not drawn; rather, many mixtures are recognized but not treated as fixed and absolute. For example, in Mexico, "Mestizo" is a broad, vague category, and persons can be more or less "Mestizo" or "Indian" depending on the clothes they wear and the language they speak.

The nature of the beliefs held by members of each group about themselves and other communal groups, about their preferred sociopolitical arrangements, and about the appropriate ways to attain as well as sustain those arrangements help shape their relations with other groups. Communities vary in the content and strength of their ethnocentrism and in their norms about tolerance. Finally, they vary in the degree of separation and integration they want with others with whom they live.[8]

Relative Position of Groups

The relative size, economic well-being, and political influence between each pair or among the entire set of communal groups within a political entity, geographic territory, or economic market are critical in shaping their relationship. Note that their relative position depends on the systemic boundaries in which they are related; each can be a minority in one setting while a majority in another. For example, Israeli Jews have seen themselves as a minority in an immense Arab-Islamic region, while Palestinian Arabs have seen themselves as vulnerable and weak in the face of Israeli strength as part of the West. Tamils in Sri Lanka see themselves as a vulnerable minority in a Sinhalese-dominated country, while the Sinhalese see themselves as threatened by the Hindu Tamils of Southern India and Sri Lanka.

The relative standing of communal groups is also affected by the multiplicity of identities that everyone has. Each person has an ethnic, religious, linguistic, local, occupational identity, as well as many others.[9] Their relative salience varies over time, in different social settings, and with the way others relate to that person. All these identities do not neatly coincide, and the way they overlap helps form crosscutting ties among various communal groups. The multiplicity of communal memberships also means that in some contexts people share interests and even identities, although in other contexts they do not.[10]

System Context of Groups

The social context within which the communal groups function profoundly shapes their relations. The context includes the structure of governance within which the groups interact, the cultural understandings they share, and the relations each has with external allies and supporters. The governance structure may embody recognition of communal differences with various forms of autonomy and power sharing, or it may deny them.

The social system to which antagonistic parties belong often has procedures for managing conflicts and ways to redress grievances. These procedures may be highly institutionalized, with official agencies to protect minority rights and active civil organizations to defend and advance minority concerns.

POSSIBLE POLICIES

In deciding what kinds of proactive methods to use to avoid conflicts from becoming destructive, the goals being sought must be considered. Table 2.2 is based on two time periods. One period is the current one, with four different phases of conflict intensity. The other period is the future condition of a conflict, with five possible goals. Combining the two dimensions yields twenty cells, in which possible proactive policies are identified. Most policies fit into many cells, but I have usually identified each policy in the one or two cells in which it is especially relevant. Some cells are left blank because the policies located in them would be relatively long-term or require intervening phases.

All strategies cannot be carried out by everyone. Some policies are usually conducted by one of the adversaries in the conflict and others by actors not directly engaged in the conflict as partisans. Some tend to be conducted by official representatives of one of the major antagonists in the conflict and some by officials of other governments or international organizations acting as intermediaries. Still other policies tend to be enacted by private persons belonging to one of the adversary camps or an intermediary body such as a religious organization, a university, or a humanitarian nongovernmental organization.

Table 2.2

Policies to Prevent Destructive Conflicts

Phase	Preferred Goal				
	A To Correct Underlying Conditions	B To Prevent Destructive Acts	C To Prevent Escalation	D To End Fighting	E To Move Toward Resolution
I. Conflict Emergence	economic growth; dialogue; reduced inequality; integration; shared identity	use legitimate institutions; dialogue; conflict-resolution training	crosscutting ties; nonviolent training; unofficial exchange	—	—
II. Threat or Isolated Destructive Acts	—	deterrence; reassurance; external mediation or intervention; crisis management; precise policies; nonviolent action; peacekeeping	nonviolent action; noninflammatory information; mediation; limiting arms; tit-for-tat; humanitarian assistance; peacekeeping	negotiation; reframing conflicts; confidence-building measures; mediation	negotiation; mutual reassurance; unofficial exchanges; superordinate goals; problem-solving workshops
III. Extensive Destructive Acts	—	—	changing expectations of victory/defeat; intervention; constituency opposition; limiting arms	mediation; external intervention; limiting arms; negotiation	superordinate goals; inter-dependence; confidence-building measures; problem-solving workshops
IV. Protracted and Extensive Destructive Acts	—	—	—	GRIT; problem-solving workshops; unofficial exchanges; negotiate step-by-step; constituency opposition	superordinate goals; acknowledging hurts; no humiliation; external enemy; mutual recognition; shared identity

Not every policy identified in table 2.2 is discussed here. Rather, I discuss several major ways a conflict might be prevented from deteriorating to greater violence from the various levels already reached. In the final section, I consider two cases in which such policies were pursued successfully and one case in which they were not and the conflict consequently deteriorated.

Reducing Conflict-Generating Conditions

Many conditions are frequently mentioned as sources of destructive communal conflicts. Among these are (1) increasing power, economic, and status inequalities; (2) deteriorating economic conditions; (3) lessening of intercommunal interaction and communication; and (4) dissolving of shared institutions and identities.[11]

As indicated in cell IA, policies to correct those conditions would therefore include reducing inequalities, improving economic and social conditions, integrating immigrants, improving dialogue among different peoples, and enhancing shared identities.[12] Pursuing some of the policies, however, has its own set of risks—as does not doing so. Reducing inequalities may raise unfulfilled expectations among the relatively deprived and threaten the relatively advantaged, thus increasing mutual animosities. This can be controlled if the general social and economic conditions are improving, if communication among peoples is enhanced, and if shared identities are made more salient. Stressing shared identities, however, may be experienced by some society members as forced assimilation into the dominant group's identity. The shared identity must be open to all citizens and not require the abandonment of subdominant groups' basic self-identities. In actuality this is rarely if ever fully achieved.

Another set of proactive policies affecting general social conditions may be directed at inhibiting violence, even aside from ameliorating the underlying conditions generating conflict. As shown in cell IB, these include developing official and nonofficial mechanisms for managing disputes. Within a country this ranges from having elected governing organs ensuring each community's representation to establishing local centers that foster intercommunal conciliation.[13] In international affairs, strengthening regional and global institutions and collective security measures are ways to prevent violence. Within and among countries, developing ongoing ties among leaders and rank-and-file persons from diverse communities can be helpful. Finally, widespread familiarity with nonviolent means of pursuing and resolving conflicts can foster their use and so avert violence without acquiescence to oppression.

Other proactive policies affecting general social conditions may be directed at inhibiting conflicts from escalating into high levels of violence, as seen in cell IC. These include promoting norms against the use of violence and having successful experiences with nonviolent means of struggle. They also include the development of cross-cutting ties of association and interest so that divisions based, for example, on region, political ideology, social class, religion, and ethnicity do not correspond and reinforce each other.[14]

Limiting Threats or Isolated Destructive Acts

Once conflicts have emerged so that at least one communal group or country has begun to threaten another with violence, additional policies may be necessary to avert the eruption of violence, which may become self-sustaining. These policies are often those regarded as preventive.[15] The recourse to threats of violence usually reflects the sense that alternative ways of redressing grievances are not available or are ineffective. They may also be derived from widespread feelings of resentment, shame, and profound anger or from the belief by leaders that such feelings can be aroused and drawn on to gain support for themselves in fighting against an enemy people.

The traditional policy for dealing with threats from an enemy is to issue counterthreats, presumably with the intention of deterring the foe (see cell IIB.) Of course, the risk here is that the other side interprets the deterrent counterthreat as confirmation of the dangers it believes are posed by the enemy, requiring even greater threats. A destructive spiral is then underway.

More constructive policies include carefully calibrated, limited responses by one or more of the antagonistic parties. This is best coupled with reassurances recognizing the other side's essential interests to help avoid the conflict's destructive deterioration. Reassurance to the other party that its interests and values are not endangered may be conveyed by unilateral statements and actions, as has been the case with Macedonian leaders after the breakup of Yugoslavia.[16] Reassurances may also be demonstrated by negotiating, concluding, and implementing mutual confidence-building agreements (CBMs).

External interventionists, or government officials in the case of a country, may serve to facilitate negotiations and agreements to settle a dispute or provide alternative ways to reach an accommodation. The Organization of Security and Cooperation in Europe (OSCE) has developed mechanisms to perform such services. External intervention, especially by a legitimate government within a country, may be able to impose a cease-fire. Even internationally, the United Nations or regional organizations may threaten sanctions or promise benefits to contain an escalating conflict.

Finally, nongovernmental agents can provide other preventive services. For example, external mass media attention can arouse wide support for intervention by governmental bodies and inhibit a conflict's escalation. In addition, nonofficial intermediaries may provide another channel for adversaries to exchange information and ideas about possible ways to prevent destructive conflict escalation.

Looking further ahead to prevent an escalation of violence, other, longer-term policies may be effective, as identified in cell IIC. These include an adversary using self-limiting means of struggle such as nonviolent action. Ensuring the provision of non-inflammatory information may also be useful, and this might well be done by external agencies. To stop escalation, one party may pursue a tit-for-tat strategy, initiating a conciliatory measure and then reciprocating the other side's actions at about the same level, cooperation for cooperation and confrontation for confrontation.[17]

Outside intermediaries may help prevent further escalation by several policies. They may provide a variety of mediating services, including persons or organizations acting in nonofficial capacities who explore with the adversaries the possibility of entering de-escalating negotiations; they also include governments and international organizations that engage in mediation using their resources to encourage settlement of matters of dispute. In addition, other governments or international governmental organizations may intervene and provide peacekeeping forces, when agreed to by the antagonistic communal groups.

Looking still further ahead, several additional methods can help to stop violent fighting, as may be seen in cell IID. A fundamental policy is to reframe or to reconceptualize the conflict so that it appears to be a shared problem, a problem less significant than other conflicts, or a block to the achievement of mutual positive goals. Such reframing can be fostered by external intermediaries and also by dissident groups within one or more of the adversary parties. Ultimately, the leadership, perhaps a new one, of one or more of the adversaries adopts and begins to act in terms of this new conception of the conflict.[18]

Considering moves toward resolving the conflict, in cell IIE, we can identify policies such as developing superordinate goals for the adversaries; this sometimes means finding a common enemy against whom they can unite. If the conflict has not escalated very far, mutual reassurances by the adversaries that they do not seek each other's destruction or that they only seek to protect what they have may help resolve the conflict. At least they help provide the bases for negotiating a settlement that can lead to further agreements and ultimately a resolution. Nonofficial as well as official intermediaries can be helpful in undertaking these policies; this may be done by organized exchanges between members of the different communal groups.

Halting Extensive Destructive Acts

Once intense and large-scale violence has developed, inhibiting further escalation until one side is suppressed by the other is of course extremely difficult. The dynamic of escalation takes over. To the adversaries the choice seems to be simply victory or defeat. For extremists this means the destruction of the enemy; the moderate position is to hurt the other side only enough to prove that it cannot win and then negotiate a settlement.

In a sense, prevention is no longer the goal. But proactive policies include measures to stop and reduce violence; continuing violence often means its institutionalization and an increased intractability. Averting such developments can result from a variety of policies, identified in cell IIIC. One policy, more effective if pursued by external actors than by one of the adversaries, is to make it evident that the defeat of one side by the other will not be possible if it threatens the defeated group's existence. If a stalemate seems certain, the adversaries may well settle sooner rather than later. A quite different policy is to make it clear that defeat for one of the adversaries is certain unless it accepts what is acceptable to the other side. Finally, resistance within one of camps to the conflict's continuation also may inhibit its escalation and perhaps hasten its end.

In cell IIID, policies are identified which may lead to an end of the fighting. Intermediaries, official and nonofficial, may identify and suggest options that allow adversaries to envision a satisfactory way out. One such method is changing the mixture of parties involved in the settlement. For example, in the 1980s, several Central American countries were racked by internal conflicts based on ideological and class differences, as well as ethnic differences. These long-lasting and interlocked conflicts made it difficult to settle any one of them in isolation. A large move toward resolution was made by the accord reached among the presidents of the five Central American countries meeting in Esquipulas, Guatemala.[19] Sometimes called the "Arias Plan," the accord included three components to be implemented simultaneously and according to a fixed time schedule. The formula included ending violent conflicts, promoting democracy, and fostering economic integration.

Long-term resolution of the conflict is likely to require additional policies. As identified in cell IIIE, these include confidence-building measures and unofficial problem-solving workshops. Furthermore, increasing integration and developing superordinate goals can be useful, as former adversaries see the possibility of shared benefits through cooperative endeavors.

TRANSFORMING PROTRACTED AND EXTENSIVE DESTRUCTIVE ACTS

Many conflicts persist for many years, even generations. Such protracted struggles appear intractable, and even periods of relative quiescence are viewed as interludes in an ongoing struggle. Transforming such intractable conflicts into tractable ones is extremely difficult. They need to be halted and the underlying conditions perpetuating and sustaining the conflicts corrected.

Only a few policies are noted in row IV of table 2.2: those stressing conflict resolution ideas and experiences that may move parties out of the intractability in which they have become mired. These actions can help to interrupt and resolve such conflicts.

Much depends on the protagonists themselves. For example, constituency weariness with a protracted conflict may become the basis for resistance to continuing a costly struggle. The destruction itself may undermine the legitimacy of the struggle. Constituency opposition to persisting in a conflict may be expressed through protest demonstrations and marches. Some leaders may respond to such changes, particularly if there have also been informal contacts with the opposing side indicating that an acceptable way out may exist. One way to communicate convincingly to the opponent that a mutual accommodation may be possible is to announce and make a conciliatory move and persist in unilateral conciliatory moves, anticipating reciprocation. This is the graduated reciprocation in tension-reduction (GRIT) strategy.[20]

One matter that tends to perpetuate a communal conflict is the apparent denial of the other side's right to exist. The mutual recognition of that right is an essential step in settling such conflicts, as occurred with the 1993 mutual recognition of Palestinians and Jews by the Palestine Liberation Organization and the State of Israel. To resolve a conflict so that it does not recur, one side should not humiliate or shame the other and thus provide fuel for later efforts at revenge.

External changes are important here, and these depend on the actions of parties who are not one of the conflict's primary adversaries. As other conflicts increase in salience for one or more other adversaries, they tend to reduce the salience of the conflict they have with each other; thus, internal conflicts may lessen in the face of threats from a shared external enemy.[21]

The involvement of intermediaries can also foster mutual recognition and reassurances. This includes activities such as problem-solving workshops, extended dialogue groups, educational programs, participation in ritual acts of reconciliation, and investigations and trials of individuals who had perpetrated gross human rights violations.

Three cases of successful and unsuccessful attempts at preventing destructive conflict escalation will be briefly discussed. The emphasis will be on the prevention of such destructive conflicts before high levels of direct violence developed.

Canada

The conflict between French-speaking Quebec and the rest of Canada has been long-standing and exacerbated by the economic dominance of English-speakers over French-speakers in Quebec.[22] The political context, however, has provided legitimate channels for pursuing the conflict and moderating it; for example, the federal system allows for significant provincial authority. Furthermore, although Quebec has long had provincially based parties, country-wide parties have always been important, and these often have had long-lasting leadership by someone from Quebec (for example, Pierre Trudeau of the Liberal Party). Furthermore, official and non-official policies were directed at building and sustaining a Canadian identity, one that incorporated and extolled its ethnic mosaic nature.

In the 1960s the Quebec separatist movement grew rapidly, and the Front de Liberation du Quebec (FLQ), a tiny Maoist organization, conducted bombings and robberies for funds. This culminated in October 1970 with the kidnaping of two officials, one of whom was killed. Prime Minister Trudeau invoked the War Measures Act, and the FLQ was made illegal; the government's actions were forceful but not indiscriminate. Violence as a means of gaining independence was generally repudiated, even by advocates of independence.

Even earlier, some of the underlying social, political, and economic inequalities between French- and English-speaking Canadians were addressed through the modernization efforts of the Liberal Party known as the Quiet Revolution, which was begun in 1960; but that modernization generated stronger sentiments for independence. Some concerns related to protecting French-speakers, particularly outside of Quebec, were responded to by the Official Languages Act, passed in 1969. The Party Québécois, on attaining power in 1976 in Quebec, strengthened the act and introduced other measures to enhance the role of French-speakers in Quebec.

Many meetings have been held to find a new formula for the

relations between Quebec and the other provinces of Canada, including the Meech Lake Accord of 1987. None of the many efforts to reach a resolution of the conflict between Quebec and the rest of Canada has yet been accepted by majorities of all the required parties, whether for confederation or for separation, and dissatisfaction is widespread. Nevertheless, the conflict has been pursued using institutions generally regarded as legitimate. The 1980 and 1995 referenda in Quebec, whatever their ambiguity, provided additional channels for the struggle over the future of Quebec to be conducted. On the whole, the parties to the conflict continue to seek a negotiated settlement that will be acceptable to the adversaries and enable them to work together in the future. The interdependence is evident, and the search for a formula to satisfy the interests and preferences of most people within each camp continues, even as some groups would be willing to abandon that effort. In any case, despite considerable frustration and the failure up to now to reach a stable resolution, violence and compulsion are disavowed and unlikely. The process seems not awful compared to places where ethnic or other communal struggles have escalated into very destructive conflicts.

South Africa

South Africa, after decades of predictions that a very bloody and long violent struggle would convulse the country, has achieved a resolution of the conflict between the dominant white communities and the subordinated black and colored communities.[23] In the transition, there was considerable violence, but it was not organized in a large continuing manner, nor was it mainly between the white and black communities.

The actions that many people in South Africa and outside it had taken over the preceding few decades modified the underlying conditions. This has helped to prevent either massively violent suppression by the government or large-scale armed revolution from below. Despite apartheid, there had been growing economic integration and mutual dependence among blacks and whites. The economy had grown well for many years, but in the 1980s its growth was hampered by apartheid and the sanctions imposed by much of the rest of the world.

The legitimacy of the apartheid system was undermined by the moral opprobrium with which it was viewed by people outside South

Africa and even by increasing numbers of the more educated white South Africans. For example, the Dutch Reformed Church passed a resolution in October 1986 that the forced separation of peoples could not be considered a Biblical imperative. Moreover, in the 1980s the resistance of blacks in the form of consumer and rent boycotts made it clear to most whites that apartheid could not be sustained without economic and social costs that were unacceptable. Repression had failed. Yet at the same time, the armed struggle strategy of the African National Congress (ANC) also failed during the 1980s. Bases to conduct the struggle in Mozambique and other neighboring countries were lost under extreme pressure from the South African government.

Significantly, new strategies pursued by the adversaries became increasingly reassuring to each other as they turned to find nonviolent alternatives to settle their conflict. The ANC, which in the early 1960s had sanctioned armed struggle, avoided terrorism.[24] Instead, in recent years, rent strikes and trade union actions were actively pursued. The ANC and trade unions consistently stressed their nonracist goals. In 1984, white business leaders began meeting with ANC leaders, unofficially and outside South Africa, prior to the official negotiations. The shared identity of being South Africans was important to many, at least of the elites of the major communities.

Direct, mediated, and indirect conversations were held between South African government and ANC leaders to explore formulas for possible resolutions. Mutual understandings were attained, and after the ANC was unbanned and Nelson Mandela was unconditionally released from prison in 1990, extended negotiations were conducted. The negotiations resulted in agreements and procedures to ensure the protection of all the communities of South Africa. This included avoiding threats to endanger the whites' economic well-being, despite their loss of political dominance.

Nelson Mandela and the ANC and President Frederik W. de Klerk and the government cooperated in staging events and meetings to reassure each other's constituencies as well as their own. These included recognition of the importance of moving toward healing and reconciliation, including expressions of guilt and understanding. The establishment of the Commission on Truth and Reconciliation was an important part of such movement.

Of course, many particular conflicts persist, and new ones have arisen that engage the peoples of South Africa. But they are in a different context, and the fundamental conflict that was epitomized by apartheid is ended.

Yugoslavia

Yugoslavia is an example of a horrible failure to prevent terrible violence. There had been warnings that this disaster would occur, and yet the actions and inactions of many parties propelled the opposing factions toward escalating violence rather than preventing it. Even in retrospect, it seems hard to say what might have been done by intermediaries to prevent what happened.[25]

Many conventional explanations stress long-standing mutual hatreds among the ethnic communities of the former Yugoslavia and the loss of central authority to keep the enemies from each other's throats. Such explanations miss important components, ones that were modifiable with policies of early prevention.

Certain actions might have been taken to correct the underlying conditions. Thus, direct acknowledgment of the communal hurts of the past might have been helpful; for example, if trials were held after World War II of persons alleged to have committed atrocities during the war, some of the desire for revenge that was available for mobilization might have been reduced.

Reducing economic and political inequalities related to region and ethnicity was difficult since the regions of the country differed greatly in their economic conditions. Fostering equality became even more difficult when economic conditions deteriorated in the 1980s.

Policies to increase the salience and significance of the Yugoslav identity would have been helpful. In the past, many Yugoslavians felt pride for having stood up to the Soviets in 1948 and creating a new and effective economic system, publicly owned and worker-managed firms operated in a market system. As pride in such matters dissipated, new reasons for pride as Yugoslavia would have been useful. Perhaps its successful multiethnic character should have been claimed. Another, less attractive option would have been to find a new external enemy.

Other policies might have helped contain the conflicts and fostered their pursuit by nonviolent means. More organizations might usefully have been established to directly address ethnic-related grievances and promote individual and collective human and social rights. Furthermore, if Yugoslavia had developed countrywide political parties in addition to the League of Communists of Yugo-slavia (LCY), the collapse of the LCY would not have led so easily to ethnically based parties. The Yugoslav army might have remained a countrywide institution, but it failed to be one and came to act as the Serbian army.

Long-term policies that would have reduced the scale of and emphasis upon armed force might have been helpful in preventing the rush to violence. Through socialization and training, alternatives to the reliance on guns and other tools of violence might have been promoted, for example, education about and training in conflict resolution and nonviolent action.

Contrary to these policies, the political leaders often pursued policies that undermined Yugoslav identity and institutions. Slobodan Milosevic and other claimants to leadership resorted to appeals, provocations, and manipulations to garner support on ethnic grounds. The public, in many cases, were resistant to the policies but unable to stop the step-by-step deterioration.

Once the conflicts had moved to the threat of armed force and violent acts had been committed, additional policies might have prevented the escalation of the violence. The new government of Croatia, headed by President Franjo Tudjman, could have reassured ethnic Serbs living in Croatia that their communal rights would be recognized and protected.

External actors, such as the European governments, the OCSE, and UN mediators, might have striven to manage the conflict in a more comprehensive and coherent fashion than dealing with each conflict as merely between two or three parties at one time. They might have given more reassurances to threatened parties and offered more opportunities for trade-offs. Some efforts were made, but the governments often pursued different policies, supporting different groups in what had been Yugoslavia. They could not themselves assure people that their rights would be protected and did not effectively threaten those who endangered others' rights.

CONCLUSIONS

The analysis presented suggests seven points. First, it is important to examine successful proactive policies that successfully prevented conflicts from erupting or deteriorating destructively. Studying how matters go badly does not automatically inform analysts and policy-makers about what might make matters go well.

Of course, success is never total; therefore, we should examine conflicts that did not go as badly as they might have. Attention should be given to averting a disaster and doing well under the prevailing circumstances.

Second, the application of proactive policies should be extended in time. Attention should be given to long-term policies to block the emergence of destructive conflicts. Public understanding of prevention needs to be increased so that governmental and nongovernmental policies that take a long time will have added support. This includes developing norms and institutions that foster mutual respect of different communal groups and developing interpersonal networks and bonds across communal divides. International nongovernmental organizations are often able to sustain long-term policies, focusing as they do on specific matters with a committed constituency. This is illustrated by the persistent efforts in regard to human rights and humanitarian assistance.

Third, attention should be given to proactive policies that have long-term peace-building consequences. Policies aimed only to halt killing may freeze a conflict, only to have it erupt again later. This means that a multitrack strategy should be planned. For example, economic development projects may be undertaken in ways that foster cooperation across communal lines. In addition, policies should be pursued that encourage forming an identity that is held in common by contending communal groups.

Fourth, preventing a conflict from becoming destructive depends most importantly on the protagonists in the conflict. Intermediaries from the outside frequently have only a limited effect. Intermediaries can, however, play useful, even critical roles at crucial junctures in a conflict. Furthermore, some intermediaries may powerfully channel a conflict; for example, this is usually the case for a legitimate government not closely identified with either of the contenders in a communal struggle, intervening in the conflict between them.

Fifth, no single policy is likely to be adequate to reach any of the goals set forth here. Preventing conflicts from deteriorating and becoming increasingly destructive requires many policies being pursued by various actors. Combinations that are mutually supportive need to be chosen, involving nongovernmental as well as governmental players. The efforts of various intermediaries should be coordinated, both as they are conducted sequentially and as they carried out at the same time. Effective coordination may be done in many ways, including particular intermediaries clearly taking the lead role and regular consultations among the intermediaries.[26]

Sixth, proactive policies as practiced by intermediaries rely not only on providing facilitation and using persuasion; they also rely on threatening negative sanctions and promising future benefits. Various combinations of inducements may be effective, depending on the nature and phase of the conflict and its particularities. Familiarity with a variety of possible policies and the circumstances of the conflict of concern is essential; such familiarity increases the likelihood of choosing the best policy for a given time. No policy is right for every conflict at all times, but one or another proactive action may well be appropriate at each particular time in a conflict's course.[27]

Finally, we should recognize that policies are inevitably significantly shaped and selected in terms of values and preferences and not only by beliefs about the course of any given conflict or of conflicts in general. Thus, whether action should be taken to deter an adversary rests not only on beliefs about the consequences of such efforts but also on the readiness to resort to violence and to accept certain injustices. This needs to be emphasized, since avoiding violence is rarely the only goal of partisans or observers. But the frequent failure to avoid mutual losses in destructive conflicts should spur us all to discover constructive ways of conducting struggles.

NOTES

1. Earlier versions of segments of this paper were presented at the International Studies Association annual meeting in Acapulco, Mexico, March 1993, and at the International Society of Political Psychology annual meeting in Cambridge, Massachusetts, July 1993. An earlier version of this chapter appears in Carment and James, eds., *Wars in the Midst of Peace: The International Politics of Ethnic Conflict* (Pittsburgh: University of Pittsburgh Press, 1997). I wish to thank the following persons for comments about previous versions of this material: Allan Griffith, Herbert C. Kelman, Stephen P. Koff, Gene Sharp, Carolyn M. Stephenson, and John C. Western.

2. The literature in this area is extensive, particularly focusing on ethnicity. See, for example, Agnew (1989), Anderson (1991), Horowitz (1985), Smith (1971), Connor (1994), and Lund (1996b).

3. This issue between what has come to be called primordialism and

constructionism has been a fundamental one in discussions about ethnicity. See, for example, Comaroff (1991), Gordon (1978), and Brass (1991).

4. Several ways of distinguishing the kinds of relations among communal groups have been put forward; with reference to them, see Shibutani and Kwan (1965), Nordlinger (1972), and McGarry and O'Leary (1993).

5. See Licklider (1995).

6. Ascriptive roles are ones assigned by birth and generally not selected by the incumbent; this is usually conceptually distinguished from achieved roles, which incumbents attain by their own actions. For example, gender, ethnicity, and even class origin are ascribed, but occupational role (in a noncaste society) is an achieved role. See, for example, Parsons (1951).

7. For recent discussions of the concept of race and its social construction, see Winant (1994) and Gregory and Sanjek (1994).

8. For a review and synthesis of the literature on ethnocentrism, see Levine and Campbell (1972). For an analysis of the current distribution of the various goals of politicized minorities in the world, see Gurr (1994).

9. Some of these identities are neatly nested within each other and generally reinforce each other, for example, city, province, and national identities. Others generally crosscut each other, for example professional and ethnic identities. How much they are experienced as consistent or as inconsistent depends on the content of the identities and particularly on their exclusivity. Some identities include expectations of multiple identities, but others would deny the appropriateness of dual loyalties, for example to nationality, exclusively defined.

10. Political leaders may try to reduce communal conflicts among their constituencies by stressing shared identities, sometimes in opposition to outside adversaries. For example, the government officials of many new nations strive to emphasize their state identity and the external threats to it. The emphasis on national identity is more likely to supersede communal antagonism if the nation is defined in civic and territorial terms rather than in ethnic or other communal terms (see Smith 1991).

11. See for example, Paige (1975), Hechter (1975), Tiryakan and Rogowski (1985), and Neuberger (1986); relevant case studies include Zamir (1990), Snyder (1982), Peretz (1990), and Clark (1984).

12. The success of the West German government in absorbing and integrating the German refugees from areas of Czechoslovakia, Poland, and East Germany undercut the risks of irredentist policies; on the other hand, the resistance in nearly all Arab countries to absorbing Palestinian refugees exacerbated the Israeli-Palestinian conflict (Kriesberg 1989).

13. This policy may be fostered by organizations in other countries, introducing such approaches. For example, with the end of Soviet domination of Eastern Europe, many organizations based in the United States have assisted in conflict resolution training and in developing local insti-

tutions to provide conflict resolution services.

14. On the role of crosscut ties in inhibiting conflict, see Dahrendorf (1959) and Kriesberg (1982).

15. See discussion in Lund (1996).

16. For example, see Ackerman (1996).

17. For an extended discussion of the tit-for-tat strategy, see Axelrod (1984); and for a test of the strategy and others in international relations, see Goldstein and Freeman (1990).

18. For example, when Anwar Sadat became president of Egypt after Gamal Nasser died, he undertook a different strategic approach, believing that the previous approach had failed. He shifted the relative importance of the issues dividing the Arabs and Israel and the means to attain the highest priority matters. He reduced the primacy of leadership of the Arab nation and believed Egyptian goals would be better achieved through Washington than through Moscow. See Kriesberg (1992).

19. For analyses of this strategy, see Hopmann (1988) and Wehr and Lederach (1991).

20. The strategy was discussed by Osgood (1962) in relation to the Cold War and has been analyzed largely in relationship to international conflicts. For example, see Goldstein and Freeman (1990).

21. This idea is discussed by George Simmel.

22. For an analysis of the francophone-anglophone conflict in Canada, see McRoberts (1988); and for the 1970 events, see Breton (1972).

23. For analyses of the transformation in South Africa, see for example van der Merwe (1989), Kane-Berman (1990), Adam and Moodley (1993), and Sparks (1995). For comparative analyses, see Giliomee and Gagnio (1990).

24. Nelson Mandela (1994) discusses the ANC decision in the early 1960s to sanction the establishment of MK, the Spear of the Nation, to conduct an armed struggle. He explains the choice of armed struggle: "For a small fledgling army, open revolution was inconceivable. Terrorism inevitably reflected poorly on those who used it . . . . Guerrilla warfare was a possibility, but since the ANC had been reluctant to embrace violence at all, it made sense to start with the form of violence that inflicted the least harm against individuals: sabotage. Because it did not involve the loss of life, it offered the best hope for reconciliation among the races afterward" (530).

25. For an account of the collapse of Yugoslavia, see Glenny (1992), Kaufman (1994/95), and Cohen (1995). For discussions of possible conflict resolution applications to the conflicts in the former Yugoslavia, see Kuzmanic and Truger (1992). The conflict became intractable once the leaders of Serbia, Croatia, and Slovenia had mobilized their constituents into positions that threatened the other communities. External intervention would have to have been extraordinarily well timed, threatening and

reassuring at the same time to be effective; see Kaufman (this volume) and also Owen (1996).

26. The problems of coordination and ways of solving them are discussed in Kriesberg (1996) and Lund (1996).

27. The literature on the timing of de-escalating actions has been growing. See Kriesberg and Thorson (1991) and Zartman (1989).

REFERENCES

Ackerman, Alice. 1996. "The Former Yugoslav Republic of Macedonia: A Relatively Successful Case of Conflict Prevention in Europe." *Security Dialogue* 27, no. 4: 409–24.

Adam, Herbert, and Kogila Moodley. 1993. *The Negotiated Revolution*. Johannesburg: Jonathan Ball.

Anderson, Benedict. 1991. *Imagined Communities: Reflections on the Origin and Spread of Nationalism*. Revised edition. London: Verso.

Axelrod, Robert. 1984. *The Evolution of Cooperation*. New York: Basic Books.

Brass, Paul R. 1991. *Ethnicity and Nationalism: Theory and Comparison*. New Delhi, Newbury Park, Cal., and London: Sage.

Breton, Raymond. 1972. "The Socio-Political Dynamics of the October Events." *Canadian Review of Sociology and Anthropology* 9: 33–56.

Clark, Robert P. 1984. *The Basque Insurgents, ETA, 1952–1980*. Madison: University of Wisconsin Press.

Cohen, Leonard J. 1995. *Broken Bonds: Yugoslavia's Disintegration and Balkan Politics in Transition*. Boulder, Colo.: Westview.

Comaroff, John L. 1991. "Humanity, Ethnicity, Nationality: Conceptual and Comparative Perspectives on the U.S.S.R." *Theory and Society* 20: 661–87.

Conner, Walker. 1994. *Ethnonationalism*. Princeton: Princeton University Press.

Coser, Lewis. 1956. *The Functions of Social Conflict*. New York: Free Press.

Dahrendorf, Ralf. 1959. *Class and Class Conflict in Industrial Society*. Stanford: Stanford University Press.

Giliome, Hermann, and Jannie Gagiano, eds. *The Elusive Search for Peace: South Africa, Israel and Northern Ireland*, edited by Cape Town: Oxford University Press.

Glenny, Misha. 1992. *The Fall of Yugoslavia*. New York: Penguin.

Goldstein, Joshua, and John R. Freeman. 1990. *Three-Way Street: Strategic Reciprocity in World Politics*. Chicago: University of Chicago Press.

Gordon, Milton. 1978. *Human Nature, Class, and Ethnicity*. New York: Oxford University Press.

Gregory, Steven, and Roger Sanjek, eds. 1994. *Race*. New Brunswick, N.J.: Rutgers University Press.

Gurr, Ted Robert.1994. *Minorities at Risk*. Washington, D.C.: United States Institute of Peace Press.

Hechter, Michael. 1975. *Internal Colonialism*. London: Routledge and Kegan Paul.

Hopmann, P. Terrence. 1988. "Negotiating Peace in Central America." *Negotiation Journal* 4: 361–80.

Kane-Berman, John. 1990. *South Africa's Silent Revolution*. Johannesburg: South African Institute of Race Relations.

Kaufman, Stuart. 1994/95. "The Irresistible Force and the Imperceptible Object: The Yugoslav Breakup and Western Policy." *Security Studies* 4 (Winter): 281–329.

Kriesberg, Louis. 1982. *Social Conflicts*. Revised edition. Englewood Cliffs, N.J.: Prentice-Hall.

———. 1989. "Transforming Conflicts in the Middle East and Central Europe." In *Intractable Conflicts and Their Transformation*, edited by Louis Kriesberg, Terrell A. Northrup, and Stuart J. Thorson. Syracuse: Syracuse University Press. 109–31.

———. 1992. *International Conflict Resolution*. New Haven and London: Yale University Press.

———. 1996. "Coordinating Intermediary Activities." *Negotiation Journal*. vol. 12, no. 4: 341–52.

——— and Stuart J. Thorson, eds. 1991. *Timing the De-Escalation of International Conflicts*. Syracuse: Syracuse University Press.

Kuzmanic, Tonci, and Arno Truger, eds. 1992. *Yugoslavia War*. Ljubljana and Schlaining: Austrian Study Center for Peace and Conflict Resolution, Schlaining, and Peace Institute, Ljubljana.

Levine, Robert A., and Donald T. Campbell. 1972. *Ethnocentrism: Theories of Conflict, Ethnic Attitudes and Group Behavior*. New Haven and London: Yale University Press.

Licklider, Roy. 1995. "The Consequences of Negotiated Settlements in Civil Wars, 1945–1993." *American Political Science Review* 89 (September): 681–90.

Lund, Michael S. 1996b. "Early Warning and Preventive Diplomacy." In *Managing Global Chaos,* edited by F. Hampson, C. Crocker, and P. Aaal. Washington, D.C.: U.S. Institute of Peace Press, 1996, 379–403.

———. 1996. *Preventing Violent Conflicts*. Washington, D.C.: U.S. Institute of Peace Press.

Mandela, Nelson. 1994. *Long Walk to Freedom*. Boston: Little Brown.

McGarry, John, and Brendan O'Leary, eds. 1993. *The Politics of Ethnic Conflict*. London and New York: Routledge.

McRoberts, Kenneth. 1988. *Quebec: Social Change and Political Crisis*.

Third edition. Toronto: McClelland and Stewart.

Neuberger, Benjamin. 1986. *National Self-Determination*. Boulder, Colo.: Lynne Reinner.

———. 1990. "Nationalisms Compared: ANC, IRA, and PLO." In *The Elusive Search for Peace: South Africa, Israel and Northern Ireland*, edited by Hermann Giliome and Jannie Gagiano. Cape Town: Oxford University Press. 54–77.

Nordlinger, Eric. 1972. *Conflict Regulation in Divided Societies*. Cambridge, Mass.: Harvard University Press.

Osgood, Charles E. 1962. *An Alternative to War or Surrender*. Urbana: University of Illinois Press.

Owen, David. 1996. *Balkan Odyssey*. New York: Harcourt Brace.

Paige, Jeffery M. 1975. *Agrarian Revolution: Social Movements and Export Agriculture in the Underdeveloped World*. New York: Free Press.

Parsons, Talcott. 1951. *The Social System*. New York: Free Press.

Peretz, Don. 1990. *Intifada*. Boulder, San Francisco, and London: Westview.

Ross, Marc Howard. "The Language of Success and Failure in Ethnic Conflict Management." In *Conflict and Change*, edited by Valerie Morgan. New York: United Nations University Press, forthcoming.

Shibutani, Tamotsu, and Kian M. Kwan. 1965. *Ethnic Stratification: A Comparative Approach*. New York: Macmillan.

Smith, Anthony D. 1991. *National Identity*. Reno, Las Vegas, and London: University of Nevada Press.

———. 1971. *Theories of Nationalism*. New York: Harper and Row.

Snyder, Louis L. 1982. *Global Mini-Nationalisms, Autonomy or Independence*. Westport, Conn.: Greenwood.

Sparks, Aliser. 1995. *Tomorrow Is Another Country: The Inside Story of South Africa's Road to Change*. New York: Hill and Wang.

Thompson, Richard H. 1990. *Theories of Ethnicity: A Critical Appraisal*. New York: Greenwood.

Tiryakan, Edward A., and Ronald Rogowski, eds. 1985. *New Nationalisms of the Developed West*. Boston: Allen and Unwin.

Van der Merwe, Hendrik W. 1989. *Pursuing Justice and Peace in South Africa*. London and New York: Routledge.

Wehr, Paul, and John Paul Lederach. 1991. "Mediating Conflict in Central America." *Journal of Peace Research* 28: 85–98.

Winant, Howard. 1994. *Racial Conditions*. Minneapolis: University of Minnesota Press.

Zamir, Meir. 1990. *The Formation of Modern Lebanon*. Ithaca, N.Y.: Cornell University Press.

Zartman, I. William. 1989. *Ripe for Resolution: Conflict and Intervention in Africa*. Second edition. New York: Oxford University Press.

Part 2

Conflict Prevention: Regional and International Approaches

3

Preventive Diplomacy, Conflict Prevention, and Ethnic Conflict

STEPHEN RYAN

INTRODUCTION

The end of the Cold War induced a period of optimism about a stronger role for the UN in international relations. Preventive diplomacy (along with peace enforcement and humanitarian intervention) was one area in which it was felt that the UN could enhance its status as the protector of international peace and security, and calls for an improved conflict prevention role have since emerged from a wide range of perspectives. The idea was one aspect of Gorbachev's "new thinking" in the USSR's post-Cold War foreign policy, and Soviet diplomats argued that the UN might adopt an early warning system and deploy UN observer posts in potential trouble spots around the globe (Belanogov 1990). From a perspective of a lifetime's work within the UN, Urquhart (1990) argued that "a new determination to give the UN a capacity to watch for, and anticipate, critical situations should also increase its capacity for contingency planning and timely action" (205).

This chapter will subject this interest in preventive diplomacy in general, and preventive peacekeeping in particular, to critical scrutiny. It is divided into five parts. Part one briefly defines the key ideas of ethnic conflict, conflict prevention, and preventive peacekeeping. Part two explores the interest that has been expressed in these ideas since 1989. Part three argues that the "technical" approach to conflict prevention adopted by the UN and the Organization for Cooperation and Security (OSCE) is not sufficient to stop outbreaks of violent ethnic conflict because it ignores deep structural causes. These include tension between the principle of national self-determination and multicultural reality; the difficulties of ensuring stability in an unstable international environment; inequalities in the distribution of wealth; and the structural changes that occur in the parties to ethnic conflict once they experience significant intercommunal violence. Part four studies the issue of the timing of interventions in ethnic conflict. The fifth, and final, part will offer some policy suggestions that could improve the international community's effectiveness in its attempts to prevent violent ethnic conflict.

First, what are the implications of labeling a conflict as "ethnic"? Here ethnic conflict refers to conflict between groups who define themselves as distinct because of cultural differences. This interpretation is consistent with Kriesberg's concept of communal groups (Kriesberg, this volume). Differences can arise from a combination of factors that include a distinctive language, religion, and history. The term *ethnic conflict*, however, is not meant to imply that violent conflicts between these distinct groups are caused by their sense of difference. When we talk about interstate conflict we do not imply that the cause of war is the existence of separate sovereign states. To say that ethnic conflict arises because there are distinct ethnic groups is, at best, tautological. We need to identify the specific factors that move communities from nonviolent to violent confrontation. There is no reason, therefore, to assume that ethnicity is necessarily destructive, nor is the label *ethnic conflict* much help in identifying the root causes of major interethnic violence.

Most, if not all, serious ethnic conflicts arise because the parties concerned believe there to be incompatible interests between them. These may be about the constitutional status of the groups, the degree of autonomy groups are to enjoy, the future destiny of particular regions, or the sense of injustice that can arise when there is not deemed to be a fair allocation of resources. Thus, Ennals (1989) has identified several "areas of conflict" that can trigger ethnic violence: land, participation in government, educational provisions (or the lack of them) and culture (17–21). He claims

> Until governments appreciate that internal conflict is caused by real grievances and not invented by agitators, there will be no solutions. When constitutions do not

allow the full and equitable participation of people in their own governance, the seeds of discord and conflict are being planted, and will grow.... When certain groups are excluded from the benefits of common wealth and real political participation, violence will result.

However, to understand fully why it has proved so difficult to prevent violent ethnic conflict, perhaps we need to dig even deeper. Why is it that these conflicts of interest arise so frequently between ethnic groups? Part of the reason is, no doubt, cultural. The presence of different groups living in close proximity, or even intermingled together, may have resulted in a historical legacy of fear, hatred, and distrust. Who was it who said that history had dug a ditch for the Irish which was now so deep that they could not climb out of it? Historical experiences (real or imagined) can result in a denial of a common humanity, which is what Yevgeny Yevtushenko may have been hinting at when he claimed that only masks hate each other.

Before I proceed, however, it is important that the key concepts of conflict prevention and preventive peacekeeping are addressed. Since all peacekeeping is concerned to prevent violence, why do we need a separate category of preventive peacekeeping? What are we trying to prevent? As Kaufman observes later on in this volume, preventive peacekeeping serves many different purposes.

The definition of peacekeeping that I shall adopt in this chapter is that offered by the International Peace Academy (IPA). This definition is identical in most important respects to that found in chapter 1 of the current volume:

> the prevention, containment, moderation and termination of hostilities between or within states, through the medium of a peaceful third-party intervention organized and directed internationally, using a multinational force of soldiers, police, and civilians to restore and maintain peace.

Three points need to be made about the definition. The first is that it defines peacekeeping in a very broad way in terms of participants and tasks. It recognizes that police and civilians (e.g., human-rights monitors, election supervisors) as well as soldiers can play an important role in peacekeeping.

If there is to be more to peacekeeping than border patrols it is likely that international forces will find themselves in complex and difficult situations with which military personnel are not always equipped to deal. There is no doubt that the way that UN peace-keeping is evolving in practice means that forces have to engage in a large number of military and nonmilitary tasks. A report by the United States Institute for Peace points out that peacekeeping tasks now include "civil functions, disarming militias, providing security to the population, rescuing 'failed' countries, organizing elections, launching preventive deployment, encouraging peace settlement, providing humanitarian assistance, or security for delivery of humanitarian assistance" (1994: 8). These roles can be accommodated within the IPA definition.

The need for nonmilitary contingents was recognized in the Cyprus case, where a small civilian police contingent (UNCIVPOL) was deployed alongside UNFICYP to deal with police matters that had an intercommunal content. In ethnic conflict situations in which the state is the representative of the dominant cultural group (the so-called "ethnocratic state") and other groups are challenging the legitimacy of this state, indigenous police forces are likely to be seen as part of the problem rather than part of the solution. Insensitive policing at the intercommunal interface can result in resentment and hostility and can produce charges of illegal shooting, harassment, biased courts, and torture and inhuman treatment in detention. In many cases of intercommunal conflict, therefore, an international police force could be an effective mechanism for reducing the opportunities for violent ethnic conflict. Indeed, in some circumstances such a force might have more to contribute to conflict prevention than military contingents.

Secondly, the IPA definition restricts international peacekeeping to multiparty intervention, organized and directed internationally. The term international direction is rather vague but would exclude, for example, the Indian Peacekeeping Force in Sri Lanka, which was composed exclusively of Indian troops and was directed from New Delhi. It would also cast doubt on the legitimacy of Russia's recent peacekeeping missions in the so-called "near abroad." But would this definition also exclude the multinational force that was sent to Beirut by the US, France, Italy, and the UK? This was a multiparty operation, but it was not under "international" direction in the sense that it was answerable to an international organization.

Thirdly, the International Peace Academy definition allows for a preventive role for peacekeeping. This is an underdeveloped area for the UN and for other international organizations, which have tended to use peacekeeping forces for the management of conflict (i.e., the containment, moderation, and termination of hostilities). This raises the question, however, about what is meant by prevention.

The concept of preventive diplomacy could be applied both to attempts to stop new conflicts becoming violent and to attempts to stop the reemergence of old violent conflicts that are presently being managed by peacekeeping operations deployed to monitor and implement cease-fire agreements. In this sense all peacekeeping forces are trying to prevent conflict. So as well as the preventive deployment of UN troops in Macedonia, the concept of preventive peacekeeping could also be applied to the work of the United Nations Force in Cyprus (UNFICYP) or UNIFIL in Lebanon. So why do we need a separate category for preventive peacekeeping?

An Agenda for Peace states that the aim of preventive diplomacy is to "ease tensions before they result in conflict."(13) This seems to be an unrealistic goal, and we should resist attempts to define conflict prevention in this way. Rather, one should think of stopping not all conflict, but destructive conflict—where ethnic groups become locked into violent behavior. Banks makes this point in an attack of the "peace as harmony" idea. He writes:

> Most of us, however, cannot live in a world without conflict, physically or even mentally. Nor would we wish to do so, for conflict is both inevitable and necessary. It is inevitable because both people and groups have basic needs, expressed in society through competing values and clashing interests. It is necessary in order to provide the catalyst for social processes without which life would hardly be worthwhile: stimulus, challenge, change and progress.... Realistic peace education must start from a recognition of these facts. Its aim must not be to abolish conflict, but to facilitate its healthy expression and to bring it under social control. (1987: 260)

Therefore, the problem that conflict prevention has to address is not the conflict per se but the destructive course that certain conflicts take. This seems to match the description of conflict prevention offered by Rupesinghe (1992): "a situation where conflicting goals exist is controlled to avoid the development of violent conflicts" (92).

Prevention, in this chapter, means action that is taken to stop destructive conflict developing, not action that is taken after the destructive conflict is underway. Therefore we can distinguish between preventive peacekeeping and "traditional" peacekeeping because the former tries to stop destructive conflict from occurring while the latter responds after destructive violence is underway. It is, therefore, not the tasks of conflict prevention that distinguish the two types of peacekeeping but the timing of intervention in the conflict. Here we can draw on an analogy from the medical world. All medicine tries to prevent illness, but there is a clear difference between the clinical model, which emphasizes the treatment of sick people, and the public-health model, which aims to prevent the occurrence of illness by dealing with environmental factors that cause disease and sickness. Conventional peacekeeping can be seen as the clinical approach, preventive peacekeeping as part of the environmental approach.

As there are so few examples of deployment to prevent new violent conflicts from erupting, most of the lessons we can learn have to be inferred from existing attempts to prevent the reemergence of violent conflict by what can be termed traditional peacekeeping forces. But one should be wary about setting out guidelines for peacekeepers in too dogmatic a fashion. One of the strengths of UN operations in the past has been their flexibility and the pragmatic attitude that has been adopted to each specific situation in which they have been deployed.

THE END OF THE COLD WAR AND GROWING INTEREST IN CONFLICT PREVENTION

Dedring (1992), from a perspective within the UN Secretariat, has examined the new roles the UN secretary-general played in the field of conflict resolution in a renewed flurry of activity in the late 1980s. Rikhye (1992), someone with considerable peacekeeping experience, [1] found it especially galling that the UN "has yet to prevent the worsening of an emerging conflict" and has tended to be "reactive, not pro-active" (2). He wants to see the UN contribute more effectively through the use of peacekeepers, early warning, and observers and monitors. From an academic perspective, Thakur (1993) has written that the "UN needs to sharpen its skills at identifying potential conflicts before the fact ... disputes are much harder to resolve when they have matured to fully-grown conflicts"

(19). Rupesinghe has pointed out that there "needs to be a mechanism which requires early and timely intervention" and believes that the UN should draw up "a comprehensive contingency plan ... for entire regions of conflict" (95). A relatively upbeat assessment of UN peacekeeping can also be found in Croate and Puchala (1990). But this optimism about a new role for the UN climaxed with the former UN secretary-general's *An Agenda for Peace* document of 1992, in which Boutros-Ghali set out his ideas about an enhanced role for the UN. Boutros-Ghali (1992b) argued that "a new era has brought new credibility to the United Nations" and that there were rising expectations that the organization "will take on larger responsibilities and a greater role in overcoming pervasive and interrelated obstacles to peace and development" (89). As Saito (1993: 115) has noted, the *Agenda* is a manifestation of a growing realization that if the UN was to meet current challenges it had to develop a comprehensive repertoire of constructive interventions in conflict.

In retrospect *An Agenda for Peace* was a wide-ranging and flawed attempt to produce a general role for the UN as the key protector of international peace and security in the contemporary international system. I do not have time to examine all aspects of it here. Instead I shall concentrate on sections II and V, which deal with the concepts of preventive diplomacy and peacekeeping, respectively. The former is based on the idea that "the most desirable and efficient employment of diplomacy is to ease tensions before they result in conflict—or, if conflict breaks out, to act swiftly to contain it and resolve its underlying causes" (par. 23). This would involve a wide range of strategies: confidence building, fact-finding, early warning, and the establishment of demilitarized zones. It is also clear from the document that peacekeeping can be seen as part of preventive diplomacy. Paragraph 21 argues that peacekeeping "is a technique that expands the possibilities for both the prevention of conflict and the making of peace"; and paragraphs 28–32 refer to the preventive deployment of UN contingents in interstate and intrastate conflicts.

The UN is not the only international forum in which preventive diplomacy has received sustained scrutiny. The OSCE seems to have done even more to apply the preventive approach to conflict. It has, for example, created a mechanism for consultation with regard to emergency decisions at the OSCE, and a Conflict Prevention Center has been established in Vienna as a result of a decision made at the November 1990 Paris Summit. This center was given the responsibility of gathering information on the application of the arms embargo on the former Yugoslavia. This conflict was the main focus of the OSCE's work at its inception. The OSCE also sent a mission of rapporteurs to the six republics (and Vojvodina and Kosovo) in 1991–92. This was followed up by another mission, organized by the Conflict Prevention Center, to Belgrade and Kosovo in mid-1992. Later that same year, "missions of long duration" were sent to the Serbian regions of Kosovo, Vojvodina, and Sanjak to contribute to the prevention of violent conflict. OSCE missions have also been sent to troubled areas such as Georgia, Estonia, Tajikistan, and Nagorno-Karabakh. Also, the newly created OSCE High Commissioner on National Minorities is meant to act as an instrument of conflict prevention and is supposed to provide early warning of tensions involving national minorities (see, for example, Griffiths 1993: ch. 5).

There have also been attempts to implement preventive diplomacy ideas at the UN. The organization has sent observers to South Africa and Haiti and fact-finding missions to Moldova and Nagorno-Karabakh. The most dramatic example of UN action in this field has been the dispatch of a peacekeeping force to Macedonia after the president of Macedonia, with the support of Cyrus Vance and David Owen, requested the deployment of UN observers in his state.

Macedonia declared its independence in April 1992 and has borders with Serbia, Bulgaria, Albania, and Greece, all of whom have territorial claims against it. A volatile situation in the region appeared to be worsening in November 1992 when there were clashes between ethnic Albanians in Macedonia (about 21 percent of the total population) and police. It was then the government of Macedonia and the UN and European Community (EC) mediators requested UN involvement. In response to the request, the secretary-general sent a group of military and civilian personnel to the area, and on the basis of their report recommended to the Security Council that UNPROFOR's mandate be expanded to include a conflict prevention role in Macedonia. On 11 December 1992, Security Council resolution 795 authorized the dispatch of military, civilian, and police personnel. At the end of 1992, peacekeeping troops were sent to Macedonia in the first large-scale deployment of peacekeepers to stop violent conflict from erupting. By July 1993 there were about one thousand UN soldiers engaged in this work, seven hundred from Scandinavia and three hundred from the US (Operation "Able Sentry"). The UN's work in Macedonia has been complemented by the OSCE, which deployed a civilian mission in Skopje and established two regional monitoring centers in Tetovo and Kumanovo.

The UN has also engaged in preventive diplomacy in South Africa, where it has attempted to ease the transition from apartheid to a pluralist democracy. Security Council resolution 772 of August 1992 has already authorized the establishment of the UN Observer Mission in South Africa (UNOMSA). Fifty observers were sent to all parts of South Africa in what the chief of the UN operation has called "a unique application of preventive diplomacy" (King 1993: 10).

Yet the period of optimism about preventive diplomacy has not lasted long. After what appear to be at best mixed results in the former Yugoslavia, Somalia, Angola, and Rwanda, hopes of a more peaceful global order have been replaced by fears and anxieties. In the mid-1990s a poll found that in the UK, US, Germany, and Japan more people thought the world had become more dangerous rather than safer since the end of the Cold War.[2] There is now a growing skepticism about the ability of international organizations to respond effectively to potentially destructive conflict.[3]

One reason why the UN has been so ineffective is that it lacks leverage over local actors, especially the warlords who have become such a striking feature of many recent ethnic conflicts. Here it is becoming clear that the end of the Cold War was not without certain negative consequences for conflict prevention. The removal of Soviet hegemony over Eastern Europe and of the threat to Yugoslavia, together with the collapse of the USSR itself, created a window of opportunity for long-suppressed nationalist movements to stake their claims for autonomy or independence. Furthermore, during the Cold War the superpowers were forced to play a crisis management role because of a fear that they would be dragged into a major military confrontation on opposite sides. In this sense the superpowers were what Aron called "enemy partners." He pointed out how "the Cold War ... is subject to unwritten laws, which the protagonists have recognized by degrees, applying them spontaneously and almost unconsciously" (1954: 171). They were able to exert their power on regional clients to restrain and suppress conflicts in order to avoid the breakdown of the nuclear deterrence system and ensure that the "long peace" lasted throughout the Cold War (Gaddis 1987). Williams (1976) has also explored this phenomenon and shows how the idea of crisis management, which is virtually unique to the nuclear age, is important in enabling us to understand superpower crises. In the post-Cold War world, the job of crisis management has now been taken up by bodies like the UN, the OSCE, and NATO. Preventive capacity is being developed within the OAU, OAS, and ASEAN. Although the UN has always played the lead role, more and more emphasis is being placed on regional capacity. In many ways the whole peacekeeping project can be seen as a child of the Cold War, and the paralysis on the Security Council and regional organizations that was the result of superpower competition has now been lifted. During the Cold War the UN was not central to crisis management work; nor were regional organizations, save NATO. Now the UN is key, but it lacks the leverage of the superpowers. Furthermore, since the threat of both mutual nuclear annihilation and superpower intervention has receded, states lack the sense of urgency that once existed to stop possibly violent situations from escalating out of hand. This is true even though the great powers are becoming increasingly involved in UN peacekeeping work. Another change involves the breakdown of certain clearly defined norms in the international political system. The general hostility to secession and an unlimited right to self-determination now appears to be softening, as is the principle of nonintervention in the internal affairs of member states.

In this more uncertain international environment it is clear that one of the most urgent tasks facing the international system is the creation of stable, democratic multiethnic states. For ethnic conflict not only threatens to spill over into interstate conflict, it also leads to gross violations of human rights and to massive refugee problems. But the growing pessimism about the chances of constructive third-party involvement in ethnic conflicts has encouraged some to believe that the best way to respond to ethnic conflict is through partition. This is not an inherently flawed idea, as divorce is sometimes a less painful option than the "separate bedrooms" arrangement. However it is a "solution" that involves surrendering to the arguments of extreme nationalists, who are sometimes willing, if a situation does not allow for an easy, clean break, to endorse policies of ethnic cleansing and genocide. In order to counter these policies the international community needs to devise mechanisms that can promote peaceful multiethnic states.

FACTORS PROMOTING VIOLENT ETHNIC CONFLICT

However we regard it, preventive peacekeeping has to compete with more negative factors that work against constructive responses to ethnic conflict. Before we can make informed suggestions about how to promote stable and democratic multiethnic states through preventive peacekeeping we need to understand some of the factors that frustrate such initiatives.

Cultural issues are certainly important in understanding the roots of violent ethnic conflict, but they may not be the complete explanation. In an analysis of intercommunal relations in Northern Ireland, Ruane and Todd (1991) have critically examined what they term the "cultural approach" to the "Troubles." This would emphasize the way the communities have become trapped within their own myths, beliefs, and tribal loyalties that has led to intolerant and uncompromising positions. It follows that if this is the real explanation for the conflict, solutions should concentrate on cultural areas, also: through reconciliation, education, and mutual understanding. Such an approach, however, does not satisfy Ruane and Todd. To counter it they propose a "structural approach" that concentrates on the broader picture and can point to factors contributing to the violence, which were beyond the control of the parties themselves. The constitutional partition of the island and the political structures this created would be one such factor. The partition of the island of Ireland was regarded as illegitimate by the majority of Irish people and a significant minority within Northern Ireland itself. Economic inequality between the communities is another structural factor the authors identify. One might want to quarrel with the way Ruane and Todd regard the cultural and structural explanations as competing approaches, but they do alert us to the presence of "deeper" factors that can promote violent ethnic conflict. We can now say something about the main structural influences that work against preventive peacekeeping in ethnic conflict situations.

THE TENSION BETWEEN MULTICULTURAL REALITY AND THE NATIONALIST DRIVE FOR HOMOGENEITY

There is clearly an important relationship between the existence of an ethnic group and the development of a nationalist ideology (see Smith 1991). For nationalism takes the existence of cultural distinctiveness and turns it into a major political principle. So, as Gellner (1983) has pointed out, the key idea of nationalism is "one nation, one state." In other words, the cultural boundaries of the ethnic group should coincide with the territorial boundaries of the state. Hence the concept of national self-determination, which is one of the key legitimizing principles of the contemporary international political system. As Ignatieff (1993) notes, nationalism is a doctrine that holds "(1) that the world's peoples are divided into nations, (2) that these nations should have the right of self-determination, and (3) that full self-determination requires statehood" (110). In fact, ever the since the French Revolution, nationalists have believed that a state's legitimacy depends on it representing the popular will of the nation, though Hobsbawm (1990) has rightly noted that what the French revolutionaries meant by nation may not be the same as what contemporary ethnonationalists claim it to be. He argues that for French and American revolutionaries in the eighteenth century the concept of the nation was closer to our idea of state citizenship. Yet, however nationalism is defined, there is no doubt that some states are clearly better placed than others. But nationalists are not likely to be deterred from applying their ideals even in situations such as that in the former Yugoslavia, which a decade ago appeared to be very stony ground on which to sow such principles.

Self-determination is referred to in numerous international documents, including the 1941 Atlantic Charter, articles 1(2) and 55 of the UN Charter, article 1 of both the 1966 Covenant on Economic, Social and Cultural Rights and the Covenant on Civil and Political Rights, article 8 of the Helsinki Final Act, and paragraph 1 of the 1960 Declaration on the Granting of Independence to Colonial Countries and Peoples. It also has been referred to many times in General Assembly resolutions on, for example, the rights of Palestinians.

It must, of course, be noted that the UN Charter refers only to the principle of the self-determination of peoples, whereas later documents refer to the right of national self-determination. It should also be noted that the UN has never intended that all ethnic groups should be entitled to such a right. But attempts to limit the applicability of the right have not been very successful in practice, and it is an idea that can have disastrous implications for multiethnic states.

For the adoption of nationalism by one or more of the ethnic groups within such a state creates real problems of legitimacy. It was John Stuart Mill (1972) who argued that "free institutions are next to impossible in a country made up of different nationalities" (361). This view has been supported by many other writers (see Ryan 1990: ch. 2).

While it is easy to understand the reasons for nationalism in societies long denied their own identity and history by "foreign" rule, it is also important to note that the idea of national self-determination, which is such a central feature of nationalist thought, can undermine multiethnic societies. It is this double-edged nature of nationalism that we have to recognize: it is a way both of creating and destroying communities. It can be linked with freedom and independence but also with oppression and chauvinism. It destroys multiethnic communities in two main ways. First it encourages ethnic minorities to seek full independence or suffer what Gellner once called the "psychic humiliation" of not having a homeland of one's own. In the absence of more "rational" explanations, perhaps this explains why there was such an urge in Slovakia for an independent state. The idea of national self-determination also gives minorities an interesting counter to the claims of dominant groups. For if such groups are entitled to their self-determination, why should the principle not be applied to ethnic minorities as well? So, for example, when Moldova proclaimed its independence on 27 August 1991, the "left-bank" ethnic Russians of the Trans-Dniester region, who had been part of Ukraine until 1940, countered with their own declaration of independence in December 1991. In so doing the Russian community was rejecting Moldavian nationalism and affirming their own link with a larger Russian community. The Turkish Cypriots used the principle of self-determination to counter Greek Cypriot demands for *enosis* (union with Greece), and some Northern Ireland Protestants would prefer to work for an independent Ulster than accept a united Ireland.

National self-determination can also have a major impact on the attitude of dominant groups in certain states to ethnic minorities within their borders. Young (1985) has pointed out the conflict that can exist between the normative ideal of the nation-state and cultural and political reality. Dominant groups have sought several solutions to this dilemma. Unfortunately, these "solutions" often exacerbate the conflict (Ryan 1988). Lord Acton (Dalberg-Acton

1909) had recognized this problem several decades ago. He stated:

> The greatest adversary of the rights of nationality is the modern theory of nationality. By making the state and the nation commensurate with each other in theory, it reduces practically to a subject condition all other nationalities that may be within the boundary. It cannot admit them to equality with the ruling nation which constitutes the state because the state would then cease to be national, which would be a contradiction of the principle of its existence. (297–98)

Van den Berghe (1981) has also argued that "any recognition by the state of ethnic sub-groups with a special relationship to the state ... would be inconsistent with the idea of popular sovereignty" (347).

The ideology of nationalism, then, can result in a desire to establish an ethnonationalist or ethnocratic state that is particularly strong when a dominant culture has obtained its freedom from foreign rule or when it has experienced a particularly traumatic recent history. Thus we see that most of the national "revolutions" in history have resulted in the persecution of ethnic minorities within the newly created "nation-state." The French Revolution is the classic example of this. Despite its proclaimed support for the rights of nations, the new regime became the "Jacobin" state that adopted a policy of forced assimilation of non-French-speaking groups. From there we can trace a line of similar cases through the Hungarian and Turkish national revolutions to contemporary examples of Zionism and Sinhalese nationalism. Examples of this phenomenon are numerous.

One common response by the idealized, and fictitious, nation-state is to deny the existence of a distinct cultural group so as to question the legitimacy of its claim to self-determination. This is what Turkey attempted to do with the Kurds, who were officially designated "mountain Turks." But Turkey is not unique in adopting such a policy of denial. Many Jews in Israel have attempted to deny the existence of a distinct Palestinian nation. When Bulgaria adopted a policy of assimilating its Turkish minority in the mid-1980s it argued that these were really ethnic Bulgarians who had been forced to convert to Islam by the Ottoman Empire.

Other popular responses by the nation-state are forced assimilation (or cultural genocide); expulsion—or "ethnic cleansing," as it has come to be called; and genocide. We can see the first of these strategies being used by Franco's regime in Spain against Basques and Catalans, by China in Tibet, and by the late communist government in Bulgaria against its Turkish minority. Examples of expulsion include the transfer of over 1 million Greeks from Asia Minor to Greece in the early 1920s and the ejection of seventy-four thousand Asians from Uganda in 1971. Genocide is also still found in state responses to ethnic minorities, as was the case in Burundi in 1972 and East Timor since 1975 (see, for example, Fein 1992; Kuper 1981; and Van den Berghe 1990).

THE SEARCH FOR POLITICAL STABILITY IN AN UNSTABLE INTERSTATE ENVIRONMENT

It is not just the ideology of nationalism that affects a dominant group's response to minorities. Also important is the regional and global system of power relations within which a particular state is located. International politics has been described as a decentralized self-help system in which each state is responsible for its own survival. In such a system, which some have described as "Hobbesian," there is an ever-present fear of attack. This tends to breed suspicion, distrust, and uncertainty. All states have to prepare for war. But in war situations there is a decreased tolerance for internal dissension, especially when an ethnic minority has links with another state that the state might exploit for its own geopolitical reasons. Even more explosive are double minority situations, in which the dominant group in one state is actually a minority itself in the wider regional context. So Jews are a majority in Israel but a minority in the Middle East. Greek Cypriots are a majority vis-à-vis Turkish Cypriots but a minority vis-à-vis Turkey. The Sinhalese are a majority on Sri Lanka, but with forty million Tamils in nearby India they are also a minority. The same is true of Protestants, who are a majority in Northern Ireland but a minority on the island of Ireland.

In such situations minorities may be seen as Trojan horses who serve the interests of foreign powers and undermine the security of their resident state. This can be seen in Jewish attitudes to Palestinians, Protestant attitudes to Catholics in Northern Ireland, Nicaraguan attitudes to the Meskito Indians, the Chinese in Vietnam, the Sikhs in the Punjab, and so on. In all these cases minorities have been associated with threats to the security of the state, and this, in part, explains why they have been denied some basic rights.

The threat to the security of the state can be raised in a number of ways, as just a quick analysis of the situation in the former Soviet Union will reveal. Here we find secession movements (e.g., Chechniya, Abkhazia), irredentism (Romania-Moldova and the so-called Bessarabian question, Pan-Turkism in Turkic areas), refugees (from Azerbaijan to Iran Northern Caucuses), disputed territories (Nagorno-Karabakh between Armenia and Azerbaijan and Crimea between Russia and the Ukraine), and the threat of external involvement in any of the above situations (Turkish and Iranian threats to intervene in the Armenia-Azerbaijan conflict).

A final feature of the interstate system that should be noted is its lack of sympathy for the issue of minority protection. Since many states feel threatened by claims arising from their own minority groups it is unlikely that intergovernmental organizations or international law (still predominantly formed by states) will respond with enthusiasm to requests to enshrine rights of minorities. This is reflected inter alia in the deliberate omission of an article on minority rights from the Universal Declaration of Human Rights and the lowly position of the Sub-Commission for the Prevention of Discrimination and the Protection of Minorities in the UN hierarchy. Furthermore, even when states do take measures to protect minority groups there is no reason to suppose that these states will have the will to make such measures effective. The 1948 Genocide Convention, for example, makes it an international crime to engage in genocidal acts, but there has been a reluctance to invoke it against governments engaged in genocidal activities (see Kuper 1985). The only exception to this is the UN's decision to establish a war crimes commission to punish war criminals from the former Yugoslavia. One of its functions is to detect breaches of the 1948 Genocide Convention.

COPING WITH ECONOMIC PROBLEMS

There seems little doubt that interethnic stability can be affected by economic factors, but there is no real agreement about the extent of the influence. There are some who would attempt to explain the impulse to identify with an ethnic group in economic terms. Such writers tend to see ethnic conflicts as arising over the rational pursuit of scarce resources, where the ability to mobilize an ethnic constituency increases one's access to wealth and power (see, for example, Hechter 1975 and Nairn 1977). Connor (1990), how-ever, argues that economic explanations undervalue the depth and intensity of ethnic feeling. We do not have the time or space to do justice to this debate here, but we can point out that economic issues do frequently seem to encourage ethnic conflicts and eco-nomic grievances and disagreements over development are a factor in most protracted ethnic conflicts even if they are not the only cause of the violence.

A rather common feature of multiethnic societies is an uneven distribution of wealth. Where there are such inequalities there will arise claims of unfair treatment and exploitation. Ironically, though, very often these claims arise from well-off areas, where they can be an important factor in promoting secessionist demands. Here a rela-tively prosperous area starts to feel resentful that its wealth is being expropriated by the central state. Such an attitude developed among the Basques in Spain, in the oil-rich Ibo region in Nigeria, in Slovenia and Croatia in Yugoslavia, and in the mineral-rich area of Bougainville in Papua New Guinea. It also seems to have been a factor in the drive for independence in the Baltic republics and in the Ukraine at the start of this decade. Where the focus of resent-ment is a failed central state, such as the former Yugoslavia or the USSR, which lacks the resources to buy off discontent in the re-gions, then the pressures within the relatively prosperous regions to secede will grow even stronger. There is no simple relationship, therefore, between economic development and violence, and, as McGarry and O'Leary (1993: 15) have noted, secession demands can arise in both economically advanced groups (e.g., Basques, Slovenes, Sikhs, Tamils) and economically backward communities (Kurds, Karens, Slovaks).

STRUCTURAL CHANGES CAUSED BY THE DYNAMICS OF ETHNIC VIOLENCE

Several writers have identified the onset of destructive processes that emerge when violent conflict breaks out between ethnic groups. Such processes include the militarization of conflict, the physical and psychological separation of the parties, increased ethnocen-trism, entrapment, economic underdevelopment, and a sense of powerlessness and victimization. Kuper (1977) has examined the different aspects of polarization during conflict in plural societies. They include the aggregation of the parties into hostile groups; escalation through reciprocal violence; and the contraction of the middle ground. Wehr (1979) has written about the way conflict triggers a move from specific to general issues, the distortion of information, reciprocal causation, and the emergence of extremist leaders. Mitchell (1981) shows how conflicts produce tunnel vision, premature closing of options, misattribution of motives, stereotype bolstering, and polarization.

Given these destructive processes, it is not surprising that Pruitt and Rubin (1986) have developed a "structural change" model, which claims that the way the conflict is pursued results in "residues" in the form of changes in the parties. These changes can occur at the psychological (dehumanization, deindividuation), group (increased cohesiveness), and environmental (polarization) levels.

PROBLEMS OF TIMING

The idea of intervening in ethnic conflicts before they become violent seems a good one, given the destructive processes that can be released when violence does erupt. However, when it comes time to transform knowledge of an impending violent conflict into action, we have to ask whether the parties to the conflict will be willing to accept external intervention at an early stage. There are at least two writers who might cause us to adopt a pessimistic attitude to the idea of conflict prevention.

The first writer is Zartman (1989). His concept of the "hurting stalemate" is an important contribution to the literature on third-party involvement in conflict, but it is an idea that seems to suggest such involvement will only be effective when a "ripe moment" exists. This ripe moment exists when there is a mutually hurting stalemate, when unilateral solutions are blocked and the parties recognize that continuing violence will damage all sides. He claims that

> Conceptually, the moment stands out, but in reality it is buried in the rubble of events.... Like any metaphor, the idea of the ripe moment should not be taken too literally. Moments, when ripe, do not fall into one's hands; they have to be taken with skill.... Thus, for the conciliating power, it is a question not only of correctly identifying the right times to move but also of moving the times with skill. (273)

One implication of the idea of the hurting stalemate is that constructive involvement before this point in the conflict is reached is not likely to be fruitful. If this is true there may be very few opportunities to engage in preventive peacekeeping. The idea of the hurting stalemate has been tested and refined by Stedman (1991) in an excellent study of the negotiations that ended white minority rule in Rhodesia. Stedman reinforces the claim that the idea of the hurting stalemate should have a central part in the theory of conflict resolution and attempts to bring in an intraparty dimension to how the concept is applied. The idea of timing is now central to an understanding of interventionist strategies (see Kriesberg, this volume).[4]

The idea that the experience of violence is an important factor in provoking people to react against it is also found in Kant's idea of unsocial sociability. His work on perpetual peace may lead one to think that this supreme example of Enlightenment thinking was a naive optimist. Yet he fully realized that there was a conflict in us all between our need for sociability and our need for freedom. He also recognized that reason alone would not force societies to take the steps necessary to establish the conditions for peace. This would be provided by the experience of war itself. In *On the Commonplace: That May Be Correct in Theory but Is Useless in Practice*, Kant writes:

> Nevertheless universal violence and the evils arising from it, at last force a people of necessity to resolve to subject themselves to the constraints of public law, which is the very means that reason itself prescribes; and thus to form and enter into a civil or political Constitution. And, in like manner, the evils arising from constant wars by which the States seek to reduce or subdue each other, bring them at last, even against their will, also to enter into a universal or cosmopolitan Constitution. (quoted in Forsyth et al. 1970: 196)

In this way, he concluded in the First Supplement to *Perpetual Peace*, "the great artist Nature" visibly "exhibits a design to bring forth concord out of the discord of men, even against their will" (Forsyth et al. 1970: 217).

A major problem for the supporters of preventive diplomacy in general and preventive peacekeeping in particular, therefore, is to gain support from the parties to the conflicts before they have learned through bitter experience the need to deal constructively with their differences. This may not be possible in many cases, and so those wishing to engage in constructive intervention will have to adjust their strategies and lower their expectations. One of the most interesting developments in contemporary conflict resolution theory is the idea that conflicts progress through certain stages and that intervention strategies that work at one stage of the conflict will be unsuccessful if applied at other stages.

This is a theme taken up by Rupesinghe (1992). He has developed an approach to constructive conflict intervention that relates the strategy used to the stage that a conflict has reached. His arguments have been summarized in the form of a table.

Table 3.1

Phases in the Conflict Process

1.	conflict formation	early warning
2.	conflict escalation	crisis intervention
3.	conflict endurance	empowerment and mediation
4.	conflict improvement	negotiation/problem solving
5.	conflict transformation	new institutions and projects

At any one time different ethnic conflicts will be at different stages. In winter 1994 Rwanda was at stage two. In 1995 Bosnia was at stage three. (Rwanda in the spring of 1994 moved to stage three as well), which is defined by Rupesinghe as the "phase in the process where the parties to the conflict have entered a state of war where the reproduction of violence becomes pathological" (92). In 1997, Bosnia was at stage four. Cyprus is at stage four, and South Africa, Palestine, and Lebanon have moved on to stage five. There is always a danger, of course, that conflicts can move back a stage or stagnate. The former happened in Angola, where disputed elections resulted in a reemergence of large-scale violent conflict. The latter occurred in Somalia, where the conflict appears to be stuck in phase three. The place for peacekeeping has traditionally been seen as stage two, crisis intervention (though, once deployed, UN forces tend to remain through stages three and four as well). However, there is no reason why peacekeepers cannot have a significant impact at stages one and five. This chapter is concerned with stage one, and it is to this issue that we can now turn.

TOWARD REAL PREVENTIVE DIPLOMACY?

The concentration on structural factors in this chapter should not be taken as an excuse for resignation in the face of problems caused by interethnic relations. Of course, if these factors are deeply embedded in the political and economic structures of the contemporary world they will not be easily addressed. As we are all probably too aware, there are no easy solutions to protracted ethnic conflicts. However, it is precisely because these problems are so deeply embedded that we need enlightened, flexible, and imaginative responses from political leaders. Personalities and policies can make a substantial difference. Compare, for example, what happened in Yugoslavia under Tito and Milosevic. Or consider the role played by Mandela and de Klerk in South Africa. One reason why South Africa is moving toward a multiethnic society whereas Northern Ireland has remained locked into continuing violence is that in the former case there have been leaders of vision and ability to take advantage of the sense of hurting stalemate that has developed after years of fighting and destruction.

The analysis presented here suggests that an enlightened response to ethnic conflict prevention in multiethnic societies would involve the following factors. It can be seen that in each category there is a need for a mixture of technical measures and action directed at structural problems. At the technical level, of course, there need to be improvements in early warning systems. Initiatives have to be taken to restrict the flow of weapons to trouble spots. The spread of conflict resolution skills through training should be encouraged. However, these measures will have to be supported by deeper changes if they are to have long-term success. There is a danger in emphasizing the role of preventive peacekeeping divorced from other conflict resolution strategies. Peacekeeping is really a form of conflict management, not a mechanism to resolve conflicts. At best it can ensure the "pacific perpetuation of disputes," which can contribute to a period of relative calm to allow the parties an opportunity to negotiate a resolution. As Thakur (1987) has noted, "the goal of peacekeeping units is not the creation of peace, but rather the containment of war so that others can search for peace in stable conditions" (489). Furthermore, it is a form of management that involves the separation of the parties. In fact, it can be seen as a way of legitimizing this separation, as may have been the case in Cyprus and is certainly true in the former Yugoslavia.

Therefore, it is important to note that if peacekeeping is not matched by positive developments in the areas of peacemaking and peacebuilding it could be used as a form of conflict control to shore up a problematic or even unjust situation. Thus Cordovez (1987) has pointed out that if peacekeeping is "not properly coordinated with the necessary peacemaking efforts, they may provide a false sense of security and perpetuate *de facto* situations without removing smouldering potential causes for renewed violence" (173). This is really pacification, not the establishment of a lasting peace. Baer (1993) has expressed concern that this is what Russian "peacekeeping" forces may be doing in the so-called "near abroad." At the very best preventive peacekeeping used in isolation would be a short-term palliative for troublesome symptoms. Therefore, it is important that peacekeeping be seen as one strategy in the conflict resolution process, not as an isolated "law and order" technique. If we want to move beyond even the strategies of conflict resolution to conflict prevention, then we have address the structural aspects of ethnic violence. Four issues seem to be significant here: (1) denationalization of the state; (2) recognition and dealing with the interstate dimension of ethnic conflicts; (3) dealing with economic inequalities; and (4) assessment of the proper role of sanctions.

It is vital that the state is not made the instrument of a dominant cultural group but becomes the agent for pluralism and tolerance of diversity. This will involve the cultivation of a civic-territorial nationalism based on equal rights and common citizenship to counter demonic ethnic-nationalism, which is exclusivist and intolerant of difference. Smith (1991) has shown how this demonic nationalism is created "from below" by excluded intelligentsia using cultural resources to mobilize a community into political action. When, and if, such a group does obtain political power the state tends to develop a powerful ethnic nationalism. Smith believes that this type of nationalism represents the "vast majority of active nationalism today" (123).

A strong civil society is needed to counter the exclusivist nationalist claims by an ethnocratic state, but it has to be a civil society sensitive to ethnic difference. Much of the classic liberal literature on civil society is of little help here, since it does not address this issue of cultural pluralism. If one thinks of Rawls's *A Theory of Justice* (1972), for example, one of the most influential liberal texts of this century, one finds that a central virtue of his system is that a person is ignorant of his or her place in society when determining what would constitute a just society. Cultural identity is ignored.

As well as supporting the establishment of a culturally sensitive civil society, the UN could help create new international norms for minority protection. Certain international documents do exist already. The Genocide Convention was adopted by the General Assembly in 1948, but, as we have already noted, it has been invoked by the UN twice only, in response to events in the former Yugoslavia and Rwanda. In 1992 the UN also passed a Declaration on the Rights of Persons Belonging to National or Ethnic, Religious or Linguistic Minorities. In article 1 it calls on states to protect the existence and identity of minorities and to adopt appropriate legislation to achieve these ends. This, however, is not legally binding. In addition, international law could become more open to ideas of group rights and autonomy (see Hannum 1990). It may even have to reassess its hostility to the right to self-determination outside of the colonial context (Halperin et al. 1992).

The strategies used to form a strong, denationalized civil society may not be centrally linked to preventive peacekeeping. However, one could easily envisage a role for such a peacekeeping force in the early attempts to establish such a society. It could, for example, monitor human rights compliance and elections or provide safe escort for parties wanting to meet to discuss common issues, etc. The OSCE, in particular, as we saw at the start of this chapter, has attempted to link peace with human rights through the creation of monitoring and fact-finding missions and the work of the High Commissioner on National Minorities.

In cases where there is an affective link between another state and a minority, the interstate dimension of ethnic conflict must be recognized. Policies of tolerance and mutual accommodation (as suggested just previously) may in themselves help to ease cross-border relations. But perhaps the only truly effective way to handle the interstate dimension is by settling the territorial destiny of disputed regions.[5] This means satisfying the demands of internal and external actors. Although this will not be easy, it is not an impossible task. Here we can learn much from the examples of the South Tyrol (German-speaking minority in Italy) and the Aaland Islands

(Swedish minority in Finland). In both cases the minorities in question accepted the jurisdiction of the state they were living in and implicitly renounced any irredentist desire, in return for substantial local powers to run their own affairs. The success of such an approach depended on the maintenance of good relations between the host state and the parent state (Italy-Austria in the case of the South Tyrol and Finland-Sweden in the Aaland Island case).

One way of reducing the fears of external involvement is to deploy a peacekeeping force to play a sort of "trip wire" function along a frontier (see Kaufman, this volume). Any invading army would then have to face the international outrage that would follow from an assault through peacekeeping positions. Of course the record of the UN in deterring invasion has not been a good one. Just think of how Turkey invaded Cyprus in 1974 despite the presence of UNFICYP and how the Israeli Defense Forces marched through UNIFIL lines in their 1982 invasion of Lebanon. Clearly, therefore, the mere presence of such UN troops is not enough. They need firm backing from the Security Council in order to be an effective deterrent. Possible interveners have to know that tripping the wire will bring about effective action from the international community. One way to do this is to attach troops from the permanent members of the Security Council to preventive peacekeeping operations. There is evidence, for example, that the presence of British troops in UNFICYP did deter Turkish attacks on certain parts of Cyprus, most notably at the Nicosia International Airport. In this context it is interesting to note the US contribution to UNPROFOR in Macedonia. The presence of US troops on the ground there probably altered the calculations of regional actors, although it has become a truism that one of the problems with conflict prevention is how to know if it has been successful. If violence does not break out, how can you show that this was the result of successful conflict prevention initiatives? How can you prove a counterfactual?

Especially important with respect to economic inequalities is Stavenhagen's idea of "ethno-development." He has defined ethno-development as "redefining the nature of nation-building and enriching the complex, multicultural fabric of many modern states, by recognizing the legitimate aspirations of the culturally distinct ethnics that make up the national whole" (1990: 90–91).

Some states have begun to link the aid they give to such considerations. The Swedish government stopped its Forest Development

Project in the Chittagong Hill Tracts of Bangladesh because the government was not employing enough local people. The Australian government abandoned a road-building project in the same region because it could be used by troops deployed in a military offensive against the indigenous people (Chaudhuri 1991: 149).

The 1992 Declaration on the Rights of Persons Belonging to National or Ethnic, Religious or Linguistic Minorities also addresses this issue. Article 4(5) declares that states "should consider appropriate measures so that persons belonging to minorities may participate fully in the economic progress and development in their country." Article 5 proclaims that national policies and programs, and programs of cooperation and assistance among states, should be planned and implemented "with due regard for the legitimate interests of persons belonging to minorities."

Two interesting tests of the link between development and peace will arise in Palestine and South Africa. In the former case the international community has realized that any deal between Israel and the PLO about the Occupied Territories will have to be underwritten by the west. Large amounts of aid have already been pledged to help with the economic development of Gaza and those parts of the West Bank that will be granted autonomy. In South Africa it may be that the move to a democratic system of government will be a lot easier than the resolution of the problems that will arise because of the huge disparities in wealth that exist between blacks and whites. The long-term success of democracy in South Africa may be determined by the ability of the new government to address this issue. The ANC has adopted a "Reconstruction and Development Programme" to address issues such as housing, education, and employment in the townships, but this may depend on western economic assistance for it to be successful.

It is also interesting that *An Agenda for Peace* does not include sanctions in its discussion of preventive diplomacy. These actions instead are included under peacemaking as something to be implemented after a conflict breaks out. This seems a serious omission, especially if we accept Zartman's point that effective mediation requires leverage on the parties.

So where does this leave the role of conflict prevention? On the one hand, the existence of all of these negative influences would tend to make us cautious about an optimistic prognosis. On the other hand, the wide range of negative influences and the diverse strategies needed to address them alerts us to the rich possibilities for constructive UN involvement in ethnic conflict. Many of these could have a peacekeeping element. But whether one adopts a pessimistic or an optimistic approach to ethnic conflict there will still be a role for peacekeeping and preventive diplomacy. Pessimistic analyses tend to support the separation of ethnic groups, and the new entities that emerge from such separation may need their security guaranteed by some form of peacekeeping deployment (Macedonia). Optimistic analyses tend to favor the bringing together of conflicting groups. Here the role of peacekeepers is to establish an environment that can facilitate such contacts and to reduce damaging third party interventions. These challenges, involving greater diversity and comprehensiveness, will only be met if there is substantial improvement in areas of training, planning, funding, coordination between agencies, predictive ability, and greater integration of peacekeeping, peacebuilding, and peacemaking approaches. The UN will also need stronger support from its own member governments.

International Alert (1993) has pointed out the need to develop and cultivate broad-based coalitions to prevent internal conflicts. In so doing they have listed the nongovernmental actors who could implement what they term nonmilitary prevention: humanitarian agencies, development agencies, citizen-based peace movements, the business community, and the media. They also include the military in their list. We are now at the stage when we should encourage a sustained dialogue between UN peacekeepers, diplomats, and these other actors about how to enhance effective and coherent prevention strategies.

NOTES

1. Indar Jit Rikhye was a senior officer in the Indian army when he became the first commander of the first UN peacekeeping force in the Sinai (UNEF). He has also been military adviser to the UN secretary-general. In 1969 he founded the International Peace Academy and acted as its president until 1989. He has published extensively on UN peacekeeping.

2. The four-nations poll was conducted for the *Guardian*, *Asahi*, *Shimbun*, *Der Spiegel*, and the *New York Times*. It was conducted the same week in the UK, US, Germany, and Japan, and the same questions were asked to a chosen and balanced cross-section of electors. The results were reported in the *Guardian* on 2 April 1994.

3. See, for example, Hella Pick's article "10 Days at the Sharp End" (*Guardian*, 9 January 1993) or Jonathan Eyal's "The Undoing of the UN" (*Guardian*, 4 December 1992).

4. See also: R. J. Fisher, "Pacific, Impartial Third Party Intervention in International Conflict"; Regan, "Conditions of Successful Third Party Intervention in Intrastate Conflicts"; Lake, "Containing Fear"; Dixon, "Third Party Techniques for Preventing Conflict Escalation and Promoting Peaceful Settlement."

5. "Territorial destiny" is taken from the work of Alcock (e.g., 1986). He uses it to argue that it is very difficult, if not impossible, to successfully implement constitutional provisions for minority regions until sovereign jurisdiction is agreed upon. Settling the territorial destiny is therefore an important precondition for the successful management of ethnic conflict.

REFERENCES

Alcock, Anthony. 1986. Contributions on South Tyrol and Aaland Islands to *Coexistence in Some Plural European Societies*. Minority Rights Group Report, no. 72. London: Minority Rights Group.

Aron, Raymond. 1954. *The Century of Total War*. London: Derek Verschoyle.

Baer, P. K. 1993. "Peacekeeping as a Challenge to European Borders." *Security Dialogue* 24: 137–50.

Banks, Michael. 1987. "Four Conceptions of Peace." In *Conflict Management and Problem Solving*, edited by J. D. Sandole and I. Sandole-Staroste. London: Pinter: 259–74.

Belanogov, A. M. 1990. "Soviet Peace-keeping Proposals." *Survival* 22: 206–11.

Boutros-Ghali, Boutros. 1995. *An Agenda for Peace: An Addendum*. New York: United Nations.

———. 1992a. *An Agenda for Peace: Preventive Diplomacy. Peacemaking and Peacekeeping*. New York: United Nations Press.

———. 1992b. "Empowering the United Nations." *Foreign Affairs* 72: 89–102.

Bremmer, I., and R. Taras, eds. 1993. *Nationalism and Politics in the Soviet Successor States*. Cambridge: Cambridge University Press.

Chaudhuri, B. 1991. "Ethnic Conflict in the Chittagong Hill Tracts." In *Economic Dimensions of Ethnic Conflict*, edited by S. W. R. de Samarsinghe and R. Coughlan. London: Pinter: 135–55.

Coate, R. A., and D. J. Puchala. 1990. "Global Policies and the United Nations System: A Current Assessment." *Journal of Peace Research* 27: 127–40.

Connor, Walker. 1990. "Ethno-nationalism and Political Instability: An Overview." In *The Elusive Search for Peace*, edited by H. Giliomee and J. Gagiano. Cape Town: Oxford University Press.

Cordovez, D. 1987. "Strengthening UN Diplomacy for Peace: The Role of the Secretary-General." In *UNITAR: The United Nations and the Maintenance of International Peace and Security*. Dordrecht: Nijhoff: 161–75.

Dalberg-Acton, J. E. E. 1909. *The History of Freedom and Other Essays*. London: Macmillan.

Dedring, J. 1992. "Silently: How UN Good-offices Work." In *New Agendas for Peace Research*, edited by E. Boulding. Boulder, Colo.: Lynne Rienner.

Diehl, Paul F. 1993. *International Peacekeeping*. Baltimore: John Hopkins University Press.

Dixon, W. J. 1996. "Third Party Techniques for Preventing Conflict Escalation and Promoting Peaceful Settlement." *International Organization* 50, no. 4: 653–81.

Ennals, Martin. 1989. "International Conflict Resolution." In *Waging Peace in the Philippines*, edited by E. Garcia and C. Hernandez. Philippines : Alteneo Centre for Social Policy and Public Affairs.

Fein, Helen, ed. 1992. *Genocide Watch*. New Haven: Yale University Press.

Fisher, R. J. "Pacific, Impartial Third-Party Intervention in International Conflict: A Review and an Analysis." In *Beyond Confrontation*, edited by J. Vasquez et. al. (Ann Arbor: University of Michigan Press, 1996): 39–59.

Forsyth, M. G. et al., eds. 1970. *The Theory of International Relations: Selected Texts from Gentili to Treitschke*. London: Allen and Unwin.

Gaddis, J. L. 1987. *The Long Peace*. Oxford: Oxford University Press.

Gellner, Ernest. 1983. *Nations and Nationalism*. London: Basil Blackwell.

Griffiths, S. I. 1993. *Nationalism and Ethnic Conflict: Threats to European Security*. Stockholm: SIPRI.

Guelke, Adrian. 1992. "Policing in Northern Ireland." In *Northern Ireland. Politics and the Constitution*, edited by P. Hadfield. Buckingham: Open University Press.

Halperin, Morton H., et al. 1992. *Self-determination in the New World Order*. Washington, D.C.: Carnegie Endowment for International Peace.

Hannum, Hurst. 1990. *Autonomy. Sovereignty and Self-Determination*. Philadelphia: University of Pennsylvania Press.

Hechter, Michael. 1975. *Internal Colonialism: The Celtic Fringe in British National Development 1536–1966*. London: Routledge and Kegan Paul.

Hobsbawm, E. J. 1990. *Echoes of the Marseillaise: Two Centuries Look Back on the French Revolution*. New Brunswick, N.J.: Rutgers University Press.

International Alert. 1993. "Preventive Diplomacy: Recommendations of a Round Table on Preventive Diplomacy." London. January: 28–30.

King, A. 1993. "Free and Fair." *Track Two* 2: 10–11.

Kuper, Leo. 1981. *Genocide*. Harmondsworth: Penguin.

———. 1977. *The Pity of It All*. London: Duckworth.

———. 1985. *The Prevention of Genocide*. New Haven: Yale University Press.

Lake, D. A. 1996. "Containing Fear: The Origins and Management of Ethnic Conflict." *International Security* 21, no. 2: 41–75.

McGarry, John, and Brendon O'Leary, eds. 1993. *The Politics of Ethnic Conflict Regulation*. London: Routledge.

Mill, John Stuart. 1972. *Utilitarianism. On Liberty and Considerations on Representative Government*. London: Dent.

Mitchell, Christopher R. 1981. *The Structure of International Conflict*. Basingstoke: Macmillan.

Nairn, Tom. 1977. *The Break-up of Britain: Crisis and Neo-Nationalism*. London: New Left Books.

Pruitt, Dean G., and J. Z. Rubin. 1986. *Social Conflict*. New York: Random House.

Pugh, M. C. 1992. *Multinational Maritime Forces: A Breakout from Traditional Peacekeeping?* Southampton: University of Southampton Press.

Rawls, John. 1972. *A Theory of Justice*. Oxford: Clarendon Press.

Regan, P. 1996. "Conditions of Successful Third Party Intervention in Intrastate Conflicts." *Journal of Conflict Resolution* 40, no. 2: 336–59.

Rikhye, I. J. 1992. *The United Nations of the 1990s and International Peacekeeping Operations*. Southampton: University of Southampton Press.

Ruane, J., and J. Todd. 1991. "Why Can't You Get along with Each Other? Culture, Structure and the Northern Ireland Conflict." In *Culture and Politics in Northern Ireland, 1960–1990*, edited by E. Hughes. Buckingham: Open University Press.

Rupesinghe, Kumar. 1992. "Conflict Transformation in Multi-ethnic Societies." *Estudios Internacionales Revista del IRIPAZ* 3: 81–95.

Ryan, Stephen. 1990. *Ethnic Conflict and International Relations*. Aldershot: Dartmouth.

———. 1988. "Explaining Ethnic Conflict: The Neglected International Dimension." *Review of International Studies* 14: 161–78.

Saito, N. 1993. "The Role of the UN in a Post-Cold War World." In *Prospects for Global Order*, edited by S. Sato and T. Taylor. London: Royal Institute for International Affairs.

Smith, Anthony D. 1986. "Conflict and Collective Identity: Class, Ethnic and Nation." In *International Conflict Resolution*, edited by Edward Azar and John Burton. Boulder, Colo.: Lynne Reinner.

———. 1993. "A Europe of Nations or the Nation of Europe." *Journal of Peace Research* 30: 129–35.

———. 1991. *National Identity.* Harmondsworth: Penguin.

Smith, Graham. 1990. *The Nationalities Question in the Soviet Union.* London: Longmans.

Stavenhagen, Rudolfo. 1990. *The Ethnic Question.* Tokyo: United Nations University.

Stedman, S. J. 1991. *Peacemaking in Civil War: International Mediation in Zimbabwe 1974–1980.* Boulder, Colo.: Lynne Rienner.

Thakur, Ramesh. 1987. "International Peacekeeping, United Nations Authority and United States Power." *Alternatives* 12: 461–92.

———. 1993. "The United Nations in a Changing World." *Security Dialogue* 24: 720.

United States Institute for Peace. 1994. *The Professionalization of Peacekeeping: A Study Group Report.* Washington, D.C.: United States Institute for Peace Press.

Urquhart, Brian. 1990. "Beyond the Sheriff's Posse." *Survival* 22: 196–205.

Van den Berghe, Pierre. 1981. "Protection of Ethnic Minorities: A Critical Appraisal." In *Protection of Ethnic Minorities: Comparative Perspectives,* edited by R. G. Wirsing. New York: Pergamon.

———, ed. 1990. *State Violence and Ethnicity.* Niwot: University Press of Colorado.

Wehr, Paul. 1979. *Conflict Regulation.* Boulder, Colo.: Westview.

Williams, Philip. 1976. *Crisis Management.* London: Martin Robertson.

Young, Crawford. 1985. "Ethnicity and the Colonial and Post-Colonial State in Africa." In *Ethnic Groups and the State,* edited by Paul Brass. Totowa, N.J.: Barnes and Noble.

Zartman, I. W. 1989. *Ripe for Resolution.* New York: Oxford University Press.

4

Ethnic Conflict and European Security

What Role for NATO and the EC?

DAVID G. HAGLUND AND CHARLES C. PENTLAND

INTRODUCTION

In the fall of 1997 it is possible to hope that an end to Bosnia's troubles is in sight. The price of peace, however, is international acceptance of ethnic partition and the corresponding demise of multinationalist principles. Regardless of whether (and how) the endgame is played, it is surely time to begin assessing the broader significance of this Balkan tragedy for the future of Europe's evolving security institutions. Part of that exercise must be to determine the extent to which Yugoslavia represents a precedent for, or a prototype of, conflicts likely to confront us elsewhere in post-Cold War Europe.[1]

Agreement among governments and public opinion across Europe and elsewhere that Yugoslavia is a test-case, foreshadowing issues soon to crowd into Europe's security agenda from other quarters of the continent, would have serious implications of at least two kinds. First, it would affect the force and confidence with which ethnic claims are advanced and borders challenged in the latent conflicts of which we are already aware, especially in Central and Eastern Europe. The more such claims are realized, the more others are encouraged to escalate their own demands. Irredentists and potential "ethnic cleansers" everywhere will take heart. This "demonstration effect" may even extend beyond the perceived zone of insecurity in the East to heighten the aspirations of relatively quiescent groups in Western Europe. Secondly, if Yugoslavia is widely accepted as a fair—and failed—test of how European institutions are likely to perform in future, the damage to their credibility may be beyond repair, with serious long-term consequences for regional security. Such an erosion of credibility is already evident in comment on the OSCE and the European Union (EU) in particular.

Therefore, if the case can be made for the Yugoslav crisis as an exception to the likely pattern of post-Cold War European conflict, it should be made with some urgency but without wishful thinking and with minimal violence to the facts. This chapter is a modest attempt to accomplish that objective. It also suggests how continuing efforts to construct a pan-European security architecture might nevertheless be informed by recent Balkan experience.

Whatever we might have believed when European institutions first became involved in Yugoslavia's internal turmoil over five years ago, each new unfolding of the crisis revealed the case as increasingly hopeless and Western objectives as unattainable. It seemed impossible either to keep the federation together, to ensure the peaceful sequential secession of various republics, to control the civil war, or even simply to alleviate the all-too-visible human suffering.

Since we are discussing the death-agony not just of a European state (which, in itself, may not make us weep) but, more importantly, of an experiment in multiculturalism and of the communities and individuals who embraced it, a medical metaphor is perhaps not out of place. Initially, European institutions came as physicians to Yugoslavia's bedside in hope of a quick cure through the usual patent medicines, although they soon came to be persuaded of the need for selective amputations. When it became clear that there was in fact little hope for the patient, the issue became how to ensure a dignified death. The best efforts of the peacemakers— Carrington, Vance, Owen, and Stoltenberg—who labored mightily in an impossible situation could not disguise the triumph of atavistic ethnicity over the principle of the multicultural state represented—however imperfectly—by Bosnia-Herzegovina and its capital, Sarajevo.

In the aftermath of the Balkan crisis, the evident threat to Europe's security from ethnic conflict therefore suggests a twopronged response, aimed both at isolating the Yugoslav case conceptually and at immunizing Europe institutionally. In that spirit the next section of this chapter will examine some of the arguments about the character of the Yugoslav conflict, underlining those elements which made it sui generis and questioning its status as a precedent or prototype. A second section then will assess one international, institutional response to the conflict, focusing on the pivotal and illustrative role of the EU. A third section will reflect on NATO's prospects of assuming the central role in managing future ethnic conflicts. A concluding section will explore the transatlantic fabric of the alliance as it seeks to position itself in respect of, and possibly respond more effectively to, the kind of conflict likely to confront it in the coming years, especially in Central and Eastern Europe.

None of the tasks facing the EC/EU and NATO is easy, to say the least. Both institutions must learn the right "lessons" from history, doubly difficult when the history is so recent and controversial and the consequences so immediate and traumatic.

YUGOSLAVIA: EXAMPLE OR EXCEPTION?

Any attempt to establish the uniqueness of the Yugoslav case and, hence, its inappropriateness as a prototype of post-Cold War European conflict, must begin by taking a critical look at some tempting but unsatisfactory arguments that purport to do so. Pfaff (1993c), for example, argues that "Yugoslavia's ... is a war of histories not ethnicity" that is "waged among three communities possessing no distinct physical characteristics or separate anthropological or 'racial' origins. They are the same people" (81). Ramet (1992) writes that the war was "about land, not religion" (81). Either argument is potentially the basis of a claim that Yugoslavia is an exceptional case, not appropriate as a precedent for truly ethnic conflict elsewhere in Europe. But surely what has made it a war about histories or about land is each community's subjective sense of its ethnic distinctiveness, destiny, and insecurity regardless of how artificial and recently invented this may be. The Yugoslav civil war is an ethnic conflict because those involved believe it to be.

Treverton (1991–92) makes a more systematic effort to establish Yugoslavia as a "particular case," although he recognizes that it has "resonance elsewhere in eastern Europe." Yugoslavia's "ethnic antagonisms," he argues, "are especially intense, its borders particularly artificial, its populations intermingled, all of its republics' economies—except possibly Slovenia's—invisible on their own. And none of its leaders are likely candidates for the Nobel Peace prize, to put it diplomatically" (105). These five points constitute a reasonably persuasive case for Yugoslavia as an exception, although each calls for some qualification.

First, although Yugoslavia's history during World War II provides ample evidence of long-standing ethnic hatreds that are excessive even by Eastern European standards, and which subsequently were masked and repressed under Tito's rule, ethnic antagonisms in general seem especially prone to rapid escalation. We cannot be entirely confident that, in certain circumstances, the same scenario might not be played out in, say, Romania. The relatively amicable divorce of Czechs and Slovaks may, in fact, be the real exception.

Secondly, the claim that Yugoslavia's borders were particularly "artificial" is not very convincing when we reflect that there is virtually no state in Central and Eastern Europe whose borders have not, since World War I, been changed several times with little regard to "natural" geographic or ethnic criteria. Indeed, to stand up at all this argument must be read in conjunction with Treverton's third point about the intermingling of populations. Given the patchwork demographics of Serbia, Croatia, and especially Bosnia-Herzegovina, it is easy to see the artificiality of many, if not all, of Yugoslavia's internal boundaries. A more significant consequence of this complex distribution of population, however, has been the great variety and intensity of localized patterns of conflict, which have made overall solutions difficult to visualize, let alone impose.

Fourth, while none of Yugoslavia's former republics is viable economically on its own, it is not clear that in this respect they are very different from most of post-Cold War Central and Eastern Europe. The difference between Serbia, on the one hand, and Slovakia, on the other, does not seem that great. If any of these states is to survive economically it must establish trade and aid relationships, necessarily dependent on Western Europe. In that respect, perhaps, the former Yugoslav republics are temporarily and exceptionally disadvantaged, having been offered nothing like the arrangements presently in place for the former CMEA countries.

The point about leadership, finally, is difficult to deny. Ethnic conflict, however, does seem to bring out the worst in people and in politics. We cannot be confident, therefore, that extreme situations elsewhere in Europe would not produce leaders of a similar character.

Treverton's arguments, therefore, are helpful in establishing the distinctiveness of the Yugoslav crisis, although they do not by themselves add up to a decisive case against invoking it as a precedent. That case can be strengthened, however, by three other points.

In the first place, the Yugoslav conflict is unique in its multilateral, all-against-all character. Most of the other potential ethnic flashpoints in Europe involve bilateral disputes which, regardless of the intensity they might attain, have limited potential to replicate the complex pattern of local tactical alliances and antagonisms among Serbs, Croats, and Muslims in Bosnia-Herzegovina. This complexity, and the direct linkage of the Bosnian conflict to parallel struggles in Croatia and elsewhere, make the Yugoslav situation uniquely unmanageable.

Secondly, Yugoslavia's geographical location, size, and ethnic diversity mean that its internal conflicts have a particularly dangerous potential for regional spillover. Of the seven countries with which the former Yugoslav federation had borders, five have more than a passing interest in the fate of ethnic kin in Yugoslavia's successor states and warring regions, not least because their own internal equilibria and relations with other neighbors may be at risk. No other ethnic dispute in Europe has the same potential for explosive ramification. Hence the special importance and unusual difficulty of containing and managing the Yugoslav conflict in all its manifestations.

It can reasonably be argued, finally, that the violent breakup of Yugoslavia caught Europe's institutions at a time when their collective capacity for intervention was constrained or underdeveloped. Skeptics may reply that the moment never seems to be right, but it is worth noting that in mid-1991, when the conflict flared up, NATO was still deliberating on its new vocation and strategy, the EC was preoccupied with the run-up to Maastricht and attendant issues of how to make and execute a common foreign and security policy, and the OSCE had not yet fully implemented the institutional arrangements for conflict-management decided at Paris a year earlier. Clearly the excuse that Europe's "security and defense identity" is still under construction cannot be sustained for long, and the failure of institutions (as distinct from their member-states) can never be the whole story, but there is something to the claim that Yugoslavia caught the rest of Europe at a unique juncture in its institutional development. The next section looks more closely at how European international institutions responded to the first major crisis of post-Cold War Europe.

EUROPEAN INSTITUTIONS AND THE YUGOSLAV CRISIS

In mid-1991, when the Yugoslav conflict was beginning to assume international dimensions, something of a consensus emerged that collective management by European institutions was appropriate. This was the view from Washington, fueled by a mix of post-Gulf War euphoria and preelection wariness about commitment to a new and potentially more problematical foreign intervention. There was as well the sense that this was an issue, in contrast to the Persian Gulf, as to which European governments could make no credible excuses to evade or limit their responsibilities for peace and security. Europeans anxious to establish the capacity and legitimacy of their emergent regional institutions, particularly the OSCE and the EC, in matters of security tended to concur.

There was, moreover, a sense that UN involvement was neither appropriate nor likely. With the marginal exception of Cyprus, the UN had never been involved in European peacekeeping. For most of the postwar period that job had been done through the bipolar alliance structure with its mix of deterrence and détente and through occasional intrabloc conflict management on each side. Since 1989, it was widely held, Europe had been evolving toward a panregional security community with a panoply of indigenous institutions that would, at the very least, work out among them a division of labor in the security field. The conceit could be sustained not only that the UN would continue to be for other, less sophisticated parts of the world, but also that the new Europe would serve, in interwar parlance, as a "producer" of security for the rest of the world through UN peacekeeping and peacebuilding.

The first focus for expectations of a "European solution" to the Yugoslav crisis was the OSCE. Early German proposals centered on convening the new "crisis mechanism" and seeking the 35 members' agreement on sending a peacekeeping or observer force to Yugoslavia. In the event, agreement was limited to passing the torch, in the summer of 1991, to the European Community. Beyond providing a formal mandate to the EC to mediate in the conflict, the OSCE did little but become the stakes for a quarrel between the seceding states and the rump Yugoslav government over each other's rights to membership and act as a forum for the airing of European governments' views as the crisis evolved. The meetings, in July 1992, of the OSCE's Parliamentary Assembly in Budapest and its Helsinki summit later that month continued the debate about membership and resulted in the temporary suspension of Belgrade from OSCE activities. In addition, the assembly approved a lengthy declaration that, while condemning violence on all sides in the former Yugoslavia and the continued violations of the Paris Charter, placed most of the blame on Serbia and the Bosnian Serbs. Action was limited, however, to expressions of support for UN activities and for the work of the International Conference on the Former Yugoslavia, exhortations to various governments and parties to the conflict, and recommendations that OSCE observers be deployed to various prospective flashpoints in the region. Some observer teams subsequently were sent, most notably to Kosovo.

On the whole, however, the OSCE's performance fell short of expectations, especially those raised by the signing of the Charter of Paris. As MacFarlane and Weiss (1992) note, "its rules of decision by consensus, coupled with the diversity and divergent interests of its members, rendered it useless as a means of addressing the crisis in Croatia.... Moreover it lacked any significant institutional infrastructure or resources, a situation that does not appear likely to change soon" (28). Specifically, the OSCE's pan-European inclusiveness and inflexible voting rules enabled the Belgrade government itself, and a Soviet/Russian government protective of Serbia and concerned about precedents for intervention into domestic ethnic quarrels, to block it from acting. In Joffe's judgment the OSCE, "unable to bring either security or cooperation to the Balkan ... looks destined for the oblivion that befell the League of Nations...." (1992–93: 43). Pierre Lellouche goes even farther, arguing that the Yugoslav case shows that the OSCE, a useful channel for East-West dialogue during the Cold War, "no longer meets security needs, notably in Central Europe" (1992: 11).

What the OSCE was prepared, in mid-1991, to hand on, the EC was eager to take on. Lord Owen remarked on the eagerness with which the EC took up the task, some even believing that it could replace the UN in the peacekeeping role: "At first Europe wanted to stand on its own feet—Yugoslavia was the virility symbol of the Euro-federalists" ("Future of the Balkans" 1993: 6) It helps to understand this enthusiasm if we recall, that in mid to late 1991 the EC's Intergovernmental Committee on Political Union was intensely engaged in formulating the structures and procedures for a common foreign defense and security policy to be incorporated into the Maastricht Treaty. In the process the EC was concerned to stake out its claim vis-à-vis the WEU, NATO, and the OSCE to best represent Europe's "security and defense identity."

At the outset of its involvement, the EC's aims, like those of most of the international community, were to mediate a new constitutional agreement for the Yugoslav federation that would better accommodate Croatian and Slovenian demands for increased autonomy with traditional Serbian centralism. By the end of 1991, however, the EC's position—again, like that of the vast majority of the OSCE's member-states—had tilted against the Serbs and the Yugoslav federal government. The EC found itself in an increasingly contradictory and unworkable position—on the one hand, recognizing Slovenia and Croatia (and later Bosnia-Herzegovina) as independent states and imposing sanctions on the Serbian-dominated remains of Yugoslavia while, on the other hand, continuing its OSCE-mandated task of mediating and trying to keep the peace.

The EC's first concrete action, at the end of June 1991, was to mount a "diplomatic rapid reaction force" to Belgrade, consisting of the foreign ministers of its past, current, and next president-countries—at the time, Luxembourg, the Netherlands, and Portugal (Freedman 1991–92: 33). Their efforts to forestall military action and to initiate negotiations were fruitless. Through the summer and fall the EC, via its Dutch presidency and then through its special representative, Lord Carrington, negotiated a series of short-lived cease-fires between Serbs and Croats. At the same time it suspended arms sales and economic aid to Belgrade, while pressuring the Serbs to accept EC mediation. In what seemed at the time a promising innovation, the EC sent teams of peace observers into various parts of Croatia, including the city of Dubrovnik, while Lord Carrington labored to convene peace talks based on a draft plan for the settlement of territorial issues.

For reasons having to do both with the civil war itself (particularly the evidence of Serbian ambitions, behavior, and military success) and with growing divergence of views among its members, any remaining semblance of balance in the EC's position had dissipated by late autumn. The shelling of Dubrovnik and the consequent withdrawal of the EC observers from that city, and the Serbs' rejection on 5 November of Lord Carrington's peace plan, probably were decisive in turning the EC from a tacit to an overt partisan of independent Croatia and Slovenia. On November 8 it took the lead in imposing selective economic sanctions on Serbia.

The EC's efforts to mediate continued, assumptions about equidistance and impartiality having been replaced by a belief that the reality of immediate economic sanctions and the promise of ultimate economic reward would combine to compel Serbia to the negotiating table. This belief survived even the fiasco of formal recognition. Pressured by Germany and despite French, British, and other reservations, the EC agreed on 17 December to recognize Croatia and Slovenia by 15 January 1992. Six days later Germany jumped the gun and extended recognition unilaterally. The balance of motives in Bonn's actions—historical ties, the presence of a large Croatian émigré community in Germany, commercial aspirations, even a genuine belief that recognition would strengthen the seceding states, remove any remaining legitimacy from Serbia's claims, and solve the problem—can be debated. Its immediate effect, however, was that the EC gave up a negotiating asset whose only power flowed from it being a promise to one side and a threat to the other.

Regardless of the resulting further diminution of its credibility as a mediator, the EC persisted in the first half of 1992 in mixing partisanship with peacemaking. On the one hand, it continued to recognize seceding republics of the former Yugoslav federation, first Bosnia-Herzegovina in April (along with the US) and then Macedonia in late June (after accommodating Greek objections). It also reacted to the Serbian-Montenegrin claim to be the legitimate successor to the old Yugoslavia by recalling its ambassador from Belgrade. In late May, responding to Belgrade's intervention on behalf of the Bosnian Serbs, the EC imposed a trade embargo on the rump Yugoslavia and took the lead in advocating UN sanctions. On 30 May the UN enacted a trade embargo and a freeze on Yugoslav financial assets abroad. In effect Brussels had passed formal responsibility for peace enforcement to New York.

In the same way, while the EC persisted through the spring in its efforts to establish cease-fires and to convene peace talks, it was becoming clear that Brussels was gradually abandoning its claims to the lead role in managing the Yugoslav conflict. The UN already had begun to introduce peacekeeping forces, first into Croatia in February and, subsequently, in increasing numbers to protect the relief operation in Bosnia-Herzegovina. After a last, short-lived, success by Lord Carrington in reconvening the peace talks in April, the EC moved to acknowledge the UN's presence, indeed its primacy, in the peace process. It is a little harsh to say, as Joffe (1992–

93) does, that by the end of May the EC had "essentially dumped the problem into the lap of the United Nations" (32). More accurately, the EC was admitting that its reach had exceeded its grasp and was undertaking belatedly to share the risks and responsibilities of Balkan peacekeeping with the UN. Symbolic both of the deflation of the EC's pretensions and of determination nevertheless to stay the course was its appointment of Lord Owen to succeed Lord Carrington and to work with the UN's envoy, Cyrus Vance, in negotiating a peace plan for Bosnia-Herzegovina. This new joint EC-UN mediatory structure was put in place under the authority of the International Conference on the Former Yugoslavia (ICFY) held at the end of August in London.

As the international body designated to oversee the search for peace in the former Yugoslavia, the ICFY is the formal successor to the earlier EC conference from which Lord Carrington's mandate had derived. It is to remain in session in Geneva until a settlement has been reached. At the London meeting the participants agreed, albeit with some ambiguity on the part of the Bosnian Serbs and Muslims, on a statement of principles and a set of working groups to support the preparation of a peace settlement for Bosnia-Herzegovina.

From that point on the UN assumed prime responsibility for enforcement of sanctions and the protection of international relief effort, principally through the establishment in October of the no-fly zone over Bosnia and in November of the naval blockade in the Adriatic. In both cases the actual work of enforcement devolved to NATO's aircraft and ships. Compared to the growing presence of the UN peacekeepers—UNPROFOR's complement had exceeded twenty thousand by the spring of 1993—the EC's few observer teams in the former Yugoslavia seemed wholly symbolic, although they were not totally without effect. It is worth recalling, as Lord Owen has done, that up to the end of 1992 the EC had "shouldered the biggest burden ... in terms of refugees, humanitarian aid and military forces committed to the United Nations, with lives lost" ("Future of the Balkans" 1993: 4). Nevertheless, from the fall of 1992 onward the EC as an institution had determined to focus its efforts on the Vance-Owen mission and to leave the rest to the UN and NATO.

In October 1992, Vance and Owen produced their draft plan for a Bosnian settlement based on cantonization into ten relatively autonomous provinces, along with provisions for supervised elections, demilitarization, freedom of movement, human rights, and adjudication of disputes. The plan also set out detailed military provisions for the region and proposed a set of principles to be embodied in a future Bosnian constitution. In January 1993, the parties convened to negotiate on the basis of the Vance-Owen plan. Only the Bosnian Croats were disposed to sign. The Bosnian Serbs were unhappy because the plan offered them less territory than they had conquered, while the Muslims refused to accept a partition based on conquest and ethnic cleansing. Both appeared, nevertheless, to have signed on by May 1993, but the Muslims subsequently backed out. A revised plan—proposed by the Croatian and Serbian presidents—for a tripartite Bosnia has been the basis of discussion since midyear. The Vance-Owen formulas for a decentralized Bosnian state "seek to reconcile the principle that aggression and ethnic cleansing cannot prevail with the fact that there is no way to restore Bosnia to its condition before the onslaught of the Serbs" (Gotlieb 1993: 73).

No international security organization involved in the ethnic imbroglio of the former Yugoslavia has emerged with its credibility intact. The only exception to date might be NATO, whose involvement has been focused and operational; its prospects for the longer haul are discussed in the next section. Certainly the EC, whose initial pretensions were greatest and whose diplomatic presence has remained significant, has had a sobering, if not traumatic, experience with respect to both its formal role and the substantive solutions it ended up brokering. The EC's role, as we have seen, evolved into something less than preeminent, exclusive, and comprehensive, while the peace proposals it found itself backing, admittedly *faute de mieux*, were defined by the minimum common denominator of ethnicity.

To some extent, then, the Yugoslav case is a rebuff to the idea of the EC as a regional solution to European ethnic problems through the exercise of "civilian power." The short-term, sometimes contradictory, efforts at peacekeeping (the observer groups), peacemaking (Carrington to Owen), and peace enforcement (economic sanctions), while not without effect, have fallen well short of initial expectations. Propositions about the longer-term peacebuilding role of economic assistance, market-access, and the lure of ultimate EC membership for the former Yugoslav republics remain, of course, untested.

In the euphoria that followed the revolution of 1989 it was easy to assume that regardless of whether one read the new distribution of power in post-Cold War Europe to be unipolar (with America the only remaining superpower) or multipolar (with Germany up, Russia down, and the US at least partially out), conditions henceforth would favor peacemaking and peace enforcement through multilateral institutions. The "climate of the times," moreover, marked by the seeming triumph of economic liberalism, democracy, multilateralism, and the notion of a virtuous circle of markets, democracy, and international security encouraged the vision of a benign ramification eastward of the Brussels-centered (EC and NATO) European security community. "Brusselization" surely was destined to triumph over Balkanization.

Unlike the OSCE, in mid-1991 the EC seemed ready and willing to assume the central role allocated to it in the scheme of things. It was ready, in the sense that it had both in its economic foreign policy processes and in the mechanisms of European Political Cooperation well-established means of making collective decisions. Insofar as implementation of its decisions was concentrated on economic means such as sanctions, enforcement was manageable. The fact that Maastricht's provisions for foreign-policy and security cooperation were not in place did not seem to matter. As time went on, however, the limits of economic peace enforcement became increasingly evident and the internal effects of the Maastricht debate increasingly debilitating.

As far as the EC's willingness to act was concerned, we have noted the zeal with which it took up the OSCE's mandate. The broad consensus on the need to act, and on the importance of a "European" approach to the Yugoslav crisis, however, could not long conceal internal divisions flowing from differences of national interest, principally between the Germans on one side and the French and British on the other. These divisions surfaced in the debates over (a) recognition of seceding republics; (b) the distribution of blame and, hence, of sanctions, among the parties; and (c) the use to be made of various international institutions. It did not help that the cleavage over what to do about Yugoslavia tended to reinforce rather than to cut across the tension over Maastricht and the destiny of the EC as Europe's defense and security identity. France's campaign for the ICFY and for a greater UN role, for example, had to do with both of these issues.

The role that the EC has come to play in the former Yugoslavia can thus be explained in part by its painful discovery of the limits of "civilian power" and in part by differences of national interest among its members. What has made the Yugoslav case especially, perhaps uniquely, difficult for the EC is that the intensity of its ethnic forces makes questionable the essentially rationalist premises underlying the EC's economic influence, while the multifaceted, transnational character of its conflicts cannot but exacerbate the EC's own domestic debates.

NATO AND THE CHALLENGE OF ETHNIC CONFLICT

Is there any reason to assume NATO would serve as a more effective antidote to the poison of ethnic nationalism in Eastern Europe than the EU? For that to happen, much will depend not only upon how the alliance manages to resolve its twofold eastern "dilemmas" through expansion but also upon whether it is able to complete its "transformation" from a military to a political entity without in the process discarding the transatlantic military-strategic infrastructure that both informed and gave credible meaning to the security guarantee provided to allies. That infrastructure was, and likely remains, the alliance's chief bonding agent. Specifically, it is upon the nature and believability of the ongoing North American (but mainly US) "commitment" to European security that our analysis of this aspect of NATO's current challenges is concentrated.

It is our thesis that NATO faces a set of challenges today that may render it of less, not of more, relevance to the resolution of crises inspired by ethnic conflict in Europe. *Pace* those in the Visegrad countries who see in NATO a remedy for their own security puzzles, we suspect that the alliance's capacities are only marginally greater than those of the EU in responding to the challenges of ethnic conflict in Europe. This is a sobering suspicion, for the stakes could not be higher, both for the alliance and Europe. NATO may continue to show itself capable of surmounting the difficulties that were afflicting it in late 1994 and could go some way to restoring what some were then taking to be its flagging viability, should NATO's Implementation Force (IFOR) and Stabilization Force (SFOR) prove capable of maintaining a modicum of calm in Bosnia. But as a means of dealing with the roots of ethnic conflict in Europe, NATO will almost certainly not suffice (though it has shown it can arrange cease-fires more effectively than other organizations). Either some alternative arrangement for dealing with ethnic conflict will be found (perhaps a sphere-of-influence according primacy to a resurgent Russia), or no solution at all will be on offer. Neither can be an inviting prospect.

We might be excused for concluding that Europe's current security funk should bode well for NATO's quest for ongoing viability. The recent relapse of part of Europe into something resembling more a charnel house than a common house should, in a macabre sort of way, be a welcome development for those who would keep NATO alive well into the next millennium. The reality of the moment, however, is that the alliance's post-Cold War existential dilemma has not been resolved by the succession of events in Europe over the past five years, and it may actually have been compounded. NATO's problem, one highlighted by recent fighting in Yugoslavia and the general uncertainty about security elsewhere in the region from the Oder to the Urals (and even further east), does not reside on the "demand side." If the health of a club is solely a function of the number of membership applications it receives, then this institution's future has never looked brighter.

Instead, NATO's troubles appear to defy easy resolution—although it must be conceded that its prospects for enduring appear more favorable in 1997 than they had twenty-four months previously. These troubles are in large if not exclusive measure "eastern" ones, stemming from two extraordinarily complex policy questions:

(1) What is to be done about the former Yugoslavia after NATO's departure?

(2) How should the allies respond to the former adversaries of the Warsaw Treaty Organization (WTO) as they grapple with security challenges that had been kept in storage during the Cold War?

Each question, in its own way, goes directly to the most profound of NATO's contemporary challenges, namely the matter of how or even whether the alliance might transform itself and transcend its mandate of providing collective defense to the Western Europeans (and, in a different sense, the North Americans) without in the process sabotaging the internal solidarity of the current membership.

WHAT TO DO ABOUT YUGOSLAVIA?

Alliances without a foe become subject to terminal decay, victims of the dual blows of lost mission and growing indifference on the part of their own members. At least that is what a number of international relations theorists profess to believe, and in their profession they are supported by a historical record that reveals no alliance having long outlived the passing of the adversary that brought it into being. It is in this sense that NATO's late secretary-general, Manfred Wörner, was right to have identified the danger of loss of credibility to which the alliance would be exposed should it fail to involve itself somehow in a meaningful role in Yugoslavia.[2]

Initially, NATO responded to Yugoslavia in a way that managed not to drive wedges between the Western allies or lose the support of Western publics that desired to help sort out the Balkans tragedy without incurring high costs for themselves. In the longer term, NATO also appears to be on its way toward solving its "inclusion" predicament, encapsulated by the issue of eastward expansion. If it fails to become more of a factor in the security of Eastern Europe, it is hard to see how it can continue to be much of one even in Western Europe.[3]

The two challenges, in sum, constitute NATO's "Eastern dilemmas." How—or whether—it can become for the inhabitants of the continent something more than it has been (namely a collective defense mechanism for the Western Europeans alone) is perhaps the only meaningful question one should ask about the alliance at this time. It is that question to which we turn our attention in this and the following section, in which we observe that collective defense no longer seems capable of cementing the alliance; collective security remains what it always has been—a distant promise; and peacekeeping—a possible salvational mission for the alliance—carries with it a set of risks that are not yet fully understood, notwithstanding the current apparent success in Bosnia.

NATO officials and policy-makers in the member states have assuredly been attentive to the requirements of continued alliance existence in an era when "chaos" and not the Soviet Union constitutes the threat (or, as it is more often put, the "risk"). The first significant landmark on NATO's road to its "transformation" (presumably from a predominantly military alliance to more of a "political" one) was the "London Declaration on a Transformed North

Atlantic Alliance," issued by the heads of state and government in July 1990. Between that time and the meeting of NATO foreign ministers in Oslo nearly two years later (in June 1992), a succession of declarations and announcements would testify to the need felt by all to make the alliance's force structure respond to the requirements of crisis management (inter alia by abandoning Cold War doctrines and weapons—especially short-range nuclear ones—and embracing the logic of multinational and ostensibly rapid intervention forces and even at Oslo signing on to a new mission, peacekeeping).[4] Two prominent accompaniments to these declarations of transformation were significant institutional innovations, the first being creation in December 1991 of the North Atlantic Cooperation Council (NACC), the second the adoption of the Partnership for Peace (PFP) slightly more than two years later.[5]

Since early 1993 NATO had become more directly involved, almost on a daily basis, in the Yugoslav crisis. First came the announcement in February by Secretary of State Warren Christopher that the US would participate in a UN/NATO peacekeeping force in the Balkans to broker and police a cease-fire arranged under the Vance-Owen plan for dividing Bosnia-Herzegovina into a loose federation of ten autonomous provinces structured on the basis of ethnicity (Pick 1993: 1, 7; British American Information Council 1993: 1–2). The peace plan engendered bitter debate both within the former Yugoslavia and in the West before it was euthanatized in late May in favor of carving up Bosnia into three unequal ethnic entities, as discussed above.

Significantly, there was a role either for NATO or for some of the allies individually no matter what one's views on the merits of Vance-Owen. To the proponents, the plan could have worked if and only if a cease-fire between Bosnia's Serbs, Croats, and Muslims (i.e., the government) were preserved by a large force of peacekeepers, supplied by NATO members and other countries and under NATO operational command and overall UN authorization. Estimates of the number of troops needed for this mission ranged from as few as forty thousand to as many as three hundred thousand. Although the Vance-Owen Plan died, the Dayton Accord of late 1995 brokered by the US resulted in the dispatch of a sixty-thousand-strong peacekeeping force to Bosnia, bringing a semblance of peace to that tragically war-torn land.

For a time in early 1993 it appeared as if a more active role than peacekeeping was being envisioned. To those who denounced Vance-Owen, NATO or even individual allies had a vital role to play, either by arming the Bosnian government forces and letting them look after their own security or by more energetically punishing the Serbs who had been emboldened by successive triumphs in their campaign of ethnic cleansing. We now know that NATO's potential role was constrained not, as some believed, by UN unwillingness to approve "collective security" measures against the Bosnian Serbs but by irresolvable divisions within NATO's own midst (Hastings et al. 1994: 4).

At least, the divisions appeared irresolvable as long as Western Europeans believed that they could not count upon America to demonstrate a vigorous leadership, ratified by the deployment of ground forces, in respect of what was increasingly being termed a "European" problem (and debacle).

For more than two years prior to the decision to let partition tacitly occur in Bosnia (which is one meaning of Dayton), the alliance had been becoming incrementally involved in the conflict. In July 1992 NATO Airborne Early Warning (NAEW) aircraft began monitoring naval operations over the Adriatic. Three months later, NAEW aircraft began to enforce the UN ban on military flights over Bosnia-Herzegovina. NATO tactical aircraft began in mid-April 1993 to enforce the no-fly zone decreed over Bosnia at the end of 1992. In early 1994 NATO's responses became bolder, involving attacks on Serbian fighter aircraft and selected ground targets. But up until the late summer of 1995, even the boldest actions would quickly be followed by gestures intended to demonstrate an unwillingness to move beyond incrementalism.

Although it was commonplace to blame the British and French (and Canadians)—all of whom with troops on the ground at risk of Serbian reprisals—for the incremental and ultimately unproductive NATO armed responses, other "culprits" could be singled out, as well (Lewis 1994: 4). The UN, and its penultimate commander Sir Michael Rose, did at times give the impression that they believed a moral equivalency could be established between the aggressors and the victims in the Bosnian conflict, and acted accordingly. (Hoffmann 1994: E19). More to the point, in light of what would transpire the US could be singled out for direct responsibility, since NATO's incrementalism could never have been replaced by a more forceful interventionism so long as American leadership and resolve were lacking. Until the combination of Croatian offensives and Serb atrocities in the summer of 1995 made continued abstention unwise, the case for caution in Yugoslavia remained a strong one in Washington. In the end, the administration acted, and did so in a decisive enough manner that it had many analysts wondering if a renewed, credible, American commitment to European security was going to be in the offing.[6]

Why should the Western European members of NATO have been worrying so much at the start of this decade about the security difficulties of Eastern Europe? After all, the Cold War had just been ended, rather favorably from the western perspective since its alliance had held together while its adversary's had collapsed. Indeed, not only had the foe's alliance shattered, so did the Soviet Union itself. So what was the worry?

Most broadly, two kinds of "threat" were felt liable to be exacerbated if appropriate responses could not be developed or applied. First was the threat of generalized ethnic conflict spilling over into Western Europe. Second was the possibility of Russia becoming the effective equivalent of the Soviet threat of yore. In the early 1990s, the first appeared to be the more immediate menace; today, with the prospects of antiwestern forces coming decisively to power in Moscow, it is the second that looms largest.

Let us examine for a moment the first threat scenario. In respect of this, there has clearly already been a direct (and in one country, temporarily very worrisome) impact on security created by the refugee crisis. Antiforeign violence in Germany during the early 1990s provides a compelling example. However, one should refrain from jumping to the conclusion that the reaction to imported social problems with an Eastern provenance would lead inevitably to strains among the Western Europeans themselves. Ironically, worries about the stability of Germany could have the effect of reinforcing the desire of Germany's most important neighbor, France, to seek closer economic, political, and military integration with it—if only better to control it.[7]

There are also indirect effects of generalized chaos to the east, notably the real prospect of political conflict among the Western Europeans as a result of differential assessments both of the problem in the East and the measures needed to address it. Does anyone require reminding of the tensions that were produced among the Western Europeans late in 1991 and early in 1992 as a result of a very different understanding of the need for early recognition of Slovenia and Croatia? This intra-alliance (intra-EC, really) tension over the wisdom of early recognition in turn contributed to increasing concern over the "renationalization" of Western European foreign and security policy (Honig 1992: 122–38).

Differential "contributions" to resolving the security problems in the East can also be guaranteed to sow discord among the European allies and with the US. Until recently, a central problem was thought to lie in constitutional limitations on German use of force for multilateral crisis management. Even Chancellor Helmut Kohl, who believes Germany must do its share in maintaining security out of the NATO theater of operations with armed forces if need be, used to draw a very sharp line at Yugoslavia for historical reasons. That line (and the "Kohl Doctrine") has blurred of late, and if the Germans still cannot deploy ground forces to Bosnia, their commitment of airpower to that theater, coupled with the more momentous dispatch of logistical support units to Croatia, demonstrates that fears of German strategic immobility were misplaced.

One of the ironies of the early post-Cold War era was the refusal of that old war-horse of the alliance, the "burdensharing" debate, to amble off to the conceptual glue factory. In a new guise, burden sharing looked as if it was going to continue to serve as a source of intra-alliance wrangling, perhaps even more so than during the period of East-West strife. No Western European country would likely have been more affected by the resurgence of that debate than Germany, unless, of course, the US so deemphasized its interest and role in European security management as to become a less exigent *demandeur* of the European allies. This question we explore below.

NATO'S INCLUSION PREDICAMENT

Germany also figures—albeit as hopeful analogy, not as source of sorrow—in the second kind of threat mentioned earlier, namely that of a spurned Russia becoming for the alliance the equivalent of the former Soviet Union (Glaser 1993). According to some, much will have been sacrificed if the current opportunity to incorporate Russia somehow into a West-facing security structure is bungled. The new, less pleasant Russia that would emerge would not generate the level of commitment to cooperative security demonstrated by its recent foreign- policy shapers. Gone would be the promise of what the most prominent of those, former foreign minister Andrei Kozyrev (1993), called the "new partnership strategy."

In this context the German analogy is of possible utility. The prospects of democracy, prosperity, and stability in Germany and, by extension, all of Western Europe were substantially advanced as a result of the Western embrace of Germany after its second great military defeat of this century. This contrasts starkly with the consequences of the Entente and Associated Powers' rejection of Germany at Versailles in 1919.[8] An alliance structure, in this case NATO after 1955, proved to be the vehicle not only for defending Germany against its Eastern foe but for reassuring Germany's Western neighbors that they could count on and work with it to build a community of security and prosperity. NATO was in this sense an implicit collective-security structure, or at the very least a powerful and necessary "confidence-building" mechanism (Haglund and Mager 1992).

For some time there has been an advocacy, in the US as elsewhere, that the West move emphatically to embrace the new Russia. The embracers have usually stressed the need for and logical merits of economic assistance, but there have been those who have argued as well that bringing Russia into an alliance with the US was a necessary precondition of any lasting rapprochement.[9] Usually, however, the logic of embrace stops far short of actually admitting Russia into the alliance; doing that, it is said, would render the latter irrelevant for any mandate. Compounding the issue, of course, is the desire of those Central European ex-allies of Moscow—Poland, the Czech Republic, Hungary, and possibly Slovakia—who have sought early admission (some successfully) to NATO and whose entries were, until recently, apparently considered necessary by Germany and some other allies.

Thus is posed, though hardly resolved, NATO's second major Eastern dilemma. Given that embracers have carried the day both in the US and in other major allied countries, it is far from evident that the Russians themselves would welcome an invitation to join NATO in any form. Admittedly, such quondam pro-Westerners as the departed foreign minister Kozyrev had broached the thought that to consummate the new partnership strategy an alliance with the West would have to be concluded. To Kozyrev (1993), the path to success was held to lie "in alliance between a strong new Russia and other democratic states. That is why we see the NATO nations as our mutual friends, and in future allies" (4).[10] But the foreign minister's views did not prevail in the internal Russian debate, and even President Boris Yeltsin has inclined away from Kozyrev's earlier position.

Apart from possible Russian objections to an expanded NATO, there is another, more philosophical, difficulty with the attempt to "solve" the Russian problem by relying on NATO as deus ex machina. In essence, NATO's problem is that collective defense seemed by mid-decade to be obsolete, while collective security remained out of reach. Thus a few observers were beginning to wonder whether something in between the two conceptual poles, namely peacekeeping, might not become NATO's new mission.[11]

Because of the intractable nature of the Eastern dilemma, alliance leaders tried by 1994 to create a halfway solution to their problem by offering something to the Central and Eastern European states without extending them full membership. With time, full membership was proffered. For example, in October 1993, at a NATO meeting of defense ministers at Travemünde, Germany, US Defense Secretary Les Aspin (1993: 2) proposed that the expansion-of-membership issue be shelved, in exchange for a series of bilateral alliance agreements with the former members of the WTO (Vogel 1993: B4). Dubbed the "Partnership for Peace," this proposal stopped short of offering security guarantees as provided by article 5 of the NATO treaty, but provided a forum for consultation, under the treaty's article 4, which states that the parties to the treaty "will consult together whenever, in the opinion of any of them, the territorial integrity, political independence, or security of any of [them] is threatened" (quoted in Simon 1993: 33). There was also an enhanced program in this formula for some technical assistance measures. There existed as well the possibility of Eastern cooperation with NATO in peacekeeping, crisis management, and search and rescue missions. This proposal was embraced by alliance leaders at their Brussels summit in January 1994, which also ostensibly committed the alliance eventually to enlarge itself.

Whether the PFP compromise constitutes a long-term solution to NATO's Eastern dilemmas remains to be seen. Its short-term effects have served to smooth over some of the current tensions among alliance members, albeit at some cost to the Poles, Hungarians, and Czechs—the so-called "Visegrad countries." Over the longer term, however, one might be permitted more than a little skepticism about the alliance's ability to resolve successfully the contradictions looming to the East. If those Eastern headaches were all that afflicted the alliance, they would be bad enough. Significantly, there is a transatlantic aspect to NATO's contemporary woes, to which we now turn our attention.

A TALE OF TWO "CANADIANIZATIONS": WILL NORTH AMERICA REMAIN COMMITTED TO EUROPEAN SECURITY?

Statements made in the first two years of the Clinton administration by both former Secretary of State Christopher and President Clinton that Europe was no longer the most strategic part of the world for the US caused many in Europe to worry about the long-term sustainability of the US "commitment" to their security. In early to mid 1994, however, it looked as if the tilt away from Europe had been arrested, and American energies in brokering the Dayton cease-fire, coupled with a resolve to send ground troops to Bosnia, had some in Europe once again taking solace in the smothering—if not altogether happy—embrace of the US.

To some of those following the issue prior to the recently postulated turnaround in America's European policy, an analogy was being drawn with Canada, and those who drew it did so out of fear. We argue, however, that there really were and remain two relevant analogies, which we call the two "Canadianization" theses. The first holds that the US eventually will withdraw militarily from Europe, just as Canada did when it canceled in February 1992 its stationed-forces commitment in Germany. The second, in contrast, maintains that the US might stay in Europe, as is Canada apparently, by dint of a concentration on peacekeeping as a mission to replace the now-obsolete rationale for troop stationing developed during the Cold War, i.e., collective defense on the "Central Front."

We start by examining the first thesis. Decisions made in Ottawa rarely are of major moment for European security. Thus it came as something of a surprise to witness the alarm set off by the announcement, made in February 1992, that Canada would be removing all its stationed forces from Germany rather than leave in place a task force of eleven hundred soldiers, as had been announced in September 1991 (Government of Canada 1992: 8–9). Although policy-makers in National Defence Headquarters quickly proclaimed that the end of stationing would not weaken the country's "commitment" to either NATO or Europe—and pointed to the large Canadian contingent slated for peacekeeping duties in what used to be Yugoslavia as proof of this—the immediate reaction from some European allies was a feeling of abandonment and panic (Sallot 1992; Fisher 1992; Pick, et al. 1992).

The sense of abandonment was perhaps more understandable than panic over the ultimate implication of the Canadian pullout, but the latter is of more significance. For some reason perhaps known only to Europeans, there has been a linkage imputed between the Canadian stationed forces and the much more important American ones: it has become an article of faith that as Ottawa goes, so too might Washington, hence the urgency with which NATO officials and European allies alike set to work (unsuccessfully) trying to persuade Ottawa to reverse its decision (*Ottawa Citizen*, 31 March 1992: A6). Washington, it should be recalled, tends not to take its cues from Canadian decisions when matters regarding the future of Europe are at stake: it did not do so in 1914, when Canada entered the First World War simultaneously with Great Britain, while the United States remained neutral for nearly three more years; it did not do so in 1939, when Ottawa hesitated all of a week to join the fray, while Washington needed the Pearl Harbor attack to trigger its belligerency; and it will not do so in the remainder of the 1990s and beyond.

That being said, those who linked the Canadian decision with a potential American one were not completely misguided. There may be no direct causal connection between Ottawa's and Washington's policies on troop stationing, but there could well turn out to be an indirect connection, more an analogy than anything else. Washington will act as it decides to act: that is both a tautology and a truism. Yet it is our thesis that the ultimate result of the decisions it makes independently may look amazingly familiar to those who have followed the history of Canadian troop stationing in Europe. We may well expect to see, and sooner rather than later, an effective "Canadianization" of American policy regarding European security.

What does this Canadianization thesis entail? It involves the ongoing search for a plausible rationale and optimal level for stationed forces of a distant North American power on what was once the Central Front of the Cold War. As the Canadian example shows, the quest can be a troublesome one for policy-makers on both sides of the Atlantic. Once Canada's troop commitment to Europe—in the 1960s nearly ten thousand soldiers and airmen, but subsequently fewer than seven thousand—was deemed more important for its political "symbolism" than for operational effectiveness, it became exceedingly difficult, and eventually impossible, for Ottawa to resist the logic of reducing troop levels in a bid to save money.[12] After all, according to that logic, if seven thousand soldiers could do the job of securing symbolic relevance, then surely five thousand could as well; and if five thousand could, why not eleven hundred? Once a low enough figure had been attained, it became quixotic indeed to bother distinguishing the floor from the ceiling, with the result being the contention that one still could be symbolically significant with *no* troops. Besides, only six of the alliance's sixteen nations have ever seen fit to participate in the stationing regime (Haglund and Mager 1992).

The US is argued to be a long way from the threshold below which operational effectiveness becomes unimaginable, save in the most benign threat environment; that is to say, even one hundred thousand US troops—the number promised by President Clinton at the Brussels summit of January 1994—must surely constitute a formidable fighting contingent, barring an eruption of something equivalent to the First or Second World War. Nevertheless, it is not apparent (at least to us) that the one hundred thousand level can be maintained in coming years; thus the "Canadianization" threshold could be approached more rapidly than many might imagine, should the American ground and air forces get drawn down from the 1991 level of three hundred thousand to perhaps some fifty thousand or so by the end of this decade.[13] Here the Canadian experience might bear pondering: for Ottawa did not intend, not even as late as three years ago, to withdraw totally from Europe. Once its force levels got sufficiently minuscule, however, it would have required Herculean powers of persuasion to resist the temptation to rescue some defense programs (in the "capital-expenditure" category) by sacrificing the stationing presence (Johnston 1993).

If those Europeans who now doubt that Canada continues to have a "commitment" to Europe are to be believed, then the litmus test for what remains of the North American commitment is to be found in the future of the US stationed forces. But there is another way of addressing the issue: it may be that there cannot be a sufficiently powerful rationale to sustain an ongoing, indeed permanent, North American troop presence in Europe, but it should not be assumed that other, perhaps more meaningful means of remaining committed to European security cannot be found. This, at least, is the burden of the second "Canadianization" thesis.

If Europeans worry about the US following Canada and decamping with its stationed forces, there are many in Ottawa who are hoping that the US will "Canadianize" its European security policy by showing a disposition to involve itself heavily—like Canada—in peacekeeping and humanitarian assistance efforts in the former Yugoslavia and perhaps elsewhere in Eastern Europe.

It is rarely remarked in Europe, especially by those who lament the "faithlessness" of their Canadian ally, that Canada has played what is by any reckoning an outsized role in the dimension of security known as "peacekeeping." Of the forty-four thousand or so armed forces serving in UN peacekeeping missions around the world at the beginning of 1993, some ten percent were Canadian. To be sure, not all these forces were deployed in Europe; however, the bulk of the Canadian blue-helmeted presence was assigned to Europe, either in Croatia and Bosnia, or Cyprus (although this latter mission is now terminated). It is true that the size of the Canadian blue-helmet contingent in the former Yugoslavia had shrunk to about two thousand by 1995, but even that level contrasted favorably (in the minds of the Europeans) with the American forces on the ground in the region (more than five hundred in the Former Yugoslav Republic of Macedonia in 1994).

To some of those who subscribe to the second version of "Canadianization," causal significance is associated with this commitment: specifically, it is held that the US will be likely to show itself more interested in collective security measures in the former Yugoslavia because of the efforts made by Canada there. In this sense, the future of transatlantic security relations will continue to involve the future not only of the UN but of NATO as well. It will, however, only be a happy future if NATO so transforms itself as to become relevant in the part of Europe that has the greatest need of its involvement, the East. To do so, NATO presumably would need to become less of a collective-defense and more of a collective-security organization. Thus, to the proponents of this second "Canadianization" thesis, far from being a disloyal ally, Canada is doing the one thing in Europe that best assures NATO will have a meaningful future, even if for a while it was doing it under UN auspices: it is showing the allies what needs to be done to safeguard their individual and collective interests. This second version of the "Canadianization" thesis, need it be remarked, looks today to have been dealt a setback by the UNPROFOR experience in Bosnia—an experience that revealed what had not been so clearly highlighted earlier; namely, that "humanitarian-assistance" missions might serve as the antithesis of collective-security roles, not as precursors to such roles.

As we indicated above, if it is true that NATO was never intended to be a collective-security organization, it is no less true that it has served such a function, in making it less likely that the formerly disputatious Western European states would ever go to war against each other again. NATO has not constituted, because of the Greco-Turkish problem within its midst, a "security community"; nevertheless, it is at least arguable that it has played a necessary part in the creation elsewhere in Europe of the security community that evidently does exist. It takes nothing away from NATO's founding mandate to defend Western Europe from Soviet aggression to make the point that it has been a reassurance mechanism for the Western Europeans against themselves (Joffe 1987: chap 5; Nerlach 1979).

CONCLUSION

It is important to reiterate that should the US choose to emulate Canada, in whichever version of the "Canadianization" thesis one prefers, it will do so for reasons of its own, based (presumably) on a serious debate about how involved it needs to remain in European security arrangements in this post-Cold War era.

It is also important to stress the extraordinary nature of the American post-Cold War strategic position. On the one hand, there is a widespread view that the country's own physical security is less imperiled today than it has been in more than fifty years; the same can be said of Canada (Jockel and Sokolsky 1993). What one can expect to see flow from this perception is the increasing "Australianization" of US security and defense policy, by which it is argued that, like its far-off Pacific friend, the US can afford to deemphasize the role of defense policy because it lives in a neighborhood untroubled by bullies. On the other hand, there is a no less general perception that the planet is increasingly unraveling and becoming less capable of being managed in any general interest. Jowett (1991: 15) persuasively argues that the "Leninist extinction" of the post-1989 years can be expected to propel the global system into a period of chaos that resembles nothing so much as the world described in the Book of Genesis, where the major concerns will be "naming and bounding." In this post-Leninist period, the "emerging international environment's primary characteristic will be turbulence of an order not seen during the Cold War," and one can confidently expect a rising incidence in civil and interstate warfare often inspired by ethnic tensions.

Among the American public and political class—who can blame them?—the dominant trend is to emphasize the "Australianization" thesis and downplay the "Genesis" one. To shed the costly obligations of foreign policy for a renewal of domestic socioeconomic prospects seems to make perfect sense to most Americans (Pfaff 1993a; Cohen 1993). Even if there is a reluctance to revert openly to a policy of isolation, many aspire to obtain what isolation evidently promised in the past: safety, economy, and nonentanglement. And while it may be a mistake to attribute the appeal evidenced by Patrick Buchanan in his 1996 race for the Republican presidential nomination as being based mainly or exclusively on his well-known nationalist, isolationist proclivities, there is nevertheless a case for interpreting Buchanan's rise as revealing a fundamental desire to have done with the world's woes.

Analysts and policy-makers alike in Canada have similarly been expressing concern about isolationism taking root in that country. That either North American country could or should remain "committed" to European security in the same fashion as during the collective-defense era is doubtful. Whether either can afford not to involve itself intimately in the security affairs of the old continent, significantly, is beginning to be debated more seriously today than at any time in the past few decades. In Canada, one can in some quarters detect the onset of a reaction against the idea that open-ended commitments to peacekeeping can or should have a steady claim on the country's dwindling military resources.[14] For the US, the problem is that balance-of-power internationalism of the Eurocentric variety appears to have lost its relevance, while at the same time Americans are resistant to the call for something like a Wilsonian vision of world order (Pfaff 1993). It appears more and more as if the US will have to choose either to find a new purpose in a revitalization of multilateral security organizations and collective internationalism or relapse into something that looks at least a bit like the isolation of the interwar period. For the moment at least, the latter looks to be far more likely than the former.

Much depends, for Europe and for North America, upon which version of the "Canadianization" thesis shows itself to be more applicable. NATO may continue to survive, even should the strains currently imposed on it grow. It may, and almost certainly will, take on a more "European" flavor—indeed, doing so might be a necessary condition of its short-term survivability. But if it proves incapable of surmounting the dual challenges of remaining a credible factor in the East while retaining the engagement of its transatlantic partners, it assuredly will survive as yet one more feckless acronym—perhaps anachronism?—in a European security landscape already overcrowded with "interlocking" institutions. To date, none of these has proven particularly adept at responding to the challenges posed by ethnic nationalism. That the EC/EU has so far bungled the job even more than has NATO should be scant consolation for leaders of the alliance.

NOTES

1. In Central and Eastern Europe the concern is not that Poland, for example, will attempt to seize parts of Germany or that its 97.9 percent Polish population is itself threatened. The suppression of minority rights and ethnic confrontations are virtually nonexistent in ethnically homogenous Poland (and in the Czech Republic and Hungary to a lesser degree). However, it must be kept in mind that no matter how numerically small they are now, the groups that were at one time Poland's largest ethnic minorities have either been deported or exterminated over the course of the twentieth century. In Eastern Europe, though not exclusively, the problem is heightened by significantly lower levels of institutionalization than that of Central Europe and by unresolved disputes involving the Russian diaspora spread throughout the periphery of the former Soviet Union. Potentially explosive spots are in the so-called Dniester Republic, Ukraine, and the Baltic States. These Russian minorities exist side by side the remnants of the Soviet Armed Forces. The possibility of ethnic clashes is not isolated to these areas. Antagonisms within Russia proper, i.e. Tartarstan, North and South Ossetia, Donbass and the Crimea, and the Trans-Dniester region have been ongoing [editor's note].

2. In late April 1993 Woerner told a Canadian reporter that the many "reasons for the existence of NATO ... will not be sufficient to prove the need for NATO in public perception if we fail to deal effectively with [this crisis] on our doorstep" (quoted in Koring 1993: A1, 14).

3. On this point, see Pfaff (1993a: 4); also see Mather (1993: A11).

4. See Barrett (1993), Peters and Barrett (1993) and Shea (1993).

5. NATO has a number of conflict prevention instruments at its disposal. Articles I and IV of the 1949 Washington Treaty establish the commitment to consult together when the territorial integrity, political independence, or security of any of the parties is threatened. The Washington Treaty itself can be considered as a statement of conflict prevention, because it declares the political willingness and legal obligation to defend collectively against armed attack. In brief, NATO's current conflict prevention policy framework consists of the commitment to the expansion of the alliance through bilateral and multilateral linkages, the Alliance Strategic Concept, and to the concept of mutually reinforcing institutions. Since the launching of the NATO Partnership for Peace (PFP) at the NATO Summit held in January 1994, twenty-six nations have signed the Framework Document. Twelve states have concluded their follow-on Individual Partnership Programmes (IPPs), with a range of activities such as provision of NATO technical documentation on standardization, adapting airfields to NATO standards, and exercises in compatible command and control systems. The program has moved from peacekeeping exercises to defense review planning, an important transparency and confidence-building measure.

6. One analyst laments what he labels the "Japanization of America's foreign policy," by which is meant a policy fixated selfishly on domestic issues and only those foreign-policy ones of a primarily economic nature. See Bertram (1993: 6).

7. France similarly attempted to contain Germany's apprehended eastward "drift" a decade ago. See Haglund (1991: 77–78).

8. The analogy is made between Western policy toward Germany in the Weimar Republic and after World War II and the current situation regarding the proper means of aiding Russia in Skorov (1993: 6) and Smith (1993: 8); also see Treverton (1993).

9. Prominent examples include Nixon (1992, 1993), Kirkpatrick (1992), Hoagland (1993), Brzezinski (1993), and Iklé (1991–92).

10. For a discussion of this question, see MacFarlane (1993).

11. For a critical examination, see Martin (1993).

12. For a good discussion, see Rempel (1992).

13. See Allen (1993), Bracken and Johnson (1993), Snider (1992–93), and Clarke (1993–94).

14. Notes one Canadian analyst, "it reached the point last autumn where every Canadian combat soldier (at the very best there are no more than ten thousand of them) was either coming home from a war zone, caught in the middle of one, or preparing to strap on a flack jacket and head overseas" (Fisher 1993: 11); see also Government of Canada (1994).

REFERENCES

Allen, William W. 1993. "The United States Army in Europe, 1995 and Beyond: Determinants for a Dual-Based, Smaller, yet Substantive Force." In *From Euphoria to Hysteria: Western European Security after the Cold War*, edited by David G. Haglund. Boulder, Colo.: Westview.

Asmus, Ronald D., Richard L. Kugler, and F. Stephen Larrabee. 1993. "Building a New NATO." *Foreign Affairs* 72: 20–40.

Barrett, John. 1993. *Conflict Prevention and Crisis Management: The Approach of NATO.* Brussels: NATO International Staff, Political Affairs Division.

Bertram, Christoph. 1993. "There Is a Foreign Policy." *International Herald Tribune* (17 November): 6.

Bracken, Paul, and Stuart E. Johnson. 1993. "Beyond NATO: Complementary Militaries." *Orbis* 37: 205–21.

British American Information Council. 1993. "Major Powers Give Little Backing to Vance-Owen Plan." *Basic Reports* (16 April): 1–2.

Brzezinski, Zbigniew. 1993. "The Way forward for an Inspired NATO." *International Herald Tribune* (2 December): 4.

"Canada Will Be Asked to Reconsider European Troop Exit." 1992. *Ottawa Citizen* (31 March): A6.

Carment, David. 1995. "NATO and the International Politics of Ethnic Conflict: Perspectives on Theory and Policy." *Contemporary Security Policy* no. 4 (Winter): 347–79.

Clarke, Jonathan. 1993–94. "Replacing NAT." *Foreign Policy* 93. 22–40.

Cohen, Richard. 1993. "Americans Are Inclined to Let the Bridges Fall." *International Herald Tribune* (15 November): 6.

Conference address by David Haglund, U.S. Security Horizons in the 1990s, Centre for International Relations, Queen's University, Kingston, Canada, 16 May 1991.

Diehl, Paul F. 1993. *International Peacekeeping.* Baltimore: John Hopkins University Press.

Drozdiak, William. 1993. "NATO Likely to Slow East Europe's Entry," *International Herald Tribune* (6 October): 2.

Fisher, Marc. 1992. "Europeans Ask: If Canada's Troops Leave, Can GIs Be Far Behind?" *Washington Post* (11 March): 16.

Fisher, Matthew. 1993. "Souring on Peacekeeping," *Ottawa Sun* (23 November): 11.

Freedman, Lawrence. 1991–92. "Order and Disorder in the New World." *Foreign Affairs* 71, no. 1: 33.

"The Future of the Balkans: An Interview with David Owen." 1993. *Foreign Affairs* 72: 6.

Glaser, Charles L. 1993. "Why NATO Is Still Best: Future Security Arrangements for Europe." *International Security* 18: 5–50.

Gotlieb, Gidon. 1993. *Nation against State.* New York: Council on Foreign Relations.

Government of Canada. Department of National Defence. 1992. *Canadian Defence Policy.* 8–9.

Government of Canada. 1994. Department of National Defence. "1994 Defence White Paper."

Haglund, David G. 1991. *Alliance within the Alliance? Franco-German Military Cooperation and the European Pillar of Defense.* Boulder, Colo.: Westview.

Haglund and Olaf Mager. 1992. "Bound to Leave? The Future of the Allied Stationing Regime in Germany," *Canadian Defence Quarterly* 21: 35–43.

———. 1992. "Homeward Bound?" In *Homeward Bound? Allied Forces in the New Germany,* edited by Haglund and Mager. Boulder, Colo.: Westview, 273–85.

Harries, Owen. 1993. "The Collapse of the 'West.'" *Foreign Affairs* 72: 41–53.

Hastings, Adrian, Norman Stone, Mark Almond, Noel Malcolm, and Bronka Magas. 1994. "On Bosnia, Washington Should Stop Deferring to London and Paris." *International Herald Tribune* (November 29): 4.

Hoagland, Jim. 1993. "Security, Not Economics, Is Still the Central U.S.-Russian Issue." *International Herald Tribune* (8 April): 6.

Hoffmann, Stanley. 1994. "What Will Satisfy Serbia's Nationalists?" *New York Times* (December 4): E19.

Honig, Jan Willem. 1992. "The 'Renationalization' of Western European Defense." *Security Studies* 2: 122–38.

Iklé, Fred C. 1991–92. "Comrades in Arms: The Case for a Russian-American Defense Community." *National Interest* (6 October): 2.

International Herald Tribune. 1993. "Aspin Tells Allies to Proceed Slowly on New Members." (21 October): 2.

Jockel, Joseph T., and Joel J. Sokolsky. 1993. "Dandurand Revisited: Rethinking Canada's Defence Policy in an Unstable World." *International Journal* 48: 380–401.

Joffe, Josef. 1987. *The Limited Partnership: Europe, the United States, and the Burdens of Alliance* Cambridge, Mass.: Ballinger.

———. 1992–93. "The New Europe: Yesterday's Ghosts," *Foreign Affairs* 72, no. 1: 43.

Johnston, William R. 1993. "The Canadian Military Commitment to Europe: Political Smoke, Military Mirrors?" In Haglund, ed., *From Euphoria to Hysteria,* 93–115.

Jowett, Ken. 1991. "After Leninism: The New World Disorder,"
    Journal of Democracy 2: 15.
Kirkpatrick, Jeanne. 1992. "Give Top Priority to Preserving Democracy
    in Russia." *International Herald Tribune* (25 February): 6.
Koring, Paul. 1993. "Europe's Lack of Will Condemned." *Globe and
    Mail* (1 May): A1, A14.
Kozyrev, Andrei. 1993. "The New Russia and the Atlantic Alliance."
    NATO Review 41: 3–6.
Lellouche, Pierre. 1992. Interview in *Le Quotidien de Paris* (16 March);
    reprinted in *FBIS-WEU-82-075 17 (April)*: 11.
Lewis, Anthony. 1994. "NATO Discredited by Its Members." *Interna-
    tional Herald Tribune* (November 29): 4.
MacFarlane, S. Neil. 1993. "Russia, the West, and European Security."
    Survival 35: 3–25.
MacFarlane and Thomas G. Weiss. 1992. "Regional Organizations and
    Regional Security." *Security Studies* 2: 28.
Martin, Laurence. 1993. "Peacekeeping as a Growth Industry." *Na-
    tional Interest* 32: 3–11.
Mather, Ian. 1993. "NATO, the Toothless Tiger." *Ottawa Citizen* (17
    August): A11.
NATO Office of Information and Press. 1992. "Ministerial Meeting of
    the North Atlantic Council in Oslo, Norway, 4th June 1992." *Press
    Communique M-NAC-1 92. 51.*
"NATO: Plums for Poland?" 1993. *Defense Media Review* 7: 1.
Nerlich, Uwe. 1979. "Western Europe's Relations with the United
    States." *Daedalus* 108: 87–111.
Nixon, Richard. 1992. "We Are Ignoring Our World Role." *Time* (16
    March): 72.
———. 1993. "The West Can't Afford to Let Yeltsin's Russia Fail."
    International Herald Tribune (8 March): 6.
Notes of panel discussion. 1993. Thirtieth Munich Conference on
    Security Policy. Munich, 6 February.
Peters, Hans Jochen, and John Barrett. 1993. "NACC and the CSCE: A
    Contribution in the Context of the Concept of Interlocking Institu-
    tions." Ebenhausen: Stiftung Wissenschaft und Politik.
Pfaff, William. 1993a. "The Allies Should Get Used to the New Isola-
    tionism." *International Herald Tribune* (19/20 June): 4.
———. 1993b. "If NATO Can't Guarantee Security in Europe, What
    Good Is It?" *International Herald Tribune* (2 November): 4.
———. 1993c. "Invitation to War." *Foreign Affairs* 72, no. 3: 97–109.
———. 1993d. "Rehabilitating Wilson Is an Attitude but Not a Policy,"
    International Herald Tribune (12 November): 9.
Pick, Hella. 1993. "Enforcing the Plan." *Manchester Guardian Weekly*
    (7 February): 1, 7.

Pick et al. 1992. "Canada Plans to Pull All Its Troops Out of Europe." *Manchester Guardian Weekly* (8 March): 1.

Platt, Erika. 1993. "NATO's Ostpolitik." *Defense Media Review* 7: 6–7.

Ramet, Sabrina Petra. 1992. "War in the Balkans." *Foreign Affairs* 72: 81.

Rempel, Roy. 1992. "Canada's Troop Deployments in Germany: Twilight of a Forty-Year Presence?" *Homeward Bound?*, 213–47.

Safire, William. 1994. "Arm Muslim Fighters and Bomb Serbian Positions." *International Herald Tribune* (November 29): 4.

Sallot, Jeff. 1992. "Canadian Troop Pullout Upsets Allies in NATO." *Globe and Mail* (5 March): A1, A2.

Shea, Jamie. 1993. "NATO's Eastern Dimension: New Roles for the Alliance in Securing the Peace in Europe." *Canadian Defence Quarterly* 22: 55–62.

Simon, Jeffrey. 1993. "Does Eastern Europe Belong in NATO?" *Orbis* 37: 33.

Skorov, George. 1993. "The West Must Decide What It Intends for Russia." *International Herald Tribune* (25 June): 6.

Smith, Gaddis. 1993. "Russia: Much Like Weimar, but with a Fortunate Difference." *International Herald Tribune* (11 October): 8.

Snider, Don M. 1992–93. "US Military Forces in Europe: How Low Can We Go?" *Survival* 34: 24–39.

The Transformation of an Alliance: The Decisions of NATO's Heads of State and Government. 1992. Brussels: NATO Office of Information and Press.

Trenin, Dmitri V. 1993. Linking Transatlantic and Eurasian Security: Prospects for Peace Operations, NATO Defense College, Occasional Paper, no. 1.

Treverton, Gregory. 1991–92. "The New Europe." *Foreign Affairs* 71, no. 1: 105.

———. 1993. "Finding an Analogy for Tomorrow." *Orbis* 37: 1–20.

Vogel, Steve. 1993. "U.S. Proposes Pact Nations Join NATO as 'Partners.'" *Montreal Gazette* (21 October): B4.

5

Trial by Fire

International Actors and Organizations in the Yugoslav Crisis

Michel Fortmann, Pierre Martin, and Stéphane Roussel

INTRODUCTION

The end of the Cold War, it is widely believed, did not bring the harvest of international peace and cooperation hoped for after decades of superpower confrontation over a divided Europe. Initially, the fall of the Berlin Wall generated some degree of optimism about the prospects for peace, reflected in proposals for a new system of European security (Kupchan and Kupchan 1991; Treverton 1991; Bennett and Lepgold 1993). Suddenly, a lasting peace seemed possible in Europe, and this perception contributed to heightened expectations. But the proponents of a "realist" approach have never shared this optimism. The end of the bipolar stalemate, realists predicted, would spark uncontrollable ethnic conflicts that would endanger the stability of Europe as a whole (Mearsheimer 1990). Confronted with these new threats, the realists argued, existing institutions and frameworks of international cooperation developed in the period of the "long peace" (Gaddis 1987) would be more or less irrelevant.

At first sight, the bitter breakup of Yugoslavia and the protracted conflict that ensued among its various ethnic groups would seem to vindicate these predictions. Few weeks have passed in recent years without a reminder in the media of the incapacity of international actors to put an end to a conflict whose complexity escapes the grasp of most Westerners. As early as 1991, analysts painted a gloomy picture of the international community's incapacity to intervene effectively in a situation that was degenerating into a major European civil war.[1]

For the pessimists, the new architecture of European security was badly flawed, as it seemed to rest upon the shaky foundations of a hopelessly divided Europe and an indifferent America. Some even suspected the resurgence of old alliances that recalled bitter memories, such as that between Germany and Croatia or between Serbia and France (Brenner 1992; Larrabee 1992; Joffe 1993). Inside the former Yugoslavia itself, images of the Chetniks and the Ustase came back to haunt the daily reporting of events.

The first years of the conflict gave plenty of support to pessimistic views of the new European security institutions. Too many foreign governments held on for too long to the hope of saving the moribund Yugoslav federation and thus failed to take in due time the more radical actions that the crisis commanded. Some commentators even noted ironically that European security institutions seemed to act more in competition than in concert (Nerlich 1992: 7). Many others believed that European action suffered from a deplorable lack of leadership and a "total absence of a vision of the future" (Julien 1993). Although the Dayton Accord represents an important breakthrough in the quest for peace in the Balkans, the pessimists still seem to have the upper hand, and the Yugoslav crisis continues to symbolize the problematic nature of direct international intervention in a domestic crisis.

Can international security institutions contribute effectively to manage, and hopefully to prevent, the new breed of conflicts brought about by the end of the Cold War? Measured against the high expectations generated by this historic event, it is, of course, easy to write off the efforts of the international community in Yugoslavia as a dismal failure. But is it realistic to use the ideal of a quick and definitive end to all hostilities in the Balkans as the only yardstick with which to measure the success or failure of the international community? In our view, analysts and practitioners need a more realistic basis to assess international actions.

In this chapter, we seek to evaluate the performance of international actors and organizations as they were confronted with the Yugoslav crisis. First, we survey the evolution of the issue since 1989. This summary shows how a spiraling conflict shattered the expectations that many had placed in a peaceful transition to a new "architecture of security" in Europe. We note, however, that the pervasive sentiment of defeat that long prevailed in assessments of international action was determined partly by the unrealistically high level of these expectations. Then, we survey the numerous stages in the long search for a political solution to the conflict, from the first concerted international efforts to the conclusion of the Dayton Accord in the end of 1995. The final sections present an evaluation of the various dimensions of international cooperative action in the Yugoslav conflict that emphasizes its overall coherence and normative consistency.

We conclude on a cautiously optimistic note. The roots of conflict in the Balkans are very deep, and the international community may be unlikely to eradicate them altogether. Nevertheless, there is no doubt that the international community has succeeded in maintaining a reasonably coherent line of action vis-à-vis the conflict, containing violence that conceivably could have been much worse and preventing its spread to other regions of Europe.

THE EMERGING SECURITY ARCHITECTURE IN THE NEW EUROPE

On 12 December 1989, just a few weeks after the fall of the Berlin Wall, US Secretary of State James Baker spoke to the Berlin Press Club. On this occasion the idea of a new architecture of security for Europe was formulated for the first time. In concrete terms, this architecture referred to a complex set of institutions that, ideally, would work in concert to ensure European security in the post-Cold War era. In Secretary Baker's own words,

> This new architecture must have a place for old foundations and structures that remain very valuable—like NATO—while recognizing that they can also serve new collective purposes. The new architecture must continue the construction of institutions—like the European Community—that can help draw together the West while also serving as an open door to the East. And the new architecture must build up frameworks like the CSCE process—that can overcome the division of Europe and, at the same time, can bridge the Atlantic Ocean.

This concept required some time to take shape, but it came to be commonly accepted during 1990. Indeed, although the notion was unclear at the outset, it soon became compelling because the image of a new architecture captured the need for new structures to replace the crumbling edifice of a Europe divided in two blocs. The old structure, in which an uneasy stability resulted from bipolar confrontation, would have to give way to a new framework of cooperation based on a variety of institutions and an enlarged conception of regional security.

In this new environment, the North Atlantic Treaty Organization (NATO) would still serve its primary functions as a defensive alliance and as a foothold for the United States in Europe, but it could progressively move toward new political roles, including a strategy of openness and dialogue with Central and Eastern Europe. This political role was consolidated at summits in London and Rome in 1990, at Copenhagen in 1991, and by the creation of the North Atlantic Council of Cooperation (NACC) in 1991 and NATO's Partnership for Peace (PfP) in 1994.

In parallel, however, an institution such as the Conference for Security and Cooperation in Europe could act within this new architecture on the basis of a wider definition of security. Although the CSCE remained a forum for arms-control negotiations, its actions concentrated mainly on the development of democracy and human rights in Central and Eastern Europe. For the CSCE, the Charter of Paris, signed in November 1990, was seen as a foundation for a new European security order and planted the seeds of a permanent and effective organization. The charter confirmed the CSCE's pivotal role in the definition of the norms and principles governing relations between states but also between governments and their citizens. To make this normative framework effective, a series of mechanisms were instated at the Paris Summit and later gradually improved, notably at the 1992 Helsinki meeting. This process of institutionalization was completed when the CSCE became the Organization for Security and Cooperation in Europe (OSCE) on 1 January 1995.

Finally, in this new architecture, the European Union (EU) would symbolize not only the political and economic integration of the Western part of the continent but also the desire of Europeans in general to regain control of their destiny in matters of security and foreign policy. The signing of the Maastricht Treaty in December 1991 strengthened the idea of a common external and security policy (CESP), but even the rapid progress toward unification could not entirely mask the remaining divergence. In the same period, spurred by the insistence of France, the Western European Union (WEU) jumped on the bandwagon of a common security policy, appointing itself coordinator of Western Europe's common defense.

Underlying this whole edifice, the notion of architecture suggested that the various actors in the emerging structure of European security should work together in a spirit of cooperation. This need for collaboration led to the idea that the new architecture of security should be based upon an interlocking of existing actors and institutions.

This rapid evolution of a structure with multiple, overlapping players was bound to produce frictions, especially when it came to establishing a hierarchy of European security institutions. Indeed, throughout 1991 there was an intense debate between the "Atlantists," who wished to preserve NATO's role as the key center of decision, and the "Europeanists," who wanted to see a clean break from Cold-War structures and thus called for a more distinctly European security system centered around the European Community (Fortmann 1993). In spite of frictions between governments pursuing their national goals, there was a genuine desire to achieve results, which led to major concessions from each participant.

In sum, during the two years between the fall of the Berlin Wall and the breakup of Yugoslavia, a genuine and politically effective security structure had begun to take form as a result of a multitude of small adjustments between existing organizations. This emerging structure, however, was not immediately able to fulfill all the expectations that it had helped engender, and the process is far from complete.

In December 1995, just as the Dayton Accord was being countersigned in Paris, European governments still clashed over some of the same issues that they had been discussing in 1991: What should be the role of the United States in defending Europe when the continent is increasingly insisting upon forging its own "security identity"? How can the states of Eastern and Central Europe be integrated into the Western defense system without provoking Russia or jeopardizing relations between allies in NATO or the WEU? The December 1995 meetings of the EU, the WEU, and NATO were still dominated by debates between the Atlantists and the Europeanists, along with debates over the eventual eastward enlargement of NATO and the EU. In many ways, nonetheless, the institutional network and mechanisms of cooperation in existence today are closer than ever to the kind of "security regime" that many envisioned immediately after the end of the Cold War (Roussel and Fortmann 1994).

In the meantime, the notion of architecture almost became obsolete or disappeared from the vocabulary of leaders or analysts (for an exception, see Claes 1994), in large part because of the harsh judgment passed on international institutions involved in the Yugoslav conflict. In our view, however, the main reason that institutions were perceived so negatively was the fact that the expectations engendered by the onset of the post-Cold War European security order in 1990–1991 were vastly exaggerated.

HIGH HOPES, SHATTERED EXPECTATIONS

The new international order in Europe has found its concrete expression in the development of institutions that have recast relations between states in a more cooperative framework. This emerging regime has faced enormous challenges, however, as the end of the Cold War brought about what many have called a resurgence of history or, to be more precise, a regression of political reason (Ramonet 1993) toward aggressive micronationalisms.

Unleashed by the fall of communist regimes, ethnic and ultranationalist tensions proliferated in Eastern Europe. In addition to the Yugoslav case, tensions have also appeared between Romania and Hungary, the Czech Republic and Slovakia, Albania and Serbia (Kosovo), and Macedonia and Greece, not to mention many of the former Soviet republics. Taken individually, these trouble spots may not present great risks for the stability of Europe as a whole, but the danger resides more in the possibility (however small) for a chain reaction. Indeed, particularly if violence appears to bring rewards, the transformation of one of these conflicts into an open war could serve as a catalyst for others (Pfaff 1993; Mayall 1992). This type of conflict could also bring great powers to abandon the common goal of regional security in favor of shortsighted notions of immediate self-interest (Mearsheimer 1990).

The crisis in the former Yugoslavia is thus a real challenge to European stability. Moreover, it takes place at a time when the security regime is still in construction and when the norms, principles, and rules that guide it are still, for a large part, inherited from the Cold War. In other words, an entire regional "system," still in a process of rebuilding, had to confront a severe crisis at a time when individual countries were forced to thoroughly and simultaneously redefine national policies, collective interests, and common values (De Montbrial 1992). As Richard Betts (1992) argued, it is only in times of crisis that the efficiency of a system of security can really be tested. The Yugoslav crisis represented precisely such a test for international institutions in the early 1990s.

EVALUATING INTERNATIONAL COOPERATION

It is well known that the verdict of most commentators on the management of the Yugoslav crisis is extremely severe. Is this harsh judgment on the performance of the European security system an expression of zeitgeist, a reflection of some kind of sinister fin de siècle mood, or is it an objective reading of the situation? Thierry de Montbrial (1992: 101) has, in fact, implicitly answered this question by emphasizing that no evaluation of international actions toward Yugoslavia can be complete without accounting for the positive dimensions.

We would tend to go even farther: the early analyses of how international organizations acted in the Yugoslav crisis were marred, in many cases, by the militant involvement of their authors. To be sure, the daily reports of atrocities from Bosnia and Croatia were hardly conducive to adopting a moderate outlook. Such dramatic images, however, largely overshadowed the considerable efforts deployed by the EC and by the greater international community in response to the Yugoslav tragedy. Perhaps because of this somber general mood, the more impartial commentators tried to find excuses for the apparent international incapacity to end the fighting rather than to highlight the positive aspects of the concrete actions that had been undertaken (Edwards 1992).

In our view, the militant and passionate involvement that has driven much of the analyses of the conflict tended to create false hopes and erase the distinction between what is desirable and what is achievable. Thus, in contrast to what the press suggests, particularly in the German-speaking countries,[2] it is not possible for international organizations to impose peace upon conflicting parties. As in the case of an acrimonious divorce, for which legal, social, or religious institutions can suggest solutions to facilitate a settlement but cannot impose any, a conflict of such magnitude can only be solved with the full consent of the disputing parties.

In other words, if international actors seek to end a conflict of the kind that we are discussing here, their task can only go as far as making all possible efforts to bring the belligerents to face each other and engage into a dialogue. Of course, the success of mediating institutions rides for a large part on the attitude of the parties. As Kalevi Holsti notes, there is often no room for successful mediation or conciliation as long as the warring parties refuse to recognize the impossibility of conquest by force. Holsti also notes that violent nationalist movements seek capitulation or conquest. They are notoriously unable to accept compromise solutions until the harsh realities of a war that no one can win changes their calculations and attitudes (Holsti 1992: 113–14). Despite all good intentions and even extraordinary efforts, international organizations can help, but they cannot act as substitutes for the conflicting parties.

This leads us to a truism the self-evidence of which was confirmed by the Yugoslav conflict: One can only expect the warring parties to stop the killings when they no longer perceive that it is in their interest to fight, not when some third party tries to impose a cease-fire (Lefebvre and Jakubow 1993). External actors cannot force belligerents to lay down their arms any more than they can dictate a political solution to the leaders of the torn federation. The idea of using military force to impose peace inspired an ironic comment from the former US Secretary of Defense, Richard Cheney, who asked wryly: "How many Yugoslavs are we prepared to kill to prevent them from killing one another?" (*International Herald Tribune*, 17 September 1992).

The use of force by external actors to impose peace in the former Yugoslavia presented several problems. Serious questions can be raised as to the level of tolerance of Western governments and their publics confronted with the hazards for their soldiers of a "peace-making" operation. The interventions in Lebanon in the 1980s and in Somalia more recently have shown this level to be extremely low, as the loss of even a few lives can lead governments to backtrack from their commitments. Moreover, the remoteness of a conflict and the difficulty to perceive its potential effects on the security of other states can make it even harder to sell a costly and hazardous operation to the Western publics and their political leaders (*The Economist*, 26 February 1994: 19).

Domestic constraints can weigh heavily on the international community's capacity to act. Publics sometimes send conflicting messages to their leaders; pressing for action when confronted with the horrors of foreign wars but calling for retreat when these actions lead to casualties (Mueller 1995: 722–24). The situation can be even more complex when the appropriate attitude to adopt toward a conflict becomes an issue in domestic political battles, for reasons often quite remote from the conflict itself. The American and Russian cases readily come to mind. In the United States, the arms embargo against Bosnia was but one of the contentious issues in a high-stake confrontation between a Democratic president and a Republican Congress. In Russia, the conciliatory tone adopted toward Western initiatives became a key argument of the ultranationalists in their relentless criticism of the government. Such pressures led Moscow to distance itself from many of these initiatives, notably those that involved the use of force (Thibault and Lévesque 1995).

In general, for states and international institutions, these constraints greatly limited the room to maneuver when the use of force was at stake. For a long time, they had to limit their action to idle demonstrations of force such as the military and naval presence in the Adriatic or the deployment of the Rapid Reaction Force (RRF). Air raids were also attempted, as during "Operation Deliberate Force" in August and September 1995, but the risk associated with these operations was minimal compared to the involvement of ground troops.

Finally, analysts of the crisis in the media and elsewhere created the illusion that international unanimity was necessary to put an end to the conflict.[3] In fact, it is not at all clear that a Europe speaking with one single voice would become much more efficient. Moreover, unanimity very seldom if ever occurs in politics, especially in a situation in which state interests diverge to such an extent. It already is remarkable that some form of consensus developed around the Yugoslav situation, not only among European governments but also in the United Nations and among the five nations of the Contact Group (Britain, France, Germany, Russia, and the United States). Thus, we now turn to an examination of the concrete actions taken by international organizations in the Yugoslav crisis, drawing attention to positive elements that characterize these efforts.

THE COORDINATION OF INTERNATIONAL ACTION

What is perhaps most striking when one considers the joint actions of the Europeans, beyond the gloomy headlines, are the very positive features that few observers noted. Thus, contrary to the general perception, all foreign policy-makers in Europe followed the events in Yugoslavia closely. In spite of reluctance to intervene in a complex internal political situation, European governments and the United States clearly had indicated that the situation was of great importance to them. They all openly expressed their concerns in the spring of 1991, even before the crisis erupted in Belgrade (Edwards 1992: 165). When judging the initial reaction, one must keep in mind the fact that international attention late in 1990 and early in 1991 was largely focused upon war in the Persian Gulf, that Germany was still recovering from the "shock" of unification, and the Soviet Union was entering a period of instability that was to lead, in August 1991, to its own dismantlement. Moreover, in its early phase the crisis was still an internal Yugoslav affair, and thus European states could not invoke OSCE principles to intervene.

When the conflict could no longer be construed as an internal affair, Europeans reacted quickly through the OSCE, the EC, the Council of Europe, and the WEU.[4] The entry of the Soviet Union or Russia on the scene was delayed by domestic turmoil, while the United States and the United Nations initially preferred to let Europeans make the first move. The UN took its first actions in the winter of 1991, while Washington waited until the end of 1992 to join, cautiously and gradually, the international effort.

From the sound of the first gunshot, Europeans did not remain idle. They acted through their security organizations in accordance with precise rules, notably the patient search for consensus, gradualism, coherence, perseverance, and a respect for diversity of approaches and perspectives. Five key observations stand out.

First, one of the most notable aspects of Europe's action was the persistent will to act in concert, not only among the twelve members of the EU but also among the European nations as a whole. Thus Central and Eastern European governments became involved in the search for a solution. This approach was notable within the framework of the OSCE and that of the United Nations. There, countries such as Russia, Ukraine, Poland, and the Czech and Slovak republics, along with Sweden and Finland, were able to participate, particularly in collective peacekeeping operations. They also joined their efforts in preventive surveillance actions in some of the hot spots of the former Yugoslavia, such as Kosovo, Macedonia, Sandjak, and Vojvodina.

The arrival of the United States and Russia did not compromise the will to reach the largest possible consensus. There was still much divergence on issues such as the arms embargo against Bosnia, the modalities of proposed peace plans, or the resort to air strikes. In spite of this, states generally avoided taking unilateral actions that could have led to an escalation of the conflict. States engaged in the international effort also managed to avoid creating new acrimony among themselves that could have had lasting effects on European security.

In general, by channeling the reactions of nonbelligerent states, existing institutions certainly prevented the "pursuit of separate policies" (De Montbrial 1992: 102). Indeed, no European state openly and extensively supported, materially or politically, any of the parties to the conflict, even when narrow notions of "national interest" could have justified such support. Such support would no doubt have helped to intensify the conflict or make it spread to neighboring zones (Roussel and Fortmann 1994). On this last count, the Yugoslav case contrasts with the Spanish civil war in the 1930s, where the involvement of foreign powers exacerbated tensions between great powers.

Even if some countries in the region felt more directly than others the effects of the crisis, which directly challenged the cohesiveness of European policy positions, organizations such as the EC were able to make the required efforts to preserve solidarity. The German, Austrian, and Greek reactions to the crisis serve as examples of this active search for solidarity.

The second observation is that the Yugoslav crisis confronted Europeans with a whole new situation: this was the first civil war on the continent since the one in Greece. Consequently, they attempted to act gradually, initially giving priority to political means and then moving progressively to military pressure and sanctions, then to a limited use of force. This kind of approach, which many have described as displaying a lack of courage, simply reflects the perception that all possibilities must be offered to the parties in conflict so they can arrive at a negotiated settlement with a minimum of external intervention.

Indeed, if an external intervention is not accepted by the belligerents, it can aggravate rather than solve the problem, as the external actor actually becomes party to the conflict. It is only in 1993 that western states begun to designate—albeit most often implicitly—the Bosnian Serbs as the aggressors, in spite of Russia's objections during most of the conflict. Similarly, diplomatic recognition of the secessionist republics was a necessary step before more direct action. It was necessary inasmuch as this recognition would authorize the international community to consider the Yugoslav crisis no longer as the internal problem of a sovereign state but as an international conflict that threatened peace and security, as stipulated in chapter VII of the United Nations Charter. Indeed, actions by international organizations could be represented as a knot that is slowly tightening itself, progressively constraining the belligerents' margin to maneuver.

Third, the degree of coherence that characterized international action toward the Yugoslav crisis is, in our view, quite striking. The various organizations involved in the conflict, particularly the EU, NATO, the OSCE, the UN, and the WEU, demonstrated a large measure of agreement, which tended to muffle the discordant voices of individual states. Thus, international institutions served as forums in which states could express their positions and attempt to reconcile their differences. From this standpoint, institutions fulfilled an essential function, which was to facilitate adjustment of conflicting national policies (Roussel and Fortmann 1994).

Moreover, the collective actions of Europeans were largely complementary, each specializing in one or several roles. The EU thus took the leadership in negotiation of a political solution. The OSCE centered its actions around prevention and information, notably with respect to issues of human rights. The United Nations, for its part, concentrated efforts on finding ways to stop the fighting on the field, helping to channel humanitarian aid, overseeing the security zones. NATO, for its part, provided the military might to ensure compliance with the arms embargo, the no-fly zones, and the security zones, as well as to help implementing the Dayton Accord after December 1995. Even organizations that had competed with each other in the past, namely the WEU and NATO, found ways to cooperate (albeit in a rather minimal fashion) over the maritime embargo begun in July 1992. Moreover, the UN, the OSCE, and the EU worked in concert in a variety of domains, including preventive diplomacy, investigations on human rights violations, and the search for a political solution. This attempt at coordinating actions between organizations reinforces the image of coherence concerning the logic of progression, which marked international efforts toward resolution of the crisis.

Fourth, it must be pointed out that the various international organizations playing a role in the crisis employed not just one method but a whole arsenal of approaches. These tactics, in some cases, remained without effects. Nevertheless, as we will demonstrate below, they reveal the scope of efforts at the political, juridical, economic, and military levels toward putting an end to the conflict.

Fifth, and finally, we note that collective efforts around the Yugoslav situation did not seem to take any slack throughout the evolution of the crisis. This shows a rare perseverance in dealing with an extremely complex problem without an obvious solution. This perseverance finds its expression not only in the sustained participation of the Europeans but also in the actions of the UN Security Council—which voted eighty resolutions from September 1991 to November 1995—and in the dozens of peace plans presented throughout the conflict.

Therefore, international involvement in the Yugoslav civil war shows, on the surface, some positive features that call for a more thorough examination, to which we now turn.

A COHERENT NORMATIVE FRAMEWORK

One often neglected aspect of international intervention in Yugoslavia is the effort by all European governments, particularly through the OSCE and the UN, to adapt the principles of the Charter of Paris to the realities of European politics. Perhaps the principles were too optimistic, but these efforts were pursued in the years following the charter's signature. As Adam Rotfeld (1992) notes, both the Helsinki Act and, fifteen years later, the Charter of Paris reflect principles and norms which remain largely valid (570ff). Nevertheless, each document is based upon assumptions and approaches that were made obsolete by the course of events.

In our opinion, the Yugoslav situation, as well as the collapse of the Soviet Union and the conflicts that it sparked, call for a renewed analysis of the normative framework underpinning European security. Economic and political development is still the cornerstone of stability. In order to make this development possible, however, it has become increasingly important to ensure the stability of regions threatened by social, ethnic, or religious breakdown and preserve the most basic gains of the Helsinki process in terms of human rights.

The OSCE is perhaps the European security institution that lost the most credibility during the Yugoslav conflict. In addition to its apparent incapacity to implement the principles detailed in its own documents, this organization was often paralyzed by its consensus requirement, even in spite of the more recent adoption of a "unanimity minus one" rule. This loss of credibility was reflected notably by the neglect of the Bosnian crisis in the December 1994 Budapest Summit's final document and, more generally, by the fact that the OSCE was literally left on the sidelines from 1993 to 1995, even if the Dayton Accord reserved a role for the OSCE.

Nonetheless, we have to underline the fact that the OSCE, far from being complacent with its own operational shortcomings, has contributed to redefining the normative framework that made the organization a source of legitimacy for any action toward conflict resolution, peacekeeping, or peacemaking on the Continent (Ghebali 1992). The documents of Prague (January 1992) and Stockholm (December 1992) and, above all, that of Helsinki (adopted in July 1992 by the fifty-two members of the CSCE), insist notably on the indivisible character of peace and on the importance of solidarity in matters of security. In particular, the OSCE considers that "aggressive nationalism, intolerance, xenophobia and ethnic conflicts" threaten the stability of the whole region under its watch and thus should be a central preoccupation of all its member states (Helsinki Conference 1992: 4).

In this context, security no longer can be viewed in a restrictive way. It must be understood as an issue involving a whole array of economic, social, and political dimensions. Moreover, any violation of commitments taken under the human rights dimension of the OSCE is not within the exclusive domestic jurisdiction of a member state. Instead, it is considered a matter of direct and legitimate concern for all member states (Helsinki Conference 1992: 2).

This is how the OSCE provided a foundation of legitimacy for pressures and interventions from abroad in situations such as that of Yugoslavia. The Organization thus makes a show of solidarity that sends a clear message to all of the new states—and there seems to be no shortage of them—that face similar situations or are likely to confront them in the future. Indeed, one of the main risks that Europe must face in the wake of the Soviet Union's collapse is gradual closure of the former Soviet republics to the outside world. This new isolationism comes in part from Europe's failure to demonstrate more solidarity in matters of security by reacting more cohesively to the situations that developed in Georgia, Azerbaijan, Armenia, Ukraine, Tajikistan, and elsewhere.

From this vantage point, the OSCE acted appropriately by making respect for human rights and for minority rights the top European security priorities. It should be underscored that the creation of a position of high commissioner for national minorities was consistent with this new emphasis; it promised more rapid reactions from the organization when tensions linked with national minorities have the potential to erupt into violent conflicts. It also is notable that, in December 1992, the council of the CSCE gave even more prominence to the human rights issue by holding "governments responsible, before the international community, for acts that they would have committed against their own citizens as well as citizens of neighboring countries." The same decision also designates "authors of war crimes and those who violated international human rights as being individually responsible for their actions" (Stockholm Council Meeting of the CSCE 1992: 3). It was the United Nations, however, that put this idea into practice by creating, in May 1993, an international tribunal to prosecute war crimes. The tribunal was set up in September 1993 and held its first audiences in November of the next year.

In general, the actions of nonbelligerent states and international organizations in the Yugoslav crisis largely have benefited from the normative foundation created by the OSCE. Throughout the crisis the principles defended by this organization—such as democracy, human rights, territorial integrity, peaceful settlement of disputes, and many other related principles—were reaffirmed consistently in each of its numerous efforts toward conflict resolution.

Another important dimension of the normative framework put into place in recent years is the series of cooperation measures adopted within NATO, essentially by the NACC and the PfP. More pragmatic than the OSCE principles, the normative elements of the NACC and the PfP aim at orienting cooperation between members of NATO and other states involved in security issues. One of the key goals of the NACC and the PfP is to foster stability and trust between states by acting as a forum for discussion, the exchange of information, and military cooperation. Two aspects of their activities are relevant to the Yugoslav conflict. On the one hand, these programs aim at preventing the outbreak of new conflicts by encouraging their members to respect the norms instated by the OSCE and by reinforcing democratic controls over the armed forces. On the other hand, the PfP contributes to establish the operational standards of peacekeeping and crisis-management activities. From this point of view, the creation and the deployment of the Implementation Force (IFOR) after the conclusion of the Dayton Accord was the first concrete result of this cooperative effort.

In practice, Europe deployed peace efforts within the normative framework outlined above. These efforts involved several complementary dimensions that seldom are perceived as parts of a coherent whole. Here we distinguish five initiatives that illustrate these various dimensions and examine them in turn: the search for a political solution; the task of peacekeeping; the gradual resort to military force; the use of sanctions; and humanitarian assistance.

THE SEARCH FOR A POLITICAL SOLUTION

At first, the European Community took the lead in the search for a political solution to the conflict. To this end, the EC tried its whole arsenal of diplomatic instruments. Its interventions included offers to serve as mediator or arbiter, the design of peace plans, and the organization of special missions or international conferences.

Throughout the conflict, one of the consistent features of European diplomacy was the assignment of special emissaries such as the European Troika,[5] Henry Wijnaendts and Jose Cutileiro (from the WEU), Lord Carrington, Marrack Goulding, David Owen and Carl Bildt (from the EU), and the UN's Cyrus Vance and Thorvald Stoltenberg. Hardly a week passed during the thick of the conflict without a diplomatic shuttle of some sort. The United States also participated in these efforts, with emissaries such as Jimmy Carter and Richard Holbrooke. Because of the high ranking of these diplomats and brokers, the peace efforts remained constantly under the spotlight of world media. Moreover, the fact that these emissaries came from a variety of international organizations, in our opinion, underscores the global character of the conflict management enterprise around the Yugoslav crisis.

In addition to the Brioni agreement of 7 July 1991, which was negotiated by the European Troika and marked the end of fighting in Slovenia, no less than ten initiatives to search for a political settlement to the conflict were launched by various emissaries (GRIP 1994). Here we review the most important of these initiatives.

The Carrington Plan

The first conference on the future of Yugoslavia, presided over by Lord Carrington, opened at the Hague on 7 September 1991. This conference led to the establishment of three working committees[6] between the six republics and to the creation of a commission for legal arbitration of disputes chaired by French jurist Robert Badinter.[7]

The fall 1991 conference at the Hague saw the last attempt to rescue the idea of some form of Yugoslav federation, with a proposal to this effect sponsored by the EC on October 18. This plan included, notably, a formal recognition of the independence of all the republics of the former Yugoslavia and an offer from the EC to give the republics preferential economic treatment, along with a promise of rapid integration within the Common Market. In exchange, the European Community insisted that there should be a complete and immediate cessation of armed hostilities. The EC also required that the republics agree among themselves to maintain a minimal level of formal linkages, consisting mainly of four common institutions: a joint Supreme Court, which would hear individual citizens' complaints on human rights issues, and three executive councils dealing, respectively, with economic cooperation, foreign and security policy, and legal issues (FBIS 1991: 3).

This ambitious plan was immediately rejected by Serbia, because it more or less confirmed the end of Yugoslavia as it had existed. The conference met several more times during the spring of 1991, however, and its work helped in the definition of a framework for an initial attempt at negotiating a settlement to the conflict in Bosnia-Herzegovina in the spring of 1992.

The Vance Plan

The second initiative, commonly referred to as the "Vance plan," was considerably different from the Hague conference. The Vance plan's objective was to center the efforts to solve the conflicts between Serbs and Croats around the deployment of a peacekeeping force that would position itself between the belligerents. This force would be particularly concentrated in the regions contested by Serbs living within Croatia: Krajina and Slovenia. This plan was first introduced in November 1991 and eventually adopted by the UN's Security Council under Resolution 743 (21 February 1992). This resolution gave the signal for the deployment of the United Nations Protection Force (UNPROFOR) in four distinct sectors of the former Yugoslavia. The initial mandate of UNPROFOR was twelve months, and it was regularly renewed—not without difficulties—until fall 1995. Although the Vance plan deserves special mention among the various peace efforts, its implementation did not move beyond the confines of a narrowly defined UN peacekeeping operation. This is the reason why we do not address it in more detail here.

The third phase of international efforts to find a solution to the conflict occurred in the spring of 1992. At that time, Bosnia-Herzegovina was preparing a referendum on independence, which soon would be followed by the outbreak of war. In this new phase of international mediation, Lord Carrington oversaw talks among Bosnia's three main ethnic groups: Serbs, Croats, and Muslims. This role later was filled by the Portuguese diplomat Jose Cutileiro.

Talks at Brussels and Lisbon led to propositions to divide the new state into districts along mostly ethnic and economic lines and agreements on its political structures. Thus, Bosnia was to become a sovereign state composed of three largely autonomous constituent units. The central Bosnian government would have constitutional authority over finances, foreign policy, and macroeconomic policies, but its most important decisions would have to be approved by a four-fifths majority within a chamber of the constituent units. The plan eventually was rejected, but this time by the Bosnian authorities themselves. In spite of the best efforts of Cyrus Vance and Lord Carrington to bring the fighting to an end, it was impossible to reach any form of compromise agreement among representatives from the three communities (RFE/RL Research Report 1992).

The London Conference and the Vance-Owen Plan

The fourth attempt to find a political solution to the conflict came in two steps, starting in the summer of 1992. The first measure, somewhat neglected by commentators, was perhaps the most interesting. These efforts consisted of convocation of an international conference, held in London on 26–27 August 1992, which would bring together more than forty states or international organizations as well as representatives from the Yugoslav communities engaged in the conflict and leaders of the newly independent republics.

This project was particularly interesting in that it sought to bring negotiations to the forefront of international attention and forced the belligerents to deal with one another before the international community. Most of all, an international conference of such magnitude was seen as a way to bring the belligerents to openly accept a long list of rules, including: termination of violence; search for a negotiated solution; unencumbered distribution of humanitarian assistance; elimination of detention camps; and nine other prescriptions concerning items ranging from mutual diplomatic recognition and human rights to trade.[8]

Documents from the London Conference also enumerated a list of specific principles that could be applied to the resolution of the Bosnian conflict and particularly to the "new Yugoslavia" (i.e., Serbia and Montenegro). The importance of international sanctions to put pressure on the dissenting states also was reaffirmed in separate conclusions, and some form of organizational structure was proposed to monitor the work of the conference.

Thus, an executive committee was created to oversee the implementation of the conference's resolutions that included representatives from the EC and the OSCE, the UN secretary-general and the Security Council, and the former Yugoslav republics. Chaired by Cyrus Vance and David Owen and located at the UN offices in Geneva, this committee was composed of six working groups dealing with political, military, legal, and economic issues.[9]

Clearly, this was far from an improvised affair. Indeed, it was a sophisticated and coherent enterprise, which proposed both a normative and an organizational framework that seemed to go about as far as it conceivably could go to foster negotiations. In other words, if the parties had any willingness to talk to each other, they could hardly have found a better framework.

Unfortunately, this attempt, like all others, eventually led to an impasse. The second phase of negotiations in Geneva from September 1992 to January 1993 only managed to produce a very partial solution: the Vance-Owen plan, which advocated the division of Bosnia into ten provinces, a balanced ethnic repartition, and the demilitarization of Sarajevo. Although the Serbs rejected the plan definitively in May 1993, it had at least served as a basis for negotiations in the meantime.

In spite of such disappointing results, we maintain that international efforts to solve the Yugoslav crisis reflect undeniable persistence and a rare level of coherence on the part of international actors and organizations. Nonbelligerent states, however, probably deserve some blame for a certain lack of unity in their actions. Indeed, Washington was publicly critical of the Vance-Owen plan before it finally decided to endorse it (February 1992), and it may be argued that this hesitance had something to do with the rejection of the plan by the Serbs.

The Common Action Program

This program was another expression of the nonbelligerent states' will to maintain a common front in spite of pressures for division. At a meeting held in Washington on 22 May 1993, the United States, Russia, France, Britain, and Spain developed a "common action program" to avoid the tensions that followed the presentation of the Vance-Owen plan. The aim was to give a new momentum to negotiations but also to end the fighting and to prevent its extension into other areas. With this goal in mind, they agreed on a series of measures to ensure the implementation of sanctions, to protect the six security zones designated by the UN in April-May 1993, and, finally, to reinforce the international presence in sectors likely to be drawn into the conflict (such as Croatia, Kosovo, and Macedonia).

The Owen-Stoltenberg Plan

Submitted in August 1993 by David Owen and Thorvald Stoltenberg (who replaced Cyrus Vance as UN negotiator), this plan sought to reinvigorate peace talks on the basis of elements of the Vance-Owen plan, notably the notion of transforming Bosnia-Herzegovina into a confederation, divided in three autonomous republics (52 percent of the territory would go to the Serbs, 30 percent to Muslims, and 18 percent to Croats). The plan also called for common institutions, including a parliament, and stated rules regulating relations between republics. The UN would have had an extensive role in the implementation of this plan, with the participation of about fifty thousand blue helmets. After several weeks of discussions, the plan was rejected on 28 September by the Bosnian Muslims, who claimed that land conquered by force by the Serbs and Croats should be returned; the other two groups flatly refused.

The Contact Group Plan

It is notable that this plan and the Dayton Accord were developed outside the institutions that had from 1991 made the bulk of the peace efforts. This reflected a will on the part of the major players to make the process more flexible and to recast it in a different framework. In April 1994, the United States, Russia, France, Britain, and Germany joined together in an informal forum called the "Contact Group." After the creation of a Croat-Muslim federation in Bosnia was announced in May 1994, the group tried to restart the negotiations on the basis of the EU plan and the Owen-Stoltenberg plan. On 5 July 1994, the group proposed a plan to create a federation of republics united in a Bosnian state. Land was to be divided in two almost equal parts (49 percent for the Serbs, and 51 percent for the Croats and Muslims), and the transition would be overseen by an international force with a strong American participation. The Croats and Muslims accepted the plan, but the Bosnian Serbs rejected it in a referendum on 27–28 August 1994. This drove a wedge between the Bosnian Serbs and Serbia itself, whose leaders wished to see a relaxing of economic sanctions.

The Dayton Accord

This last episode was the product of an American initiative, but it was largely inspired by the previous plans and by Russian, French, and Canadian proposals. After months of diplomatic shuffle, US Deputy Undersecretary of State Richard Holbrooke managed to convince the warring parties to negotiate a new accord to put an end to hostilities on the whole territory of the former Yugoslavia. The talks began on 1 November in Dayton, Ohio. Under US supervision, President Tudjman of Croatia, President Milosevic of the Federal Republic of Yugoslavia, and President Izetbegovic of Bosnia-Herzegovina sat at the negotiating table along with representatives from members of the Contact Group and the EU.

There were a large number of problems to solve, and negotiators needed several weeks to clear all the hurdles. On 10 November, a major step was taken when the parties agreed to create two federated republics, one Croat-Muslim, the other Serbian, each with the same proportion of the land as under the Contact Group plan. Under this agreement, Bosnian Serbs could not join the Federal Republic of Yugoslavia. On 21 November, after three weeks of deliberations, the three presidents initialed the General Framework Agreement for Peace in Bosnia. Under this agreement, Bosnia was to become a federation of two republics, with Sarajevo remaining a distinct common area. The central government was to be headed by a collegial presidency (one Serb, one Croat, one Muslim) and a legislative assembly, and its institutions would also include a central bank, a common currency, and a constitutional court. Persons accused of war crimes could not hold political office. The OSCE had to supervise presidential and legislative elections within six to nine months of the signing of the agreement. A multinational Implementation Force (IFOR, later known as SFOR) was deployed to supervise the return of refugees, to monitor human rights, and to oversee the formation of a new police force in Bosnia. Economic sanctions and the arms embargo against Serbia were to be abandoned. Finally, corridors were established between Sarajevo and Gorazde and between Banjo Luka and Serbia.

All the plans summarized above show that the international institutions and the nonbelligerent states never abandoned their efforts in the search of a negotiated solution. Media commentators often complained about the apparently slow pace of the process, but this slowness was a reflection of the constraints that international actors had to confront. An important constraint to insure the success of the plan was the necessity to search for a minimal consensus, not only between the belligerents but also between key outside states. All the states involved also had to take public opinion into account and domestic pressures, notably in Germany, Russia, and the United States, which often left foreign-policy makers very little room to maneuver.

THE CHALLENGE OF PEACEKEEPING IN THE ABSENCE OF PEACE

It must be noted that the search for a political solution to the conflict was only one of the many types of intervention by international actors. Indeed, this type of intervention could develop only in parallel with a whole set of efforts aimed at ending hostilities first in Slovenia, then in Croatia, and finally in Bosnia. In these cases, also, we can observe the full arsenal of measures, the negotiation of countless cease-fire agreements, often broken within hours of signature; missions of observation and surveillance; the interposition of UN blue helmets; offers of disarmament or disengagement; arms transfer embargoes; and the maintenance of order in surveillance zones.

It soon became clear that observers from the EC and from the OSCE, who were sent first to Slovenia and then to Croatia and Bosnia, could hardly do any better than to provide surveillance in their zones of affectation since July 1991. Their main roles, in this respect, were to assist the UNPROFOR in its tasks and to report to international authorities about the situation in the field. Another key role of these observers was to play a preventive, or sometimes deterrent, role in the zones judged explosive, such as Kosovo, Macedonia, Sandjak Vojvodina, and the regions bordering with Hungary, Bulgaria, and Albania (CSCE/CPC 1993: 3–5).

The work accomplished by the relatively small contingent of observers (less than four hundred) from the EC and OSCE was very useful. They were also well integrated with the overall effort toward stabilization. Peacekeeping itself remained mostly under the responsibility of UNPROFOR. This task had several dimensions, such as demilitarization of the zones under UN protection, border surveillance, and supervision of local police forces—to insure their impartiality and prevent human rights violations. In addition, the UN blue helmets also had to serve as intermediaries in local conflicts or tensions. They also had the delicate responsibility of protecting cities designated as "security zones" by the UN Security Council (Srebrenica, in April 1993; Sarajevo, Tuzla, Gorazde, Bihac, and Zepa, in May).

United Nations forces also saw their role extended three times in Croatia, and two new commands were established in the fall of 1992, in Bosnia-Herzegovina and Macedonia. From that moment, the mission of the blue helmets in Bosnia was mostly limited to escorting humanitarian aid convoys rather than peacekeeping proper (CSCE/CPC 1993: 23–24). In March 1995, UNPROFOR was reorganized and divided in three distinct forces: UNPROFOR itself would concentrate its operations in Bosnia, the United Nations Confidence Restoration Operation (UNCRO) was assigned to Croatia, and the United Nations Preventive Deployment Force (UNPREDEP) was given the role of preventing new hostilities in Macedonia.

Indeed, there is little doubt that UN forces accomplished important tasks in the former Yugoslavia. During almost three years, they managed to maintain a relative peace in Croatia (Krajina and Slavonia). The forces deployed in the highly unstable zones of Macedonia probably helped prevent a propagation of the conflict that could have had severe international repercussions because of the potential involvement of Greece and Albania. Of course, the UN forces were heavily criticized, notably for their passivity in the face of aggressions against civilian populations or because their presence was seen by some as a caution for Serbian military progress. In spite of these criticisms, however, the UN's actions undeniably contributed to easing some of the human suffering associated with the conflict. Finally, in general, the presence of the UN blue helmets helped to maintain a climate favorable to keeping alive the search for a political solution.

All in all, one should not overlook the fact that about forty countries participated in UNPROFOR I and II and that the costs of these UN-sponsored activities in the former Yugoslavia were in the range of $2.7 billion for 1992–94 plus another $2 billion for 1995 alone, according to UN estimates. To simply argue that international efforts in this crisis were materially insufficient would be, in our opinion, short-sighted and misleading.

Obviously, the principal mission of the thirty-nine thousand UN troops (in April 1995), deployed mostly in Bosnia and Croatia, was only partially accomplished. After more than three years of relative calm in Krajina, the Croats took the offensive again to regain control of the territory in August 1995, thus rendering obsolete the presence of UNCRO. In Bosnia, the fighting went on almost without interruption from April 1992 to November 1995, except for a few short cease-fires—the longest, following Jimmy Carter's mediation effort in December 1994, lasted four months. Thus, it may not be entirely unfair to claim that the UN forces at some point became part of the problem. Indeed, they were probably used, mostly by the Bosnian Serbs, in attempts to neutralize the international community. These attempts included hostage taking, warning shots fired to intimidate UN troops, and obstacles in the channeling of humanitarian aid.

In Bosnia, UNPROFOR showed the vulnerability of this type of mission when belligerents have no intention to give up fighting. Several times, outside states resorted to air strikes or to the deployment of the Rapid Reaction Force (RRF) to protect the blue helmets, who were supposed to protect civilian populations. The UN and its blue helmets took a final blow with the conclusion of the Dayton Accord. On 20 December 1995, the UN forces had to make way for NATO's IFOR, in part because of the US reluctance to place its troops under foreign command.

Although the UN perhaps lost some of its credibility as a conflict solver in the former Yugoslavia and in Somalia, NATO's credibility was enhanced. Since 1993, it had become clear that the capacity to use force effectively was a key to success, and the alliance seemed in this context to be the only organization militarily capable of doing the job. Thus, after having played the supporting role for the UN for some time, NATO became one of the main—if not the main—institutional players.

SANCTIONS, PRESSURES, AND USE OF FORCE

In the Yugoslav conflict, international organizations were not merely instruments of mediation or providers of peacekeeping services. All available methods of conflict resolution systematically were put to work, and the same can be said for the arsenal of international pressures and economic sanctions. From the outset of the crisis in June 1991, gradual pressures were exerted on part of the former Yugoslavia. Recognition of Slovenia and Croatia, followed by economic sanctions, was used to mount pressure upon Serbia.

It perhaps should be underscored that economic sanctions were used in a constructive way to give some of the republics an incentive to behave more cooperatively, notably when it came to human rights issues. Sanctions thus came hand-in-hand with negotiations, progressively tightening the pressures upon Belgrade. These gradual measures included: the suspension of humanitarian assistance (July 1991); an arms embargo (September 1991); the recognition of secessionist republics, the suspension of Yugoslavia's membership in the OSCE, the GATT, and the EFTA (June–July 1992); the reinforcement of economic sanctions (June 1992); the exclusion of Yugoslavia from the UN General Assembly (September 1992); the establishment of a no-fly zone over Bosnia (October 1992); a maritime embargo (November 1992); and the formation of an international tribunal on war crimes committed in Yugoslavia (February 1993). Further intensification of this involvement occurred throughout 1993 and 1994. Measures included the intimidation of Serbia and the Bosnian Serbs through military maneuvers in the Adriatic in 1993.

For many, these sanctions did not have enough bite, and the targets, Serbia and Montenegro, seem to have ignored them. If one considers the economic effects of the total embargo imposed upon Serbia, however, it is evident that the burden of war is very heavily felt there and that the leadership of Milosevic often has had to confront well-organized opposition movements (Andrejevich 1992).

The end of sanctions against the Federal Republic of Yugoslavia was used repeatedly as a "carrot" by those in the international community who wanted to drive a wedge between the Bosnian Serbs and their allies in Belgrade. This approach was often criticized for being too slow, but it yielded results nonetheless. Thus, after the Bosnian Serbs rejected the Contact Group plan (20 July 1994) and following a reinforcement of sanctions by the members of the Contact Group, Belgrade finally consented to break its relations with the Pale government (4 August) and to let the UN monitor the border between the FRY and Bosnia (14 September). This gesture, which was a turning point in Belgrade's attitude toward the Bosnian peace process, led to a temporary lift of the sanctions and then to a definitive end after the Dayton Accord.

The arms embargo, however, was a major source of tension between the Americans and the Europeans. In the US, Congress was pressing the White House to lift the embargo on arms sales to the Bosnian forces. This led the Clinton administration to adopt, albeit reluctantly, a series of measures in this direction, including the removal of the US naval forces enforcing the embargo in the Adriatic (November 1994). The threat of lifting the arms embargo was also used without much success to bring the Bosnian Serbs to adopt a more conciliatory position. The impact of these American declarations on lifting the embargo was mostly felt in the relations between the US and its allies. Most of the countries that had large contingents of blue helmets in Bosnia, such as Britain, France, Canada, and others, were vehemently opposed to these measures, which also created friction between Washington and Moscow. The roles were reversed, however, when the Europeans suggested lifting, even partially, the sanctions against Belgrade in exchange for its participation in the peace process. Until September 1994, the United States had refused to consider European demands of lifting the sanction against the FRY, even in exchange for its participation in the peace process. These differences were part of the reason why Washington was reluctant toward the Vance-Owen plan in January 1993.

The other issue that fed debates and divisions between nonbelligerent states was the use of force. With hindsight, one could argue that a more vigorous intervention in the very early stages of the conflict might have favored a quick solution (see Harvey, this volume). The key states and institutional actors, however, chose to pursue a negotiated solution that would be freely accepted by all the parties to the conflict. At the time, this seemed to be the least costly solution in terms of human lives and the most likely to lead to a durable peace. There was also a perception that an escalation of the fighting could have jeopardized the civilian populations and the troops in the region. In short, there were serious doubts that active military engagement by outsiders would solve anything. As David Hogg noted, "There is no cavalry coming over the hill; the only way this killing is going to stop is by negotiation." Similarly, the French president, François Mitterrand, replied to those in his country who were calling for military intervention: "Adding war to war serves no purpose" (FBIS-WEU-92–158 1992: 7).

The degeneration of the conflict and the repeated provocations against the blue helmets, however, brought international actors to consider this solution. Troops from the nonbelligerent states were called upon to help implement certain Security Council resolutions and to put pressure on the warring parties. As for other measures, the use of force was employed gradually: Starting in 1992, outside actors sent ultimatums and used intimidation tactics;[10] beginning in February 1994, actions were taken to enforce the no-fly zone over Bosnia; increasingly severe air strikes were conducted in 1994 and 1995; and the Franco-British Rapid Reaction Force was deployed in June 1995. Most of these measures had a limited effect, and it was only in September 1995 that a major show of force—Operation Deliberate Force—managed to convince the Bosnian Serbs of the international community's determination.

Opponents of forceful intervention, which included notably Russia and Canada, resisted for a long time this escalation of international involvement. Both in the case of sanctions and when it came to consider the use of force, however, it is important to point out that this divergence did not lead to the adoption by the dissenting states of unilateral policies that could have short-circuited the search for a negotiated solution.

INTERNATIONAL ACTION AND HUMANITARIAN ASSISTANCE

The fifth and last dimension of the international effort to deal with the effects of the Yugoslav crisis—faute de mieux, as the world was waiting for a negotiated solution—is that of economic and humanitarian assistance. Such assistance was given, on the one hand, to populations adversely affected by the war and, on the other hand, to the republics that have shown a desire for peace. Refugees from the former Yugoslavia numbered in the millions throughout the crisis, and Germany itself had admitted more than two hundred thousand even by the summer of 1992. The German government also gave more than DM 200 million in humanitarian assistance, and the EC voted in July 1992 a budget of 120 million ecus to help refugees (FBIS-WEU-92–141 1992: 12–13). Convened at Geneva the same month, an international conference on refugees managed to collect $100 million from fifty-two countries (FBIS-WEU 1992: 2).

Every participant in the UNPROFOR also contributes largely, in one way or another, to efforts to channel and distribute aid to refugees within the Yugoslav republics themselves. The airdrops of food and medical supplies to besieged communities in eastern Bosnia also was a part of this effort. Humanitarian assistance came from several other organizations, such as the Red Cross, the UN High Commission on Refugees, the UNICEF, the WHO, and dozens of nongovernmental organizations (NGOs) working in the field and channeling the most urgent forms of aid, including medical supplies and health services (CSCE/CPC 1993).

This review of the five dimensions of international involvement in the Yugoslav crisis draws attention to the scope and the diversity of the efforts deployed by the international community and to the perseverance of outside actors. In spite of the problems that the crisis engendered for China and Russia (Thibault and Lévesque 1995), for example, the UN Security Council adopted more than eighty resolutions on various aspects of the conflict, including: peace plans, peacekeeping operations, humanitarian assistance, refugees, security zones, bringing war criminals to justice, economic sanctions, and the arms embargo. The UN secretary-general himself commissioned no less than twenty reports on the conflict and, along with his special envoys Cyrus Vance, Thorvald Stoltenberg, and Yasushi Akashi, actively participated in several efforts to end the fighting. Throughout the war, all major European security institutions and several other international institutions kept the Yugoslav conflict on or near the top of their agendas.

IN CONCLUSION: A POSITIVE ASSESSMENT ... AND A FEW LESSONS

This brief overview of the various dimensions of actions by international organizations in and around the Yugoslav crisis allows us to conclude that the principal critiques addressed to the international community were not all well founded.

First, international organizations may not be as ineffective or impotent as they frequently have been portrayed in the Western media. These accusations have to be reconsidered when one realizes that international and regional organizations involved in the crisis played their role while displaying a singular capacity to adapt to the demands of the situation. Indeed, the sense of initiative displayed by these organizations was surprising, given their relative inexperience. Some of the concrete realizations of the international community that often go unmentioned are its success in preventing the crisis from spreading in the eastern regions of the Balkans and its capacity to keep Russia in the mainstream of international efforts, in spite of its well-known sympathy toward Serbia.

In short, the evaluation of the performance of international organizations depends upon the conception that we have of their nature and of their role. Organizations are not independent actors. They can help states exchange information, coordinate their efforts, or even lead states to leave aside their short-term self-interest for long-term common goals. In this sense, they played their role well in the Yugoslav crisis, notably by ensuring that states would not "forget" the conflict. Organizations, however, could not substitute themselves for states, particularly the greater powers.

Second, we hear frequently that international organizations are "profoundly" or even "irremediably" divided. These problems are often little more than minor incidents, however, when compared to the cohesion of action, the spirit of cooperation and the general sense of consensus that characterize the decisions and actions of the main international actors toward the Yugoslav conflict.

Finally, the "lack of leadership" that some commentators and analysts have noted has to be balanced with the observation that the management of the crisis was mostly coherent and cohesive. This degree of coordination was somewhat impressive, for crisis management often depended upon a multiplicity of decision centers (themselves constrained by their own decision rules).

Although these conclusions may be encouraging, we must nonetheless accept the fact that the unity and the coherence of international actions in the Yugoslav case were not predestined. They were the results of circumstances, particularly the revitalization of international security organizations in the wake of the end of the Cold

War and the collective intervention against Iraq. In this perspective, it is useful to keep in mind at least five lessons from the Yugoslav conflict that, although they contrast with the general pessimism of journalistic accounts, are no less imperative.

First, it is likely that, for reasons quite unrelated to whatever international actors do, the tensions that were at the source of the Balkan conflict will linger on for years, and it could take some time before violence is ruled out among the main forces involved. Still, if the international community manages to limit the adverse humanitarian effects of the resurgence of violence, and if it continues to successfully contain the spread of violence to other countries, these outcomes should be viewed in a very positive light. In other words, the test for international actors and organizations is not whether they can eliminate the sources of conflict—that is up to the conflicting parties themselves—but whether they can adequately contain violence and deal with its consequences.

Second, the Yugoslav crisis has shown that states and international organizations are the two unavoidable and inseparable dimensions of international action. In other words, international organizations cannot act or decide, they can only facilitate the actions and decisions of governments by promoting consultation and fostering consensus. By contrast, any collective action in such a context needs a common framework to assure its own legitimacy and coordination between actors. In consequence, although Europeans sometimes have found the management of the crisis difficult, they probably have no other choice but to go ahead with the construction of a common security policy regarding both the Balkans and the former Soviet Union.

Third, the crisis has demonstrated that the United States could not simply leave the management of the situation to Europeans. This is not due to the latter's incapacity to rise to the challenge, but because the Balkans are too important strategically to represent merely a regional interest. If coordination of European policies is already a daunting task, the harmonization between Washington and the European capitals makes the task of crisis management even more complex. But it nevertheless remains vital.

Fourth, one of the effects of the crisis, which was perhaps unexpected, has been to stimulate new thinking and institutional reform within several security organizations. The Yugoslav situation thus brought the United Nations to rethink its role in matters of peacekeeping and peace enforcement. We also underscored that the OSCE evolved rapidly during the crisis. In the period between 1992 and 1995, however, the organization showed its limitations and was relegated to a secondary role.

Organizations such as NATO and the WEU, though they could have been expected to play peripheral roles in the conflict, nonetheless took the opportunity to engage in a serious reflection about their future roles. Such an effort was manifest in the studies undertaken by the NATO on its role in the area of peacekeeping and in the work of the WEU. This kind of effort should continue in the future to further reinforce the complementary nature of European security institutions. The WEU's move to Brussels should facilitate its cooperation with NATO, notably in the area of peacekeeping.

This leads us to our fifth and last point. In our opinion, the unpleasant reason why we must remain somewhat pessimistic in our overall assessment of the Yugoslav conflict is as simple as it is painful: Perhaps more than anything else, the Yugoslav conflict has shown that brute force is still, and is likely to be for some time to come, a viable instrument in international relations. As the *Guardian* noted soon after the outbreak of the conflict, "Brute force still pays in Europe; Serbia successfully defied an entire continent" (*The Guardian*, 8 August 1991). For this reason the European Union probably will have to resolve itself to assume all the necessary attributes of effective political action, including the use of military force when necessary. If the European Union cannot take this step and a common defense capacity cannot be established, the impressive edifice that grew out of the European architecture of security might turn out to be a house of cards.

NOTES

1. See especially Nijenhaus (1991: 1), Klambauer (1991: 3), Brenner (1992), Julien (1993), and Nerlich (1992).

2. Joffe (1992) has been one of the most acerbic critics of international action.

3. The notion of a hesitant and divided Europe is expressed by Nerlich (1992: 7–13) and Brenner (1992: 601).

4. A typical illustration of the early European reaction to and close monitoring of the crisis is the fact that in the first month of the crisis, July 1991, the foreign ministers and the principal foreign-policy makers of the EC met no less than nine times. A simple look at the reports from the WEU is enough to reveal the intensity of diplomatic consultations throughout the crisis.

5. The European Troika consists of the president of the European Council, elected for a six-month term, along with his predecessor and successor.

6. These included a group on the constitutional future of Yugoslavia, one on the issue of minority groups, and a third dealing with economic relations between the republics.

7. On this subject, Legault (1992: 59) has noted that the EC's ministers had decided that this commission would be composed of five members, three named by the EC and two by the Yugoslavs. Because the latter could not agree on candidates, the seats of the two missing members were coopted by EC members. In addition to the French chairman Badinter, members included Roman Herzog (Germany), Aldo Corasaniti (Italy), Irène Petry (Belgium), and Francisco Tomas Valiente (Spain).

8. The nine other items proposed at the conference were as follows: obligation to collaborate fully with international organizations to carry out UN Security Council resolutions on human rights and economic sanctions; diplomatic recognition of the state of Bosnia-Herzegovina by all other ex-Yugoslav republics; respect for present territorial integrity, unless there is mutual consent for border changes; recognition by all of minority rights according to the UN Charter and the OSCE accords; negotiation of a fair solution to the problem of displaced persons and refugees; development of democratic political and legal structures that would include guaranteed rights for minorities; the end of cross-border interventions by the republics; respect for treaties and international agreements; and finally, resumption of normal commercial relations among neighboring republics.

9. These six groups respectively held the following responsibilities: (1) promote the termination of hostilities in Bosnia and the conclusion of a constitutional accord; (2) solve humanitarian and refugee issues; (3) find possible solutions to manage ethnic problems in the republics; (4) resolve issues linked with successor states emerging from the former Yugoslavia; (5) study the economic issues raised by the breakup of the former federation; and (6) define ways to manage arms transfer, arms control, and arms reduction (1992: Document LC/C4).

10. On 25 December 1992, the United States threatened Belgrade in the event of a Serbian aggression against Kosovo. Military deployments included maneuvers by the *J. F. Kennedy,* the *Clémenceau,* and the *Ark Royal* in the Adriatic in January 1993.

REFERENCES

Andrejevich, Milan. 1992. "What Future for Serbia?" *RFE/RL Research Report* 1, no. 50 (December): 7–17.

Bennett, Andrew, and Joseph Lepgold. 1993. "Reinventing Collective

Security after the Cold War and Gulf Conflict." *Political Science Quarterly* 108: 213–37.

Betts, Richard K. 1992. "Systems for Peace or Causes of War? Collective Security, Arms Control, and the New Europe." *International Security* 17: 5–43.

"Bosnia: A Text Written in Blood." 1994. *The Economist* (February 26): 19.

Brenner, Michael. 1992. "The EC in Yugoslavia, a Debut Performance." *Security Studies* 1: 586–609.

Claes, Willie. 1994. "L'OTAN et l'architecture de sécurité euro-atlantique." *Revue de l'OTAN* 42: 3–7.

Conference for Security and Cooperation in Europe, Conflict Prevention Center. 1993. *International Organizations and Institutions Operating on a Permanent Basis on the Territory of the Former Yugoslavia or in Adjacent Countries*. Vienna: CSCE/CPC.

De Montbrial, Thierry. 1992. "L'architecture européenne et la crise yougoslave." *Revue des deux monde* 5–6: 95–96.

Diehl, Paul F. 1993. *International Peacekeeping*. Baltimore: John Hopkins University Press.

Edwards, Geoffrey. 1992. "European Responses to the Yugoslav Crisis: An Interim Assessment." In *Toward Political Union: Planning a Common Foreign and Security Policy in the European Community*, edited by Reinhardt Rummel. Boulder, Colo.: Westview.

FBIS-WEU-91–202. 18 October 1991: 3.

FBIS-WEU-92–141. 1992: 12–13.

FBIS-WEU-92–147. 30 July 1992: 2.

FBIS-WEU-92–158. 14 August 1992: 7.

Fortmann, Michel. 1993. "In Search of an Identity: Europe, NATO, and the ESDI Debate." In *From Euphoria to Hysteria: Western European Security after the Cold War*, edited by David G. Haglund. Boulder, Colo.: Westview.

Gaddis, John Lewis. 1987. *The Long Peace*. New York: Oxford University Press.

Ghebali, Victor-Yves. 1992. "Towards an Operational Institution for Comprehensive Security." *Disarmament* 15, no. 4: 1–12.

Helsinki Conference for Security and Cooperation in Europe. 1992. *Challenges of Change*. Prague.

Holsti, Kalevi J. 1992. "Paths to Peace? Theories of Conflict Resolution and the Realities of International Politics." In *International Conflict Resolution*, edited by Louis Kriesberg. Boulder, Colo.: Westview.

Joffe, Josef. 1992. "Collective Security and the Future of Europe." *Survival* 34, no. 1: 36–50.

———. 1993. "The New Europe: Yesterday's Ghosts." *Foreign Affairs* 72, no. 1: 29–43.

Julien, Claude. 1993. "Les dangers de la non-interventio." *Le Monde diplomatique: Manière de voir* 17: 39–41.

Klambauer, Otto. 1991. "The EC: A Total Failure in the Balkans." *Kurier [quoted in FBIS-WEU-91–179*: 3.

Kupchan, Charles A., and Clifford A. Kupchan. 1991. "Concerts, Collective Security, and the Future of Europe." *International Security* 16: 114–61.

Larrabee, F. Stephen. 1992. "Instability and Change in the Balkans." *Survival* 34: 2.

Lefebvre, Stéphane, and Roman Jacubow. 1993. "War Termination Prospects in the Former Yugoslavia," ORAE Project Report 629. Ottawa: Department of National Defence, iii-iv.

Legault, Albert. 1992. "The U.N. and the Year 1991–92." Paper presented to the fifth annual meeting of the Academic Council on the U.N. System (ACUNS), Washington, D.C. 18–20 June: 59.

London Conference. 1992. Documents LC/C2, C4, C5, and C8.

Mayall, James. 1992. "Nationalism and International Security after the Cold War." *Survival* 34: 19–35.

Mearsheimer, John. 1990. "Back to the Future: Instability in Europe after the Cold War." *International Security* 15, no. 1: 5–56.

Mueller, John. 1995. "Le concept de puissance et la politique internationale depuis la fin de la guerre froide." *Études internationales* 26: 711–27.

Nerlich, Uwe. 1992. "Indifference or Engagement: Roles for the Atlantic Alliance within the Evolving System of Multinational Crisis Management." Paper presented at the Fifth Conference on the Future of the Alliance. Ebenhausen, Germany. 7–8 March.

Nijenhaus, Hans. 1991. "EC Entangled in Its Own Mediation Plan." *Handelsblad as quoted in FBIS-WEU-91–157*: 1.

Pfaff, William. 1993. "Invitation to War." *Foreign Affairs* 72, no. 1: 97–109.

Ramonet, Ignacio. 1993. "Une régression de la raison politique." *Le Monde diplomatique: Manière de voir* (17 February): 6–7.

RFE/RL Research Report. 1992. 23 (June 1): 6–7.

Rotfeld, Adam D. 1992. "European Security Structures in Transition." *SIPRI Yearbook 1992.* Oxford: Oxford University Press.

Roussel, Stéphane, and Michel Fortmann. 1994. "Eppur, si muove: Le régime de sécurité européen, les États non belligérants et la guerre en ex-Yougoslavie." *Études internationales* 25: 729–62.

Stockholm Council Meeting of the CSCE. 1992. (December 15): 3.

Thibault, Jean-François, and Jacques Lévesque. 1995. "La politique étrangère russe en ex-Yougoslavie." *Relations internationales et stratégiques* 19: 113–21.

Treverton, Gregory. 1991. "A New European Security Order." *Journal of International Affairs* 45: 91–112.

Part 3

Dimensions of Peacekeeping

6

Peacekeeping and Ethnic Conflict

Theory and Evidence

ALAN JAMES

INTRODUCTION

The circumstances of some ethnic conflicts are more suitable than others for the ameliorative use of traditional peacekeeping. But ethnic conflict tends to be so intense and all-embracing as to leave relatively little room for the helpful use of this device. The inability to achieve much by this route may result in a temptation, in certain quarters, to take a tougher line with the disputants—to embark on assertive peacekeeping. However, due to such peacekeepers being perceived as benefiting one side more than another, their efforts are likely to be even less useful than traditional peacekeeping.

If states could be persuaded to be more welcoming to peacekeeping of a traditional kind, a somewhat bigger role would open up for that activity. But it would still be limited in its impact. Sometimes it would seem that the most obvious way to end ethnic conflict is for the group in question to secede. But that is much easier said than done.

This chapter unfolds as follows: Concepts and the basic problem posed by peacekeeping as related to ethnic conflict are introduced. Both traditional and assertive peacekeeping are explored. Finally, prescriptions are offered.

CONCEPTS

Ethnicity

The terms *ethnic* and *political* are widely deemed to connote concepts of a dissimilar kind. A political belief is generally thought to be just that—a belief that an individual may adopt or abandon somewhat in the manner in which an item of dress may be donned or doffed. By contrast ethnicity seems often to be conceived as something inherent (or almost so) in the human condition. Whether the preferred criterion is race, language, clan, tribe, nation, culture, or even—in many contexts—religion, the suggestion is usually that ethnicity is something one cannot get away from. For better or worse, one is marked from birth by one's ethnic identity. And it is not infrequently judged, especially nowadays, to be a mark of Cain (see for example Kriesberg, this volume).

Yet all the above-mentioned criteria are extraordinarily elusive. Perhaps partly for this reason they also appear to leave a measure of scope for an individual to choose—and abandon—an ethnic identity. Not too long ago, the "British race" was, among the inhabitants of Great Britain, a favored category. No more! Throughout the last six decades, most individuals in the state of Yugoslavia appeared to espouse the concept of "Yugoslavism," as well as that of their own intra-Yugoslav nationality (the state officially recognizing six such designations). In the last five years that war-torn country has had a very different referent. It is as if the individual is dealt a hand of ethnic cards and then decides which one to designate as personal "trumps." Moreover, this decision may be varied from time to time, or the cards may even be thrown in, indicative of a wish to opt out of the ethnic game. Such decisions and developments are probably far from instantaneous. But it remains that the element of choice, of consciously adopted belief, is present. Moreover, the coherence and strength of any ethnic group is very largely dependent on the enthusiasm with which the relevant affiliation is espoused. Some objective commonality may be required at bottom. But it is the subjective factor which imparts vitality.

Ethnicity therefore shares more than a little with politics. Furthermore, as echoes from the contemporary scene testify all too often, some political groups are ethnically based. Indeed, one might be forgiven for thinking that since the end of the Cold War, international politics has been taken over by ethnicities, so prominent have such groups been in the news bulletins. More specifically, UN peacekeeping missions—of which there has been a dramatic quantitative increase—have to a hugely greater degree than hitherto been elicited by what widely is recognized as ethnic conflict.

Presumably, however, a line remains between "straightforward" international conflict and that designated as ethnic. But where is it to be drawn? A convincing determination is not easy, as many international issues can be presented as having some ethnic character. For the purposes of this chapter a dispute between two well-established states that has no significant aspects or nuances that may easily be seen as ethnic will be treated as international, even if the states in question are ethnically differentiated. Thus, the disputes over water between Israel and certain adjacent Arab states would be excluded from consideration, whereas the Palestinian struggle would be regarded as eligible for comment. The nuclear preoccupations of India and Pakistan with each other fall into the former category, their differences over Kashmir into the latter. It is not the most satisfactory of distinctions, but it is thought to have some plausibility.

Peacekeeping

This concept, too, has been subject to inflationary tendencies (see Carment and James, this volume, and Morrison, this volume). The reason, however, lies not in its imprecision but in its favorable resonance. The twentieth century has witnessed the elevation of the idea of peace to a remarkable height. Nothing more is heard of the glory to be gained in war; ministries "of war" appear to have become extinct; and only "peace-loving" states may enter the kingdom of the United Nations (the original members having had to demonstrate their zeal in this respect by declaring war on the about-to-be-defeated powers by a certain date). In this context few activities could be more estimable than keeping the peace—in a word, peacekeeping. Accordingly, there has been some competition to affix this label to more than one type of peace-related operation.

It was not ever so, for two reasons. Firstly, because the activity in question was only conceptualized as peacekeeping in the late 1950s; and secondly because it tended to be linked with the UN, and UN operations were rather few. Thus for a few decades the term peacekeeping had a fairly precise meaning: impartial and non-threatening military (or chiefly military) action in support of peace—which in this chapter will be referred to as "traditional" peacekeeping. (It is thus distinguishable from peace making as that term has, until very recently, been generally understood: good offices, conciliation, and mediation.) The first such peacekeeping force (which spurred the process of abstraction and so gave rise to the concept) was that sent to Egypt in the wake of the Anglo-French-

Israeli assault on the Suez Canal (and more) in 1956. Other such forces were later established, often in connection with the Arab-Israeli conflict, as were observer missions.

Lately, however, the relative purity of these conceptual waters has been muddied. The war to expel Iraq from Kuwait has, not unnaturally, been seen as an exercise in keeping the peace. And lesser operations—notably in Bosnia-Herzegovina and Somalia—have had a prickly aspect that may distinguish them from the traditionally more pacific variety of peacekeeping. In this chapter the term is intended to refer to the type of activity with which it initially was associated, on the basis that enforcement of the kind seen in Kuwait (and earlier in Korea) is a very different enterprise from the quiet observation, patrolling, and inspection that go on, for example, at the eastern edge of the Golan Heights between the forces of Israel and Syria. Equally, the sort of operation that took place in Cambodia in 1992–93, although much bigger and displaying greater variety than the Golan type of mission, is fairly clearly in the same category. Even prickly operations so far tend to find a niche towards the pacific rather than the enforcement end of the spectrum and may therefore be termed exercises in what in this chapter will be spoken of as "assertive" peacekeeping.

Within that spectrum, however, there has been one notable change of emphasis during the last five years: in the locale of peacekeeping operations. For overwhelmingly, operations of recent dates have functioned within all or part of the host state's jurisdiction or in relation to some domestic problem rather than at the border between two jurisdictions. As it happens, and contrary to popular belief, it is an error to assume that earlier such activity was only rarely if ever of this kind (James 1993a). But recently the balance has swung heavily in the internal direction, no fewer than twenty-five UN missions established between January 1988 and the end of 1996 fall into this subcategory.

As might be expected of operations which relate to immediately internal problems, the ethnic factor has been prominent in some of the situations that have attracted peacekeeping attention. And as, unhappily, might also be expected, a number of these ethnically related operations have run into trouble (James 1993a, 1994).

THE PROBLEM

The reasons for the sort of difficulties sometimes encountered by peacekeepers when they try to ameliorate ethnic conflict are not far to seek. For such difficulties arise from the fundamental character of ethnic conflict, from the fact that it generally reflects an attempt by a minority to secure a safer place for itself inside or, ideally, outside an existing polity. Naturally, the relevant authorities tend to resist this attempt to dilute their control or, worse, to lessen the extent of their state's territory.[1]

Four aspects of this general argument may be identified. The first relates to the likelihood that in ethnic conflicts local passions may be running high. Civil wars are sometimes said to be nastier, at the human level, than international ones—and the violence in Bosnia-Herzegovina and Croatia does nothing to counter that view. This will of necessity pose extra problems for the peacekeepers— both in terms of their day-to-day operations and also in relation to the likelihood of a successful overall outcome.

Secondly, this problem may be compounded by the parties' undertakings being marked by a high degree of fragility. In part this has to do with the fact that internal agreements between ethnicities do not have the status of those reached internationally: even a government, therefore, may view such an undertaking less strictly than it might an international agreement. It may also reflect the fact that at least one of the parties will have no international standing and will therefore probably have little to lose at that level. Finally, some of those signing an internal agreement—guerrilla leaders and the like—may be far from having their followers firmly under control (the situation in South Lebanon comes immediately to mind). On all these grounds, therefore, the cooperation promised to peacekeepers may be appreciably less than fully forthcoming.

In the third place, the context of an ethnically related operation may be particularly difficult, in that the political situation (like all political situations) is subject to an almost definitional fluidity. The balance of influence changes frequently. Willy-nilly, therefore, and in full compatibility with their efforts to behave impartially, what the peacekeepers are doing may result in their being seen by the parties as an ally or an impediment on the internal political scene. A party that sees its fortunes as assisted by the UN mission, for example, will look much more benignly on the mission than a party which sees the situation to which the UN is contributing as slipping away from its grasp. The altering attitudes to the UN's attempts to mount a self-determination exercise in Western Sahara are an example of this. Thus peacekeeping operations will be buffeted by the hazards of the local and oft-changing political context.

Finally, these last two points are given additional weight by the greater intensity of the competition for the prize. Paradoxically, and to the extent that such comparisons are possible, it will probably be more highly valued than the stakes that are involved in straightforward interstate conflict over a border. In the latter case, there will naturally be much concern to maintain the integrity of one's territory and to recover—tomorrow if not today—any that has been lost. But the existence of the state itself is unlikely to be in jeopardy. Internally, by contrast, the object of the ethnopolitical battle will probably be the seat of government.

That is a very considerable prize indeed, carrying much by way of power, perks, and prestige. Securing it may colloquially be referred to as a "life and death" matter, and in some contexts that may be so even literally. A peacekeeping operation will try to avoid having a direct impact on that outcome. But what it does will almost necessarily have some impact on the result. If, for example, it succeeds in restoring order, the question arises as to who is going to benefit by inheriting the improved situation. Or, if a reconciliation plan has been accepted by an important party on the assumption that the plan's implementation will result in that party assuming the reins of government, a change in the balance of forces may lead to a revision of its view about the acceptability of what the UN is doing. Thus there can be great temptations to withdraw cooperation that was promised at an earlier stage.

Except, therefore, in the most promising of circumstances—which are not the most frequent—too much should not be expected of what can be contributed by peacekeeping to the calming or resolution of ethnic conflict. It is no panacea. Sometimes, however, it will certainly be able to assist in one of those directions, especially the former.

EVIDENCE: TRADITIONAL PEACEKEEPING

The two key elements that may be expected to promote successful peacekeeping activity in relation to ethnic conflict are, firstly, the occupation by each ethnicity of an at least roughly distinct territorial area; and, secondly, the existence of a viable agreement between the parties, even if it is only of an interim kind. Contrariwise, territorial intermingling is likely to present a considerable problem for peacekeeping; and this problem may well be compounded if there is no understanding about the way forward.

This gives rise to four possible configurations. The most promising is the conjunction of the two key elements, and the least promising is the absence of both. So far as the other two possibilities are concerned, it would appear that the mere existence of an agreement is, unhappily, no assurance of a rosy future for peacekeeping. For if the parties are physically intermingled, the agreement may be honored more in the breach than in the observance. On the other hand, if the parties coexist in their own generally acknowledged, unfragmented, and roughly separate territories, there may well be a route to effective peacekeeping help, notwithstanding the absence of a substantive agreement between them. This could be so even if the demarcation between the parties has come about through force of arms. For if it receives some degree of acceptance, however grudging, peacekeepers should be able to sustain a reasonably secure and successful foothold.

While, therefore, a written agreement is almost certainly required for the solution and maybe also for the control of an ethnic conflict, the most basic requirement for both its control and its solution would seem to be the existence of a reasonably clear territorial division between the ethnicities.

DIVIDING AGREEMENTS

The three outstanding instances in which the UN has been able to contribute to the solution of ethnic conflict by deploying impartial and nonthreatening personnel on the ground meet both the criteria set out above. The first concerns Eritrea. This Ethiopian province had been struggling fiercely for independence since its loss of autonomy in the early 1960s. Following internal developments in Ethiopia a new government in effect renounced the province, and its future was left to be decided by a referendum. This was held in April 1993 and watched over by a UN mission (UNOVER). Given the circumstances, there was never any doubt about the outcome— which had been encouraged by the expulsion of about 125,000 non-Eritreans. The new sovereign state of Eritrea was created and promptly admitted to the UN.[2]

A few years earlier a broadly similar series of events took place in Namibia, the former South West Africa. This territory had never been a part of South Africa, and virtually since its establishment the UN had been trying to wrest it from South African control. On the ground, the indigenous inhabitants had been fighting a guerrilla war toward the same end. Eventually, as part of a wider deal, South Africa's withdrawal was agreed. During 1989–90 a multifaceted peacekeeping force (UNTAG) watched over this process and made a significant contribution towards its eventual success. Without the UN acting as a kind of intermediary the enterprise could very easily have come off the rails. But as it happened there emerged a new state with sovereign status (James 1990b: 257–68).

The final such instance also concerns the appearance of a new sovereign state: Bahrain. Plans for the ending of its long-standing British protection, which would enable it to play a full international role, were clouded by the reactivation of Iran's claim to this Arab territory. But a diplomatic solution was engineered, a key part of which was the confirmation by a UN mission (GOMB) that the Bahrainis had no wish to become Iranian. This cleared the way for Bahrain's entry on to the international stage in 1971.[3]

TERRITORIAL DEMARCATION ALONE

Where there is a distinct territorial division between conflicting ethnic parties and they are content to respect it, at least for the time being, there is a good chance that UN peacekeepers will be able to assist in that cause. Their employment for that purpose, of course, makes no direct contribution to the settlement of the basic conflict; it may not make an indirect one either; and it is often argued—contentiously—that keeping an issue on ice in this way actually obstructs the eventual emergence of an agreement. Nonetheless, this sort of peacekeeping action may well exercise a calming influence. It may be thought to be no bad thing.

A case in which UN peacekeepers have often been hailed for their success in settling an internal conflict with ethnic connections is that of the (Belgian) Congo (formerly Zaire). Underlying some of the problem that a large UN force and a significant civilian element (ONUC) faced in the early 1960s was a very complex tribal structure. Although often blurred at the edges, the tribal divisions were territorially based. But, unlike Lebanon a few years earlier, nothing that even looked like a substantive agreement emerged. In the event (as the result of the UN force going beyond the usual peacekeeping bounds and acting to enforce the central government's authority), the UN left a formally united state. But it is a moot question whether this should be regarded as a success for the UN. (This peacekeeping episode will be discussed further below, in section 4 of the chapter.)

A long-standing example of UN peacekeepers watching over an equally long stalemate is provided by the problem of Kashmir, which arose out of the ethnoreligious division of the Indian subcontinent in 1947. The peacekeeping mission (UNMOGIP) is still there, although because it has not received any cooperation from India for more than twenty years, other than by her continuing to play host, its value during that period has been reduced. That also happens to be roughly the period during which a territorial stalemate has existed in Cyprus. The UN force (UNFICYP) undoubtedly makes an important contribution to the maintenance of calm. But this is one case where, partly for financial reasons, the UN as an organization and most of its members who have contributed troops to the force are getting fed up with their role. In consequence the force has been much reduced in size. Whether the end of the Cold War will be a sufficiently strong brew to dissolve intra-Cypriot tensions and mistrust is a fascinating question for the future. One would hesitate to put much money on it.

Another stalemate occurred in the early 1990s in the former Spanish colony of Western Sahara. Morocco has established a very firm physical grip on much of this territory, which is fairly clearly divided in two by a long sand wall. After a few years of negotiations an agreement for a referendum, in which the UN was to play an important part, was reached, and the UN set about establishing its mission (MINURSO) in 1991. But subsequent difficulties, largely emerging from the Moroccan side, justify the statement that here there is no real agreement between Morocco and Polisario—the representative of the Saharwi people. Thus the UN vanguard has been twiddling its thumbs uncomfortably in the desert for most of the 1990s.[4]

In northern Iraq, since the end of the Gulf War in 1991, a small contingent of UN guards (UNGCI) have tried to provide some protection for the Kurds against their political masters.[5] But it has been a tenuous activity. Doubtless Iraq, when it has somewhat reduced the incubus of defeat, will endeavor to reassert itself against what is surely one of the unluckiest ethnicities of modern times.

In ex-Yugoslavia UN forces watched over Macedonia's borders with the Yugoslav rump and with Albania in the hope of preventing an overspill of ethnic excess (UN Documents S/26099 1993). About one-third of Macedonia's population is ethnic Albanian, which is overwhelmingly the ethnic makeup of the neighboring Yugoslav/Serbian area of Kosovo—which, however, is dear to the Serbs on historical grounds (see Kaufman, this volume).

In Georgia the Abkhazian people have fought their way to de facto independence as a territorially distinct entity, and following a cease-fire agreement, the UN established an observer mission (UNOMIG) in August 1993 to watch over it. The Abkhazians hoped that these events would herald the birth of another sovereign state but have found that Georgia, naturally, and international opinion—lining up as usual behind the existing sovereign—have taken a different view. In these circumstances, although both sides have said that they would like the UN presence to be upgraded to the level of a peacekeeping force, it is not surprising that initially they could find little agreement about its terms of reference. The Abkhazians wanted a force deployed in a manner which emphasizes their distinctness; Georgia wanted the force to operate on the premise that the Abkhazian area is fully a part of Georgia (UN Document S/ 1994/253, 3 March 1994: 19–34). Under these circumstances the UN could play only a limited peacekeeping role.

AGREEMENTS AND INTERMINGLING

When an agreement has been made between two conflicting and, in one degree or another, intermingled ethnic groups, the prospects for any attendant peacekeepers are less than wholly favorable. Of course, a lot will depend on the exact terms of the agreement, and if it provides for some communal autonomy for each of the parties, that will offer a measure of hope for the future. But unless the parties are able, at the political level, to put their ethnicity aside—which is unlikely often to happen—the outlook probably will be gloomy. For ethnic groups that have been at each other's throats frequently find it difficult to coexist harmoniously within the same polity, however carefully checks and balances have been introduced into its constitution.

A problem that was partially, and maybe fully, ethnic arose in 1958 in Lebanon, when divisions between the Muslims and the Christians were conjoined with wider developments to produce a crisis. The activities of a UN observer group (UNOGIL) helped to produce an internal agreement, and the substantially intermixed communities seemed to resume the coexistence on which Lebanon's considerable prosperity was based (Curtis 1964). In the mid-1970s, however, the fragility of this edifice was cruelly exposed, and for fifteen years the once apparently happy country was ravaged by civil war—and much else (Skogmo 1989). It remains to be seen whether the progress towards internal peace which has been made in the last few years will be lasting.

The case of Cyprus offers little comfort in this respect. Its 1960 constitution tried to erect an intricate power-sharing arrangement between the Greek majority and the Turkish minority, so as to satisfy the essential needs of both. Within a few years it had collapsed. A UN force (UNFICYP) was brought in to assist in the maintenance of internal order, and for a decade the unity of the state was preserved, albeit alongside the increasing withdrawal of the Turks into their own enclaves. In this the UN force made an exceedingly valuable, and arguably essential, contribution (Harbottle 1970). But in 1974 an armed intervention by the state of Turkey in support of its ethnic compatriots resulted in the complete division of the state and the movement of many of its people to create two ethnic communities that to all intents and purposes are ethnically pure. (The situation since then has been discussed above.)

The long civil war in Angola after that state achieved sovereign status in 1975 was brought to a formal end in conjunction with the late 1980s agreement on Namibia. A reconciling agreement followed, and national elections were held under it in 1992. A UN mission (UNAVEM II) watched over these and then stayed on to foster the peace process. But the process foundered dramatically with the resumption of civil war by the losing side, and as of September 1994 the conflict rumbles on (UN Document S/26872 1993). The Security Council has imposed an arms embargo against the nongovernmental side and keeps threatening it with further measures unless progress is made in its negotiations with the government.

The Angolan conflict has been overwhelmingly presented to the world as ideological in character. But it has distinct ethnic aspects too. Much the same could be said of the equally long civil war in the other former Portuguese colony in southern Africa, Mozambique—where the situation is further complicated by the dominant role in the economy of non-Africans. Here too a UN mission (ONUMOZ) was established (in 1992) to assist in the implementation of a peace agreement and by early 1994 had more or less reached its expected military strength of about seven thousand.

At that time a thousand-strong police component of ONUMOZ was authorized.

In Rwanda more than a generation of ethnic conflict between the dominant Hutus and the Tutsis was formally laid to rest in August 1993, and two months later a UN mission (UNAMIR) was established to assist in the reconciling process (UN Document S/26927 1993; see also Carment and James, the introduction to this volume). However, widespread bloodletting resumed early in April 1994, and all but a token number of the UN's peacekeepers made a disorderly departure (*The Times* [London] 21–22 April 1994). The conflict has since spilled over into Zaire through refugees who fled Rwanda. In the fall of 1996, Canada led a truncated peacekeeping mission to forestall the unfolding humanitarian disaster with the unintended consequence of succeeding in placating the refugees and encouraging their resettlement in Rwanda. At the same time, a conflict with a similar ethnic complexion continues to simmer in neighboring Burundi (*New York Times*, 25 March 1994). In 1994 a UN fact-finding mission was dispatched to investigate massacres that had occurred late in 1993 and to consider what sort of further help could be given by the UN (UN Information Centre, London *News Summary*, NS/10/94, 24 March 1994). It is hard to resist the conclusion that in the context of such deep-seated ethnic conflicts as these, there is little that outsiders can do—not, at least, until the immediate fighting has died down.

Turning to West Africa, another civil war with ethnic associations—in Liberia—was brought to a formal end, and a UN group (UNOMIL) was established in September 1993 to monitor compliance with the peace agreement (UN Document S/26422, 9 September 1993). This arrangement owed not a little to the assertive activity of an allegedly peacekeeping force set up by the Economic Community of West African states, with which the UN group was in principle to cooperate. Since 1994 there have been significant hiccups in the implementation of the peace agreement, and at the time of this writing there is little reason to be optimistic that the conflict will be satisfactorily resolved.

Given the pessimistic overtones of the preceding analysis, this section of the chapter can end on a relatively positive note. For there was cautious optimism actually—and remarkably—in the air over South Africa, bolstered by the award of the Nobel Peace Prize to the unlikely pair of Nelson Mandela (the African National Congress leader) and President F. W. de Klerk. UN observers (UNOMSA—which the UN does not count as a peacekeeping body) fostered and watched over the reconciliation process. It would be folly to overlook the fact that ethnic problems of considerable magnitude remain to be surmounted; the most recent spate of violence in the townships is indicative of unresolved tribal differences. But it is not unreasonable to hope that following the overwhelming support for Nelson Mandela in South Africa's general elections and basic agreements on power sharing among South Africa's major political parties, this intermingled society could, after long simmering conflict, achieve a warm peace. If it does, the process, especially with respect to power sharing and democratization, will repay careful study in case it offers clues to its possible replication.

INTERMINGLING AND NO AGREEMENT

The least promising prospects for peacekeeping in relation to ethnic conflict exist where there is no agreement between the parties, and they are territorially intermingled. Animosity and entanglement are an ominous combination in any context. Where the flammable constituent is ethnicity, the least spark may set off a considerable blaze.

In the normal way, a UN peacekeeping group is unlikely to be dispatched to such a problem in the absence of an agreement. But occasionally the political pressure for something to be done is sufficient for a mission to be established where nothing remotely like a genuine agreement exists. Or an agreement that gave rise to a mission may have collapsed, leaving the peacekeepers high and dry— for the UN is always reluctant to draw the conclusion to which these circumstances seem to point.

Something of this last sort occurred in Lebanon after a UN force (UNIFIL) was sent to the southern part of that country in 1978 (see above). For besides acting as a kind of buffer between the Israeli and Syrian armies (the poor Lebanese state counted for nothing), the force also had to cope with the Israeli-Palestine Liberation Organization antagonism, the fact that the PLO was hardly welcome in southern Lebanon, and the destabilizing activities of two competitive anti-Israeli Muslim groups—Amal and Hezbollah. The latter group is still a force to be reckoned with (see Kaufman, this volume).

From 1993 to 1995, the (Catholic) Croats and the (Orthodox)

Serbs were busily and bloodily carving out their own areas of Bosnia-Herzegovina for themselves. In the aftermath of that conflict the Muslims managed to hang on in a number of areas, but their geographical dispersion does not bode well for the state's future, even after the Dayton accords and the establishment of a NATO peacekeeping force to oversee the settlement into the unforeseeable future. In its twilight moments of late 1995, the UN peacekeeping mission in Bosnia repeatedly tried to negotiate effective cease-fires and did what it could to ensure the continued delivery of humanitarian aid. Since 1995, however, only NATO's flexing its air muscle against the Serb cause led to relief and some credible commitment from the international community (see Harvey, this volume).

The difficulty encountered at the latter stages of the conflict—indeed, the virtual impossibility of curbing the continuing violence at an acceptable cost—is one reason why, with respect to the conflict between Azerbaijan and its Armenian-dominated enclave of Nagorno-Karabakh, the UN went no further than dispatching a couple of fact-finding missions and a representative of the secretary-general. Allegedly, units of neighboring Armenia's army were initially involved. In response to its bombardment with paper by the parties and the close concern of a number of member states, the Security Council periodically wrung its hands, issued strong words—and tried to pass the buck to the unlikely agency of the Organization for Security and Cooperation in Europe (OSCE).

Meanwhile, in respect of conflict in another successor state of the Soviet Union, Tajikistan, fact-finding and good-offices missions were sent by the UN in efforts to alleviate the fierce fighting, which has resulted in about half a million refugees (UN Document S/26744 1993). Ideological issues are also involved here, but so are ethnoreligious ones, the rebels being Islamic militants who receive support from neighboring Afghanistan. Russian troops have long been present in the guise of peacekeepers (further testimony to the concept's favorable resonance) but are generally seen by outside observers as chiefly designed to support the pro-Moscow regime. UN fact-finding missions have also been sent to a another such state—Moldova—following tension arising out of the large Russian minority (the majority are ethnic Romanians) and the continuing presence of Russian (ex-Soviet) troops (King 1993). Here, as in Tajikistan, something like a Russian military protectorate emerged, presaging a settlement and hard fought but fair elections in 1996.

Finally, consider Somalia—a state which not long ago was regularly noted for an unusual characteristic, especially in the context of Africa: its national homogeneity. But in the early 1990s it collapsed into clan warfare. A 1992 peacekeeping initiative of the UN (UNOSOM I) to watch over a cease-fire and provide security for the UN relief operation ran into considerable opposition from the local factions (UN Document S/24859 1992). The UN also found that the extra troops that had been called for were very hard to raise from the member states. Accordingly, at the end of the year it was decided that the operation should stand aside. In its place the Security Council authorized more assertive measures—which will be discussed in the chapter's next section.

ASSERTIVE PEACEKEEPING: THEORY AND EVIDENCE

In the scheme of things as established by the UN Charter, the Security Council has a very significant place. If articles 24 and 25 of the Charter are taken in conjunction with chapter VII, what emerges, so far as security issues are concerned, is the scaffolding of a world state—and hence a theoretical threat to, at the least, a most important aspect of domestic jurisdiction. In 1945, when the UN was the victorious alliance writ large, this was acceptable. Then, with the early collapse of wartime unity, the charter's grand scheme became in essence redundant. Subsequently the council recovered something of a positive role in connection with the establishment and continuation of peacekeeping operations. But that role was nonmandatory.

The end of the Cold War, however, has given some life to the Security Council. And this has found reflection in rather more than just greater activity. The strength of the tone has gone up a notch or three. In the euphoria of the post–Cold War era, economic sanctions found new favor; having been imposed on a number of states— for example, the former Republic of Yugoslavia, Libya, Liberia, and Haiti, and on rebels in Angola. And in the specific area of peacekeeping the council was fairly free with ringing declarations that it was acting under chapter VII—notably in respect of Bosnia-Herzegovina and Somalia.

This development raises large questions at three different but connected levels. Most generally, there is the issue of the kind of role which the Security Council should assume. What was anticipated in 1945 is not necessarily welcome fifty-two years later. And in fact, in the very differently constituted UN of the late 1990s, the council's recent approach has not been enthusiastically received by the membership at large. Quite clearly there is a concern that the council might get overly authoritarian, that it might take too close an interest in certain internal matters and ignore others (such as Rwanda in 1994) and that it is already showing some disdain for the UN's noncouncil members. Put differently, the council, through its enhanced yet differentiated and selective role in keeping the peace, is seen to be assuming something of the spectral aspect of a threat to sovereignty.

More specifically, there is the issue of whether, in respect of states which have been brought by ethnic conflict to a condition of virtually complete collapse, the UN should step in and assert control. "Trusteeship" is the word—some might see it as the euphemism—that has been aired in this connection (UK House of Commons, Session 1992–93, Foreign Affairs Committee). Partly because many members would look very warily on any such development, it may be doubted whether the council will assert de jure control over a (previously) sovereign state. For the same reason, it is likely to be exceedingly cautious about exercising de facto control. Another factor that points in the same cautionary direction is the difficulty of the task when the organization would be faced with something close to anarchy, such as in Somalia, Liberia, or the Congo.

This leads to the second question. It concerns the efficacy of assertive activity as a means of curbing or quenching ethnic conflict. It is thought that considerable doubt is in order on this score. Any conflict that has reached the stage at which outsiders are led to ruminate about forceful intervention is, by the same token, likely to be an extremely bitter one. Each party will probably see itself as at war in defense of the group and its territory—including territory that is not yet held but which, on one ground or another, is deemed to be rightfully theirs. Such a war is not one merely for property but for dominance—and hence will be seen as one to the death. It will therefore give rise in a much more acute form to all the problems that arise for peacekeeping in any ethnic context (which were considered in the second section of this chapter) (Houweling 1994).

Peacekeeping may sometimes be able to play a useful role in an ethnic conflict that has not developed to this dire stage, as has been seen in the preceding section. It may also be able to make a contribution, in association with state-building activity, where ethnic ambition and distrust are eventually on the wane. But at the height of an all-out conflagration there seems little prospect of outsiders being able swiftly to douse the ethnic fires through the use of superior force. All that may occasionally be possible is for force to be used for two limited purposes. Firstly, to ensure the supply of humanitarian assistance—but even that is less easy than it sounds, and faced with many political hazards. And secondly to impose the restoration of some kind of order. The problem with that last task, however, is that the order that may perhaps be so obtained is, almost by definition, only temporary. It is just a holding down of the lid of the boiling kettle. Underneath, the waters will be as turbulent as ever—and one day, presumably, the interveners are going to leave, permitting the resumption of the fundamental battle.

This draws attention to the third question raised by the issue of assertive peacekeeping. It concerns its political practicality. In its present mood and configuration the Security Council may sometimes be minded to authorize this type of activity. And if such cases are relatively exceptional (in terms of both their extremity and their infrequency), the General Assembly will probably be willing to agree to their funding and be wary of their application. But that does not mean that the requisite numbers of men and dollars will be forthcoming. Member states have a legal obligation to pay their assessed shares of the peacekeeping bill. But that obligation is not self-executing, and some of the sums assessed may in fact not be paid. However, that problem is likely to be noticeable only some way down the road. The immediate difficulty may well be the supply of military personnel—and, later, the maintenance of that supply. Member states are under no legal obligation to provide this kind of assistance and may find a number of practical and political reasons for being reluctant to do so, even on the assumption that the potential host state is willing to receive a peacekeeping force.

Indeed, that willingness may be a part of the problem for possible contributors. For although it gets over the hesitation states feel about intervening in another state's domain without its consent, no matter how desperate its internal condition, it points to another problem. It is that in the context of ethnic strife, the government will in all probability be, in effect, one of the parties. Its readiness to play host to assertive peacekeepers will therefore almost certainly reflect the expectation that they offer support against its rivals or at least have the indirect effect of bolstering the governmental side. If that appearance is actually given by the peacekeeping force, its members will thereby be seen by the government's opponents as part of the enemy. In consequence the peacekeepers will probably be at some physical risk.

Even, however, if that is not the exact scenario, the outcome is likely to be roughly the same. In a violent ethnic conflict, any third party can easily give offense to one side or the other, or both, no matter how earnest the search after impartiality. It follows that states may be cautious about contributing troops—and keep any contingents that are volunteered under close control, even though that offends the principle that they have been placed under UN (or some other multinational) command. In a conflict in which no clear national interest is involved, which has no obvious term, and where there is considerable lack of clarity about the precise way in which the peacekeepers are able to contribute to peace, it would be unrealistic to expect anything else of potential and actual contributors. No government can ignore the fact that its political base lies in its domestic constituency, where criticism of seemingly superfluous risks and casualties can speedily arise.

These issues are well illuminated by three ethnically related cases in which, in a peacekeeping (as distinct from an enforcement) context, there has been some question about whether the UN was behaving or should behave in a clearly assertive manner. The first of these concerned the UN force in the Congo in the early 1960s, which had been established to help usher the intervening Belgians out and to assist the government in the restoration of order. This last task was complicated by the fact that the Congo had an intricate and divisive tribal (i.e., ethnic) structure. Before long the UN, with some justification, was charged with undermining the power of one of these groups (which, in Cold War terms, was Eastern-oriented) to the benefit of another (which was pro-Western). This led a number of states to withdraw their contingents from the force. Then the UN was accused by the Congolese authorities of taking a high-handed attitude toward them (the word *trusteeship* was being bandied about), which led to substantial local difficulties. And finally, strong UN action—effectively on behalf of the government—against a secessionist (and tribally distinct) province led to some international uproar. The success of this move meant that the UN was able to leave a formally united state, on which grounds it received many plaudits (and also fulsomely congratulated itself). But underneath the disunity persisted—so much so that now, thirty years on, the Congo seems in hardly much better condition than it did when the UN first entered the country (James 1994a).

These events left a deep impression on the UN and its member states. They led to peacekeeping being embarked on much more cautiously; many African states became very suspicious of the whole concept; and members of the UN Secretariat subsequently looked warily at anything which could become "another Congo." And in fact more than a generation was to go by before the UN became embroiled in anything at all similar. It occurred in Somalia.

Reference has been made in the preceding section of this chapter to the UN's early travails in that country. Because of them, the UN accepted its voluntary eclipse by a thirty-thousand-strong (non-UN) humanitarian relief operation (the Unified Task Force—giving rise to a possibly misleading acronym: UNITAF) led by the United States, which provided about four-fifths of the troops. When this operation was brought to an end in May 1993 the UN had another go, its force (UNOSOM II) of twenty-eight thousand having the ambitious mandate of reestablishing civil society, fostering political reconciliation, and enforcing disarmament on the warring Somali factions. The United States was the largest troop contributor. However, it also tended to go its own way and got involved in a costly hunt for a troublesome warlord. The UN endorsed this approach only to find that after a battle in Somalia's capital in which eighteen American soldiers were killed, the United States changed its tactics. It sought talks with the warlord, to the public annoyance of the now more belligerently minded UN secretary-general. But the Security Council backed this new approach, and gradually the UN abandoned its brief enthusiasm for assertiveness.

An important reason for this was that the US president had made it clear that the heavily armed American contingent would be withdrawn early in 1994. Other states with powerful military equipment at their disposal were also planning on withdrawal. The UN secretary-general said that he was still in favor of a confrontational line if necessary. But he recognized "unmistakable signs of fatigue among the international community" (UN Document S/1994/12 1994: 46) and recommended a nonbelligerent option. This was accepted by the Security Council in a resolution which, while continuing to intone chapter VII of the charter, actually spoke in a different tongue. Reference was made to a "revised mandate," under which the UN force would not go beyond "encouraging and assisting" the Somali parties and trying to provide humanitarian relief (Security Council Resolution 897, 4 February 1994).[6]

As it happened, the reversion to this more traditional peacekeeping role was accompanied not just by the American withdrawal but also by some apparent progress at the political level. Somali leaders agreed on a Declaration of National Reconciliation and set a date for a conference that was to elect a president and for another to discuss the establishment of a legislative assembly (UN Information Centre, London, *News Summary* NS/11/94, 30 March 1994). In retrospect there was a huge gap between the words and the deeds of Somalia's clan leaders. But at least the political process and the humanitarian mission in Somalia proceeded without the distraction of an interfering—and very possibly an unhelpfully interfering—outsider. Instead, the UN placed itself in a secondary role, offering a hand to offer such help to the factions as they are willing to accept.[7]

In the topographically very different state of Bosnia-Herzegovina there was great, and understandable, reluctance to try to impose a peace on the ground. The Vance-Owen plan of early 1993 was, it may be remembered, said to require in the region of seventy thousand troops to ensure its implementation—and that was on the assumption that it was accepted by all three parties! However, in face of local frustration and international displeasure the essentially humanitarian UN operation—UNPROFOR I—edged towards the limited use of force.[8] But the sort of measures which states were most willing to authorize—the relatively "safe" device of the use of airpower—are also the least likely to have the desired dampening effect on the ground.[9] Thus the ban on military flights was quite effectively supported by NATO but did not seem greatly to have inconvenienced the parties in their efforts to claim territory. The UN's 1993 proclamation of half a dozen "safe areas," and the eventual and much-publicized preparations for NATO air strikes against the Serb threats to one or two of them in the early months of 1994 (*The Times* [London], 23 April 1994), seemed to have had a deterrent effect (see Harvey, this volume).[10]

However, the most assertive peacekeeping can do is to freeze the status quo, and it may prove to be not very successful in that. Moreover, there is the danger that tough action will jeopardize the maintenance of both the UN's humanitarian work and the security of its personnel.[11] The organization came to be seen by the Serbs and the Croats and Muslims as the enemy. Under such circumstances, the UN force could not but expect to continue to meet large problems. In retrospect it was unrealistic to assume that the ethnic militia could be held in check or surmounted by increasing the size and strength of the UN forces on the ground. Arms do indeed determine the pattern of territory held by indigenous ethnic groups (see Kaufman this volume).

Significantly, that seems better recognized by the UN's local officials than by those who are at a distance from the conflict. It may be noted, though, that the former UN secretary-general described the situation in Bosnia as "characterized by massive mistrust among the communities.... all the parties tend to blame each other; mutual recriminations abound; the cycle of violence is escalating; ... [and] the parties hold conflicting and contradictory views on almost all aspects of the conflict." He concluded that the idea of a peacekeeping force was therefore "not feasible" (UN Document S/23836, 14 April 1992: 22, 23, 27). That conclusion, however, was expressed before it was decided to deploy UNPROFOR in Bosnia. There can be little doubt that in humanitarian terms the UN force had considerable value. But in political terms, and whether one is thinking of traditional or assertive peacekeeping—and especially in regard to the latter—the secretary-general's assessment was, broadly speaking, equally valid.

All three instances of assertive peacekeeping therefore suggest that this particular tool, which has been enthusiastically received in some quarters, leading almost to euphoria about what has been termed "second generation" (Mackinlay and Chopra, 1993) peacekeeping, is not well suited for the ethnic context. Trying to frogmarch warring ethnicities down this or that path, or trying to bar them from certain routes, seems likely to reap little long-term profit. It may well be that the international community's peacekeepers will be able to offer useful, valuable, and maybe even essential help to the contestants at certain stages of some ethnic conflicts. In other words, there may be scope for traditional peacekeeping. But even that option has so far had only limited success. Assertive peacekeeping, however, has had a good deal less. The basic reason for this seems to be that an effective settlement between contesting ethnic groups is one that emerges from the parties. They need to map out their own future, both figuratively and literally. It does not seem to be something that can be done for them or forced on them. Agreements appear to come from within, not from without. There may well be some opportunity in this process for third-party peacemakers to wield carrots and sticks of an economic and diplomatic kind. But assertiveness on the part of those who are supposed to be maintaining the immediate ethnic peace seems unlikely to have a positive impact of a lasting kind.

PRESCRIPTION

The final section of this chapter addresses the question of whether, notwithstanding all the cautionary and perhaps discouraging remarks which have gone before, it may still be possible to find some comfortable words about the possibility of a contribution by peacekeepers to the calming and even the resolution of ethnic conflict.

Peacekeeping

On the issue of whether some improvements could be made in the procedures for peacekeeping, there is much that can be said (James 1994) but little which, in the present context, demands saying. The word *much* refers to the close scrutiny being given in a number of quarters to the UN's arrangements for the mounting and management of peacekeeping operations, and to the question of the extent to which advance planning for peacekeeping is desirable. The word *little* reflects the view that the contribution that peacekeeping can make in situations of ethnic conflict is essentially of a secondary character only. That is to say, peacekeeping may well be of stabilizing value where the disputants can be persuaded to adopt a pacific disposition, whether of a long-term or interim kind. But in the absence of that disposition peacekeeping will hardly ever have anything of substance to offer, no matter how well oiled and all-embracing the peacekeeping machinery may be.

Ethnicity

Looking directly at ethnic conflict, the present writer is reduced to the obvious. If ethnic groups felt less threatened, if they felt better respected, if they were given greater autonomy, the heat of at least some ethnic problems would presumably be reduced. The obvious is often worth saying. But in this case it is also not much better than useless. For, speaking of course only for himself, the writer has little idea about how to achieve the mentioned goals.

There is no problem over drawing up on paper constitutional safeguards that the planner deems suitable. It should not, in any specific case, take more than half an hour. But there is usually every problem over persuading both sides to the conflict to accept one particular scheme.[12] Moreover, even if a plan for the balancing of ethnic ambitions receives the requisite consent, it may not be easy to be more than moderately optimistic about the likelihood of that condition subsisting over a lengthy period of implementation. For one speedily encounters the minefields of feelings—feelings of being threatened, feelings of a lack of respect, feelings that justice is not being done—against which legislation is notoriously insufficient.

On the other hand, it is manifestly the case that instances can easily be found of ethnicities coexisting satisfactorily within a single polity. To that the academic almost instinctively responds by calling for research, or for further and better research, into the matter. (How often, one wonders, does ethnic trouble erupt where there is a fairly high and fairly evenly distributed level of prosperity? Perhaps the research has already been done and is just unfamiliar to the present writer, whose intellectual burrow lies inconveniently far from the locale of any such investigations.) Be that as it may, the thought remains that the application of any positive research results may not be the simplest of tasks, not least in cases of ongoing ethnic turbulence.

Sovereign Freedom

Given the argument, developed above, that in certain circumstances peacekeeping may be able to make a limited contribution towards the calming of ethnic conflict, the question is worth asking whether there are any "unnecessary" obstacles to the acceptance of such missions by potential host states. Without question, states tend to be sensitive about the presence on their soil of third parties, especially if military personnel are involved (James 1990a). It suggests, without much room for ambiguity, that the state in question is unable to cope on its own with one of its problems. And in the case of an ethnic problem it will usually be difficult to pin the blame on another state. Peacekeeping groups are therefore generally accepted only when the state concerned is in a very tight corner. Accordingly, the light in which peacekeepers will be viewed will not be overly favorable. They will probably be seen as only the least of the available evils. And generally they will be accepted at a later rather than an earlier stage of the mounting difficulty.

Most of the factors that explain this attitude are related to the physical presence and activity of the outsiders (see Kaufman, this volume). But there usually seems also to be a conceptual element. A peacekeeping mission is conceived as an infringement of, or at least an affront to, the state's sovereignty. It follows that if states could be led to a reconceptualization of sovereignty there might be some possibility of more being done on the peacekeeping front to modify the harsh edges of ethnic conflict. Of course, all the other— and it has to be said, weightier—hesitations about playing host to peacekeepers would remain. And it also has to be recognized that states do not pay much attention to arguments of an abstract kind. They are in the business of politics, not of the intellect.

Nonetheless, for political reasons states do periodically tend to make some fuss about the abstraction that they term sovereignty. And it happens that the ending of the Cold War has created an international context singularly favorable to the idea of external involvement in a state's internal affairs. The question that has been raised is therefore worthy of a brief examination.

Sovereignty, in the sense in which it has just been referred to, consists of a state's sovereign freedom—notably, its freedom to run its own affairs as it pleases. The state is not subject to a superior constitutional authority that can, at least on certain issues, legitimately involve itself in the state's affairs. However, that does not mean that the state is likely to enjoy a completely free hand, either in political or in legal terms. It may deem it prudent to take some account of what another state thinks of as an aspect of its internal conduct—that, after all, is commonplace in any societal context. Similarly, the state may have accepted certain international legal obligations to behave in a particular way. Such obligations may even extend to giving outsiders the right to conduct specified operations on the state's territory.

So far as the legal aspects of these matters are concerned, the state is diminishing its sovereign freedom. It can be spoken of in this way because its sovereignty, in the sense of legal freedom, is not an absolute but a relative concept. It exists in degree. It may be added to, as when a state receives the right to do something in another state. Equally, it may be diminished, as when a state permits another state or an outside body to do something within its borders. Rhetoric apart, therefore, there is no need to make a fuss about, for example, peacekeepers diminishing a state's sovereignty.

In general terms the expansion and diminution of a state's sovereign freedom is a process that is going on all the time. Indeed, by giving and receiving such permissions the state concerned is exercising its most basic sovereign freedom.

There is therefore no reason in principle why states should not be more equable about giving an internal investigatory or supervisory role to outsiders. Were national cultures to become more receptive to such devices—in part, perhaps, through academics making the point that the experience of being a sovereign state in no way precludes the raising of the portcullis—there might be a greater use of peacekeeping missions in ethnic contexts. That could hardly do any damage to the cause of ethnic peace and could well bring some benefit.

However, a state would perhaps have to be relatively relaxed about itself and its international position for it so to behave. Furthermore, ethnic divides do not facilitate relaxation. And where there is a deep conflict, the idea of introducing a peacekeeping mission may come up against a brick wall—and if a mission does manage to gain entry, it may not be of great use. In such contexts it may be necessary not to think about, or just about, ways of trying to reconcile ethnically divided polities, but also about the possible sundering of such structures.

Sovereign Status

The term *sovereignty* also is employed in another way, to refer not to the extent of a state's freedom but to its status. As such the concept is absolute in its application, not relative. In this sense, a territorial entity is either sovereign or not. In principle, there is no halfway house; and in practice, too, there is hardly any such staging post. Sovereignty is either present or absent.

Sovereignty in this absolute sense is constitutional independence (James 1986). If and when the constitution of a territorial entity is not part of a superior constitution, in the way in which a colony is part of an imperial structure, that entity enjoys the status that is requisite for it to embark on the international game. In slightly different terms, it enjoys the necessary condition for it to be admitted to the international club. *Sovereignty* in this usage therefore identifies the potential participants in international relations.

It is sovereignty in this sense that is often sought by embattled ethnicities. Notwithstanding the possibility that winning it may leave them exposed as small and weak entities in a competitive environment—and therefore perhaps not having much by way of sovereign freedom—they want formally to be in charge of their own affairs. Many peoples have gained this status during the twentieth century through the breakup of many empires. Why, others ask, should they not also do so?

In relative terms—which may not be saying much—there is some ground for such ethnic groups to take heart. For, in the late 1990s, there is being called into question the confident assertion of the post–World War II period that self-determination applies only in respect to colonies and not within existing or newly emerged sovereign states. Indeed, this generally self-serving international orthodoxy was almost visibly falling apart in certain parts of the world. In large measure this is due to the extent of the obeisance that is now being paid to the idea of democracy. On many sides arrangements are being set in hand for governments better to reflect the will of their subjects. In that emerging context, it will become difficult to draw a convincing line between allowing people to choose who are to rule them within the existing polity and denying some of them the right to be ruled outside the polity. Thus states run the risk (as they will generally see it) of being hoisted by their own asserted democratic petards—rather in the manner in which, a generation or two ago, democratic colonial powers found themselves somewhat embarrassed by calls from their colonial subjects for self-rule. Having been taught the virtues of democracy and freedom, these people were—"would you believe it?"—asking that they should almost immediately exercise the concomitant rights.

Of course, that is not at all to say that states will adopt the implications of their intellectual positions. Political processes rarely reflect logical cogitation, and in almost every governmental quarter the prospect of a secession is viewed with something not far short of horror. Furthermore, in many instances there are without doubt large practical difficulties in the way of a smoothly engineered secession. Most prominently, it is not often that ethnic groups fall into neatly exclusive territorial areas, and in some cases—a citizen of the allegedly United Kingdom would think immediately of Belfast—they seem inextricably intertwined. The twentieth century has seen enough of the suffering entailed by population movements to discourage any proposals pointing in that direction. And yet, in a number of contexts it seems that it is only through the breakup of some existing sovereign entities that there lies any hope of resolving ethnic conflict.

Perhaps, therefore, policy-oriented thought should focus on the themes not just of decentralization and autonomy but also on how secession, self-determination, and power sharing might be facilitated. At bottom this is probably a cultural matter—the acceptance in national cultures that there is nothing discreditable in a people wishing to secede or share power or in allowing them to do so—and even that it is honorable for a government so to respond. There is no suggestion here that such attitudes will easily take political root, no matter to what extent they come to receive unofficial endorsement. But should secessions or less grave forms of political organization take place, resulting in the emergence of additional self-determined political entities, the international outlook will probably be brighter for them than at any earlier time during the five-hundred-year history of the international society.

In the first place, worries about the possibly destabilizing consequences of secession as an extreme case for the wider political scene have been much diminished by the end of the Cold War. Secondly, it must by now be widely appreciated that there is no necessary inconsistency between the independence brought by sovereign status, self-determination, autonomy, and economic and technological interdependence. Thirdly, the mechanisms for far-reaching international cooperation are relatively advanced. Fourth, in these egalitarian times there is no obstacle to even very small sovereignties being fully welcomed into the international society. In the early 1920s the European ministates were snubbed by the League of Nations; but in recent years all four—with an average population in the region of thirty thousand—have been warmly ushered into the UN. And finally, the legal and moral impropriety of larger states swallowing up smaller ones is now firmly established. That does not mean that such states will not be subject to telling pressures. But the likelihood of their annexation by rapacious neighbors is lower than ever before.

There is no reason at all to think it will come to that—but what would be wrong with a world of city states?

NOTES

1. See the third section of this chapter for a discussion of Ethiopia's attitude to Eritrea—which was truly exceptional, and so goes to prove the enunciated "rule."

2. It should be noted that the UN counts this operation as an instance not of peacekeeping but of peacebuilding; see *UN Chronicle* (1993: 39).

3. This, too, is an operation which the UN does not classify as peace-keeping. See further, Jensen 1985 and Parsons 1990.

4. See UN Documents S/25170, 26 January 1993, and S/25818, 21 May 1993, for the UN secretary-general's reports on the problem. It was later stated that he had proposed the withdrawal of the UN mission but that the Security Council members had rejected this idea: see *The Times* (London), 19 March 1994. Subsequently the council passed a resolution saying that if the referendum was not held by the end of the year it would reconsider the future of the UN peacekeeping mission: see UN Information Centre, London, *News Summary*, NS/11/94, 30 March 1994.

5. For the initial memorandum of understanding regarding this activity, see UN Document S/22513, 22 April 1991.

6. Editor's note: The subsequent UN Operation in Somalia (UNOSOM II), established in May 1993, was the first explicitly authorized UN peace-enforcement mission since that in the Congo in the early 1960s. The phase-out of UNOSOM II from Somalia began in November 1994 and was completed in March 1995. Given the volatile situation prevailing in Somalia, it was a complex exercise involving the departure of the fifteen thousand UN troops then deployed in the country. During the final stage of the operation, support for the withdrawal was provided by the Combined Task Forces United Shield (France, India, Italy, Malaysia, Pakistan, the United Kingdom, and the United States), whose troops landed at Mogadishu on 28 February 1995. The troubled outcome of the Somalia mission caused a rethinking of the feasibility of UN peace enforcement in a civil war. Somalia failed not because of inadequate rules of engagement but because of the absence of recognized political authorities with whom the UN could conclude agreements. Somalia's communal contenders for power would not cooperate with peacekeepers.

7. Editor's note: UNOSOM II was, in theory, to be carried out in four phases. Phase I would concentrate on the transition of operational control from the Unified Task Force (UNITAF). Military support to relief activities and the disarming of factions would continue throughout the transition. Phase II would consolidate UN operational control and would conclude when UNOSOM II was deployed and operating effectively throughout Somalia and the border regions. In phase III, major efforts would be made to reduce UNOSOM II's military activity and assist civil authorities in exercising greater responsibility. That phase would end when a Somali national police force became operational and major UN military operations were no longer required. Phase IV would concern redeployment or reduction of the UNOSOM II forces. In fact, UNOSOM II never really extended beyond phase II, the point at which the operation was terminated.

8. In response to the disintegrating situation in Yugoslavia, the UN Protection Force (UNPROFOR) was established in early 1992 as an in-

terim measure to create the conditions of peace and security required for the EC-initiated negotiation of an overall settlement to the Croatian crisis. Eventually, the operation evolved into a traditional disengagement mission in Croatia, a humanitarian support mission in Bosnia and Herzegovina, and a small observation mission in Macedonia. While UNPROFOR's tasks multiplied, mainly in response to the rapidly deteriorating situation in Bosnia and Herzegovina, the resources at its disposal lagged behind and the political process on which it relied for authority and direction all but disintegrated.

9. Editor's note: Operationally the UNPROFOR mission met with some success on the ground but at a considerable cost to UN legitimacy. This is because the political solution to the conflict would not have been possible without the support of NATO; action made possible through the passage of several UN resolutions protecting Sarajevo and other safe havens as neutral zones. The blending of two kinds of operations—traditional peacekeeping, where neutrality is the order of the day, and assertive peacekeeping, where force is the primary instrument of control—under a single UN mandate was a risky strategy for both organizations.

10. On 30 August 1995, NATO initiated a week-long series of selective air strikes against Serb positions. NATO affirmed its determination to act in the same way for the other safe areas. The six "safe areas" (Gorazde, Sarajevo, Bihac, Zepa, Tuzla, and Srebrenica) were decreed as such last year by Resolution 824 and 836 of the Security Council. The operation, called "Deliberate Force," consisted of attacks by over sixty aircraft and the artillery pieces of the newly created Rapid Reaction Force. The strikes were implemented more than two full years after Serb forces laid siege to Sarajevo and were intended to force the Serbs to remove their artillery aimed at UN-designated safe areas. On 20 November 1995 an agreement was reached and a cease-fire was obtained.

11. For example, in November 1994 UN peacekeepers were detained by Bosnian Serb forces in retaliation for the NATO bombing of Serb-controlled depots near the town of Bihac.

12. As Frederick the Great is to have said about a plan for international peace: "It is fine in almost every detail. All we need now is the consent of Europe, and a few similar trifles!"

REFERENCES

Curtis, Gerald L. 1964. "The UN Observation Group in Lebanon." *International Organization* 18: 738–65.

Dawson, Pauline. *The Peacekeepers of Kashmir.* New Delhi: Popular Prakashan/ London: Hurst, forthcoming.

Diehl, Paul F. 1993. *International Peacekeeping.* Baltimore: John Hopkins University Press.

Harbottle, Michael. 1970. *The Impartial Soldier.* London: Oxford University Press.

Houweling, Henk. 1994. "Peacekeeping after State Collapse." In *Peacekeeping: Challenges in Europe and Eurasia,* edited by Ernest Gilman and Detlef E. Herold. Rome: NATO Defense College.

James, Alan. 1994a. "The Congo Controversies." *International Peacekeeping* 1, no. 1.

———. 1993a. "The History of Peacekeeping: An Analytical Perspective." *Canadian Defence Quarterly* 23: 10–17.

———. 1993b. "Internal Peacekeeping. A Dead End for the UN?" *Security Dialogue* 244: 359–68.

———. 1990a. "International Peacekeeping: The Disputants' View." *Political Studies* 38: 215–30.

———. 1990b. *Peacekeeping in International Politics.* Basingstoke: Macmillian.

———. 1994b. "Problems of Internal Peacekeeping." *Diplomacy and Statecraft* 5, no. 1.

———. 1986. *Sovereign Statehood. The Basis of International Society.* London: Allen and Unwin.

———. 1993c. "The UN in Croatia: An Exercise in Futility?" *The World Today* 49: 5.

———. 1994c. "UN Peacekeeping Problems: Recent Developments and Current Problems." *Paradigms: The Kent Journal of International Relations.*

———. "The UN Force in Cyprus." In *UN Peacekeeping in the 1990s,* edited by R. Thakur and C. A. Thayer. Boulder, Colo.: Westview, forthcoming.

Jensen, Erik. 1985. "The Secretary-General's Use of Good Offices and the Question of Bahrain." *Millennium: Journal of International Studies* 14: 335–48.

King, Charles. 1993. "Moldova and the New Bessarabian Questions." *The World Today* 49, no. 7: 135–9.

Mackinlay, John, and Jarat Chopra. 1993. "Second Generation Multilateral Operations." *Washington Quarterly* 30, no. 3.

Parsons, Sir Anthony. 1990. "Britain and the Security Council." In *The United Kingdom - The United Nations,* edited by Erik Jensen and Thomas Fisher. Basingstoke and London: Macmillan.

Security Council Resolution 884, 12 November 1993.

Security Council Resolution 897, 4 February 1994.

Skogmo, Bjorn. 1989. *UNIFIL: International Peacekeeping in Lebanon, 1978–1988.* Boulder and London: Rienner.

UK House of Commons. 1992–93. Foreign Affairs Committee. *The Expanding Role of the United Nations and Its Implications for*

United Kingdom Policy, United Kingdom, House of Commons. 1: xxv–xxvi.

UN Chronicle, 30, no. 3: 39.

UN Documents S/22513, 22 April 1991.

UN Documents S/23836, 14 April 1992.

UN Documents S/24859, 27 November 1992.

UN Documents S/25170, 26 January 1993.

UN Documents S/25818, 21 May 1993.

UN Documents S/26099, 13 July 1993.

UN Documents S/26422, 9 September 1993.

UN Documents S/26872, 14 December 1993.

UN Documents S/26926, 30 December 1993.

UN Documents S/1994/12, 6 January 1994.

UN Documents S/1994/89, 28 January 1994.

UN Documents S/1994/253, 3 March 1994: 19–34.

UN Information Centre, London. 1994. *News Summary* NS/10/94 (24 March).

UN Information Centre, London. 1994. *News Summary* NS/11/94 (30 March).

7

Preventing Ethnic Violence

Conditions for the Success of Peacekeeping

Stuart Kaufman

INTRODUCTION

The intractable nature of violent ethnic conflict has been a continuing source of frustration for scholars and policy-makers. The Lebanese conflict, a horror for those caught up in it, was for a long time a source of despair for those trying to find a solution. The equally brutal and equally frustrating conflict in Bosnia-Herzegovina has proven Azar's contention (if it needed proof) that there is nothing unique about Lebanon: such protracted social conflict, as he calls it, is common (Azar and Haddad 1986). Lebanon and Bosnia are unusual only in the completeness with which their fragile inter-ethnic equilibria were shattered. In each instance, the international community introduced peacekeepers to try to help manage the violence; in both cases, the peacekeepers had little success. Their failure prompts an interesting question: might peacekeeping have a better chance of success if begun before violence has become serious—before, in Azar's terms, the equilibrium is shattered?

Neither theories of ethnic violence, theories of peacekeeping, nor theories of conflict resolution offer much encouragement to those pursuing the idea. Theories of ethnic violence supply most of the bad news, emphasizing its almost irremediable causes: fundamental conflicts of interest arising from processes of modernization; fears of group extinction; and political dynamics which produce extremist leaders. Those who study third-party interventions in such conflicts add that interventions more often exacerbate ethnic conflict than ameliorate it. Even when third parties are well intentioned, there is often little they can do to help.

These circumstances are not promising for attempts to use the tools of conflict resolution and peacekeeping. Peacekeeping can only work when the parties to the conflict want the peace to be kept. Conflict resolution theory (see Haass 1990; Zartman 1985) suggests some of the requirements of that desire: leaders must consider either conflict management (a "kept peace") or conflict resolution preferable to continued fighting; they must be able to convince their followers to accept that alternative; and they must enforce their followers' observance of it. But if any of the above causes of ethnic violence are present for a given case—if leaders do not want peace, their followers do not consider the terms of peace acceptable, or the people are too emotionally aroused to consider the option— then conditions for successful peacekeeping do not exist. The sad irrelevance of peacekeeping forces in Lebanon and Bosnia-Herzegovina constitutes a cautionary tale for those who would dispatch peacekeepers where conditions are not suitable.

Furthermore, peacekeeping can only be attempted if peacekeepers are invited into the conflict area by the internationally recognized authorities. Preferably, all of the parties to the conflict should be parties to the request for peacekeeping, so the conditions outlined above can be met. But why should all parties agree to peacekeeping? Governments are notoriously protective of their sovereignty and are always reluctant to call in armed forces outside of their own control. If outside forces must be invited, governments usually prefer to invite allies rather than impartial arbiters.[1] By the time a government sees the value of peacekeepers, it is likely to be because it is losing ground badly to its opponents, at which point it is too late for preventive peacekeeping.

All of these considerations suggest that peacekeepers are simply not an appropriate policy tool for preventing or ending ethnic violence. Why, then, do people continue to propose such peacekeeping missions? Sometimes it is a way of forestalling other, more vigorous actions that states are disinclined to take. In a related sense, it may be a result of habit or organizational process: peacekeeping is something foreign ministries routinely consider as an option, and something certain militaries and international organizations know how to do, so they may routinely apply it in the absence of better alternatives.[2]

This chapter argues, contrary to all of the above, that there actually are cases in which peacekeeping troops can be used preventively to forestall ethnic violence or prevent its spread. If leaders on both sides are amenable to allowing peacekeeping, then peacekeepers backed by outside pressure have a chance of successfully preventing the outbreak or spread of ethnic violence. The situation in Macedonia in the mid-1990s is an example of such a case. Not every incipient ethnic conflict is so promising, however: in the case of Croatia, neither peacekeepers nor other foreign intervention could have prevented the outbreak of war in 1991.

The argument in this chapter proceeds in three main parts. First, theories of ethnic violence and of peacekeeping are synthesized to establish a theoretical basis for this analysis. Next, case histories of peacekeeping are examined to draw out some conditional lessons of peacekeeping: what, exactly, are peacekeepers good at achieving, and what do they have more trouble doing effectively when used in internal ethnic conflicts? Building on these conclusions, the third part uses the situations in Croatia and Macedonia to illustrate the difficulty of preventive peacekeeping and the promise of peacekeeping to prevent the spread of ethnic violence.

THEORIES OF ETHNIC VIOLENCE

The key disagreement among theorists is whether ethnic violence should be understood as the result of rational calculation or of the psychology of violence. Gurr's early work (1970) argued that political violence is the result of feelings of relative deprivation, which result in frustration and then aggression. Azar's approach (1986; cf. Azar and Haddad 1986) and Horowitz's (1985) focus on a different emotion—fear. The core argument of both is that a prime motivation for extreme ethnic conflict, including ethnic violence, is an ethnic community's fear that it will be marginalized or even driven to extinction as a group. Brass (1991) points out that elites, especially if aided from outside, may have both reason and ability to manipulate such fears to increase ethnic violence—and thereby increase their own power (cf. Rothschild 1982)(see introductory chapter by Carment and James).

The opposing approach argues that rational calculation offers the best explanation for ethnic violence. Laitin (1991) argues, for example, that each of two linguistic groups may rationally conclude from an analysis of the "tipping game" that neither can be safe from assimilation and ethnic extinction unless it imposes policies threatening the other with the same fate. The logical result is extreme, often violent conflict. Tilly (1978), focusing on the collective logic of political violence, argues that when organizations, resources, and opportunity become available, people will mobilize for collective action, including rebellion, if they calculate that it is in their best interest to do so.

These approaches are in fact highly complementary, as the authors have begun to recognize (Tilly 1991, Gurr 1993). Rabushka and Shepsle (1972), using a rational choice approach, show convincingly that if ethnic groups have very intense preferences—if they prefer even a small chance of "winning" on an issue to the certainty of compromise—then it is rational for them to follow extremist leaders. Rabushka and Shepsle cannot explain why people might have these preferences, but Horowitz and Laitin can: if an ethnic group fears extinction unless it gains political dominance, then, whether that fear is rationally based or not, its preferences will be intense. Especially if one or both ethnic communities have some experience of ethnic subordination, intraethnic politics is likely to become a contest in ethnic outbidding, in which elites compete to make increasingly extreme promises of communal benefits at the expense of other ethnic groups (Crighton and Mac Iver 1991).

Third-party intervention in such ethnic disputes is ubiquitous, especially in attempts at secession (see Heraclides 1991), but it is virtually always aimed at exacerbating rather than ameliorating conflict. While third-party patrons can sometimes restrain extremist politicians, they are notoriously reluctant to do so, because it means forfeiting the political gains that motivated the patronage in the first place (see Zartman 1985; 1990). In some cases (see Kaufman 1993), external patronage may be decisive in mobilizing support for extremist elites, in providing the resources for a sustained rebellion (Heraclides 1990), or in aiding the victory of one side.

THEORIES OF PEACEKEEPING

Peacekeeping can be defined as the nonviolent use of third-party armed forces to maintain peace among belligerents.[3] Peacekeepers work by persuasion, negotiation, and reassurance—often by interposing themselves between the conflicting parties. For such tactics to work, the peacekeepers must be impartial. They are usually sponsored by the United Nations (UN), but they do not have to be: any group whose legitimacy and impartiality are accepted by the parties can sponsor peacekeepers. In practice, peacekeepers are usually sent after violence has broken out and then settled down again; they can, however, be sent before the outbreak of serious violence. If they are, their mission can be labeled *preventive peacekeeping* (see introductory chapter by Carment and James).

The UN's former peacekeeping expert, Sir Brian Urquhart (1983), argues that there are four necessary conditions for successful peacekeeping (64). First, there must be agreement on the peacekeeping effort from all major parties—both those directly involved and their external patrons. Most importantly, the state which will be hosting the peacekeepers must, according to international law, consent to their introduction. The second, and related, requirement, is that all parties must cooperate with the peacekeepers: if even one party is determined to resume or continue fighting, it can withdraw its cooperation and simply go around, over, or through the peacekeepers, who generally lack both the mandate and the capability to stop them. If the peacekeepers do try to fight, they lose their neutrality, their attempts at reassurance lose credibility, and as a result they become simply another group of belligerents. The implication is that, in practice, cooperation presupposes that all sides want the peace to be kept.

Urquhart's third condition is an appropriate mandate. While the meaning of this term will be fleshed out in the cases, one implication follows from the above logic: the peacekeepers must be policing, or helping to create, a status quo that all major parties prefer to continued violence.[4] If any party is dissatisfied enough with the status quo, it can withdraw its cooperation, resume fighting, and render the peacekeepers irrelevant.

The fourth condition for successful peacekeeping is strong motivation for the international community to act. This condition is by no means the easiest of the four to meet. On the one hand, the conflict must be important enough to create a consensus among the major powers concerned that they must act by introducing peacekeepers. On the other hand, no major power can have enough at stake that it would prefer to sponsor one of the belligerents against the peacekeepers. Such finely tuned balances of major-power interest cannot be taken for granted.

A final issue is how to define peacekeeping success. Suppose peacekeepers manage to keep the civilian population in their sector safe while fighting rages on: is that success or failure? To some degree, the answer depends on the peacekeepers' mission. For the purposes of this chapter, however, successful peacekeeping will be defined in terms of actually keeping peace. Total peacekeeping success requires that all armed conflict end: the more shooting incidents, and the more casualties there are from such incidents, the less successful peacekeeping is. If peacekeepers manage to ameliorate suffering while the fighting goes on, that is a partial success for humanitarian intervention but a peacekeeping failure.

CASES OF INTERNAL PEACEKEEPING

International peacekeeping in internal conflicts is not unprecedented. The list of major peacekeeping efforts of this sort (Karns and Mingst 1993: 193) includes the Congo (1960–64), Cyprus (since 1964), Lebanon (since 1978), Namibia (1989–90), Cambodia (1991–93), Yugoslavia (since 1992), and Somalia (since 1992). All of these conflicts include, to some degree, an ethnic dimension, so it is useful to consider what lessons can be learned from them about the use of peacekeepers in ethnic conflicts. This chapter will focus on peacekeeping efforts from the Cyprus and Lebanon conflicts, which are among the best-studied and which began long enough ago for the degree of success and failure to be clear.

Cyprus Operation

The conflict between ethnic Greeks and ethnic Turks on Cyprus has shown all of the theoretical hallmarks of protracted ethnic conflict. Both groups have histories of ethnic subordination: the Greeks suffered for centuries under Ottoman Turkish rule, while the Turks felt disfavored by decades of British colonial rule. Both groups have fears for the survival of their community as a result of a classic "double minority" situation: while Greeks outnumber Turks on the island itself, they are in turn vastly outnumbered by Turks on the mainland nearby (see Kriesberg, this volume). Finally, intraethnic politics in both communities became dominated by a process of ethnic outbidding. For example, when Archbishop Makarios, then president of Cyprus, attempted in 1963 to shore up his support among Greeks by revoking the guarantees provided to the Turks in the British-imposed constitution, he provoked the fighting of 1963–64. When Makarios was ousted by military men with an even more extremist ethnic Greek agenda, they provoked the 1974 invasion by the Turkish army.

The history of the United Nations peacekeeping force in Cyprus

(UNFICYP), in continuous operation since 1964, is punctuated by those two dates. The nature of its job changed substantially after the 1974 Turkish intervention on the island, so it is useful to consider separately the lessons of UNFICYP from before and after that intervention.

Before 1974, UNFICYP's job was more complex than it was later. Pockets of Greek and Turkish Cypriots were scattered in areas predominantly inhabited by the other group. In short, these often hostile groups often lived cheek by jowl, producing two different kinds of tensions. In many places, neighboring communities had established fortified positions manned by armed militiamen who often needed little provocation to start shooting. In other places, daily routines, such as the travel of Greek Cypriot government officials (especially policemen) through Turkish Cypriot areas, provided frequent occasions for incidents.

UNFICYP's success can be measured by the fact that, largely due to its efforts, full-scale war did not resume for a decade. It was able to restore a semblance of normal life to some areas, escorting legitimate travelers through contested territory, persuading both sides to dismantle new and provocative fortifications, and taking control over the strategic Nicosia-Kyrenia road (Stegenga 1968: 126–38). UNFICYP's usual tactic in preventing or ending shooting incidents was to interpose itself between the two sides—often directly into the line of fire—and to negotiate with the two sides to end the shooting. In at least one case, UNFICYP went beyond normal peacekeeping tactics, resorting to a threat to use force to prevent a battle: when persuasion failed to prevent a Greek attack on a Turkish village, UNFICYP deterred the attack by interposing a force stronger than the would-be attackers (Harbottle 1970: 82–91).

The crisis of November 1967 represented a classic peacekeeping success for UNFICYP. The crisis began when the Greek Cypriot military commander, General Grivas, provoked a significant battle with the Turkish forces in a disputed area, possibly intending to force an escalation to all-out war. UNFICYP's presence created pressure on the Greeks to end the attack early, and it facilitated international pressure to the same end. After the fighting ended, UNFICYP was able to calm the situation on the island, thus allowing the international community time to dissuade Turkey from intervening on that occasion (Harbottle 1970).

The peace was unstable, however. While shooting incidents were often easy to stop, it was impossible to prevent them from recurring. Terrorist acts, such as hostage-taking and intercommunal murder, were even less tractable problems: while UNFICYP's presence may have reduced the impulse to such actions, they were a continuing problem throughout UNFICYP's first decade, and UNFICYP had little success in its attempts to identify those responsible and have them brought to trial (Harbottle 1970).

The most important "failure" of UNFICYP, of course, was its inability to prevent or stop the Turkish invasion of Cyprus in 1974. The crisis began when General Grivas, now in exile in Greece, led a coup against President Makarios, installing a government intent on *enosis*, or union with Greece. The coup provoked the Turkish invasion of the island and, once established, Turkey decided to complete the partition of the island by force (see Haass 1990: 65–66). While UNFICYP troops courageously faced down a Turkish move on the Nicosia airport toward the end of the campaign, there was simply nothing UNFICYP could do, in the face of overwhelming Turkish numbers, to prevent the war.

After 1974, UNFICYP had the much simpler job of encouraging the creation of a buffer zone between the Greek and Turkish frontlines and then patrolling that buffer zone to prevent or end shooting incidents. The post-1974 task resembles interstate peacekeeping more closely than peacekeeping in a domestic ethnic conflict.

In spite of the skill and courage of UNFICYP personnel, both their successes and their failures were determined by the conditions identified by Urquhart—conditions largely out of UNFICYP's control. Strong international support was one decisive element: the force was able to take up its task in 1964 only because the United States delivered "the diplomatic equivalent of an atomic bomb" to Turkey to prevent Turkish intervention in that year,[5] while the British extracted Makarios's agreement to the UN force by commencing their own unilateral intervention. Vigorous US and other foreign remonstrations were also necessary to prevent Turkish intervention in 1967. UNFICYP made it easier for the US to make its case in 1967, but vigorous diplomatic action by the US was clearly indispensable in preventing external forces from escalating in Cyprus.

The UNFICYP task was possible in the decade from 1964 to 1974 because all sides found the situation tolerable and were therefore willing to cooperate, accepting UNFICYP mediation rather than ignoring it (as the Turks finally did in 1974). The Greek Cypriot leader, Archbishop Makarios, was reasonably happy with the fact that he had managed de facto to abrogate the constitution, ending the effective Turkish Cypriot veto on virtually all acts of his government. Thus he had the more or less unitary government he wanted. The Turkish Cypriots, on their side, had de facto partition (or *taksim*, as they call it) and autonomy from most of the Greek-dominated government's powers (see, e.g., Stegenga 1968: 183). No one was fully satisfied, but only radicals (especially Greek Cypriot advocates of *enosis*) were extremely dissatisfied. Sadly but understandably, it was they, led by General Grivas, who provoked war and the Turkish invasion of 1974 by overthrowing Makarios' government.

In short, then, the positive lesson of UNFICYP is that peacekeepers can be effective at maintaining a fragile peace even where conflicting parties live more or less intermingled across fairly wide stretches of territory. Their action need not be restricted to patrolling continuous cease-fire lines (UNFICYP's prime task after 1974). The cautionary lesson is that such actions can only be effective to the extent that all significant actors want them to be: the withdrawal of cooperation by any local or major foreign actor can lead to the resumption of war. Thus every major actor has effective veto power over the peacekeeping operation's success.

Lebanon Operations

Lebanon's drawn-out agony since 1975 is another archetypal case for the composite theory of ethnic violence. While it is too simplistic to call the war a case of sectarian violence between Christians and Muslims, the factions within Lebanon itself usually did align along that divide. Both groups have a history of ethnic subordination—the Christians under the Arab Caliphate and the Ottoman Empire and the Muslims under the Crusaders and after the nineteenth-century French colonization. The Christians feared ethnic extinction in the surrounding sea of mostly Muslim Arabs, while the poor Muslim majority grew weary of being dominated by the Christians. The Muslims were finally mobilized by a coalition of leftists and religious radicals, while the Christians, especially the Maronites, countermobilized on an ethnic extremist platform, inaugurating a period of ethnic political outflanking.

This conflict affords two contrasting examples of internal peace-keeping in a conflict with ethnic dimensions: the UN Interim Force in Lebanon (UNIFIL) emplaced in the south of the country after the 1978 Israeli invasion and the Multinational Force (MNF) emplaced in Beirut after the 1982 Israeli invasion. The contrast is instructive: the MNF had grand objectives and turned into a catastrophic failure; UNIFIL had more modest objectives and aimed in practice only to achieve some of them, and thus achieved real, if only temporary, success.

The main lesson from the MNF, especially its American contingent, is that a peacekeeping mission cannot take sides in a conflict if it is to keep the peace. The American and French contingents in the MNF—more specifically, MNF II, emplaced after the Sabra and Shatila massacres—were given the mission of aiding the Lebanese government in establishing order in and around Beirut. The trouble was that the Lebanese army was a partisan in the civil war, siding with the Maronite Phalangist militia against the Druze and most Muslim militias as well as the Palestine Liberation Organization (PLO). Thus by 1983 American naval forces found themselves shelling the same targets being shelled by the Phalangists—a sure sign to the Lebanese Muslims that the Americans were siding with the Phalangists and the Israelis (Fisk 1991; cf. Pelcovits 1991). The truck bombs that eventually forced the MNF's withdrawal were the result.

UNIFIL, in spite of its dogged persistence in southern Lebanon, might appear to be a similar failure. Deployed to help restore peace and security to southern Lebanon, UNIFIL's actual ability to keep the opposing sides from fighting has varied over the years between modest and nil (see United Nations 1985: 108–54). From 1978 to 1982, the PLO retained positions from which it could launch artillery and rocket attacks against Israel and the enclave on the Israeli border controlled by the Christian militia of Israel's ally, Maj. Saad Haddad. When the PLO did attack, Haddad's forces or the Israelis invariably responded. Thus UNIFIL interposition did not stop the fighting: the pro- and anti-Israeli sides continued to fight either in between UNIFIL positions (the UNIFIL zone is not continuous) or literally over the heads of UNIFIL. The PLO and Haddad's forces prevented UNIFIL from expanding its deployment area to hinder such attacks.

Furthermore, UNIFIL did not even have full control over its

own deployment area. Israeli intelligence estimated that in 1979 there were five hundred PLO fighters stationed in the UNIFIL area (Comay 1983: 104), and the Israelis insisted that the PLO continued to use the area as a base for operations against Israel and the Haddad forces. When Israel wanted to retaliate on the ground against the PLO, Israeli troops simply drove through the UNIFIL perimeter. Ultimately, the Israelis determined to clear the PLO out of southern Lebanon entirely, launching the 1982 invasion. UNIFIL troops were able to do nothing more than act as a nuisance to the Israeli troops (United Nations 1985: 137).

These events comprise only one side of the UNIFIL story, however. UNIFIL also achieved important successes in two areas, especially in the period from 1978 to 1982. Its major success was, in spite of the problems, a substantial limitation of conflict among the main parties. The PLO's willingness to respect the UNIFIL zone—in order to improve its diplomatic credentials (Brynen 1990: 119–20)—did reduce the number of PLO attacks from Lebanon on targets in Israel. The presence of UNIFIL as a buffer also limited direct daily contact between the PLO and Haddad forces to one narrow area, vastly decreasing the opportunity for violence between them. Most substantially of all, UNIFIL acted as a buffer during the first-ever cease-fire between Israel and the PLO in 1981–82, acting as an intermediary to settle disputes over the cease-fire (United Nations 1985: 134). The cease-fire was virtually unbroken for almost a year, collapsing only when Israel decided to change its policy and pursue more grandiose objectives in Lebanon by invading it (see Schiff and Ya'ari 1984: chs. 2–5).

UNIFIL also achieved the humanitarian success of pacifying its own area of operations. It reached a modus vivendi with the PLO, limiting the attacks launched against UNIFIL itself while persuading the few PLO gunmen in the UNIFIL area generally to behave themselves. Largely as a result, UNIFIL checkpoints managed to turn back some two thousand attempts to infiltrate into its area of operations between mid-1979 and mid-1981—also contributing to the general peacekeeping mission (United Nations 1985: 122–23). Major Haddad's forces were less cooperative with UNIFIL, but they restricted themselves to the southernmost part of the UNIFIL zone. The effect of UNIFIL's security and humanitarian operations was to make the UNIFIL zone one of the safest places for civilians in Lebanon: before 1982, there was a net migration of civilians to the zone (Heiberg and Holst 1986: 405). This migration occurred, it should be noted, in spite of the shells and rockets that frequently flew overhead between the PLO zone to the north and the Israeli zone to the south.

A crucial factor that made this conflict management possible was the improvement of discipline within the PLO in the 1978–82 period. Immediately after Chairman Arafat announced PLO acceptance of the UNIFIL deployment and of a cease-fire in southern Lebanon, Fatah units loyal to Arafat arrested over one hundred of their own people who had been about to attack the UNIFIL zone. Two months later, there were reports of a five–hundred–man Fatah force specifically assigned to assure the cease-fire (Brynen 1990: 119–20). By the time of the 1981–82 cease-fire, Arafat was able to ensure perfect PLO compliance (except for one incident a few days after the cease-fire began), in spite of what the PLO considered provocative flights by Israeli reconnaissance aircraft.

One of the chief lessons from Lebanon is a surprisingly optimistic one: skilled peacekeepers can make an enormous contribution to peace and security in their region, even under conditions of complete anarchy, to the extent that the major armed forces in the area are willing to cooperate. UNIFIL could do nothing in the city of Tyre, because the PLO kept it out; it could do nothing in Haddad's enclave, because Haddad and the Israelis kept it out. But in the area it did occupy, UNIFIL was able to act as a de facto government: it "protected the local civilian population from the militias" (Sirriyeh 1989: 52), and even mediated between the PLO and the Shi'ite Amal militia when the latter began its rise to power (United Nations 1985: 135). By and large, it was able to keep guerrillas from infiltrating into the area. Since the 1982 Israeli invasion, UNIFIL's effectiveness has drastically decreased, but it still provides something of a buffer between Israel and her enemies, and, aided by an understanding with Amal, it continues to promote order in its area of operations (James 1990: 345–49).

The lesson from the MNF is that peacekeeping missions must be truly neutral among the parties. When the French, Americans, and to a lesser extent the British sided with the Lebanese army and Phalangist militia against other militias, they lost their credibility as peacekeepers and became simply additional militias in the civil war. Given that UNIFIL's mission was supposedly to help re-establish Lebanese government authority, this fate could have befallen

UNIFIL also. Had the Lebanese army been strong enough to attempt to take control of the UNIFIL zone in 1983, UNIFIL would have been obliged to cooperate—and would have been helpless when the army brought in Christian militias to help and when those militias began to fight with the mostly Muslim population of the region. Thus UNIFIL was paradoxically saved by the factor that also made its assigned mission impossible: the weakness of the Lebanese government.

SUMMARY OF HISTORICAL LESSONS

The history of peacekeeping in ethnic conflicts affords some room for optimism, but also illustrates the importance of the conditions for peacekeeping success suggested by Urquhart. First, there must be agreement from all major parties to the peacekeeping effort. Outside powers' decisions not to accept peacekeepers' roles—Turkey in the Cyprus case, Israel in the Lebanon case—can restart wars quickly. As the 1967 Cyprus incident shows, however, quick international action (in this case, in the form of US pressure) can sometimes forestall such outbreaks. Withdrawal of agreement by local actors, as by Greek Cypriots after the 1974 coup, can provoke renewed war.

A final note about agreement concerns the consent of the state on whose territory the conflict occurs. States are notoriously reluctant to invite any international forces onto their sovereign territories; why did these two states extend such invitations? The common element was a desire to force out foreign interveners who were even less welcome. For Makarios on Cyprus, the UN was preferable to increasing British intervention and the threatened Turkish one. In Lebanon, both peacekeeping forces were invited to facilitate the withdrawal of invading Israeli forces. In neither case would peacekeepers have been as welcome in the absence of larger foreign threats. And in neither case would their presence have been possible without the fourth condition: international willingness to send them and the interveners' willingness to defer to them.

The second requirement for successful peacekeeping is that all major parties cooperate with the effort. As the UNIFIL case shows, when parties want the peacekeepers to succeed, and when they are capable of (generally) disciplining themselves, peacekeepers can maintain peace and security even in anarchic conditions. Mediation to prevent or end incidents, as on Cyprus or between the PLO and Amal in Lebanon, is the bread and butter of peacekeeping operations and is effective as long as no major party is determined to make it ineffective. Limited provocations by strong parties can be turned back by peacekeepers' perimeter forces, as UNIFIL shows, or addressed through mediation.

The third condition is an appropriate mandate. As the experience of the Multinational Force in Beirut shows, a mandate which requires peacekeepers to take a side also requires them to abandon their peacekeeping role. Since even heavily armed peacekeepers are rarely capable of forcing conflict resolution, such taking of sides spells disaster. Urquhart maintains that the mandate should be clear, but the cases above show this is not necessary. All three forces mentioned above had vague mandates; what is important is that local commanders be able to interpret their mandates to demand no more than they can accomplish. Such interpretation requires not clarity, but canny commanders and sponsoring institutions that tolerate the commanders' autonomy.

PREVENTIVE PEACEKEEPING IN FORMER YUGOSLAVIA

In contrast to peacekeeping in violent internal conflicts, international peacekeeping to prevent violent internal ethnic conflict had never been attempted before the current effort in Macedonia.[6] Historical lessons can be applied, but the only way to do so is counterfactually—to posit various "might have beens" and "might be's" and to consider what one can learn from them about the subject. I take for the source of my examples the ethnic conflicts in the former Yugoslav republics. I examine the Croatian case because if ethnic violence were to have been prevented in Yugoslavia as a whole, Croatia—the location of the first severe fighting—had to be the locus for the attempt. The Macedonian case is chosen because it is a case in which the spread of ethnic violence was and is possible but not inevitable and in which preventive peacekeeping has been most recently attempted.[7]

Croatia

The 1991–92 war between Serbs and Croats in Croatia is well explained by the composite theory of ethnic violence. Both groups had experience with ethnic repression in this century: Serbs dominated Croats in interwar Yugoslavia and, to a lesser extent, under Tito; while the Croatian fascist Ustashas dominated (and slaughtered) Croatia's Serbs during the World War II Nazi occupation. Both groups were also encouraged by the media (especially after Tito's death in 1980) to fear ethnic extinction (see Simic 1994): Serbs were taught to identify all Croats as bloodthirsty Ustashas, while Croats heard that they should deny the guilt of the Ustashas and beware attempts by the Serbs to Serbianize them. The unsurprising result was the rise of a politics of ethnic outflanking among both groups.

The process operated as follows. Slobodan Milosevic, the president of Serbia, began the cycle with heavy-handed attempts to achieve Serbian domination of Yugoslavia, arousing well-founded fears of repression among Croats and other Yugoslavs. One result was a resurgence of Croatian nationalism, which Franjo Tudjman drove to extremes while riding it to power. In the process, Tudjman kindled in Croatia's Serbs legitimate fears for their safety and well-being: he resurrected symbols associated with the Ustasha fascists; he indiscriminately fired thousands of Serbs from their jobs in government and government-controlled industry; and he allowed local police and paramilitary personnel to brutalize and intimidate Serbs in relatively remote areas of Croatia (Rusinow 1991: 155; Glenny 1992: 3, 13; Dragash 1991; Miljus 1991). Milosevic contributed to the Croatian Serbs' overreaction by providing arms, money, and advice for extremist Serb militias and political organizations in Krajina, the region of Croatia where most Serbs are concentrated (Andrejevich 1990: 39). The Serb extremists then proceeded to intimidate their moderate fellow-nationals into joining their militias (Glenny 1992: 20) and to bully their Croatian neighbors into fleeing.

Could preventive peacekeeping have stopped this process before it led to war? The crucial question concerns the fundamental requirements of peacekeeping success: might the parties have agreed to the introduction of preventive peacekeepers and cooperated with them once introduced? On the surface, the answer seems obvious: they would not have. Milosevic, along with his pawns in Krajina, was so determined to provoke violent conflict that the peacekeepers' efforts would have been futile. Indeed, Milosevic boycotted a mediation attempt by the European Community that might have led to the introduction of peacekeepers (Steinberg 1992: 16). Tudjman, motivated primarily by a nationalist determination to exert Croatian sovereignty over every square inch of Croatian soil, was also disinclined to concede any portion of that sovereignty to a neutral peacekeeping force.

As clear as these facts are, however, they are not the end of the story. Before the war began, many—perhaps most—inhabitants of Croatia were moderates who neither expected nor desired violence. As Glenny (1992) put it, "Croats and Serbs lived together in relative contentment ... [N]obody in their wildest fantasy would have predicted that ... the peaceful town of Vukovar would be levelled to the ground in one of the most merciless bombardments of modern history" (19). Part of what swept these people up into a maelstrom of violence was a security dilemma: when local extremists of the other nationality joined militias, moderates had little choice but to join their own group's (extremist-led) militia or else leave themselves vulnerable to retaliation by both sides (Posen 1993).

In a way, the embodiment of the dilemma of these moderates was the experience of Josip Reichl-Kir, the Croatian chief of police for the Osijek region in Eastern Slavonia, not far from the Serbian border. As tensions rose in late 1990 and early 1991, Reichl-Kir worked tirelessly to prevent violence, making local arrangements in village after village to calm people's fears and restrain extremists. A prominent Serb of similar inclinations was Milorad Pupovac, the leader of Croatia's urban Serbs, who also called for minimizing violence as well as for ending discrimination against Serbs (Glenny 1992: 84–85, 102–04). Pupovac's ideas had support among rural Serbs as well: as late as May 1991, on the eve of war, some Krajina Serbs demonstrated against their own extremist leaders (*RFE* 1991: 19). Surely such people as these would have welcomed the introduction of neutral peacekeepers to forestall violence as political deals were struck.

The frailty of this hope is illustrated, however, by the fates of Reichl-Kir and Pupovac. Reichl-Kir was murdered by an extremist Croat, a member of Tudjman's own party, the Croatian Democratic Union (HDZ). Pupovac was marginalized, squeezed out of influence by the extremist Serbs backed by Belgrade on one side and by Tudjman's unwillingness to make real concessions to Croatia's Serbs on the other. The brutal truth of Croatia is that the violence was elite-led.[8] Leaders like Milosevic, Tudjman, and their clients found that they could advance their careers by stoking hatred and promoting violence. Aided by the colossal arrogance and insensitivity of Tudjman, the sinister manipulations of Milosevic, and the tinderbox situation that was Krajina, they succeeded.

Furthermore, given the Serb and Croat leaders' goals, even if they had agreed to the introduction of peacekeepers, cooperation would not have been forthcoming. Such lack of cooperation would have made the peacekeepers' mission impossible in the long run—though of some value in the short run. If there were enough peacekeepers to create an adequate perimeter around Croatian territory (a difficult feat given the length of Croatia's borders), they might have been able to intercept the flow of arms—and of armed extremists—to Serb militias in Krajina. This would have had a significant effect, since many violent incidents in Croatia were perpetrated by groups based elsewhere.[9] Peacekeepers might also, by interposition, have prevented combat between overt armed groups, as UN forces did on Cyprus. They also could have reassured local residents, at least for some months, thereby buying more time for negotiators to find a way to resolve the underlying political issues.

But preventive peacekeepers in Croatia would have been able to do little to prevent terrorism, as the Cyprus example also shows. Both sides in Croatia were capable of resorting to terrorism—and did so both before and during the full-scale war of 1991–92. Peacekeepers would eventually have been rendered helpless—possibly even helpless targets—as terrorist attacks and retaliations escalated. And if not deployed in strength in Bosnia-Herzegovina as well, they might only have shifted the locus of the first outbreak of fighting. Peacekeeping, in brief, could only have helped in such troubled circumstances in the short run.

All of this also begs the more difficult question: how could the responsible governments—of Croatia, Serbia, and Yugoslavia—have been persuaded to agree to the introduction of peacekeepers in the first place? The cases of internal peacekeeping discussed above were all intended, from the viewpoint of the inviting state, to stop unilateral intervention by another state. In the Yugoslav case, no one seemed inclined to intervene against the Serbs.

The one chance for successful preventive peacekeeping would have come had someone—most plausibly, a group of NATO members—threatened military intervention. After the initial outbreak of hostilities in June 1991 (but before full-scale war began in August), one or more Western nations might have begun preparing to intervene in support of Croatia: taking initial diplomatic steps toward recognition of Croatian independence, mobilizing troops and materiel, preparing to arm the Croatian government, and so on. The Serb and Yugoslav governments could have been told that the intervention would be stopped if they agreed to the deployment of a neutral peacekeeping force. It is conceivable that the Serbs would have agreed in order to forestall the Western intervention, which would have threatened them with utter defeat. If the Serbs did agree, the Croats could have been told that the intervention was canceled: they could have the peacekeepers or nothing. They would probably have acquiesced.

The Serb-dominated Yugoslav People's Army (YPA), on the other hand, probably would not have agreed. Bitterly suspicious of the capitalist West (including such likely peacekeeping contributors as Canada), the YPA might well have blocked Yugoslav and Serb agreement to the introduction of peacekeepers and scotched the deal, determined instead to fight all out against any "imperialist" intervention. Such a reaction, of course, would have meant that the threat to intervene would have been counterproductive, leading to escalation even if not carried out.

Among the other practical difficulties with such a scheme is the problem: who, exactly, could credibly have threatened to intervene? Of the countries inclined to help Croatia, Austria and Hungary were too weak to matter and Germany was constitutionally constrained from taking effective action. The French, looking to past Franco-Serbian friendship, were not inclined to help the Croats; and Britain, fearing another Northern Ireland, was not inclined to get involved at all (Storck 1993). The Soviets, meanwhile, actively worked to deter any Western intervention against the Serbs. This leaves the United States as the only country that could credibly have threatened to intervene—but faced with the distraction of the just-ended war against Iraq, the opposition of Western Europe to American involvement, and Soviet deterrent threats, among other obstacles, the United States was reluctant to act so decisively. As Urquhart puts it, peacekeeping requires "international political necessity" to motivate outside powers for constructive action. Such necessity was absent on the Yugoslavia issue in 1991.

These obstacles to successful preventive peacekeeping in Croatia were decisive. The responsible governments were unlikely to agree to the introduction of peacekeepers unless they were compelled, and no one was likely to attempt to compel them: in the event, no one did. If any country had made the attempt, it would probably have failed and exacerbated the conflict. If the parties had grudgingly agreed to the deployment of peacekeepers, they almost certainly would not have cooperated fully: extremists on both sides were likely to resort to terrorism, and the governments capable of restraining them may not have been inclined to restrain them very long. Thus, if tried, peacekeeping might at best have helped in the short run (probably a matter of months); more likely, it would not have helped at all.

Even the best case—short-term amelioration of conflict—would have represented little real improvement. According to James (1990), peacekeeping can defuse crises; stabilize situations once defused; or aid in conflict resolution; but it does not itself resolve conflicts (4–5). Since peacekeeping could only have been short-lived in Croatia, it could only have been useful if it had contributed to a relatively quick institution of a conflict management scheme, or to real conflict resolution. But the conflict was probably not manageable or resolvable.

Kaufman (1993) argues that virtually all circumstances conspired by the summer of 1991 to make conflict resolution or management in Yugoslavia impossible. First, the policies of the main players were thoroughly deadlocked. Milosevic was determined on war if he could not gain Serb dominance in all Serb-inhabited areas (though he was willing to concede non-Serbian areas like Slovenia). Tudjman, in contrast, insisted on virtually absolute Croatian sovereignty and was willing to concede no substantial powers either to a Yugoslav government or to his own Serbian population. Worse, Milosevic's policies were not flexible because he had raised Serb expectations so high that he would have jeopardized his rule if he had compromised with Tudjman.[10]

Milosevic's situation is aptly explained by the typology proposed by Carment and James (1996). Milosevic represented the ethnically dominant group in Serbia and headed a government that was moderately constrained by political institutions. This created the most violence-prone situation possible: Milosevic was unconstrained enough to be able to arouse ethnic extremism and embark on an ethnic war, but once the extreme atmosphere was set, he found himself too constrained to be able to accept any compromise settlement should he have wished to.

Furthermore, the central Serb-Croat deadlock was bound up

with a series of other issues that also had to be solved if there was to be a stable solution to the Serb-Croat problem. First, Slovenian secession would have given the Serbs a permanent majority in the collective Yugoslav presidency, and thereby dominance in Yugoslavia. Thus the Croats had to secede if the Slovenes did—and the Slovenes were determined to secede. Second, the Croats insisted on having some kind of independent military force, and the YPA was determined to prevent the creation of any such force. Third, any agreement between Croatia and Serbia had to be compatible with a peaceful resolution of the Bosnian problem, which was probably impossible because of irreconcilable demands among the national communities in Bosnia.

Finally, any accommodation among the republics (unlikely as it was) also required that Serbia solve its Kosovo problem in a way compatible with Western human rights demands, since Slovenia and Croatia wanted integration into the European Community. But the Serbs were (and are) even more intransigent on Kosovo than on the other issues, while the Kosovo Albanians were quite fed up with the Serbs. Thus, a resolution of the Kosovo issue was least likely of all. In short, then, a resolution of the Croat-Serb dispute was only possible in the context of a comprehensive Yugoslav settlement, which would have required resolving issues even less tractable than the Croat-Serb dispute itself.

If this were not enough, the crowning obstacle to conflict resolution in Yugoslavia was the absence of a credible negotiating process. All of the key parties to the dispute, especially the Serbs, Croats, and Slovenes, had spent the previous year negotiating in such flagrant bad faith, and so flagrantly violating whatever agreements they reached, that by the summer of 1991 no one was willing to negotiate seriously. In short, not only were the Yugoslavs stymied by a number of intractable issues; they were not even willing seriously to discuss them. A Slovenian legislator summed up the situation with pithy irony: "Let us not forget that we are in the Balkans, where lies and deceit are the highest moral values" (Olive 1992).

The Croatian conflict of 1991 is a paradigmatic example of a situation in which preventive peacekeeping is inappropriate. The main parties to the conflict were unlikely to agree to peacekeeping. There was no burning international political necessity to motivate outside powers to compel the parties to accept peacekeepers. If the parties had been compelled to accept peacekeepers, they probably would not have cooperated with them. Thus, peacekeepers could at best have been effective only briefly, pending conflict resolution. And conflict resolution was almost certainly impossible in 1991.

Peacekeepers were introduced into the Krajina area in 1992, but only after the situation had changed dramatically. Essentially, the Serbs captured effective control over all of the territory they coveted and "cleansed" it of Croats, so they were willing to accept peacekeepers as a shield behind which to consolidate their gains. The Croats, by far the weaker party, were willing to accept the peacekeepers for two reasons: to stop further Serb depredations and in the hopes that the peacekeepers would help them regain control over lost territories. Meanwhile, the Croats build their army, preparing to recapture what they cannot regain peacefully (as the Maslenica Bridge incidents of 1993 demonstrate).[11]

Macedonia

The United Nations had deployed a peacekeeping force to Macedonia which, between 1992 and 1996, numbered over one thousand troops. The peacekeepers' mission, called UN Preventive Deployment in Macedonia (UNPREDEP), was to "'monitor and report any developments in the border region' [with Serbia and Albania] that could threaten Macedonia" (*New York Times* 1993). The Macedonian government was happy to consent to and cooperate with this mission for several reasons. First, UNPREDEP concerned Macedonia's external security and so implied no infringement of Macedonian sovereignty. Second, Macedonia had an extremely weak army (Troebst 1994: 34) and several serious external security threats, so it found the peacekeepers' presence enormously reassuring.

Macedonia's security situation—and the peacekeepers' mission—was, however, complicated by internal ethnic conflict. The Albanian community constitutes (depending on who is counting) between 21 and 40 percent of Macedonia's population,[12] and the conflict between it and the ethnic Macedonian majority had most of the prerequisites for extreme ethnic conflict leading to violence. The history of ethnic domination is long: Orthodox Christian Macedonians associate Turkish rule (which lasted until 1912) with the Muslim Albanians, while Albanians associate Serbian rule (for most of this century) with the Serbs' Macedonian coreligionists. Both groups felt threatened by their ethnic milieu, fearing, for different reasons, the Serbs, Greeks, and Bulgarians who surrounded and outnumbered them both. Extreme cultural differences between Albanians and Macedonians had created extreme distrust, and some degree of hatred, between them as well. Worst of all, each group had reason to fear that the other's demands might threaten its own communal survival. The tensions created by this mutual distrust were explosive: in November of 1992, rumors that an arrested Albanian youth had been killed by Macedonian police were enough to start a riot in Skopje, the Macedonian capital (Austin 1993: 24).

The Albanians' current grievances began with a perception of discrimination on practical issues: educational and media services in the Albanian language were inadequate, they did not have equal access to government jobs, and so on. Albanians also wanted more self-government—at the very least, an end to the situation in which even Albanian-majority communities were ruled entirely by ethnic Macedonians. Preferably, the Albanians said, they wanted regional autonomy in the borderlands of northern and western Macedonia (Perry 1992b; Moore 1992a; Austin 1993).

More complicated than these practical issues are related symbolic ones: the Macedonian national anthem and especially the constitution seem to exclude or degrade Albanians. The Macedonian constitution states that "Macedonia is established as the civil state of the Macedonian people, in which full equality as citizens ... is provided for Albanians ... and other nationalities." Macedonian nationalists actually preferred the phrase "national state of the Macedonian people," so this formulation represents to them a major concession. To the Albanians, however, it implies that they are second-class citizens rather than a constituent nation in a multinational state (Moore 1992a: 12; Perry 1992b: 16). The combination of practical and symbolic discrimination with a history of repression seemed to have awakened a fear among Albanians that the viability of their communities in Macedonia could eventually be threatened.

Albanian demands, however, sparked Macedonian fears about their ultimate goals: "ethnic Macedonians suspect Albanians of seeking to establish the conditions for secession and thus endangering the state." These fears were not unfounded: Albanian lawmakers have a habit of boycotting votes that they expect to go against them, apparently intending to refuse to legitimize the decisions by voting against them (Perry 1992b: 18). Much more worrisome is this type of assertion: Nezvat Halili, then chairman of the main-stream Albanian Party of Democratic Prosperity (PDP)—a partner in the ruling Macedonian coalition—had been quoted as saying that "all Albanians must 'live in one state'" (Moore 1992a: 13)—in effect, that Albanians should secede from Macedonia and join with Albania. Others in his party have said the same. This context makes the Albanian demand for the right to display their ethnic symbol, the Albanian flag, appear extremely threatening. PDP leaders deny that they really intend to secede, but it is easy to see why ethnic Macedonians doubt the disclaimer.

The one ingredient for large-scale ethnic violence so far absent from Macedonian politics is extremist outflanking in intraethnic politics. The Macedonian government, led by the politically moderate President Kiro Gligorov and Prime Minister Branko Crvenkovski, included five Albanian ministers and was committed to meeting some of the Albanians' tangible demands, such as on education and the media. And the Albanian PDP was committed to remaining in the government in an attempt at power-sharing aimed at preventing the escalation of ethnic tensions. But the leadership of both groups was under pressure from ethnic extremists. On the Macedonian side, the largest single political party is the Internal Macedonian Revolutionary Organization (IMRO), the party of extreme Macedonian nationalism. As one observer puts it, "the satisfaction of all the ethnic Albanian demands would mean virtual political suicide for the current Macedonian coalition" (Austin 1993: 25), leading to IMRO's assumption of power. The Albanians were also divided. At its February 1994 party congress, the ethnic Albanian PDP split into two factions: extremists had gained control of the party machinery and purged moderates from the leadership in December, so the moderates stalked out and held their own congress (RFE/RL 1994). The moderates remained committed to participation in the government, but there is room for doubt about the degree of their support in the Albanian community. The fact that even moderate Albanian leaders must hint at separatist goals suggests that the Albanian population has the kind of extreme preferences that respond to the siren song of extremist ethnic outflanking (see Rabushka and Shepsle 1972: 53–55).

From the Macedonian point of view, this internal threat from the Albanians could have combined with foreign threats to put the survival of Macedonia, and of the Macedonian people, at considerable risk. The foreign threats resulted from the refusal of any of the Macedonians' neighbors fully to accept them. Greece has been the most hostile of these neighbors, arguing that the very name "Macedonia" implies a territorial claim on the northern part of Greece known as Greek (or "Aegean") Macedonia. In response, Macedonian leaders have explicitly and repeatedly denied any territorial claim on Greece, going so far as to insert their denials into their constitution. But the Greeks point out that the current Macedonia was originally created by Tito as a springboard for his attempt to dismember and communize Greece in the late 1940s (*New York Times* 1994); it is not impossible, they reason, that Macedonia might in the future be used as a cat's-paw against them. Therefore, notwithstanding Macedonian denials of any irredentist intent, Greece has steadfastly refused diplomatic recognition and until 1996 imposed an embargo on Macedonia. Macedonia continues to refuse Greece's request to choose a name without the word "Macedonia" in it.

The territorial issue is bound up with the politics of ethnic identity. Greece has refused to recognize the existence of a "Macedonian" nationality; it refers to its Slavic Macedonian minority in Greek Macedonia as "Slavophone Greeks"—a community it has managed almost completely to assimilate. Macedonia professes itself interested in the ethnic rights of these people. Thus the Greeks affect fear of Macedonian interference in their internal affairs, and of course irredentism, while the Macedonians fear that Greek refusal to recognize their identity leaves them vulnerable to the fate of their conationals in Greece—assimilation and ethnic extinction.

From the Greek point of view, the issue was as much cultural piracy as national security: they insisted that the legacy of ancient Macedonia is part of Greek heritage and that the Slavic Macedonians had no right to claim any of it—neither the name nor the associated symbols (Pribichevich 1982: 239). When Greek Premier Constantine Mitsotakis seemed to be wavering on the issue of recognizing Macedonia in the face of near-unanimous foreign condemnation and a defeat on the issue of Macedonia's UN membership, he was outflanked and replaced by his socialist rival, Andreas Papandreou. Papandreou's policy innovation was to impose on 16 February 1994 an economic blockade on landlocked Macedonia, blocking Macedonia's primary trade route through the Greek port of Salonika.

The key source of tension between Macedonia and Albania is, of course, Albania's role as patron of the Albanian community in Macedonia. Albanian President Sali Berisha has gone out of his way to build good relations with Macedonia and has repeatedly counseled restraint among his brethren there, but the basic sources of tension remain (Austin 1993). Concerned about the demographic balance in their country, Macedonians have been attempting to limit cross-border traffic, especially immigration and smuggling, from Kosovo. Albanians resent this limitation on the trade that provides an essential lifeline for the economy of Albanians in Kosovo—much of which is ultimately bound for Albania. And of course, Albania is concerned about the treatment of Albanians in Macedonia, while the Macedonians resent the interference, occasionally flinging accusations of espionage across the border. A series of shootings at the Albanian-Macedonian border in 1993 contributed further to these tensions.

The Macedonians cannot fully trust Bulgaria—their most friendly neighbor—either. Bulgaria was among the first countries to recognize the independence of the Macedonian state, and it has been generous in allowing Macedonia to use its port of Burgas to handle the traffic traveling through Salonika in Greece. But the Bulgarians, like the Greeks, do not recognize the existence of a separate Macedonian nationality; they claim that the Macedonians are simply Bulgarians that reside in parts of Greece, Turkey, and Macedonia. For its part Bulgaria has its own Macedonian separatist movement. Thus when Macedonian President Kiro Gligorov was on a state visit to Bulgaria, Bulgaria's president insisted that Gligorov's remarks not be translated, arguing that Macedonian is simply a dialect of Bulgarian. This Bulgarian claim strikes right at the Macedonians' most vulnerable spot, implying doubt about Macedonia's right to exist as an independent state and possibly irredentist designs on Bulgaria's part.

In its relations with Serbia, Macedonia is caught on the horns of several dilemmas. During the Bosnian conflict, the international community expected Macedonia to enforce UN sanctions against Serbia, but doing so seriously harmed Macedonia's economy since Serbia was previously Macedonia's biggest trading partner. Large-scale smuggling from Kosovo brought an unwelcome influx of ethnic Albanians. Shutting it down was equally problematic, as it was thought that it would increase the pressure on Kosovo's Albanians to the breaking point, contributing to open violence that could easily spill over into Macedonia. Despite the end of the conflict in Bosnia, several problems remain.

The possibility of a spillover of ethnic conflict from Kosovo into Macedonia is the event some analysts fear might escalate into a renewed Balkan war. The nightmare scenario works as follows. An upsurge of violence in Kosovo (following either from an Albanian uprising or a Serbian "ethnic cleansing" offensive) would lead to a surge of Albanian refugees across the borders into Albania and Macedonia. This tide of refugees could create a backlash in Macedonia, propelling extremists into power and impelling Macedonia to join in the war on the Serb side to stem the Albanian tide. Albania might then see little to lose in entering the fighting openly, especially if it could gain Turkish backing (which is plausible if the Turkish minority in Macedonia were threatened by the fighting). Once the fighting spread to that degree, Greece and Bulgaria might also become involved; further spread to Cyprus would then be quite likely (Moore 1992b; Glenny 1993; Perry 1992b: 45). Most of the steps in this chain of escalation are unlikely, and most are irrational, but given the volatile passions of the Balkans they cannot be ruled out. Since the end of the Bosnian war, there has been a considerable relaxation of tensions in the region. Most of the countries in the Balkans are now more concerned with internal economic issues.

Still, if Macedonia were to become involved in any international conflict—and a spillover from Kosovo is the most likely cause—it might reawaken the old "Macedonian Question": the rivalry among Bulgaria, Greece, and Serbia over Macedonian territory. The Bulgarians still remember the short-lived San Stefano settlement of 1878, which awarded Macedonia to Bulgaria, and they occupied most of Macedonia during World War II. The Serbs, for their part, are still inclined to consider Macedonia to be "southern Serbia," as it was labeled between the world wars (see Banac 1984: 310–13). Thus, the Macedonians fear, the secession of their Albanian regions might spark a partition of Macedonia between Albania and Bulgaria—as happened during World War II, except with Turkey instead of Germany sponsoring the partition—although Bulgarians deny this possibility. Resistance to the Muslim Albanians, on the other hand, might mean falling back under Serbian domination (their pre-World War II situation) with Greek connivance. In the short run, the Greek embargo prolonged, and exacerbated, economic distress in the region but not enough to spark Macedonian-Albanian conflict and make these scenarios possible.

The pressures from within and without on Macedonian stability present a great challenge for peacekeeping troops, as a review of Urquhart's list of requirements shows. The first item on Urquhart's list, agreement by the parties, is not a serious problem because the most important parties—the Albanian and Macedonian leaderships—have agreed to the peacekeeping effort. And the last item, strong motivation for external parties to act, is also clearly present—a positive result of international fears of the kinds of "nightmare scenarios" mentioned above. The other two requirements, however, are more problematic.

Urquhart's second necessary condition, the parties' willingness to cooperate with the peacekeepers, is unstable. The original ouster of the moderate leaders of the ethnic Albanian PDP in early December 1993 was reportedly due to rank-and-file frustration that the leaders had not extracted enough concessions on ethnic issues for their constituents (*RFE/RL* 1993). Meanwhile, extreme nationalists among both Albanians and Macedonians formed terrorist groups (Perry 1992a: 38). They were most vocal during the Bosnia crisis, and their voices have since diminished. Today, in the relatively tense atmosphere of unresolved ethnic tension, exacerbated by economic woe, any sort of spark could set off a round of the sorts of violence—riots, terrorist attacks, or both—which peacekeepers are particularly ineffective at controlling.

If UNPREDEP were ever required to forcefully prevent escalation to full-scale civil war, then its actions would most likely resemble UNFICYP in Cyprus before 1974. Albanians live in scattered communities, but mostly in certain regions of northern and western Macedonia. Peacekeepers would be required to monitor areas of tension where armed people were facing each other and interpose themselves or negotiate cease-fires if shooting began. The existence of mixed towns including Skopje would make peacekeeping more difficult, but possible (see James, this volume).

Hypothetically, success in such an effort would depend primarily on the nature of the Macedonian government: Albanians in this scenario would be effectively autonomous; peace could be kept only if the Macedonian government were not determined to crush that autonomy (or if it were deterred from doing so by threats of foreign intervention). That condition, in turn, would require that the Macedonian moderates be able to keep the extremist forces out of power. Should the extremists come to power, bloodletting on the Bosnian scale would likely follow (even if a general Balkan war did not), and the peacekeepers would be relegated to the same degree of impotence faced by the peacekeepers in Bosnia in 1992–95.

The third item on Urquhart's list—the need for an appropriate mandate—is more ambiguous. What constitutes an appropriate mission—that is, a mission both possible and useful? In principle, UNPREDEP could have been expanded to embrace peacekeeping between ethnic groups inside Macedonia, should the need have arisen. In retrospect the peacekeepers' sponsors central hope was that the UN presence signaled to Serbia enough hardening of their flabby resolve to deter "ethnic cleansing" in Kosovo. Since the peacekeepers had no legal right to act in Kosovo without Serbian permission, that hope was, in retrospect, probably fatuous.

Today, an outbreak of severe violence in Kosovo remains a possibility. Albanian extremists in Kosovo may eventually succeed in pushing their moderate leader, Ibrahim Rugova, into stepping up violence against the Serbs, thereby provoking a Serb reaction. Alternatively but less likely is the rise to power of extremists in Serbia bent on cleansing Kosovo as well. In neither case would the Serbs be deterred by a lightly armed preventive deployment of UN troops. NATO's presence in Bosnia would surely have a more significant deterrent effect.

If the international community chooses to stay out of Kosovo itself, an expanded peacekeeping force could take on two important tasks to help prevent the conflict from spreading to Macedonia. First, it could assume primary responsibility for handling the refugee flows, keeping the refugees in Albanian-majority areas of Macedonia. This step would reduce friction between ethnic Macedonians and Albanians, thereby alleviating IMRO pressure on the Macedonian government. By relieving the Macedonian military of the necessity of working with the refugees, it would also reduce the likelihood of inadvertent conflict between the refugees—some of them probably armed—and the Macedonian army.

The second task of the peacekeepers in this scenario would be to patrol the Macedonian-Serbian border to prevent military attacks across it. In the absence of a UN presence, Albanian guerrillas could base themselves in northern Macedonia and launch raids into Serbia; the Serbs would surely retaliate against Macedonian territory, conceivably with a full-scale invasion and an attempt at annexation (possible even if Macedonia became their ally). The presence of peacekeepers (whether UN or NATO) might make it possible to create a peaceful sanctuary in Macedonia, which could be in the best interests of all sides. The Albanians would have to agree not to use Macedonia as a base of operations, in return for the safety of their refugees. The Serbs would have to agree not to attack Macedonia, in return for improved security on their southern border. And Macedonia would have to accept the refugees and peacekeepers in some regions, in return for the opportunity to maintain its neutrality and stability.

If the international community chose to address the problem in Kosovo itself, it might attempt to use peacekeepers to pacify the province. Serbia might conceivably agree to such action if it had a government more moderate than Milosevic's, which is not unlikely given the 1996 protests in Belgrade. If the alternative were full-scale war against one or more major powers, Milosevic or his successor is likely to back down at the slightest provocation. Even a moderate Serbian government, however, may feel obliged to appeal to Serbia's history of defiance of great powers and resist the foreign threat to Serbia's "Jerusalem." In this case, of course, no peacekeeping force could be deployed.

In the unlikely event the Serbs were to agree, the peacekeepers' main task would be to patrol Kosovo's border with Serbia proper to prevent the infiltration of Serb guerrillas. They would be successful if the guerrillas' chief were convinced (as the PLO was convinced in the UNIFIL case) that acquiescence was better for his cause than the alternative. The peacekeepers' second task would be to protect the local Serb population from the Albanians. Since the Albanians would have achieved their main goal—escape from Serbian administration—they would have little motivation to challenge the peacekeepers on that issue. Thus, as long as the external threat against the Serbian government remained credible and serious, the peacekeepers would be able to keep Kosovo pacified.

In summary, up until 1996, the success of preventive peacekeeping in Macedonia depended primarily on the nature of the problem they were called upon to address. If ethnic violence erupted within Macedonia, it was believed that peacekeepers could have prevented escalation to full-scale civil war (on the pre-1974 Cyprus model) if they were reinforced, and if both sides found the resulting status quo acceptable. The peacekeepers could in this case have done little to stop riots and terrorism, however, and Skopje would remain a focus of continued threats of escalation.

As of today, if Macedonia's simmering conflict was threatened by spillover from a violent conflict in Kosovo or Albania, the peacekeepers would have two options. They could contain the spillover by handling the refugee flow and patrolling the Macedonian-Serbian border. Alternatively, if the international community threatened military intervention, and if the Serbian government was susceptible to such coercion, Serbian agreement to peacekeepers' pacification of Kosovo itself might be obtainable.

CONCLUSIONS

Violent ethnic conflicts are intractable. They typically occur against a historical background of ethnic dominance and repression, so the stakes are perceived to be very high. Indeed, in many cases, one side (or both) fears that if it cannot achieve its maximal goals—often involving dominance over the other group—it is doomed to group extinction. When these conditions lead to intraethnic politics of extremist outflanking, protracted ethnic violence generally results. But if peacekeepers are introduced before ethnic outflanking goes too far—before ethnic extremists take power—they can contribute to prevention of ethnic violence.

Preventive peacekeeping can only work, however, if the conditions identified by Urquhart are satisfied. The key requirements are the agreement and cooperation of the parties: all sides must consider the status quo after the introduction of peacekeepers tolerable, and all must prefer that situation to a failure of the peacekeepers' mission. If leaders on either side are determined to end the status quo (as after the coup in Cyprus in 1974), they will succeed in rendering the peacekeepers irrelevant. In some cases, the leaders' calculus can be influenced by threats of external intervention, but as Lebow (1982) has shown, such expedients are uncertain: some leaders are simply not coercible, as the Serbs were not in 1991. In all cases, the situation must be serious enough to motivate the international community to take action, without providing any major power with an incentive to support one of the parties to the conflict against the peacekeepers.

Once these conditions are met, the details of the situation can vary. Peacekeeping is possible if the communities in conflict live interspersed with each other, as the Cyprus example shows. Thus, if the leaders of Yugoslavia had genuinely wished to find a compromise to allow their conflict to be managed, peacekeepers could have been effective in damping down the security dilemma in Krajina that fed the violence. Since they did not so wish, peacekeeping there would have been pointless.

Another case is when parties to a conflict are willing to allow specific areas to be neutralized, as the UNIFIL example from 1978 to 1982 shows. This is the reason that peacekeepers might be able to prevent the spread of any violence from Kosovo into Macedonia: all the concerned parties may conclude that neutralizing Macedonia is in their best interests.

Sadly, when ethnic conflicts reach the verge of violence, they tend to be more like Croatia in 1991 than Macedonia in 1993–96: extremists are usually in charge and hostile to the idea of introducing peacekeepers. The temptation in such circumstances is to impose cease-fires and have the peacekeepers show "resolve" by using force against violators. But any peacekeeping force that attempts to do so is likely to share the fate of the MNF in Lebanon—it will come to be perceived as a participant in the conflict. Since the parties' resolve is generally greater than the peacekeepers', such efforts will generally fail. Peacekeepers, in short, cannot make the parties want to stop fighting. If any party is determined to continue to fight, the best that peacekeepers can do is stay away.

NOTES

1. Azar (1986) argues that dependence on outside allies is typical of the syndrome of protracted ethnic conflict.

2. The organizational process model was first presented in Allison (1969). The idea of applying this model to international organizations is from Robert McCalla.

3. This definition is a simplified version of the International Peace Academy's definition of peacekeeping. For the original version, see the chapter by Ryan and the introductory chapter in this volume.

4. As noted above, conflict resolution theorists make a similar argument (see Haass 1990; Zartman 1985; 1990).

5. The phrase was Undersecretary of State George Ball's, quoted in Haass (1990: 65).

6. Probably the closest historical parallel is a series of plebiscites in Europe in the years after World War I, which were supervised by interna-

tional forces and designed to settle national boundaries essentially on ethnonational lines (James 1990: 23–36).

7. Editors' Note: The term used by Kaufman as preventive peacekeeping in Macedonia is more formally called preventive deployment. See chapters 1 and 3 of this volume for important distinctions between the general term preventive peacekeeping and the more specific term, preventive deployment.

8. Meadwell has suggested the term "elite-led nationalism," which refers to nationalism created by local elites in order to stem emigration from the areas they control (quoted in Rogowski 1985: 99). Elite-led ethnic violence is a different phenomenon: the nationalism is preexisting, and possibly quite old, but is aroused and manipulated toward violence by power-seeking leaders.

9. For example, the ambush of a Croatian police patrol in early May 1991—in some sense the first battle of the war—was probably the work of "chetniks" commanded by Vojislav Seselj and based in Bosnia-Herzegovina (*RFE* 1991: 18).

10. According to Montenegrin President Bulatovic, all six republican presidents in Yugoslavia were "captives" of their own policies by the middle of 1991 (Cohen 1993: 218).

11. The Maslenica Bridge, which was destroyed in the 1991 fighting, connected the Croatian heartland to the Dalmatian coast region. Without that bridge, Croatia was effectively cut in two, with no land link between the two portions. In January 1993 the Croatians launched an attack to recapture the bridge site and construct a pontoon bridge to reconnect its severed province. The attack succeeded and the bridge was built, but intermittent Serb shelling has forced its reconstruction several times. The fallout from the battle threatened to reignite all-out war in Croatia.

12. The 1991 census counted 429,562 Albanians, constituting 21 percent of Macedonia's population. Albanian leaders claim that many of their people did not participate in the census, partly because the census forms were available only in Macedonian (Perry 1992b: 15).

REFERENCES

Ackerman, Alice. 1996. "The Former Yugoslav Republic of Macedonia: A Relatively Successful Case of Conflict Prevention in Europe." *Security Dialogue* 27, no. 4: 409–24.
Allison, Graham. 1969. "Conceptual Models and the Cuban Missile Crisis." *American Political Science Review* 63: 689–718.
Andrejevich, Milan. 1990. "Croatia between Stability and Civil War Part II." *Radio Free Europe Report on Eastern Europe* 1: 39.
Austin, Robert. 1993. "Albanian-Macedonian Relations: Confrontation or Cooperation?" *RFE/RL Research Reports* 2: 42.

Azar, Edward E. 1986. "Protracted International Conflicts: Ten Propositions." In *International Conflict Resolution*, edited by Edward E. Azar and John W. Burton. Boulder, Colo.: Lynne Reinner.

Azar and Robert F. Haddad. 1986. "Lebanon: An Anomalous Conflict?" *Third World Quarterly* 8: 1337–50.

Banac, Ivo. 1984. *The National Question in Yugoslavia: Origins, History, Politics*. Ithaca: Cornell University Press.

Brass, Paul R. 1991. *Ethnicity and Nationalism*. Newbury Park, Cal.: Sage.

Brynen, Rex. 1990. *Sanctuary and Survival: The PLO in Lebanon*. Boulder, Colo.: Westview.

Bulgarian Academy of Sciences. 1978. *Macedonia: Documents and Material*. Sofia: Bulgarian Academy of Sciences Press.

Carment, David, and Patrick James. 1996. "Two-Level Games and Third Party Intervention: Evidence from Ethnic Conflict in the Balkans and South Asia." *Canadian Journal of Political Science* 29: 3.

Cohen, Lenard J. 1993. *Broken Bonds: The Disintegration of Yugoslavia*. Boulder, Colo.: Westview.

Comay, Michael. 1983. "UN Peacekeeping: The Israeli Experience." In *Peacekeeping: Appraisals and Proposals*, edited by Henry Wiseman. New York: Pergamon.

Connor, Walker. 1972. "Nation-Building or Nation-Destroying?" *World Politics* 24: 319–55.

———. 1973. "The Politics of Ethnonationalism." *Journal of International Affairs* 17: 1–21.

Crighton, Elizabeth, and Martha Abele Mac Iver. 1991. "The Evolution of Protracted Ethnic Conflict." *Comparative Politics* 23: 127–42.

Diehl, Paul F. 1993. *International Peacekeeping*. Baltimore: John Hopkins University Press.

Dragash, Nikola J. 1991. "Prepared Statement of Nikola J. Dragash." In *Civil Strife in Yugoslavia: The United States Response*. Hearing before the Subcommittee on European Affairs of the Committee on Foreign Relations, United States Senate. 21 February. S. Hrg. 102–12: 54–60.

Fisk, Robert. 1991. "'If We Take Fire . . . We're Gonna Return It': How a Peacekeeping Force Took Sides." In *The Multinational Force in Beirut, 1982–1984*, edited by Anthony McDermott and Kjell Skjelsbaek. Miami: Florida International University Press, 169–83.

Glenny, Misha. 1992. *The Fall of Yugoslavia: The Third Balkan War*. New York: Penguin.

———. 1993. "Is Macedonia Next?" *The New York Times*, 30 July 1993, A7.

Gurr, Ted Robert. 1993. *Minorities at Risk*. Washington, D.C.: US Institute of Peace.

———. 1970. *Why Men Rebel.* Princeton: Princeton University Press.

Haass, Richard N. 1990. *Conflicts Unending.* New Haven: Yale University Press.

Harbottle, Michael. 1970. *The Impartial Soldier.* London: Oxford University Press.

Heiberg, Marianne, and Johan Jorgen Holst. 1986. "Peacekeeping in Lebanon: Comparing UNIFIL and MNF." *Survival* 28, no. 5: 399–422.

Heraclides, Alexis. 1990. "Secessionist Minorities and External Involvement." *International Organization* 44: 341–78.

———. 1991. *The Self-Determination of Minorities in International Politics.* London: Frank Cass.

Horowitz, Donald. 1985. *Ethnic Groups in Conflict.* Berkeley: University of California Press.

James, Alan. 1990. *Peacekeeping in International Politics.* New York: St. Martin's.

Karns, Margaret P., and Karen A. Mingst. 1993. "Maintaining International Peace and Security: UN Peacekeeping and Peacemaking." In *World Security: Challenges for a New Century,* 2nd ed., edited by Michael T. Klare and Daniel C. Thomas. New York: St. Martin's.

Kaufman, Stuart. 1993. "Bush and the Mirage of Yugoslav Stability." Paper presented at International Studies Association conference in Acapulco, Mexico, March 26.

Laitin, David. 1991. "Four Nationality Games and Soviet Politics." *Journal of Soviet Nationality Studies* 2: 1–34.

Leatherman, Joanie. 1996. "Untying Macedonia's Gordian Knot: Preventive Diplomacy in the Southern Balkans." In *Preventive and Inventive Action in Intrastate Crises,* by J. Leatherman, W. De Mars, P. Gaffney, and R. Vayrynen. Manuscript under review.

Lebow, Richard Ned. 1982. *Between Peace and War.* Baltimore: Johns Hopkins University Press.

Lefever, Ernest W. 1967. *Uncertain Mandate: Politics of the U.N. Congo Operation.* Baltimore: Johns Hopkins University Press.

Melson, Robert, and Howard Wolpe. 1970. "Modernization and the Politics of Communalism: A Theoretical Perspective." *American Political Science Review* 64: 1112–30.

Miljus, Veljko. 1991. "Prepared Statement of Veljko Miljus." In *Civil Strife in Yugoslavia: The United States Response.* Hearing before the Subcommittee on European Affairs of the Committee on Foreign Relations, United States Senate, 21 February. S. Hrg. 102–12: 54–60.

Moore, Patrick. 1992a. "The 'Albanian Question' in the Former Yugoslavia." *RFE/RL Research Reports* 1: 14.

————. 1992b. "Kosovo Could Spark Another Balkan War." *RFE/RL Research Report* 1: 50.

The New York Times. 1993. "300 US Troops in Macedonia To Try To Contain Balkan War. July 13, A10.

The New York Times. "Newly Elected Rightist Pledges to 'Govern For All Salvadorans.'" 1994. April 26, A13.

Newman, Saul. 1991. "Does Modernization Breed Ethnic Political Conflict?" *World Politics* 43: 451–78.

Olive, David. 1992. *Political Babble: The 1,000 Dumbest Things Ever Said by Politicians*. New York: Wiley.

Pelcovits, Nathan A. 1991. "What Went Wrong." In *The Multinational Force in Beirut, 1982–1984*, edited by Anthony McDermott and Kjell Skjelsbaek. Miami: Florida International University Press, 37–79.

Perry, Duncan M. 1992a. "Macedonia: A Balkan Problem and a European Dilemma." *RFE/RL Research Report* 1: 15.

————. 1992b. "The Republic of Macedonia and the Odds for Survival." *RFE/RL Research Report* 1: 46.

Posen, Barry. 1993. "The Security Dilemma and Ethnic Conflict." *Survival* 35: 27–47.

Pribichevich, Stoyan. 1982. *Macedonia: Its People and History*. University Park: Pennsylvania State University Press.

RFE. 1991. *Radio Free Europe Report on Eastern Europe* 2: 23.

RFE/RL. 1993. *RFE/RL Daily Report* (December 3).

RFE/RL. 1994. *RFE/RL Daily Report* (February 17).

Rabushka, Alvin, and Kenneth A. Shepsle. 1972. *Politics in Plural Societies: A Theory of Democratic Stability*. Columbus: Charles E. Merrill.

Rogowski, Ronald. 1985. "Causes and Varieties of Nationalism: A Rationalist Account." In *New Nationalisms of the Developed West*, edited by Edward A. Tiryakian and Ronald Rogowski. Boston: Allen and Unwin.

Rothschild, Joseph. 1982. *Ethnopolitics*. New York: Columbia University Press.

Rusinow, Dennison. 1991. "Yugoslavia: Balkan Breakup?" *Foreign Policy* 83: 143–59.

Schiff, Ze'ev, and Ehud Ya'ari. 1984. *Israel's Lebanon War*. New York: Simon and Schuster.

Simic, Predrag. 1994. "The Former Yugoslavia: The Media and Violence." *RFE/RL Research Report* 3: 5: 40–47.

Sirriyeh, Hussein. 1989. *Lebanon: Dimensions of Conflict*. Adelphi Paper no. 243. London: International Institute for Strategic Studies.

Stegenga, James A. 1968. *The United Nations Force in Cyprus*. Columbus: Ohio State University Press.

Steinberg, James B. 1992. "The Role of European Institutions in Security after the Cold War: Some Lessons from Yugoslavia." Rand Note N-3445–AF. Santa Monica, Cal.: Rand.

Storck, Sylke Vonk. 1993. "European Political Cooperation: The Case of Yugoslavia." Master's thesis, University of Kentucky.

Tilly, Charles. 1991. "Ethnic Conflict in the Soviet Union." *Theory and Society* (October): 572–80.

————. 1978. *From Mobilization to Revolution*. Reading: Addison-Wesley.

Troebst, Stefan. 1994. "Macedonia: Powder Keg Defused?" *RFE/RL Research Report* 3, no. 4: 33–41.

United Nations. 1985. *The Blue Helmets*. New York: United Nations Department of Public Information.

Urquhart, Brian E. 1983. "Peacekeeping: A View from the Operational Center." In *Peacekeeping: Appraisals and Proposals,* edited by Henry Wiseman. New York: Pergamon.

Young, Crawford. 1976. *The Politics of Cultural Pluralism*. Madison: Wisconsin University Press.

Zartman, I. William. 1990. "Negotiations and Prenegotiations in Ethnic Conflict: The Beginning, the Middle, and the Ends." In *Conflict and Peacemaking in Multiethnic Societies,* edited by Joseph V. Montville. Lexington, Mass.: Lexington Books.

————. 1985. *Ripe for Resolution: Conflict and Intervention in Africa.* New York: Oxford University Press.

8

Deterrence Failure and Prolonged Ethnic Conflict

The Case of Bosnia

FRANK HARVEY

INTRODUCTION

Scholarship on Yugoslavia continues to theorize strictly in terms of ethnic conflict and ethnic mobilization. While these explanations offer very important clues about the root causes of the conflict, they are not sufficient to explain the onset (i.e., timing), escalation, and duration of the violence. This chapter examines the conflict in the former Yugoslavia through the prism of deterrence theory. Evidence shows that in almost every major encounter with the Bosnian Serbs between April 1993 and September 1994, US and European (NATO) officials failed to satisfy even the most basic strategic requirements of deterrence. These conditions include definition of unacceptable behavior, clear communication of a commitment to punish transgressors, and demonstration of intent (that is, resolve) to carry out retaliation. Instead, external powers either diluted or intentionally qualified most of their retaliatory threats. As failures mounted, Bosnian officials simply ignored subsequent efforts to control hostilities. In contrast, satisfaction of all three prerequisites for effective deterrence ultimately reestablished credibility and enabled the US and NATO to control fighting and obtain cooperation on key demands. Not only does deterrence offer a useful framework within which to describe and explain events in Yugoslavia, it also provides a set of specific policy guidelines with the potential to control hostilities and create an environment conducive to negotiating settlement of territorial claims.

As it will be shown in this chapter, there *are* instances when a situation is ripe for effective coercive diplomacy. These are conflicts that tend to be complex, intrastate disputes often equated with failed states. An extreme example is when an armed group operates outside the control of recognized political authorities and resists peacekeeping efforts (see Kaufman, and James, this volume).

The chapter unfolds in four stages. The first stage examines the theory of deterrence through a series of ten exchanges between US/NATO officials and Bosnian-Serb leaders (from April 1993 to September 1995) that constituted either immediate deterrence or compellence encounters, considers whether the prerequisites for effective use of these strategies were met, and assesses whether behavior in these cases was consistent with the theory's predictions. The second part describes the domestic and international forces that were obstacles to US/NATO involvement at the latter stages of the conflict and, in turn, leads to a discussion of policy recommendations. Stage three highlights the contributions of an approach that recommends identifying separate deterrence and compellence encounters within a single crisis, thus expanding the body of evidence that would be appropriate for testing a wide range of theoretical propositions while offering an alternative to the dominant strategy.[1] The fourth and final section concludes with a few thoughts on the enduring relevance of classical "realist" theories like deterrence to the study of international relations and ethnic conflict.

DETERRENCE FAILURE AND PROLONGED ETHNIC CONFLICT IN BOSNIA

Definitions and Methods

This section views the war in Yugoslavia through the prism of deterrence and compellence (DC) theory and strategy. The objective is threefold: (a) to isolate, for purposes of analysis, all exchanges between US/European (NATO) officials and the Bosnian-Serbs (between April 1993 and September 1995) that represent immediate deterrence encounters; (b) determine whether the behavior exhibited in these exchanges is consistent with expectations derived from DC theory; and (c) address the policy implications for US/NATO crisis management and peacekeeping efforts in a post-Cold War setting. Huth and Russett's definitions of deterrence and compellence will be used to distinguish the two categories of coercive threats:

Compellence is defined as an attempt by policy makers in state A to force, by threat and/or application of sanctions, the policy of state B to comply with the demands of state A, including but not limited to retracting actions already taken.... By contrast, in a situation of attempted deterrence, the threatened sanction is designed to prevent state B from taking actions it is considering but has not already initiated; thus the sanction would be employed only if the target undertook the action that the deterrer had sought to prevent. (1990: 475)

Although this distinction is useful there are exceptions that should be noted. For instance, if state A threatens retaliation to contain the spread of violence in a crisis, does this constitute an attempt to deter escalation or compel compliance with demands to keep the fighting to a minimum? Similarly, does one deter a state from rejecting the latest peace proposal or compel leaders to sign the accord? These questions are especially relevant in the case of Yugoslavia, because US/NATO threats attempted to accomplish both: (a) deter escalation, particularly with respect to ethnic cleansing, through the creation of "safe havens" and "no-fly zones"; and (b) compel the Bosnian-Serbs to accept the Vance-Owen peace accord or, at least, return to the bargaining table. Of course, even a relatively straightforward threat linked to protection of safe havens is problematic: Is the US trying to compel the Serbs to back away from territory bordering these "safe" towns, deter them from crossing the line or shelling the city, or both? The issue becomes even more confusing when one considers encounters that constitute examples of successful deterrence but failed compellence (and vice versa).

One advantage of breaking crises down into a series of separate exchanges, instead of assuming that the entire crisis can represent a single deterrence or compellence encounter, is that it becomes easier to pinpoint the precise time frame and exact sequence within which the appropriately designated threats, counterthreats, and responses were made. Although Huth and Russett (1990) and Lebow and Stein (1990) partially specified the class of deterrence they were concerned with (i.e., threats of military retaliation to deter military attacks), the potential for confusion is obvious. Regardless of their efforts to focus solely on features of the crisis that collectively appeared, on the surface, to be a military-security deterrence encounter, the behavioral properties associated with other classes of deterrence or compellence (e.g., economic or political) still may have influenced actions and outcomes.

The most relevant question, then, is whether US and European (NATO) encounters with the Bosnian-Serbs constituted specific instances of immediate deterrence or compellence (DC). If an immediate DC threat was not initiated, the exchange would be inappropriate for evaluating theory. Once a specific encounter is deemed relevant, the next step is to judge whether the threats succeeded or failed in accordance with the following prediction derived from DC theory: if leaders define the unacceptable behavior, communicate to challengers a commitment to punish any violation, possess the means (capability) to do so, and demonstrate the resolve to follow through with the retaliation, credibility will be high and the deterrent/compellent threat should succeed (Lebow and Stein 1989a: 53–55). If all of these conditions are satisfied but the behavior still occurs, that would constitute a case of DC failure—both in terms of theory and strategy. On the other hand, if the conditions are not satisfied, the theory predicts failure.

The first step is to identify all major statements, threats (implicit or explicit), and actions (e.g., sanctions, mobilization of force, demonstration of force, dispatch of diplomats, etc.) initiated by either the US and/or NATO between April 1993 and September 1995 to alter (deter or compel) the behavior of the Bosnian-Serbs. All major political and military responses to those threats also are identified. Special attention is given to the "timing" of the response (i.e., did it occur within minutes, hours, or days?). This is a crucial consideration when judging whether coercive threats succeeded or failed, and one that may account for discrepancies in case listings between Huth and Russett and Lebow and Stein.

The main source of data, given the current nature of the crisis under investigation, was the *New York Times* (and *New York Times Index*), which provides an excellent chronology and synopsis of events and interactions for the period in question. Detailed coverage of the crisis allows specification of the sequence of threats and an accurate assessment of provocation, retaliation, and response levels. Several additional sources were used—including *Time, Newsweek, US News and World Report* and the *Economist*—but coverage here was less specific and heavily policy oriented. It often focused on the technicalities of the peace accord without providing specific details about interactions.

None of these sources is capable of providing a definitive account of perceptions and intentions and can only offer a relatively accurate account of actions and reactions. Critics might point to the lack of information on subjective costs, benefits, and probabilities as an important problem, especially if the goal is to test propositions derived from DC theory. But leaders are constrained and encouraged by military, political, domestic, and systemic forces when making foreign policy and base their subjective estimates of costs and benefits on these concrete considerations; they do not simply pull utility estimates out of thin air. To imply that these factors are not important assumes that decisions are a product of internal psychological beliefs, perceptions, and intuition alone, with little if any connection to objective reality. If true, then we should not expect one theory to predict behavior any better than another, given the idiosyncratic nature of military and political calculations during crises.

On the other hand, if behavior appears to be consistent with theory, that would constitute an important finding. For purposes of testing DC theory, therefore, it is assumed that if a threat was issued and the proscribed behavior (noted in the ultimatum) did not take place, or if leaders were compelled to perform an act (stipulated in an ultimatum) that they previously had refused to do, that would constitute strong evidence that the threat had relevance. The onus, then, would be on critics to provide counterevidence that the threats were insignificant or offer a more compelling explanation for observed behavior.

Other skeptics might demand the use of primary documentation prior to making valid inferences about intentions or deterrence outcomes. After all, defenders (or challengers) may never have intended to retaliate (or attack) in the first place, and without access to the decision-making record it would be difficult to make those judgments. A few problems should be noted with respect to this claim. First, assuming one could gain access to such documentation (an exceedingly difficult thing to accomplish given the barriers to doing field research in Bosnia during the crisis), decision makers may not always understand their own motives or be able to articulate them (Huth and Russett 1990). Alternatively, they may be prone to articulating conflicting intentions, disguising them, or even changing their motives during official meetings. It would be a mistake, therefore, to assume that the decision-making record is essential to make valid inferences about deterrence theory.

Finally, Huth and Russett (1984, 1988, 1990), Lebow and Stein (1989a, 1990), James and Harvey (1992), Harvey and James (1994) and others have used information and data (in one form or another) obtained from primary documentation, yet all produce divergent case histories, disagree over decision-maker's knowledge, motives, perceptions, and intentions, and draw different conclusions about rational DC theory and strategy. Although the decision-making record is important, the record of actions, threats, counterthreats, and other forms of *observable* behavior (as reported in the sources used in this study) is equally important when assessing DC or, for that matter, any theory of coercive diplomacy. It certainly is true that the definitive link between theory and evidence will remain elusive without access to the minds of decision makers, but it would be a mistake then to conclude that inferences based on observable behavior are somehow prohibited simply because on occasion actions may not accurately represent intentions. This cannot possibly be true in every case, and the margin of error is likely to be sufficiently small to justify an approach that downplays that possibility. The alternative is to fully accept the inadequacy of such an approach, throw one's hands up in failure, and repudiate the entire enterprise. The relevant question is whether we would know more or less about crisis management and deterrence if we pursued that strategy.

With this in mind, the next stage reports on the ten exchanges between the US/NATO and the Bosnian Serb leadership that constituted immediate deterrence encounters. Each exchange will include a summary of events, a description of the threats and responses, a determination of the severity and credibility of the threat, and an evaluation of the outcome in terms of success and failure.

Exchange I

On 31 March 1993, the United Nations approved a plan to enforce a "no-fly zone" (NFZ) over Bosnia-Herzegovina, authorizing the use of NATO planes to shoot down aircraft or helicopters in violation of the order. The threat was designed to deter the Bosnian Serbs from mounting yet another offensive against Muslims in Bosnia and to compel Serbian political and military leaders to return to the bargaining table and sign the Vance-Owen peace accord. This was followed, the next day, with a more specific resolution threatening to impose tighter economic sanctions and trade restrictions on Serbia if the accord was rejected. On 2 April, NATO formally agreed to enforce the flight ban with jet fighters from the US, Britain, France, and the Netherlands and began patrolling the airspace over Bosnia ten days later (Riding 1993; Burns 1993).

From the point of view of satisfying the strategic requirements of compellence, the UN warnings fell short for several reasons. First, the threat of economic sanctions was directed against the leadership of the Serb Federation, namely Slobodan Milosevic, and would have affected the ability of Bosnian Serbs to continue their offensive only indirectly. Second, the list of economic sanctions in the original UN resolution was curtailed by a Russian threat of a Security Council veto. Yeltsin faced a particularly difficult position at home, most notably a 25 April referendum on power sharing in the Russian parliament. In an effort to appease hardliners who wanted to maintain a strong connection to Serbia, Yeltsin requested that the Security Council hold off on immediate sanctions until the referendum was over.

Second, the US refused to "unambiguously endorse" the Vance-Owen peace accord, ignoring strong appeals from Britain and France to offer greater support, and demanded that the resolution only "commend" the plan.[2] Third, unlike the NFZ established over Iraq, NATO pilots over Bosnia had severely limited options: Pilots were "not allowed to fire on civilian intruders or ground installations, even if they are attacked from them by missiles or antiaircraft fire" (Cowell 1993: A8). In addition, pilots were required to issue "several warnings" to unauthorized aircraft before firing. More importantly, there was no indication (or threat) that NATO planes would be used to "stop" the fighting; they had orders only to enforce the NFZ. Together, these factors undermined the ability of the UN, US, and NATO to mount a unified, credible threat of sufficient intensity (severity) to achieve its objectives. In fact, a few high-ranking UN officials believed, and stated publicly at the time, that the threats of a NFZ and economic sanctions would have a negligible affect on the ability of Bosnian Serbs to gain more territory.

The political response from the Serbian nationalist leadership was clear. Backed by a mandate from parliament, Karadzic not only refused to give even a modified conditional acceptance to the peace plan but issued his own warning that the leadership would reject any pressure to sign the accord and take retaliatory action in response to the sanction imposed on Serbia. On the military front, fighting escalated in Sarajevo and Srebrenica, with intense artillery barrages beginning "within minutes" of NATO's enforcement of the NFZ (Burns 1993: 1). The 123 reported deaths represented the largest number of casualties in a single shelling since Srebrenica came under attack seven months earlier. In addition to these battles, Bihac was reported to have suffered several casualties from attacks by some one hundred Serbian tanks around the same time.

For many of the reasons noted, neither the Bosnian Serb nor Serbian leadership in Yugoslavia took the compellent threats very seriously. With respect to the more specific deterrent threat tied to enforcement of the NFZ, there were no reported violations on the first day, although there may not have been any planned. In other words, the threat may have been insignificant because, until that point, there had been only one "verified combat violation" by Bosnian Serb aircraft since enactment of the NFZ six months earlier. However, activity and operations during the previous weeks did indicate that flights would have taken place, given unconfirmed reports from UN observers of some five hundred violations over the last four months (Lewis 1993a: A23). In any event, although the NFZ was not officially violated in the short term, there was open defiance of the ban once the NATO threat subsided and the commitment appeared to be weakening. Ironically, the decision by NATO to threaten retaliation only against flights over designated territories may have given the Bosnian Serb military more reason to step up shelling in defiance of NATO's relatively weak ultimatum.

Exchange II

On 17 April, the UN Security Council passed a resolution to impose the strongest economic sanctions on the Yugoslav Federation to date if the Bosnian Serb and Serbian leadership failed to endorse the Vance-Owen peace plan by 26 April. Intended to bring about the total economic and financial isolation of Serbia, the embargo would:

1. ban transhipment of any goods through Yugoslavia;

2. impose stricter controls on barges along the Danube River;

3. ban all ships entering Yugoslavian territorial waters and create a twelve-mile exclusion zone;

4. impound all trucks, ships, aircraft, or rolling stock in other countries; and

5. freeze all Yugoslav financial assets in foreign countries. (*New York Times*, 18 April 1993: 16)

The intent was to put direct pressure on Serbian leader Slobodan Milosevic to cut off all financial and military support of the Bosnian Serbs and, in so doing, compel them to return to the bargaining table. Although not a direct threat against the Serbian nationalists, the exchange does constitute at least two immediate compellence encounters: the UN's attempt (with strong backing from the US, Britain, and Russia) to compel Milosevic to endorse the accord, and Milosevic's subsequent efforts to pressure Karadzic to do the same (Lewis 1993).

The day after the UN announcement, the Serbian nationalist political leader stood firm on his commitment to reject the treaty, threatened to pull out of the negotiations altogether, and "waved off threats of direct military action with an air of both bravado and victimization" (Darnton 1993: A14). The official response to the UN ultimatum came in the form of a vote by the Bosnian Serb parliament on 23 April to reject the accord. On 27 April, one day after the UN deadline, Serbian forces (one thousand troops with ten tanks) mounted a new ground and artillery offensive against the Muslim town of Bihac. On the same day, the economic sanctions stipulated in the UN ultimatum took effect (Kinzer 1993a: A11).

Several things should be considered prior to making judgments about success and failure in this case. In terms of the initial compellent threat to impose a complete economic blockade on Serbia in exchange for endorsement of Vance-Owen, the threat appeared to work as predicted by the theory. The UN ultimatum was unambiguous, clearly communicated, and tied to a specific deadline. Moreover, there was a very strong commitment to follow through with sweeping economic sanctions if the presidents of Serbia, the Montenegrin Republic, and the Yugoslav Federation failed to endorse the peace plan and pressure the Bosnian Serbs to do the same. The resolve to follow through with the sanctions was bolstered by the overwhelming support the resolution received from every member of the Security Council, with abstentions from only Russia and China. In sum, the credibility of the threat was high and, from that point onward, Milosevic and Cosic expressed support for the peace accord and began a campaign to persuade the Bosnian Serb leadership to accept it as well.

This particular exchange poses an interesting empirical puzzle for those wishing to test DC theory. Conventional wisdom stipulates that once the defender follows through with the retaliatory threat, the strategy should be considered a failure. Ironically, retaliation did occur in this case, but not because the UN ultimatum lacked credibility or US/European resolve was questioned; the threat did compel Milosevic and Cosic to endorse the accord. It was Milosevic's subsequent attempt to compel Karadzic to sign the accord that failed. The threat by Milosevic to break economic and military ties with the Bosnian Serbs was not credible enough or sufficiently threatening to convince Karadzic or General Mladic that they should accept the accord. In fact, the Serbian nationalist weapons stocks were so extensive that they were actually selling arms to raise cash.

However, several things happened in the last week of April, shortly after the attacks on Bihac, that made Karadzic reconsider his position and return to the bargaining table. First, the referendum in Russia gave Yeltsin the mandate he needed to pursue a more aggressive foreign policy in the region, which included increasing the pressure on the Bosnian Serbs to return to the table. Also, on 29 April Milosevic sent a strongly worded letter to Karadzic informing him that, in light of the new sanctions against Serbia, he would be forced to cut off all military and economic aid to the Serb nationalists fighting in Bosnia (Sciolino 1993). At the same time, several high-level NATO meetings were being held to consider a more "assertive peacekeeping" role in Bosnia, which included the possible use of air strikes to stop the fighting around Sarajevo and Srebrenica. All of these pressures appeared to have an effect on Karadzic, who announced on 30 April that he now was prepared to resume peace talks in Athens.

Since the purpose of these threats was to compel Karadzic to sign the accord, the decision to resume talks could be interpreted as a partial compellence success. It should be noted, however, that as the Bosnian Serbs prepared for the new round of negotiations, their forces continued to shell Sarajevo, Srebrenica, and Bihac (Gordon 1993).

Exchange III

On 1 May, President Clinton agreed "in principle" to commit American airpower to end the fighting in the Balkans and to use US aircraft to protect Muslim areas from further Serb aggression. The threats were now being directed at the Bosnian Serb military and were designed to deter further escalation of the fighting. Although US military action at that time "was not imminent," Secretary of State Warren Christopher did warn Serb military leaders that the "clock is ticking" (Friedman 1993: A1). There also was a commitment in principle to lift the arms embargo against the Muslims and to use American fighter bombers to protect "safe havens" around Muslim villages in Bosnia. The plans were specific enough to indicate likely targets, including key bridges used for transporting military equipment and other supplies from Serbia to Serbian-held territory in Bosnia. The threats became much clearer and more specific in subsequent statements by Christopher that day. Three key demands were attached to the warnings: honor the cease-fire, stop shelling Muslim villages, and let the aid convoys continue with their missions. The assumption held by US officials was that the same "saber rattling" that brought Karadzic back to the bargaining table would deter General Mladic, the Serb military leader, from shelling Muslim villages.

On 2 May, Karadzic decided to sign the very same accord that his parliament rejected a week earlier, and he agreed to end the war in Bosnia. At the signing ceremony, Karadzic formally requested that the US drop its threats to use military force against the Bosnian Serbs. Another indication that the threat of military intervention played an important role in the decision was that several Bosnian Serb delegates stated publicly that the prospect of US military air strikes led them to reconsider support for the plan (Lewis 1993).

Exchange IV

On 6 May, the Bosnian Serb parliament voted 65–1 (with twelve abstentions) to reject the peace accord and to hold a second referendum. On the same day, Bosnian Serb gunners continued to attack Muslim areas in eastern and western Bosnia (Kinzer 1993b). In response to continued aggression, the UN Security Council designated six Muslim enclaves as protected "safe areas": Sarajevo, Tuzla, Zepa, Gorazde, Bihac, and Srebrenica (Prial 1993). The resolution, adopted unanimously, stipulated that these areas should be free of any form of military hostility, although it included no specific recommendation for how violations would be handled. Although European and Russian officials agreed with US demands for tougher action, they rejected the two main US proposals to lift the arms embargo against the Muslims and expand the air-strike mandate beyond the safe havens to enforce a more general cease-fire throughout the region. In both cases, the Europeans were concerned for the safety of their peacekeepers, who might become targets of Bosnian Serb retaliation. The Europeans recommended the stationing of US troops in Bosnia in order to reinforce the credibility of NATO threats, but US representatives on the council rejected that option. The gap between US and European interests appeared to be widening, which had a direct effect on NATO's ability to communicate a commitment to respond to Bosnian Serb aggression and to demonstrate resolve. The problem was compounded even further by a statement from the White House and State Department proclaiming that the US was doing all it could and that without European support it was unlikely that tougher actions would be taken to stop the fighting.[3] Without a serious commitment to impose costs on Karadzic and Mladic for violations, the balance of influence in the region remained with the Bosnian Serbs.

Obviously, US/NATO actions at this time did not amount to a very credible commitment to respond to Bosnian Serb aggression, and although Karadzic "promised" that they would "respect" the UN safe areas, Serbian nationalist forces broke through defense lines that surrounded Zepa, killing over five hundred people in the offensive (Prial, *New York Times* 1993). The attack did not appear to have any effect on the US or European approach toward the problem, and, as expected, the Bosnian Serb parliament voted for a third time to reject the Vance-Owen peace accord (51–2)—followed by yet another referendum in which 96 percent of the voters rejected the plan.

Exchange V

On 4 June 1993, the United Nations reinforced previous threats by authorizing air strikes to deter Bosnian Serb forces from attacking Muslim enclaves and by sending an additional twenty-five thousand peacekeepers to the region. The Russian delegation was the only cosponsor of the resolution to agree "in principle" to send ground forces to protect the safe areas, a commitment they subsequently withdrew on 12 June despite strong pleas from Britain and France. Subsequent comments by President Clinton at a news conference further undermined the credibility of UN/NATO threats:

> On Bosnia, I made a decision. The UN controls what happens in Bosnia, I cannot unilaterally lift the arms embargo. I didn't change my mind. Our allies decided that they weren't prepared to go that far this time. (quoted in *New York Times*, 1993)

On 18 June, the US began to signal its willingness to consider the Bosnian Serb proposal to partition Bosnia into three ethnic regions and began to put pressure on Itzebegovic to agree to the Serbian-Croatian partition plan, which stipulated that the Bosnian Serbs would keep most of the land acquired through the war. US officials became convinced that the Bosnian Muslims were not likely to gain back the territory lost to the Serbian forces and that the US was incapable of doing anything constructive without either European backing or stronger domestic support for a more assertive role in the region. Even European diplomats, previously convinced of the merits of Vance-Owen, began to give serious consideration to the Serbian-Croatian partition plan.

UN officials begin to state publicly that Western reluctance to carry out its threats had caused the fighting to worsen rapidly. Although Bosnian Serb political leaders promised once again to refrain from attacking the Muslim enclaves, their forces maintained regular attacks on Sarajevo, Gorazde, Bihac, Tuzla, and Srebrenica throughout June and July.

Exchange VI

On 1 August 1993, the US administration declared that it was now prepared to use airpower "unilaterally" to increase pressure on the Bosnian Serbs to end their attacks on Muslim safe havens, to allow safe passage for UN relief convoys, and to negotiate a peace settlement. More importantly, these air strikes would take place even without European support. According to a State Department spokesperson, "The United States, at this point, is determined to act in a more vigorous fashion as it relates to Bosnia" (Holmes 1993: A3). Under pressure from the US to take a more assertive role, NATO issued a formal warning to the Bosnian Serb military that if it did not cease attacks on Sarajevo and withdraw forces and heavy weapons behind the twenty-kilometer exclusion zone, NATO would engage in strategic bombing raids and air strikes against the Serbian military (Whitney 1993). This marked the beginning of a new, aggressive US strategy to mount an effective DC threat by creating consensus, not waiting for it. Also, recent Bosnian Serb attacks on French peacekeepers convinced European leaders that air strikes could actually prevent, instead of provoke, attacks on their troops. Large numbers of NATO aircraft were deployed to the region and began patrolling the NFZ, so the threat was explicit. The secretary-general, Manfred Woerner, of NATO issued a formal statement on 3 August stipulating the demands and outlining how the strikes would be coordinated. An unofficial deadline was set for the following Monday, 9 August, when NATO officials were to meet to decide whether Bosnian Serb forces "relaxed their grip on the city enough to avert western action" (Jehl 1993a).

The immediate response on 3 August was defiance, with Serb leaders warning of "dire consequences" and threatening to respond to attacks from the air with counterstrikes against UN peacekeepers on the ground (Burns 1993: A8). This was met with a retaliatory threat from both NATO and high-ranking officials of the US State Department: air strikes would be used to wipe out the nearly two thousand Serbian guns around Sarajevo, and the mission would succeed. Although some of the fighting in other areas of Bosnia continued, artillery attacks on Sarajevo stopped within hours of the NATO ultimatum. Two days later, Radovan Karadzic emerged from a meeting with UN officers to announce that he had agreed to pull the Bosnian Serb army back from the hills overlooking Sarajevo, they had begun operations to restore electricity, water, and gas services throughout Bosnia, and Bosnian Serb forces no longer would restrict relief convoys from reaching Muslims in the city.

On 11 August, the US reinforced previous NATO threats with a warning to the Serbian nationalist army that their heavy artillery must be removed from Sarajevo by 13 August or face air strikes (Jehl 1993b). Despite some diplomatic maneuvering over timing, weather problems, and the concern of Bosnian Serb commanders that a larger UN buffer force be deployed to protect retreating troops, the threat worked (Burns 1993). On 13 August the UN commander confirmed that the Bosnian Serb army indeed had pulled almost all of its troops back from the two mountain regions under dispute, pledged completion of the withdrawal by the next day, and allowed relief trucks and convoys to deliver supplies to Muslims in Sarajevo. This marked the first time since the war began that previously occupied territory had been given up by the Bosnian Serbs.

There was, however, one problem with mounting such an effective deterrent and compellent threat; it became apparent to Muslim leaders, namely Itzebegovic, that the tide of the war was changing in their favor, and that NATO threats possibly could be used to gain concessions on territory. As the US officials regained some confidence in the utility of coercive diplomacy, they began to back Muslim demands for territory. As a result, the Geneva talks broke down in August and completely collapsed in September, setting the stage for further escalation in the fighting.

Exchange VII

On 18 October 1993, in response to an increasing number of Bosnian Serb artillery attacks on Sarajevo (presumably to force the Bosnian Muslims to accept the partition plan), the US issued several "air strike" warnings (Binder 1993). But this time no schedule was established, nor were the threats backed by official statements (or costly signals) from the US State Department or NATO. The Bosnian Serb attacks on Sarajevo began as relatively minor probes to test NATO's resolve, but without a formal response the attacks increased in number and intensity over the next two months. The Bosnian Serb military became confident that the momentum for US/NATO air strikes had diminished. This was confirmed in statements by Secretary Christopher indicating that the US would be willing to send food and medicine to the region, but that no formal military response had been planned or was in the works.

It was not until 11 January that NATO issued a more formal "air strike" warning to stop the Bosnian Serb siege of Sarajevo, with European and Canadian members voicing their traditional concerns for peacekeepers and the possibility of retaliation (Apple 1994). This time NATO requested that UN commanders in Bosnia draw up plans for air support, implying that the decision was theirs to make. However, several attached regulations undermined the effectiveness and potency of the threat; UN commanders had to request air strikes and then recommend the action to the UN secretary-general. The secretary-general then would be required to issue a formal request to NATO, which would require a meeting of members for a vote.

As expected, the Bosnian Serbs ignored the warning and continued to shell Sarajevo (Sudetic 1994a). The most direct and devastating attack occurred on 5 February in a packed central market in Sarajevo, killing sixty-eight and wounding more than two hundred civilians.

Exchange VIII

On 9 February 1994, in response to the public outrage in the aftermath of the Sarajevo bombing, NATO issued an ultimatum to the Bosnian Serb leadership to end their siege on Sarajevo and withdraw forces and heavy weapons from around Sarajevo or face direct attacks from NATO bombers. This explicit threat was attached to a firm deadline of 21 February.

On 9 February (the day the threat was issued) the Serbian military commander agreed to an immediate cease-fire and to remove all heavy artillery from around Sarajevo (or place it under UN control). According to Lt. Gen. Sir Michael Rose, "it was the looming threat of NATO air strikes that had caused the Bosnian Serbs to agree to the cease-fire plan" (Kifner 1994a: A14). On 17 February, UN sources confirmed that Serb forces indeed were withdrawing from the Sarajevo area and that the withdrawal would be completed a day ahead of schedule. In Karadzic's words, "We have been withdrawing convoys and we will withdraw even more.... We have made our own desirable deadline.... We want to move as quickly as possible" (Kifner 1994b: A1). By 21 February, UN officials confirmed that almost all Bosnian Serb forces had withdrawn from Sarajevo, as occurred six months earlier under similar circumstances (Kifner 1994c). The Serbian army withdrew behind the twelve-mile exclusion zone and gave UN troops unimpeded access to the area to check for violations of the agreement. Even as the ultimatum was being met, Clinton continued to demonstrate American resolve by underscoring his intention to follow through with the air strikes should any of NATO's demands not be met and by preparing the American public (in a televised address) for the possibility of direct US involvement in the region to stop the fighting:

> Nobody should doubt NATO's resolve.... We are determined to make good on NATO's word. And we are prepared to act.... Our military goal will be straightforward: to exact a heavy price on those who refuse to comply with the ultimatum. (quoted in Cohen 1994: A1)

On 21 February, the day of the deadline, UN observers agreed that compliance with NATO demands had been complete, removing the need for air strikes. The Serbian nationalists turned in or moved to the other side of the exclusion zone 225 heavy weapons. There was some discussion that the Sarajevo experience could be used as a more general model for controlling the fighting around other safe havens.

On 28 February, US fighters shot down four Serb warplanes that were violating the UN flight ban over Bosnia (Gordon 1994). As on previous occasions, the Serbian military would wait for the pressure to subside and then initiate probes to test NATO's resolve to follow through on threats. The probes usually occurred when peace talks appeared to be heading in the right direction, inspiring European leaders to utilize a "wait and see" strategy. Unlike earlier exchanges, the immediate response by NATO aircraft this time was intended as a clear demonstration of NATO's resolve to enforce the no-fly zone.

Exchange IX

Two things happened in March 1994 that undermined the stability of NATO's deterrent threat and encouraged additional probes by the Bosnian Serbs around the safe haven of Gorazde on 9 April. First, Defense Secretary William Perry and several other high-ranking military officials publicly questioned whether threats of air strikes should be used, as they were in Sarajevo, to protect other safe havens, given differences in terrain and local grievances. The comparison to Vietnam was used to imply that US officials should consider carefully whether they wanted to become too involved in an area that is not directly tied to strategic or national interests. Second, although several US warplanes were prepared to retaliate against a Serbian attack on French peacekeepers, they were unable to respond in time because of a problem with communication in the chain of command. The original request for air strikes came from the French commander on the ground, went to the commander of peacekeeping forces in Bosnia, then to the commander of UN forces in Yugoslavia, and finally to Yasushi Akashi, the special representative of Secretary-General Boutros Boutros-Ghali, who had the power to authorize air strikes—two hours later. The UN official tried for approximately one hour to contact the Bosnian Serb military leader to inform him of the impending air strike if the attacks continued and then requested that NATO planes respond. The three-hour delay allowed the Bosnian Serb forces to escape with their weapons, and no air strike took place.

On 12 March 1994, after a mortar attack from Serb tanks against French blue-helmet positions in the south of Bihac, the UN called for intervention by NATO aviation. However, at the last minute the attack was canceled. The UN explained this was because of local atmospheric conditions and the fact the Serb cannons had stopped firing. Such intervention would have been the first allied close air support action in favor of UNPROFOR. The NATO version is somewhat different. In Naples, an AFSOUTH spokesman pointed out that the attack had not been canceled because of bad weather but simply because of the fact that UNPROFOR had not confirmed its request for an air strike. Diplomatic and military circles at the NATO headquarters in Brussels emphasized the slowness with which UN and UNPROFOR procedures were carried out as well as the hesitations in the UN's representative in Yugoslavia, who had reportedly allowed the attackers to withdraw from their positions.

Together, these events served to weaken US/NATO credibility and, after a six-week cease-fire, required that new threats be issued in response to attacks on Gorazde on 9 April (Lewis 1994). This time the threats came from the UN secretary-general, not NATO or the US, and only warned that the UN was "ready" to order air strikes. No specific deadline was set for a Serbian pullout, which, if previous actions are any indication, amounted to a threat that was not expected to have a very strong impact. The Serbs ignored the warning and continued shelling the city.

On 10 April, two NATO planes mounted a limited bombing attack (three bombs) on Serbian tank and command centers near Gorazde (Sudetic 1994b). Shelling apparently slowed down immediately after the air raid as Bosnian Serb commanders tried to assess the damage. On the morning of 11 April, after a lull in the shelling, the Serb army began another major offensive on Gorazde, which provoked a second (though more limited) bombing raid by NATO aircraft. Several direct warnings to General Mladic were issued by the UN Commander Rose, giving the general ten minutes to stop the fighting "or face another air attack." The threat was not carried out, although the Serbs did not actually stop firing until approximately two hours later (Sudetic 1994c).

The overall performance of NATO warplanes was less than impressive. A total of six bombs were dropped, two of which did not explode, and a British Harrier jet crashed in an attempt to bomb a Serbian tank. In addition, Serb antiaircraft fire shot down a French reconnaissance plane. Two UN soldiers were wounded and one died. The attacks were so limited that Mladic may have concluded that further limited damage was sustainable and that a victory in Gorazde would be worth it. It was clear from extent of damage caused by the air raids that they were no more than a "symbolic shot across the bow" (Gordon 1994: A1).

On 23 April, NATO issued a stronger ultimatum, modeled after the two Sarajevo exchanges. Two days later, the Bosnian Serb forces pulled all of their heavy weapons out of the exclusion zone, and the bombing raids, once again, were called off.[4]

Exchange X

NATO made several announcements, including the one of 22 April 1994, that if any Bosnian Serb attacks involving heavy weapons were carried out on UN designated safe areas, including Bihac, these weapons and other Bosnian Serb military assets, as well as their direct and essential support facilities, including but not limited to fuel installations and munitions sites, would be subject to NATO air strikes, in accordance with the procedural arrangements worked out between NATO and UNPROFOR following the council decisions of 2 and 9 August 1993 and a decision of 19 November 1994 authorizing air strikes in response to attacks against or which threaten the UN safe areas in Bosnia-Herzegovina. These strikes would be launched from the UN-protected areas in Croatia.

Several significant events from April to September 1995 shifted the balance of power in the former Yugoslavia away from the Bosnian Serbs. The Krajina region was recaptured by Croatian and Bosnian government forces in the most significant loss by rebel Serbs since the war began. Approximately two hundred thousand refugees relocated into Serb-controlled areas of Bosnia, producing an exodus that severely hampered Bosnian Serb military efforts in the region. Karadzic began to lose control over the political and military leadership by committing one of the biggest blunders of his career—threatening to fire General Mladic. Since few commanders shared the view of Mladic as a psychopath, his efforts failed. To make things worse for Karadzic, Milosevic joined the general in calling for his removal. Within a week, Mladic lost control of Krajina, gave up on a siege of Bihac, and was deterred from attacking Gorazde by a NATO threat of a massive air strike. NATO affirmed its determination to act in the same way for the other safe areas. The six "safe areas" (Gorazde, Sarajevo, Bihac, Zepa, Tuzla, and Srebrenica) were decreed as such in 1995 by resolutions 824 and 836 of the Security Council.

On 30 August 1995, NATO initiated a week-long series of selective air strikes against Serb positions. The operation, called "Deliberate Force," consisted of attacks by over sixty aircraft and the artillery pieces of the Rapid Reaction Force. The strikes were implemented more than two full years after Serb forces laid siege to Sarajevo and were intended to force the Serbs to remove their artillery aimed at UN-designated safe areas. On 20 November 1995, an agreement was reached and a cease-fire was obtained. The attempt by NATO to prevent attacks on Gorazde represented the strongest and most specific threat leveled against Mladic since the onset of hostilities four years earlier. The threat included a commitment to use US F16, F15E, and FA18 attack aircraft, British Tornadoes, and French Mirage fighters against three main targets:

1. Surface-to-air missiles (SAMs);

2. Troop formations and tank and artillery units; and

3. C31 installations around Pale.

The threat appeared to work, so NATO officials extended coverage to the other safe areas. In response to another Bosnian Serb mortar attack on Sarajevo, approximately one month later, NATO mounted one of the most extensive campaigns in its history. The objective was to compel Mladic to pull heavy weapons behind the twenty-kilometer exclusion zone, open the Sarajevo airport, and allow free access for relief convoys to deliver aid and supplies. The plan was given full and complete support by the UN.

On 15 December 1995, the United Nation Security Council—acting under chapter VII of the charter of the UN—adopted resolution 1031, which authorized the member states of NATO to establish the NATO implementation force (IFOR), under unified command and control and composed of ground, air, and maritime units from NATO and non-NATO nations, to ensure compliance with the relevant provisions of the Dayton peace agreement. On the one hand, the decision to deploy a sixty-thousand-person force in Bosnia was the logical next step for that organization. From the beginning of the Bosnian conflict, NATO carried out peace support operations on behalf of the UN through an enforcement of an embargo and a no-fly zone. On the other hand, the cost to the UN has been considerable. While the organization's disengagement from the Bosnian peace process is significant, a more long-term set of issues turns on the credibility and capacity of the UN to intervene on behalf of beleaguered minorities. In Bosnia, mutual hatred among the three major ethnic groups is exceeded only by their collective distrust of the UN.

The subsequent 1995 Dayton accord also came at a cost: exclusion of the Bosnian Serb leaders from the negotiating table and substantial territorial gains for Bosnian Croats in comparison to what was being offered them under Vance-Owen (see Fortman, Roussel, and Martin, this volume). In essence, territorial boundaries gained through military means were legitimate. The Bosnian Serbs' territorial stranglehold was reduced to 49 percent of Bosnian territory, with the Bosnian Croat and Muslim coalition taking the balance. By most standards, the accord merely reaffirmed what had long been recognized: Bosnia would be two effectively independent nations, and the Bosnian Muslims, although a numerical majority, would be left in the political wilderness.

LESSONS

In each encounter, the behavior of Serbian military and political officials invariably supported predictions of classical deterrence and compellence theory. Consistent with expectations, satisfaction of strategic requirements established the credibility of US/NATO threats and achieved immediate objectives. When commitments were weak or ambiguous, they would be challenged by the Bosnian Serbs. As failures mounted, both Karadzic and Mladic ignored subsequent efforts to stop the fighting, until enough support was generated to mount the next clear retaliatory threat. In sum, coercive diplomacy succeeded and failed for all the right reasons.

Comprehensive understanding of how deterrence and compellence worked in Bosnia requires analysis of the barriers that often prevented the US, NATO, and UN forces from mounting a successful strategy. Some of these impediments are specific to the Bosnian case but most are endemic to international politics in a post–Cold War world. For example, the ability to generate the international consensus required to mount an effective, credible DC threat is becoming increasingly limited. In the case of Bosnia, initial divisions within NATO forced many of the retaliatory threats to be diluted. The Europeans were reluctant from the outset to use air strikes against the Serbs because of potential retaliation against their peacekeepers. Initially, Britain and France agreed to participate in the UN force only if the US refrained from introducing airpower. The presence of their troops on the ground in Bosnia gave them what amounted to a veto over US policy. When Europeans began to reject several key US demands (e.g., lifting the arms embargo against the Muslims), the split in the alliance had a direct effect on the peace process.[5] As Weiss (1994) observed,

> Inadequate military and humanitarian action, combined with half-hearted sanctions and a negotiating charade constituted a powerful diversion. They collectively impeded more vigorous western diplomatic and military pressure to lift the arms embargo for Muslims to help level the killing field. (123)

The US was in a difficult position of having to negotiate with Serbia, Croatia, Bosnia, Bosnian Serbs, Europeans, Canadians, Russians, the UN, and NATO, each of which had its agenda and special concerns. Domestic pressures in each capital became paramount and had a direct effect on any one leader's ability to generate consensus on a wide array of issues (Lieber 1994). During the Cold War, when bargaining efforts were directed against a single opponent over a relatively straightforward set of issues, international politics was less complex. Now that the Cold War is over, demands for international consensus are increasing but our capacity to generate it is diminishing. This is precisely why it is so difficult to replace the current strategy, which is to establish short-term commitments to reach quick solutions to complex problems with only a minimum risk of casualties.[6]

In addition to debates within NATO, there were equally important divisions in (and between) the White House and Congress. Colin Powell and Warren Christopher constantly pushed for a more restrained and cautious approach to the crisis, while Les Aspin, Madeleine Albright, and NSC Advisor Anthony Lake were convinced that air strikes were needed to control the fighting.[7] The "lift and strike" policy was developed only after Congress demanded that Clinton outline an official US strategy (Berdal 1994). Of all the alternatives considered, there was never any real commitment to send US ground forces to the region. The exclusion of this option from the outset gave European and Bosnian Serb leaders the impression that there never would be a moral imperative pushing the Americans to become formally involved. As Secretary Christopher stated, "Bosnia may be a human tragedy but it does not affect our vital security interests except as we're concerned about humanitarian matters and except as we're trying to contain it" (quoted in Berdal 1994: 37). Even when there was a moral imperative to respond (as occurred in the aftermath of the 5 February market bombing), the American public remained highly sensitive to casualties and continued to reject large-scale American intervention. Clinton was placed in a position of having to "reconcile two conflicting aspirations: demonstrating resolve while avoiding measures that would place American lives at risk" (Berdal 1994: 37). The Bosnian dilemma was particularly damaging to Clinton because there was never any real political capital to be gained, even if the policy succeeded. Unlike Republicans, Democrats consistently rank foreign policy low on their list of priorities come election time (Lieber 1994).

POLICY RECOMMENDATIONS: EXTENDED DETERRENCE AND PREVENTIVE DIPLOMACY

According to George (1991), policy-relevant theory may take on three distinct qualities. It may be diagnostic, whereby emphasis is placed on describing how and why things work. It may also take the form of a conditional generalization—i.e., in situation X, if one does Y, one should expect Z. Finally, policy-relevant theory may be prescriptive, offering explicit recommendations to policy-makers faced with certain kinds of problems. Deterrence theory encompasses all of these qualities. The evidence from the ten exchanges, for example, illustrates quite clearly the utility of DC theory in both the "diagnostic" and "conditional generalization" sense; it provides a useful framework within which to describe, explain, and predict events in Yugoslavia. More importantly, DC theory is highly prescriptive in content, offering a set of specific policy guidelines with the potential to control hostilities in Bosnia and create an environment conducive to peaceful settlement of territorial disputes. This section outlines policy recommendations derived from theory and evidence.

To begin, preferences over solutions to ethnic conflict often depend on the explanations we accept for the violence. If one emphasizes root causes (e.g., primordialism, relative deprivations, pluralism, etc.), the list of possible solutions would include partition, power sharing, democratization, constitutional entrenchment of ethnic minority rights, proportional division of key offices, mutual vetoes, etc. But without an end to the fighting, debates about root causes and solutions to underlying problems will remain futile. They offer no guidelines when fighting breaks out, territory is lost, or the death toll is in the hundreds of thousands, threatening to create yet another generation of fear and war.

The recommendations offered here focus exclusively on ending the violence and creating an environment for negotiation, obviously a more immediate priority for the people living and dying in the region. As the evidence from this chapter indicates, the protracted nature of the fighting in Bosnia is not a product of pluralism, primordialism, or relative deprivation but a direct consequence of decisions by political and military officials on all sides of the dispute. Ethnicity and religion may account for the mutual hatred underlying the fighting, but the war itself was waged with specific objectives in mind—e.g., territory, access to key waterways, transportation and trade routes, or survival. Decisions by Bosnian Serb leaders to escalate the violence depended entirely on the prospects of winning and losing particular battles.

Evidence from the ten exchanges shows that whenever US and NATO leaders mounted a prolonged and stable DC threat backed by ultimatums, deadlines, and a clear commitment to punish, credibility was high and coercive diplomacy worked to stop the fighting. On the other hand, weak threats actually promoted violence. The most important lesson: do it right or not at all (Weiss 1994). Bloomfield (1994) made a similar argument:

> If the European powers (and the United States) had moved early to confront the latter-day vandals off Dubrovnik, or to actively protect relief supplies and UN peacekeepers at Sarajevo airport when first fired upon, or had consistently punished violations of their no-fly zones, things might have turned out differently. (158)

One important benefit of swift and intense retaliation is that it promises to quickly eliminate the threat that triggered the deployment, so that pressure from the public to leave can be satisfied without facing the prospect of withdrawing with the threat left hanging (Alan 1994: 204).[8] Skeptics offer Vietnam as a warning against such a strategy, but the analogy is misleading because the US was attempting to win that war, not stop the fighting.[9]

The potential benefits of such a strategy go well beyond Bosnia, as Clinton himself acknowledged in April 1993:

> I think we have an interest in standing up against the principle of ethnic cleansing. If you look at the turmoil all through the Balkans, if you look at other places where this could play itself out in other parts of the world, *this is not just about Bosnia*. (quoted in *New York Times*, 17 April 1993: 4—emphasis added)

It is imperative, therefore, that the US and NATO, with UN backing, develop a policy of extended conventional deterrence based on a comprehensive set of guidelines to prevent ethnic violence from reaching the levels it has in Yugoslavia. Policy failures in Bosnia will have a direct impact on the probability of success in other regions, so establishing a strong and credible reputation for responding (without hesitation) to protect peacekeepers and control the violence is crucial.

Alan (1994) recommended several specific strategies that would help to insure success. The general deterrent threat must be "asymmetrical in application, intense and overwhelming in its offensive, with a capability for punishment as well as denial, and extended globally through new technologies and weapons systems" (208). Punishment should be precise and tailored to the "values of the targeted regime," and "must be disproportionate in order to convey the seriousness of challenging US interests and preventing US from becoming involved in a protracted conflict"(208). All of these measures are expected to establish a stable deterrent threat by codifying commitments and resolve.[10] The core assumption, indirectly supported by evidence from the ten encounters with the Bosnian Serbs, is that a series of overwhelming US-led victories would create a period of stability "while potential adversaries search for real or perceived weaknesses in US strategy" (208).

Critics might claim that relentless US/NATO bombing at such high levels would have exacted sweeping concessions from the Bosnian Serbs, but because the policy requires such a radical shift in Western and UN attitudes, it was simply unrealistic (Gompert 1994). A crucial component of the policy, however, was an aggressive publicity campaign to sell the strategy to the public. As Bloomfield (1994) noted, "with its powers of shame, embarrassment and ridicule, publicity has become a powerful diplomatic instrument" (157–58). Publicizing the effects of Bosnian Serb shelling and ethnic cleansing, for example, would have provided US and European officials with the ammunition needed to convince the public of the merits of a more assertive role in the region.

DETERRENCE EXCHANGES IN CRISES:
AN ALTERNATIVE TO HUTH-RUSSETT VS. LEBOW-STEIN

Valid testing of rational DC theory has always depended on the ability of scholars to identify a body of evidence that would be appropriate for testing a wide range of propositions. Unfortunately, notwithstanding the many efforts to produce a suitable list of cases, cumulative knowledge about deterrence and compellence, both as theories and strategies, remains elusive. The most prominent testing strategy, designed by Huth and Russett (1984, 1988, 1990) and criticized and revised by Lebow and Stein (1987, 1989a, 1989b, 1990), recommends identifying cases of deterrence successes and failures, isolating conditions that were present during successes and absent during failures or vice versa, and, based on these differences, drawing conclusions about why and how deterrence works.

The lack of correspondence or convergence in the empirical domain of the research program represents the most significant obstacle for those using this approach. Several potentially controversial coding decisions must be made prior to testing propositions (Harvey and James 1994).[11] Given this complexity, it is almost impossible for this form of testing of deterrence theory to produce a definitive interpretation of the historical record. There are multiple reasons available to accept or reject the coding of any case. Although disputes over the accuracy of historical accounts can be useful, lingering divisions over coding have become counterproductive. Indeed, there has been almost no effort to develop alternative testing strategies or evaluate a wider range of propositions derived from the theory. Two recent exceptions are Harvey and James (1994) and Lieberman (1994).[12]

The present study offers a third alternative that recommends dissecting individual crises by identifying separate deterrence and compellence encounters. This approach expands the pool of evidence that would be appropriate for testing the theory. The problem with the approach used by Lebow and Stein (1990) is with their assumption that each crisis encompasses within it a single encounter and that as long as the particular class of deterrence or compellence is specified[13] and the sample of crises is "sufficiently alike in theoretical terms," the cases can be compared (Huth and Russett 1990: 473). But given that every crisis contains elements of different types of interactions, case selection and coding becomes extremely difficult, particularly if the researcher must pinpoint the precise time frame and exact sequence within which the appropriately designated threats and counterthreats were made (Harvey and James 1994). Most of these pitfalls do not apply here because only a single crisis, representing a series of DC successes and failures, was studied. The approach is expected to provide a more valid test of the theory that goes beyond debates over methods and case selection.

CONCLUSION: THE ENDURING RELEVANCE OF "REALIST" THEORIES

A study of deterrence, a relatively abstract theory derived from analysis of states in anarchy, has an important role in the study of ethnic conflict and development of foreign policy. State-centric models like deterrence and compellence remain central to the research program on international and interethnic relations. Not only do they provide greater theoretical clarity but more importantly, the commitment to sovereign statehood remains a common objective for both old and newly developing states (James 1993).[14] Writing more than thirty-five years ago, Wolfers (1959) concluded:

> Psychologically, nothing is more striking today than the way in which men in almost every part of the world come to value those possessions upon which independent national statehood depends ... (and) are willing to make the most sweeping sacrifices of their own well-being as private individuals in the interest of their nation. (10)

As we approach the twenty-first century, commitments to "statism" have not diminished. On the contrary, the war in Yugoslavia, demands for sovereignty by the Baltic republics in 1989–1991, ethnic turmoil throughout Central Asia and Africa, and even separatist movements from Czechoslovakia to Canada are sufficient evidence that very little has changed in this regard. Furthermore, ethnic nationalist movements—often cited as increasingly important, nonstate actors—seek statehood, not transformation of the system. Analyses of the dynamics of international politics must take into account that a great deal of global activity, particularly with respect to questions of war and peace but not limited to them, will continue to be a product of structures and strategic processes specified in the realist paradigm. To claim that Bosnian Serbs and Muslims do not represent states in the conventional sense is true but misleading, especially within the context of crisis and war; these groups possess armies, political and military representatives, institutions of government, and territorial claims.

Is the challenge to international relations scholarship today "not to contribute to the construction of universal and absolute knowledge, but to devise a *fresh perspective* useful for framing and working on the problems of the present," as Cox (1992: 132) recommended? Is it true that "we need new thinking for a veritable new world order: a post-realist critical theory of world social relations at the end of the twentieth century" (Scholte 1994: 1)? The answer to these questions, which underscores the epistemological basis of this chapter, is no. There is a tendency in scholarship on international relations, as Holsti (1985) observed almost ten years ago, "to develop theoretical innovations on the basis of recent diplomatic developments ... before these developments have assumed the character of long-term trends or patterns of behaviour" (131). The inference that nothing of value has been gained from the last forty years of research on the causes and consequences of interstate war and ethnic conflict, that nothing of substance has emerged to facilitate an understanding of the properties of this form of violence and the prospects for stability, and that a radically new approach is required to assess the implications of change and strategies appropriate to deal with it, is highly premature. We cannot assume that contemporary events are sufficient to render the contributions of an entire research program (and practically all of its underlying realist assumptions) superfluous. It would be dangerous, to say the least, to ignore the diagnostic and prescriptive qualities of deterrence and compellence theory, particularly if we want to learn how to manage the next ethnic war.

NOTES

1. Russett (1963) introduced that strategy, which culminated in the debate involving Huth and Russett (1984, 1988, 1990) and Lebow and Stein (1987, 1989a, 1989b, 1990).

2. This prompted speculation that US officials were worried about the precedent a stronger statement would set for Israeli compliance with similar UN resolutions.

3. "The White House was not in the grip of war planning and there were no special deployments of American aircraft or military personnel in preparation for action in Bosnia" (Friedman 1993: A1).

4. For a detailed discussion of the events, see Carment 1995.

5. There were serious problems with the policy from the beginning: rearming the Muslims threatened to escalate the fighting and provoke an immediate Serbian offensive to win the war in order to gain advantage before the weapons reached the Muslims. There also were several logistical problems related to delivery and training that would be difficult to overcome.

6. The strategy will continue to produce a variety of outcomes, depending on the region and the politics in question. Some cases will be easier to handle and sell to the public—e.g., protecting famine relief was easier in Somalia than in Bosnia; enforcing a no-fly zone around Iraq was easier than it was in Sarajevo and Gorazde. Although Iraq's army was more formidable, much more credible threats were mounted (Bloomfield 1994).

7. On the utility of air strikes as a deterrent force and the debate in the White House, see Engelberg (with Gordon) 1993.

8. See also George (1991), Record (1993), and Garfinkle (1991) on this point.

9. Gompert (1994) recommends conducting a cold war against Serbia, "one of indefinite duration but certain outcome—while in the meantime using NATO's military power more effectively to ensure that relief reaches Bosnia's innocent victims" (32).

10. For example, Bloomfield (1994: 157) recommends giving the international community's rule book a "sharper set of teeth" by having the UN Genocide Convention, the Fourth Geneva Convention and other laws "expanded to cover slow motion genocide" as in Yugoslavia (1994: 157).

11. These issues are dealt with extensively elsewhere (Jervis 1979; Jervis, Lebow and Stein 1987; Levy 1988; Pages 1991; Harvey and James 1994, Lieberman 1994). In addition to separating cases of attempted deterrence from those of attempted compellence, distinguishing immediate and general forms of the threat, and identifying "successes" and "failures," the approach also requires specification of attacker and defender roles, despite potential variation in the same crisis.

12. Harvey and James use a less rigid set of operational criteria to test deterrence in the domain of US-Soviet rivalry. Most of the coding controversies noted above do not apply to identification of superpower crises, because there are far fewer potentially controversial decisions to make

about whether officials perceive (1) *a threat to basic values,* with a simultaneous or subsequent awareness of (2) *finite time for response,* and (3) *high probability of involvement in military hostilities.* The findings confirm the results of this chapter, namely, that US/Soviet leaders acted in a way that confirmed DC theory. Lieberman also expanded the empirical domain of deterrence theory by solving the problem of selection bias. Instead of focusing on individual cases of deterrence failure, he argues that a valid test of DC theory requires an approach that looks at the impact of reputations on perceptions of capability, commitment, and resolve. Based on an assessment of deterrence relationships within enduring rivalries in Middle East, he concludes that Egyptian and Israeli behavior in almost every major encounter supports the theory.

13. "The sanction threatened by state A may be based on military or non-military means (economic or diplomatic, for example) and the action which state B may take in pursuit of its policy goals may entail the use of military force or be non-military in nature.... The fundamental differences in the policy instruments used by state A to deter, and the types of policy actions being considered by state B, suggest that theoretical propositions on success or failure in one class of cases *cannot readily be applied to other cases.... State B may be vulnerable to military retaliation by state A but may not be vulnerable economically"* (emphasis added). Craig and George (1990) provide a practical example of this complexity in their study of the 1973 Yom-Kippur war. Despite diplomatic efforts, "the United States was unable to guarantee Israel's security from a variety of Arab threats ranging from economic blockade to terrorists attacks to full scale offensives by conventional forces.... [T]he deterring powers found themselves forced to re-evaluate their commitments as the dissatisfied powers altered their strategies in accordance with perceived weaknesses in *these commitments"* (139—emphasis added).

14. James (1993: 23) also notes that there still is considerable impressionistic evidence in favor of state-centrism, citing Deutsch's 1988 observation regarding the "25–1 (aggregate) ratio of state spending power as compared to that of international organizations" (45).

REFERENCES

Alan, Charles T. 1994. "Extended Conventional Deterrence: In from the Cold and out of the Nuclear Freeze." *Washington Quarterly* 17: 203–33.

Apple, R. W. 1994. "NATO Again Plans Possible Air Raids on Serbs in Bosnia." *New York Times,* 12 January, A1.

Azar, Edward E., and Robert Haddad 1986. "Lebanon: An Anomalous Conflict?" *Third World Quarterly* 8: 1337–50.

Barth, F., ed. 1969. *Ethnic Groups and Boundaries: The Social Organi-*

zation of Cultural Differences. Boston: Little, Brown.

Bell, Daniel 1975. "Ethnicity and Social Change." In *Ethnicity, Theory and Experience*, edited by Nathan Glazer and Daniel P. Moynihan. Cambridge: Harvard University Press, 141–71.

Berdal, Mats. 1994. "Fateful Encounter: The United States and UN Peacekeeping." *Survival* 1: 30–50.

Binder, David. 1993. "U.S. Renews Warning to Serbs on Sarajevo Shelling." *New York Times*, 19 October, A8.

Bloomfield, Lincoln P. 1994. "The Premature Burial of Global Law and Order: Looking beyond the Three Cases from Hell." *Washington Quarterly* 17: 145–61.

Burns, John F. 1993. "Dawn Brings a Ray of Hope to a Newly Silent Sarajevo." *New York Times*, 4 August, A8.

Carment, David. 1995. "NATO and the International Politics of Ethnic Conflict: Perspectives on Theory and Policy." *Contemporary Security Policy* no. 4 (winter): 4.

Connor, Walker. 1973. "The Politics of Ethnonationalism." *Journal of International Affairs* 17: 1–21.

Cowell, Alan. 1993. "NATO Jets to Enforce Ban on Illegal Bosnia Flights." *New York Times*, 12 April, A8.

Cox, Robert. 1992. "Towards a Post-Hegemonic Conceptualization of World Order: Reflection on the Relevancy of Ibn Khaladin." In *Governance without Government: Order and Change in World Politics*, edited by J. N. Rosenau and Ernst-Otto Czempiel. Cambridge and New York: Cambridge University Press, 347–79.

Craig, Gordon A., and Alexander George. 1990. *Force and Statecraft: Diplomatic Problems of Our Time*. New York: Oxford University Press.

Crighton, Elizabeth, and Martha Abele Mac Iver. 1991. "The Evolution of Protracted Ethnic Conflict." *Comparative Politics* 23: 127–42.

Darnton, John. 1993. "Leader of Bosnian Serbs Remains Firmly against Peace Plan, despite U.N. Pressure." *New York Times*, 19 April, A14.

Despres, L. A . 1967. *Cultural Pluralism and National Politics in British Guiana*. Chicago: Rand-McNally.

———, ed. 1976. *Ethnicity and Resource Competition in Plural Societies*. Paris: Mouton.

Deutsch, Karl. 1961. "Social Mobilization and Political Development." *American Political Science Review* 55: 493–514.

———. 1988. *The Analysis of International Relations*. 3rd ed. Englewood Cliffs, N.J.: Prentice-Hall.

Diehl, Paul F. 1993. *International Peacekeeping*. Baltimore: Johns Hopkins University Press.

Engelberg, Stephen, with Michael Gordon. 1993. "Clinton Is Caught by Bosnian Dilemma." *New York Times,* 4 April, A4.

Friedman, Thomas L. 1993a. "Bosnia Air Strikes Backed by Clinton, His Officials Say." *New York Times,* 2 May, A1, A12.
—— 1993b. *New York Times,* 9 May, A1.
Furnivall, J. S. 1948. *Colonial Policy and Practice.* London: Cambridge University Press.
Garfinkle, Adam. 1991. "The Gulf War: Was It Worth It?" *World & I* 6: 70–79.
Geertz, Clifford. 1973. *The Interpretation of Culture: Selected Essays.* New York: Basic Books.
Gelner, E. 1964. *Thought and Change.* London: Weindenfeld and Nicholson.
George, Alexander. 1991. *Forceful Persuasion: Coercive Diplomacy as an Alternative to War.* Washington, D.C.: U.S. Institute of Peace Press.
Gompert, David. 1994. "How to Defeat Serbia." *Foreign Affairs* 73: 30–47.
Gordon, Michael R. 1993. "Clinton Says U.S. Pressure Nudged Serbs back to Talks." *New York Times,* 1 May, A6.
—— 1994. "The Bluff that Failed." *New York Times,* 19 April, A1.
Gurr, Ted Robert. 1991. *Minorities at Risk.* Washington, D.C.: US Institute of Peace.
——. 1970. *Why Men Rebel.* Princeton: Princeton University Press.
Harvey, Frank, and Patrick James. 1994. "Nuclear Deterrence Theory: The Record of Aggregate Testing and an Alternative Research Agenda." *Conflict Management and Peace Science* 12: 17–45.
——. 1994. "Nuclear Powers at the Brink: Toward a Multi-Stage Game of Crisis Interaction." Paper presented at the Sixteenth World Congress of the International Political Science Association, Berlin, August.
Hechter, M. 1975. *Internal Colonialism: The Celtic Fringe in British National Development, 1536–1966.* Berkeley: University of California Press.
——. 1986. "Theories of Ethnic Relations." In *The Primordial Challenge: Ethnicity in the Contemporary World,* edited by J. F. Stack, Jr. New York and London: Greenwood.
Holmes, Steven A. 1993. "U.S. May Attack Serbs Even without NATO." *New York Times,* 2 August, A3.
Holsti, Kal. 1985. *The Dividing Discipline: Hegemony and Diversity in International Theory.* Boston: Allen and Unwin.
Horowitz, Donald L. 1985. *Ethnic Group Conflict.* Berkeley and London: University of California Press.
Huth, Paul, and Bruce M. Russett. 1988. "Deterrence Failure and Crisis Escalation." *International Studies Quarterly* 32: 29–45.
——. 1990. "Testing Deterrence Theory: Rigour Makes a Difference." *World Politics* 42: 466–501.

————. 1984. "What Makes Deterrence Work? Cases from 1900–1980." *World Politics* 36: 496–526.

Isaacs, Harold. 1975. *Idols of the Tribe: Group Identity and Political Change.* New York: Harper and Row, 39–45.

James, Patrick. 1993. "Structural Realism as a Research Enterprise: Toward Elaborated Structural Realism." *International Political Science Review* 14: 123–48.

James and Frank Harvey. 1992. "The Most Dangerous Game: Superpower Rivalry in International Crises, 1948–1985." *Journal of Politics* 54: 25–51.

————. 1989. "Threat Escalation and Crisis Stability: Superpower Cases, 1948–1979." *Canadian Journal of Political Science* 22: 523–45.

Jehl, Douglas. 1993b. "Serbs Must Withdraw Promptly or Face Air Strikes, U.S. Insists." *New York Times,* 12 August, A1.

————. 1993a. "U.S. Turns Bosnia Threat into Near Ultimatum." *New York Times,* 4 August, A1.

Jervis, Robert. 1979. "Deterrence Theory Revisited." *World Politics* 31: 289–324.

Jervis, Richard N. Lebow, and Janice G. Stein. 1985. *Psychology and Deterrence.* Baltimore: Johns Hopkins University Press.

Kifner, John. 1994a. "Serbs Agree to Give up Sarajevo Guns." *New York Times,* 10 February, A14.

————. 1994b. "U.N. Reports Serbs Are Pulling Back around Sarajevo." *New York Times,* 18 February, A1.

Kinzer, Stephen. 1993a. "Serbs Attack Muslim Stronghold in Northwest Bosnia," *New York Times,* 28 April, A11.

————. 1993b. "Serbs Reject Bosnia Pact, Defying Friends and Foes and Insist on Referendum." *New York Times,* 6 May, A1, A16.

Lebow, Richard N., and Janice G. Stein. 1987. "Beyond Deterrence." *Journal of Social Issues* 43: 5–71.

————. 1990. "Deterrence: The Elusive Dependent Variable." *World Politics* XLII: 336–69.

————. 1989a. "Rational Deterrence Theory: I Think, Therefore I Deter." *World Politics* 41: 208–24.

————. 1989b. "When Does Deterrence Succeed and How Do We Know?" Paper presented at the Annual Meeting of the International Studies Association.

Levy, Jack. 1988. "When Do Deterrent Threats Work?" *British Journal of Political Science* 18: 485–512.

Lewis, Paul. 1993. "Top Bosnian Serb Facing U.S. Action, Signs a Peace Plan." *New York Times,* 3 May, A1, A10.

————. 1994. "U.N. Warns Serbs on Gorazde; Move Could Lead to Air Strikes." *New York Times,* 10 April, A1.

Lieber, Robert. 1994. "Constraints on American Foreign Policy in the Post-Cold War Era." Paper presented at the Sixteenth World Congress of the International Political Science Association, Berlin, August.

Lieberman, Eli. 1994. "What Makes Deterrence Work?: Lessons From the Egyptian-Israeli Enduring Rivalry." Paper presented at the Annual Meeting of the American Political Science Association, New York, September 1–4.

Marshal, Monty G. 1997. "The Societal Dimensions of 'Human Nature' and the Dynamics of Group Conflict: Violence, Diffusion and Disintegration in the Middle East." In *Wars in the Midst of Peace: The International Politics of Ethnic Conflict,* edited by David Carment and Patrick James. Pittsburgh: University of Pittsburgh Press.

Mason, David T. 1994. "The Ethnic Dimension of Civil Violence in the Post-Cold War Era: Structural Configurations and Rational Choices." Paper presented at the annual meeting of the American Political Science Association, New York.

Melson, Robert, and Howard Wolpe. 1970. "Modernization and the Politics of Communalism: A Theoretical Perspective." *American Political Science Review* 64: 1112–30.

Midlarsky, Manus. 1997. "Systemic War in the Former Yugoslavia," in David Carment and Patrick James eds., *Wars in the Midst of Peace.*

Nagel, Joane, and Susan Olzak. 1982. "Ethnic Mobilization in New and Old States: An Extension of the Competition Model." *Social Problems* 30: 127–43.

New York Times. 1993.17 April, A4.

Nielsen, Francois. 1985. "Toward a Theory of Ethnic Solidarity in Modern Societies." *American Sociological Review* 50: 133–49.

Olzak, Susan. 1983. "Contemporary Ethnic Mobilization." *Annual Review of Sociology* 9: 355–74.

Pages, Erik R. 1991. "The Evolution of Deterrence Theory: A Review of the Literature." *International Studies* 16: 60–65.

Prial, Frank J. 1993. "Resolution Establishes Safe Areas but Lacks Enforcement Provision." *New York Times,* 7 May, A11.

Record, Jeffrey. 1993. "Defeating Desert Storm and Why Saddam Didn't." *Comparative Strategy* 12: 125–40.

Riding, Alan. 1993. "NATO Agrees to Enforce Flight over Bosnia Ordered by UN." *New York Times,* 3 April, A5.

Rothschild, Joseph. 1981. *Ethnopolitics: A Conceptual Framework.* New York: Columbia University Press.

Russett, Bruce M. 1963. "The Calculus of Deterrence." *Journal of Conflict Resolution* 7: 97–109.

Scholte, Jan Aart. 1994. "Beyond Realism, beyond Liberalism, beyond

Marxism: Rethinking the World System Concept." Paper presented at the Annual Convention of the International Studies Association, Washington D.C., 21–25 February.

Sciolino, Elaine. 1993. "Bosnia Rivals Set New Talks as U.S. Weighs Action Plans." *New York Times,* 30 April, A1, A7.

See, Katherine O'Sullivan. 1986. *First World Nationalism: Class and Ethnic Politics in Northern Ireland and Quebec.* Chicago: University of Chicago Press.

Smith, Anthony D. 1981. *The Ethnic Revival.* Cambridge: Cambridge University Press.

———. 1986. "The Suppression of Nationalism." *International Journal of Comparative Sociology* 31: 1–31.

Smith, M.G. 1965. *The Plural Societies in the British West Indies.* Berkeley: University of California Press.

Stack, John, ed. 1981. *Ethnic Identities in a Transnational World.* Westport, Conn.: Greenwood.

———, ed. 1986. *The Primordial Challenge: Ethnicity in the Contemporary World.* New York and London: Greenwood.

Sudetic, Chuck. 1994a. "Serbs Pound Sarajevo Again and Bosnian Counterattack." *New York Times,* 12 January, A8.

———. 1994b. "Two NATO Jets Bomb the Serbs Besieging a Bosnian Haven; U.S. Warns of More Strikes." *New York Times,* 11 April, A1, A6.

———. 1994c. "U.S. Planes Bomb Serbian Positions for a Second Day: Serbs Voicing Defiance." *New York Times,* 12 April, A1, A10.

Taylor, Donald M., and Fathali M. Moghaddam 1988. *Theories of Intergroup Relations: International Social Psychological Perspectives.* New York: Praeger, 1988.

Van Evera, Stephen. 1994. "Hypotheses on Nationalism and War." *International Security* 18: 5–39.

Weiss, Thomas G. 1994. "Intervention: Whither the United Nations." *Washington Quarterly* 17: 109–28.

Whitney, Craig R. 1993. "NATO to Join U.S. in Planning Air Strikes against Serbs' Forces." *New York Times,* 3 August, A1.

Wolfers, Arnold. 1959. "The Actors in International Politics." In *The Theory and Practice of International Relations,* edited by David McLellan, William Olson and Fred Sonderman. New Jersey: Prentice-Hall, 8–19.

Zald, Mayer N., and John D. McCarthy, eds. 1987. *Social Movements in an Organizational Society: Collected Essays.* Oxford: Transactions Books.

9

International Action and National Sovereignty

Adjusting to New Realities

ALEX MORRISON

As the Cold War recedes and the hot wars advance, peacekeeping personnel are coming into more frequent contact with famine, destroyed urban infrastructure, medical catastrophes, decrepit political regimes, and the non-existence of food distribution networks. Whatever the specifics of the situation, it is sufficient that there be a need for national and international action for peacekeeping partners to be called into consultation.

Samuel P. Huntington

INTRODUCTION

This chapter proposes a new definition of peacekeeping that is broad in nature and interpretation and can possibly serve as a unifying conceptual approach to future challenges from ethnic and other conflicts. The chapter also outlines a "New Peacekeeping Partnership," describes the "Peacekeeping Umbrella," and explains "The Changing Face of Peacekeeping." It examines the Canadian approach to peacekeeping in the hope that others may profit from the Canadian experience.

The end of the Cold War has not brought about the era of universal peace, harmony, and tranquillity that many had expected. Instead it has ushered in a period of great uncertainty, setting up what Samuel P. Huntington describes as the inevitable "clash of civilizations." According to him, there is a new phase of world politics—one in which the fundamental source of conflict will not be ideological or economic but cultural. Whereas before the world witnessed "Western civil wars" between princes, states, and ideologies, in the future the greatest clashes will be along the faultlines between opposing civilizations or nations. Huntington maintains that this will be especially true in "torn countries" where different cultural groups exist, brought closer through the forces of economic regionalism.

Cultural conflict is inevitable, Huntington continues, because the perception of risk strikes at the core of identity, accentuating basic value differences. In a world that is shrinking as a result of political and economic integration, it is ironic that people are becoming more rather than less conscious of what makes them dissimilar. Add to this the processes of modernization and social change that are separating people from long-standing local identities, and what Huntington discovers is a weakening of the state in favor of revived spirituality and the indigenization of the elite. This in turn serves to build tension between "the West and the rest" on the micro or domestic level as adjacent groups along the faultlines between civilizations struggle over control of territory and each other and on the macro or international level as different civilizations compete for relative military and economic power, control of international institutions and third parties, and the access to promote their way of thinking.

According to some, the incapacity of collective efforts to manage ethnic strife is indicative of a current crisis of authority in the international system, characterized by a decline in the effectiveness of the United Nations. These emerging conflicts are cases in which new issues of intrastate relations have emerged. These issues far outpace the rules and norms that the international community has in its possession to manage them. Proponents of such views argue that the absence of a revised, overarching framework of policies on ethnic conflict management and resolution is closely connected to transformations in thinking about the nature of state sovereignty, which includes the behavior of states external to a conflict and internal changes that states are experiencing. As a consequence, prevailing international norms also are in transition.

The most notable of these changes include new justifications for intervention (including the violability of state boundaries and delegitimated sovereignty, as discussed in other chapters in this volume: see James, and Ryan, for example) and altered objectives for involvement (including efforts to end civil strife and stop genocide), as discussed below. As argued by Kaufman and James in this volume, the most insurmountable problem is that these struggles consist of competing ethnic identities that operate within the domestic political sphere and spill over into the international arena.

Other, more optimistic positions, such as the one put forth in this chapter, submit that multifaceted peacekeeping could reflect a resurgence of the UN as an appropriate tool for managing and resolving ethnic strife. Instead of going back to traditional peacekeeping, as James and Kaufman suggest, the new breed of conflicts calls for different peacekeeping strategies and new partners in the peace process.

Today, in Africa and areas of the former Soviet Union, ancient religious, ethnic, and nationalist tensions have burst once again to the surface. In addition, disputes over declining resources and the state of the world's environmental, political, tribal, cultural, and economic concerns are causing massive refugee flows with resultant social unrest. Everywhere, citizens are struggling to improve the quality of democracy in their countries. "Torn" in different directions by economic hardship, ethnicity, and other interests, war-torn regions are ripe for future battles over culture.

The former secretary-general of the United Nations, Boutros Boutros-Ghali, estimated that in 1992 there was a trend towards an excessive exploitation of nationalist tendencies ad infinitum, heightening the potential of ethnic conflict (Boutros-Ghali 1992). In 1997 this trend has leveled off somewhat (see the introduction, this volume) but the challenges are no less formidable. Today, the challenge for the international community is to develop an approach that will retain the maximum respect for national sovereignty while at the same time permit prompt and effective responses to crises of all types, even in the face of national objections.

Today there is a cautious optimism in the international community, in the UN, and, perhaps most importantly, in the UN Security Council. Despite setbacks in Bosnia and Somalia there are reasons to be optimistic. Both conflicts have provided tough lessons for peacekeepers. Some of these lessons have been painfully obvious, such as the need for high-level coordination in the face of widespread violence (Harvey, this volume), and some have been less easy to comprehend. For example, before the current East-West rapprochement, intense national and bloc rivalries had ensured that crisis management, establishment of peacekeeping missions, the

delivery of humanitarian aid of all types, effective refugee management programs, and the advancement of human rights were held
hostage to outmoded concepts of national sovereignty. Today these
impediments have been removed, yet the international community
seems unsure where to begin. On the one hand, this cautious optimism has been evident in the low number of vetoes cast by the
permanent members of the council in the past few years and in the
number of resolutions passed. There are those who say that the
resolutions are meaningless (*New York Times*, 12 December 1993).
That may be so, but only to a matter of degree; once the council
has spoken, it is up to member states to obey its dictates, as is
required of all UN members under the terms of the charter.

On the other hand, the nature of conflict has changed dramatically. Whereas before international actors were engaged at the interstate level, increasingly they are finding themselves in the middle
of messy, intrastate conflicts where the parties, objectives, and means
may or may not be well defined. Mass migration of peoples, and
the identification of cross-boundary environmental issues, together
with the loosening of bipolar constraints, are contributing to the
erosion of traditional demarcating lines between states. While "the
state" remains important as an organizing principle, it is acknowledged that its coherence and primacy are under siege. More and
more, UN military and civilian peacekeepers and aid workers are
dealing with hostile elements that blend easily into the civilian population. The lives of aid workers and diplomats are constantly at
risk. The mortar emplacement is temporary and the incoming shell
does not identify the aggressor. Deprivation of the basic necessities
of life has become a weapon. Peacekeepers find themselves in the
difficult position of presiding over the building and rebuilding of
states. Part of the trouble, of course, is that in order to preside over
the building of states, they also must preside over the dismantling
of states.

Thus in this new environment contact between peacekeeping
troops and nongovernmental organizations, out of necessity, has
increased tremendously. Close liaison and cooperation are manda-
tory. Humanitarian aid agency personnel are accepting more and
more, albeit perhaps not wholly enthusiastically, that the military
has a role to play in the delivery of aid. By the same token, the
military is increasingly recognizing and appreciating the vital role
played by the many NGOs in the field in the establishment and
maintenance of international peace and security.

The changing face of peacekeeping—exemplified by the dramatic increase in United Nations and other national and international peacekeeping operations of all types (the mandates of which go well beyond the traditional tasks), an expanding group of participants, the inability or unwillingness of the traditional peacekeeping countries to continue to supply personnel at historic levels, and the rapidly rising financial and other costs—requires that all who participate in peacekeeping be properly educated and trained so that the maximum benefit is gained from any expenditure of resources.

In the area of international peacekeeping, the UN has responded to the challenge by creating in the first five years after the end of the Cold War more peacekeeping missions than in the first thirty-eight years of its existence. Military men and women from well over one hundred countries have worn the blue beret and helmet in the service of international peace, security, and stability. Currently there are well over eighty thousand military peacekeepers on duty in more than fifteen missions. It is virtually impossible to estimate the number of civilian peacekeepers, but if one includes all humanitarian aid personnel of all types, the total is probably higher than that of the military. Peacekeepers have monitored and enforced cease-fires, verified security agreements, provided and ensured the delivery of humanitarian aid and the provision of basic governmental structures and services, and have assisted in the transition from colony to nation. Table 9.1 provides a breakdown of the number of UN peacekeeping operations since its inception up to the present. This table indicates that the UN may be experiencing "overstretch" in its application of operations.

Table 9.1

United Nations Peacekeeping Operations as of July 1995

OPERATIONS
1948 to 1995: 39
Currently underway: 16

PERSONNEL
Military personnel served 1948 to present: Over 720,000
Fatalities 1948 to present: 1,194

Military and civilian police personnel serving on 28 February 1994: 69,356
Countries currently contributing military and civilian police personnel: 77

FINANCIAL ASPECTS
Total cost to the UN of all operations to present: About $12.5 billion
Annualized cost to the UN of current operations: About $3.5 billion
Outstanding contributions to peacekeeping operations: About 1.2 billion

CURRENT PEACEKEEPING OPERATIONS

UNTSO
United Nations Truce Supervision Organization
June 1948 to present
Rough annual cost to the UN: $28.6 million
Current strength: 218
Fatalities: 28

UNMOGIP
United Nations Military Observer Group in India and Pakistan
January 1949 to present
Rough annual cost to the UN: $7.2 million
Current strength: 39
Fatalities: 6

UNFICYP
United Nations Peacekeeping Force in Cyprus
March 1964 to present
Rough annual cost to the UN: $42.3 million
Current strength: 1,183
Fatalities: 163

UNDOF
United Nations Disengagement Observer Force
June 1974 to present
Rough annual cost to the UN: $32.2 million
Current strength: 1,030
Fatalities: 37

UNIFIL
United Nations Interim Force in Lebanon
March 1978 to present
Rough annual cost to the UN: $142.3 million
Current strength: 5,146

Fatalities: 200
UNIKOM
United Nations Iraq-Kuwait Observation Mission
April 1991 to present
Rough annual cost to the UN: $63.1 million
Current strength: 1,142
Fatalities: 3

UNAVEM III
United Nations Angola Verification Mission III
June 1991 to present
Rough annual cost to the UN: $25.5 million
Current strength: 135
Fatalities: 4

MINURSO
United Nations Mission for the Referendum in Western Sahara
Operational: September 1991
Rough annual cost to the UN: $40.5 million
Current strength: 334
Fatalities: 4

UNPROFOR
This mission was reformed into three parts: UNCRO in Croatia; UNPROFOR in Bosnia-Herzegovina; and UNPREDEP in the former Yugoslavian Republic of Macedonia.

United Nations Protection Force
March 1992 to December 1995
Rough annual cost to the UN: $1.6 billion
Maximum strength: 39,789
Fatalities: 131

UNOMIG
United Nations Observer Mission in Georgia
August 1993 to present
Rough annual cost to the UN: $10.9 million
Current strength: 134

UNOMIL
United Nations Observer Mission in Liberia
September 1993 to present
Rough annual cost to the UN: $1.1 million
Current strength: 84

UNMIH
United Nations Mission in Haiti
Established 23 September 1993
Rough annual cost to the UN: $1.1 million
Authorized strength: 6,567
Current strength: 74

UNMOT
United Nations Mission of Observers in Tajikistan
December 1994 to present
Rough annual cost to the UN: $1.1 million
Authorized strength: 40
Current strength: 27

NOTE:
Figures for operational strength and fatalities include military and civilian police personnel. Operational strength varies slightly from month to month due to rotation. Costs to the United Nations of 15 of 17 current United Nations peacekeeping operations are financed from their own separate accounts on the basis of legally binding assessments of all member states. UNTSO and UNMOGIP are funded from the United Nations's regular budget. Since the mandates of most operations are renewed periodically starting from different dates, annual cost for estimates for comparative purposes are approximate.

OPERATIONS NOW CLOSED

UNAMIR
United Nations Assistance Mission for Rwanda
October 1993 to March 1996
Rough annual cost to the UN: $193.5 million
Current strength: 5,222
Fatalities: 16

UNSCOB
United Nations Special Commission on the Balkans
1947 to 1951

UNOGILP
United Nations Observer Group in Lebanon
June to December 1958

ONUCP
United Nations Operation in the Congo
July 1960 to June 1964

ONUSAL
United Nations Observer Mission in El Salvador
July 1991 to 30 April 1995
Rough annual cost to the UN: $28.9 million
Ending strength: 34
Fatalities: 3

UNSFP
United Nations Security Force in West New Guinea (West Irian)
October 1962 to April 1963

UNYOM
United Nations Yemen Observation Mission
July 1963 to September 1964

DOMREP
Mission of the Representative of the Secretary-General in the Dominican
Republic
May 1965 to October 1966

UNIPOM
United Nations India-Pakistan Observation Mission
September 1965 to March 1966

UNEF
First United Nations Security Force
November 1956 to June 1967

UNEF II
Second United Nations Security Force
October 1973 to July 1979

UNGOMAP
United Nations Good Offices Mission in Afghanistan and Pakistan
April 1988 to March 1990

UNIIMOG
United Nations Iran-Iraq Military Observer Group
August 1988 to February 1991

UNAVEM I
United Nations Angola Verification Mission I
January 1989 to June 1991

UNTAG
United Nations Transition Assistance Group
April 1989 to March 1990

ONUCA
United Nations Observer Group in Central America
November 1989 to January 1992

UNAMIC
United Nations Advance Mission in Cambodia
October 1991 to March 1992

UNTAC
United Nations Transitional Authority in Cambodia
March 1992 to 24 September 1993

UNOSOM I
United Nations Operation in Somalia I
April 1992 to April 1993

UNOSOM II
United Nations Operation in Somalia II
May 1993 to March 1995
Rough annual cost to the UN: $942.4 million
Ending strength: 9,412
Fatalities: 134

UNOMURA
United Nations Observer Mission Uganda-Rwanda
October 1993 to 1994

UNOMOZ
United Nations Operation in Mozambique
December 1992 to January 1995

To respond to these changes, there is now developing a New Peacekeeping Partnership (NPP), which is composed of military organizations; government and nongovernmental agencies dealing with humanitarian assistance, refugees, and displaced persons; election monitors and media; and civilian police personnel as they work together to improve the effectiveness of peacekeeping operations.

The members of this partnership are dedicated to ensuring the widest, most inclusive response possible to the challenges and opportunities of the post–Cold War era. They are determined to cooperate to ensure that international stability operations are as effective as possible.

This approach to peacekeeping differs markedly from traditional approaches, for it assumes that resolution is possible and that individuals and social groups, not just states, are important units of analysis in international affairs. There is an understanding that peace, like war, is a multifaceted phenomenon that demands a multimethod response. It is a complex combination of domestic and foreign policies, expectations, and human needs, which cannot be found without considering how individuals use the state and organizations positively and negatively. Psychology provides the link between action and outcome, considering how individual or micro concerns translate into macro violence. There is a recognition that Cold War attempts to diffuse hostilities at the macro level have done nothing to address the underlying reasons that conflict reaches such levels of hostility nor to prevent long stalemates such as that for twenty-seven years on the island of Cyprus or that between Arabs and Israelis in the Golan Heights. In the complex interdependent world of the twenty-first century this is not something military peacekeepers can do in isolation. They must work in cooperation with other organizations and interests if they are to peel away the surface layers of conflict and to get to the heart of on-the-ground issues. Social scientists, theorists, law-enforcement officers, and humanitarian aid workers all have a role to play.

The expansion of peacekeeping into the realm of peacemaking, peace support, and peacebuilding activities represents a move from what Kenneth Waltz (1959) terms the third image to the second image of international affairs. Recognizing the inadequacy of explaining war solely on the basis of the international environment (the third image), he suggests examining also the structure of the states involved (the second image) and, more importantly, how individuals (the first image) operate within their internal environment. Thus in an increasingly interdependent world contradicted by the breakdown of multinational states and the ensuing intrastate violence, an understanding of the roots of conflict becomes all the more important. Peacekeeping is clearly a part of the process, growing and changing to address real needs and problems within the theater of conflict in a way that those pulling strings at the negotiating table cannot. First by separating belligerents and then by developing a rapport with and between them, peacekeepers can provide grassroots support for diplomatic activities and can prove to the parties that the international community is as equally concerned with the quality of any agreement reached as with the signing of the agreement itself.

Although the members of the partnership have enjoyed a great measure of individual success in their endeavors, there appears to be room for improvement in the areas of advance planning and coordination. What remains now is for the partners to work together and in close cooperation with national governments, regional organizations, and the United Nations to ensure early detection of crises, an active and effective response, and a comprehensive follow-through program to prevent recurrences. The principles of the New Peacekeeping Partnership must be formalized and adopted at organizational, national, and international levels. Only by such a course of action can the challenges of present and future conflicts be met.

Moreover, it must be acknowledged that when one speaks of "resolving" conflict this is not to imply that all conflict between the parties can be solved, for conflict in some form is a natural part of all relationships. While specific incidents may be resolved, conflict itself is never eradicated. A "successful" course of action then, is not necessarily one which achieves "peace," broadly defined. It is more important that a diffusion of recent or potential incidents of armed violence takes place and that conflict be maintained below some mutually agreeable level. During the Cold War, conflicts central to the broader patterns of competitive international relations had the greatest potential for expansion (e.g. Turkish and Greek confrontation over Cyprus, Arab-Israel strife). Accordingly, the international community devoted a great deal of energy to their management. An important implication is that during this period some ethnic conflicts spread because bipolarity and the presence of nuclear weapons limited direct conflict between the superpowers but not among client states. As Patrick Moynihan argues in his book *Pandemonium,* both sides of the Cold War may have supported (or suppressed) ethnic struggles to further their broader foreign policy objectives. Today, it may be that some conflicts will not go away, and the UN will have peacekeepers in some locations forever (Kashmir and Cyprus). Therefore the task of the New Peace-keeping Partnership is to initiate a process whereby the parties to the conflict can reconceive their relationship in a lower-cost environment in a manner consistent with local reality. Where involved, UN peacekeepers must make their intervention appear as little like intervention as possible.

There are many competing, conflicting, yet in many ways complementary demands being made of the relatively few resources countries have available for or are willing to devote to peacekeeping. The hope that the end of the Cold War would mean the release of vast sums of money that could then be allocated to other areas of the security spectrum has not been realized. But progress has been made. As the Cold War wound down, more attention began to be paid to the nonmilitary items contained in the definition of security. Yet countries soon realized to their dismay that citizens of those states recently released from the yoke of autocratic, dictatorial communist regimes were in many instances anxious to put their pent-up energies to use by starting conflicts.

Thus, the heartstrings and the purse strings of developed countries are being pulled in many directions. To address the needs described above requires the expenditure of a great deal of time and energy. It seems as if every dollar spent on aid and other forms of humanitarian relief is a dollar not spent on UN and other peacekeeping forces and vice versa. Furthermore, it is recognized that in this era of diminishing defense budgets and emphasis on deficit reduction, no government can afford, financially or politically, to go it alone. Yet the international public demands action on both fronts—hence the necessity for coordinated action. Thus another important measure of "success" for future UN peacekeeping operations will be their affordability.

However, not everyone is so quick to embrace the new mandate for peacekeeping, cautioning that as peacekeeping becomes more deeply involved in the political and administrative aspects of states, it runs the risk of doing a little bit of everything but doing nothing well. A broader but poorly defined mandate, they point out, may create a host of problems over which peacekeepers may have little control. For example, the failure of antiterrorist operations resulting in casualties, military and civilian, could taint peacekeepers' reputation and hamper their ability to carry out other activities, undermining political consensus and increasing the danger of greater violence. As peacekeeping comes to include more proactive functions peacekeepers may indeed find themselves tangled in a complex web of state and nonstate actors (see Kaufman, and James, this volume). Yet this does not diminish the fact that in the long run, peacekeeping must be reworked within the context of a broader program of conflict resolution. This will require a rethinking of peacekeeping policy, strategy and training. Governments, by necessity, will have to be more discriminating about their sites and means of involvement and in assessing the degree to which a conflict resolution process may or may not be meaningfully initiated at that time.

THE NEW BREED OF PEACEKEEPING

In order to meet the expanding requirements and to ensure simplicity of approach and understanding, the following definition of peacekeeping is suggested:

> Actions designed to enhance international peace, security, and stability that are authorized and coordinated by competent national and international organizations and which are undertaken cooperatively by military, humanitarian, good governance, civilian police, and other interested agencies and groups.

This umbrella definition includes all forms of problem solving and conflict resolution, from discussion, mediation, negotiation, and arbitration through traditional methods of peacekeeping—delivery of all forms of humanitarian aid and provision of good governance assistance—to operations of the Gulf war type.

Some have advocated that a single definition no longer meets the requirements of the contemporary conflict resolution situation. They feel that the spectrum is now so wide that a single term cannot cover the range of activities. Peacebuilding, peace enforcement, peace establishment, peacemaking, peace support, and peace resolution are but a few of the alternative terms that are advanced to cover what heretofore has been called peacekeeping (some of these terms are covered individually in chapter 1). It may be that for certain purposes greater definitional clarity is needed. But such defining attempts ought not to interfere with efforts to address the challenges of today. Action ought not to founder on the shores of definitional morass. The very term "peacekeeping" has such a positive aura about it that attempts to change it to meet shifting circumstances and requirements may well lead to a diminution of public support.[1]

At the same time as the requirement for greater coordination among and between all the peacekeeping partners has developed, there has emerged a discussion concerning the limits of national sovereignty and whether the well-being of citizens can, in effect, be held hostage to what are regarded as traditional concepts of national sovereignty. In *An Agenda for Peace,* UN Secretary-General Boutros Boutros-Ghali, with reference to the aims and missions of the UN, said:

> The foundation-stone of this work is and must remain the State. Respect for its fundamental sovereignty and integrity are crucial to any common international progress. The time of absolute and exclusive sovereignty, however, has passed; its theory was never matched by reality.

Thus the challenge for the international community lies in developing an approach that will maintain the maximum respect for national sovereignty while at the same time permitting prompt and effective responses to crises, even in the face of national objections (*Agenda for Peace* 1992:9).

THE FOUNDING OF THE UNITED NATIONS

In many ways, the United Nations of the late 1990s is facing much the same situation the founding members encountered in drafting the charter. At that time, the world was in the midst of the Second World War and Allied leaders were attempting to create a vision and an implementing mechanism for the postwar world. Currently, the United Nations and its member states are trying to come to grips with the challenges and opportunities presented by a post-Cold War world. Before we deal with the present and future, it will be of benefit to dwell for a short time on the reasons for the founding of the UN.

The preamble to the UN Charter begins with a firm statement:

> We the peoples of the world (are) determined to save succeeding generations from the scourge of war, which twice in our lifetime has brought untold sorrow to mankind....

The first article of the first chapter of the charter outlines that the main purpose of the UN is:

> To maintain international peace and security, and to that end: to take effective collective measures for the prevention and removal of threats to the peace, and for the

> suppression of acts of aggression or other breaches of
> the peace, and to bring about by peaceful means, and in
> conformity with the principles of justice and international
> law, adjustment or settlement of international disputes
> or situations which might lead to a breach of the peace.

In 1943, during the American internal planning process that
led to the Dumbarton Oaks "conversations" and eventually to the
founding of the UN, it was clear that future wars were to be prevented by the use of force or the threat of its use by the major
victorious powers of the Second World War. They were determined
that there would not be a World War III, even if they had to go to
war to prevent it.

In late summer of 1944, when he addressed the first meeting at
Dumbarton Oaks, Mr. Cordell Hull, the American secretary of state,
made it quite clear that the UN must arrange for the

> peaceful settlement of international disputes and for
> the joint use of force, if necessary, to prevent or suppress
> threats to the peace or breaches of the peace. It is gener-
> ally agreed that any peace and security organization
> would surely fail unless backed by force to be used ulti-
> mately in case of failure of all the other means or the
> maintenance of peace. That force must be available
> promptly, in adequate measure and with certainty.
> (Morrison 1992)

It was envisioned that the UN would have its own military force
of over two million soldiers, thousands of airplanes, and hundreds
of warships. At one time, it was even suggested that this standing
military force should possess atomic weapons.

The UN was able to authorize effective military action at the
time of the invasion of South Korea due to the Soviet boycott of the
Security Council, but generally speaking there were no more ad-
vances in the military field for another fifteen years.

THE INVENTION OF CONTEMPORARY PEACEKEEPING:
A CANADIAN ENTERPRISE

In October 1956, the UK, France, and Israel attacked Egypt
and occupied the Suez Canal Zone. At the United Nations, Lester
B. Pearson, the Canadian secretary of state for external affairs, began the series of negotiations that resulted in the establishment of
the UN Emergency Force (UNEF). Mr. Pearson's suggestion that

the UN set up a peacekeeping mission to supervise the separation of the warring parties was the beginning of peacekeeping as it is now practiced. For his success, he was awarded the 1957 Nobel Peace Prize, which ensured that from that time on, the names of Canada and peacekeeping would be synonymous.

During his acceptance speech in Oslo, Norway, in December 1957, Pearson made a number of points which are germane to the subject of this paper. He said:

> What is needed is a new and vigorous determination to use every technique of discussion and negotiation that may be available, for the solution of the tangled, frightening problems that divide today, in fear and hostility, the two power blocs and thereby endanger peace. We must keep on trying to solve problems one by one, stage by stage, if not on the basis of confidence and cooperation, at least on that of mutual toleration and self-interest.

We made at least a beginning then [with UNEF I]. If, on that foundation, we do not build something more permanent and stronger, we will once again have ignored realism, rejected opportunities and betrayed the trust.

The time has come for us to make a move, not only from strength, but from wisdom and from confidence in ourselves; to concentrate on the possibilities of agreement, rather than on the disagreements and failures, the evils and the wrongs of the past.

There can be no enduring and creative peace if people are unfree. The instinct for personal and national freedom cannot be destroyed and the attempt to do so by totalitarian and despotic government will ultimately make not only for internal trouble but also for international conflict.

...if there is to be peace, there must be compromise, tolerance, agreement.

Mr. Pearson knew that there are many dispute-solving techniques to be attempted before there should be recourse to force.[2]

From observer missions such as UNMOGIP to the use of combat units on interpositional duties in Cyprus to overseeing the transition of a colony to a nation in Namibia, military peacekeeping has evolved to meet changing requirements and to take into account the changing nature of international relations. The whole area of peacekeeping writ large must now be expanded in a like manner.

SOVEREIGNTY

For most of the nearly five decades of its existence, speeches of diplomats at the United Nations always included references to national sovereignty and how the UN and other international organizations ought not, must not, take actions that would violate that principle. Yet, as has been pointed out by the UN former secretary-general, the concept has been honored more in the breach than otherwise (*Agenda for Peace* 1992). National sovereignty was always cited as the reason why peacekeeping forces could not be deployed without the consent of the appropriate national authorities and other concerned parties. Only today, as it is realized that peacekeeping forces have a far greater potential for positive action in more areas than previously envisaged, is it being accepted that consent is not a sine qua non for peacekeeping forces.

Behind the notion of consent has always been the idea, from the perspective of the parties to the conflict, that a third party—in this case, UN peacekeepers—must be able to maintain a degree of neutrality. However, as Lori M. Laubich explains in a prizewinning paper written for the Program on Negotiation Series at Harvard Law School, from the perspective of intervening third parties it is crucial to distinguish between neutrality and fairness; the two may not, in fact, be synonymous. The idea that fairness stems from neutrality and consent, she says, rests on the belief that the third party who favors one of the participants or who has a stake in the outcome will jeopardize the fairness of the procedure as well as the outcome; however, total commitment to neutrality and consent may sometimes frustrate the achievement of fundamental fairness or justice. For example, a neutral third-party intervention may result in an unfair outcome for a significantly weaker party or a satisfactory outcome for an unrepresented party. Thus for the intervenor there is a difference between being impartial and unconcerned. In both procedure and substance, therefore, it is important for the third party to be accountable to the parties at the table, to other parties not represented at the table but who will be significantly affected by any agreement reached, and, most of all, to conscience. The third party should pursue a strategy of observation and intervention of all kinds, making sure that each party concerned has equal opportunity to express its views and to make offers free from intimidation and threat in such a way that none can claim negligence, collusion, or the imposition of outside values (Laubich 1987).

Writing specifically with regard to human rights, but in words that are equally applicable to other areas, Asbjorn Eide (1987) has added that:

> To insist on the sovereignty of a state at all costs, even when the authorities in that state violate the self-determination of a people living inside its boundaries, or seriously oppresses its population through neglect of human rights, is *not* compatible with the new international legal order (3).

"Life, Death and Aid: The Mèdecins Sans Frontières Report on World Crisis Intervention," issued in the autumn of 1993, maintains that the "conventional notion of state sovereignty, which was reaffirmed at the end of the Second World War, strengthened during the decolonization period and frozen by East-West confrontation, has become outdated" (3). The report goes on to suggest that "the rights of victims" are more important than national sovereignty.

A recent report by the UN high commissioner for refugees has determined that "internal policies and practices which cause large numbers of people to flee are a threat to international peace and security." This interpretation of course means that national sovereignty need not be given undue emphasis when intervention is being contemplated.

Speaking to an audience in California in September 1991, Canadian Prime Minister Brian Mulroney said:

> ...we also favor rethinking the limits of national sovereignty in a world where problems respect no borders. Just a few days ago, Iraq blocked a UN arms inspection on grounds of national sovereignty. In the past year, countries have blocked food delivery to starving people, again on grounds of national sovereignty. Some Security Council members have opposed intervention in Yugoslavia, where many innocent people have been dying, on grounds of national sovereignty. Quite frankly, such invocations of the principle of national sovereignty are as out of date and as offensive to me as the police declining to stop family violence simply because a man's home is supposed to be his castle. (Mulroney 1991)

In June 1992, the UN secretary-general made his statement that "the day of absolute and exclusive sovereignty, however, has passed" (Boutros-Ghali 1992: 3).

While the statements above are expressed differently, what is now clear is that the international community can no longer tolerate the use of national sovereignty as an excuse to prevent positive action. There is a consensus that those states with resources and an interest in resolving conflict have an obligation to do so that overrides notions of well-defined neutrality, consent, or altruism. They must intervene early and directly to combat the problems of disease, starvation, and the gross violation of human rights. Passivity is tantamount to compliance. However, when they do so, they must be sensitive to and well versed in the conditions and needs of the local environment. This will require specialized training unlike any UN peacekeepers have had before.

THE CHANGING FACE OF PEACEKEEPING

Bearing in mind the definition of peacekeeping offered above, it is evident that the face of peacekeeping has changed considerably. The great divide that once existed between the military and humanitarian aid agencies has been bridged, and the former are directly involved with ensuring that the latter are able to accomplish their tasks. The "peacekeeping umbrella" is ever expanding to encompass activities not traditionally associated with peacekeeping. Other examples are the increasing use of civilian law-enforcement personnel and the hundreds of good governance missions conducted by election officials (see Ryan, this volume).

It is critically important that the needs of these new missions be recognized and understood. This requires the harmonization of the specific interests, approaches, and methods of operation of the various stakeholders so that peacekeeping becomes an integrated and focused means of dealing with peace and security, both regionally and globally.

THE NEW PEACEKEEPING PARTNERSHIP

Into this picture of cautious cooperation enters the New Peacekeeping Partnership. Each of the members of the new partnership is learning the characteristics and capabilities of the other. "The Peacekeeping Umbrella" has expanded in one way to include missions ranging from observation through the classical interpositional model as practiced in Cyprus and the "colony to nation" aspects of Namibia and Cambodia to the responses to the Iraqi invasion of Kuwait, and in Somalia and the former Yugoslavia. In another way, it is expanding to include the humanitarian aid agencies and the other organizations mentioned above. Such a turn in the positions of humanitarian aid agencies was not envisioned at the end of the Cold War (Weiss 1990).

Representatives of some humanitarian aid agencies have objected to placing their activities under the peacekeeping umbrella. They are of the opinion that peacekeeping per se is primarily and exclusively a military activity. They feel that *international stability operations, international development relief,* or some such term perhaps better describes their work. Yet military personnel are firm in their view that peacekeeping is an honorable activity and that the term must remain in force. In the public eye, it is certain that *peacekeeping* is the accepted word. While this definitional argument will not stand in the way of positive action, it must be borne in mind.

The former chief of the Canadian Defence Staff, Admiral John Anderson has called on "military commanders to take a holistic approach, involving all the stakeholders in mission planning and operations to ensure coordination from beginning to end" ("Canada's Agenda for International Peace and Security" 1993). Implementation of that exhortation would mean the exchange of knowledgeable personnel among and between the agencies with different mandates. Each of the partners must consider how the partnership can be enlarged. For example: Is there a place for police personnel other than members of the national force? How are the roles and contributions of maritime and air forces evolving? How can the utilization of the expertise and contacts of humanitarian aid agencies be enhanced? How can traditional peacekeeping mechanisms and modalities be put to use in nontraditional environments?

Humanitarian aid agencies can bring much of value to the partnership table. For example, their representatives are stationed in virtually every country of the world. Their very presence serves as an early-warning mechanism for impending crises. It is folly not to take advantage of that knowledge.

PEACEKEEPING'S ESSENTIAL INGREDIENTS

When a country considers its potential contribution to a peacekeeping mission, it decides the percentage of each of the following ingredients it will select: personnel, financing, materiel and equipment, and research, education, and training. Each of these must be considered against the backdrop of command, control, and communications. That is, there must be a central authority with the ability to define and oversee the entire operation.

Consider, for example, how Canada, a country often cited as the progenitor of peacekeeping, has altered its approach to peacekeeping in recent years. In the past, Canada has contributed to peacekeeping in the order outlined above. Indications are that as the government reduces the size of the armed forces while insisting that Canada remain a high-profile, significant power player of the international security stage, it will be necessary for that country's contribution to be less in the personnel and financing areas and more in the other two areas. Thus, in the future, the overall Canadian contribution will be as significant as it has been in the past but will involve the other areas to a greater degree. That is, an increase in research, education, and training (subjects on which there is now much more focus in Canada and elsewhere) can compensate for a decrease in personnel contributed and in the length of time that Canada participates in any given mission.

The potential shift in Canadian contribution categories looms at a time when many more countries than previously are anxious to become participants. In essence, other countries new to peacekeeping, such as Japan, Germany, and Brazil, will be expected to make contributions in areas where they have traditionally not been active while traditional peacekeepers such as Canada shift the burden across a variety of tasks.

THE BROADER REQUIREMENT

Generally, the military and civilian, on-the-ground peacekeeping forces have been eminently successful, and this is where greatest financial attention should be given. Where they have been unable to carry out their mandates, the Security Council has insisted that peacekeepers remain in place and function as best they can. The UN and member states are extremely reluctant to wind down a mission where there is a possibility that it could serve a useful purpose in the future. It is much easier to react efficiently if there is already a peacekeeping force in existence and deployed.

Another area badly in need of attention is conflict resolution and transformation. Peacekeeping has failed more often than many would like, chiefly because the underlying causes of conflict have not been addressed. Once the Security Council has established a force and deployed the troops, there is a tendency for politicians to enter "the era of the long sigh" or "the era of the long pause." The feeling is one of relief that the military are on the spot and thus it is not necessary to effect political solutions. More effort must be made in the area of solving the underlying causes of the conflict. In addition, there must be concerted efforts to solve political disputes before they erupt into open conflict (see Ryan, this volume).

It has been normal UN practice that contingents and HQ personnel are requested on the basis of "equitable geographic representation." That is, there must be in each force an equal or almost equal representation from the various areas of the world. This practice is often implemented without due regard for experience, expertise, or competence. In addition, the UN does not outline anything more than the basic requirement skills for each headquarters position (in many instances, only the title of the position is known) and does absolutely no checking at all that those requirements are in fact possessed by the person assuming the appointment. The first time most of the headquarters personnel meet one another is when the headquarters is set up in the new mission area. There is a definite need for standardization of talents and skills required by contingents and individuals assigned to peacekeeping duties.

It is simply an acknowledgment of the present-day realities to accept that there are two categories of military peacekeepers: (1) those from countries that have been traditional contributors and are able to put to good use in a peacekeeping environment the skills gained in other multinational military organizations; and (2) those from countries less experienced but possessed of a willingness to learn. That willingness to learn ought to be accommodated and encouraged.

It is also prudent to consider whether each of the other peacekeeping partners mentioned above ought not to be official members of each peacekeeping mission. There should perhaps be certain specified positions for them. In that manner, the commander of the force will have the experience and advice at hand when it is needed. If such is to be the case, then there is a need for advance education and training in working with individuals from other countries in a multinational setting.

There is more of a need now for cultural awareness training than has perhaps been the case in the past. In missions such as election supervision and delivery of humanitarian aid, which entail close contact with local populations, it is essential that all peace-keeping personnel are cognizant of the national and regional characteristics, habits, and customs of the country concerned.

The effective conduct of peacekeeping efforts places great reliance on commanders and leaders at all levels. Peacekeepers are ambassadors and teachers by example at one and the same time. They must be consummate diplomats and know instinctively what negotiating skills to employ in any given situation. They must know the limits of their authority and responsibility as well as the limits of their capabilities. In other words, they must be masters of the entire conflict-resolution spectrum. Canadian Lt. Col. M. D. Capstick and Maj. D. M. Last (1994) emphasize this point when they note that by the fifty-eighth rotation of peacekeepers to UNFICYP the training guide for troops consisted of just two pages. In contrast, they say, direction to units preparing for deployment to Yugoslavia (UNPROFOR) runs more than twenty pages and is backed up by instruction packages that differ for units deployed to Croatia, Bosnia, and the Canadian logistic support group. Moreover, it was the absence of such detailed instruction for missions like Cyprus that led to the preparation of a negotiation training package for Yugoslavia from first principles, building on work in the field of industrial relations, police crisis intervention, and applied social psychology.

Clearly, the task of keeping the peace has become more complex and demanding. Still with (or perhaps because of) contemporary requirements peacekeepers must know the limits of their authority and responsibility as well as the limits of their capabilities. In other words, they must be highly skilled in conflict resolution techniques. They must have tremendous self-control, know when to exercise initiative and how to determine quickly the merits of any situation and then act decisively. In other words, they need all the attributes possessed by professional soldiers.

In *An Agenda for Peace*, UN Secretary-General Boutros Boutros-Ghali's report of 17 June 1992 to the UN Security Council, he says:

> The sources of conflict and war are pervasive and deep. To reach them will require our utmost effort to enhance respect for human rights and fundamental freedoms. To promote sustainable development and social development for wider prosperity, to alleviate distress and to curtail the existence and use of massively destructive weapons.

Later, he advocates that the UN have the following aims:

To seek to identify at the earliest possible stage situations that could produce conflict and to try through diplomacy to remove the sources of danger before violence results;

where conflict erupts, to engage in peacekeeping aimed at resolving the issues that have led to conflict;

through peacekeeping, to work to preserve peace, however fragile, where fighting has been halted and to assist implementing agreements achieved by the peacekeepers;

to stand ready to assist in peacebuilding in its differing contexts: rebuilding the institutions and infrastructures of nations torn by civil war and strife and building bonds of peaceful mutual benefit among nations formerly at war (32);

and in the largest sense, to address the deepest causes of conflict: economic despair, social injustice, and political oppression. It is possible to discern an increasingly common moral perception that spans the world's nations and peoples, and which is finding expression in international laws, many owing their genesis to the work of this organization.

Near the conclusion of *An Agenda for Peace,* the former secretary-general continues his thoughts on the broader context of peace-keeping:

Democracy within nations requires respect for human rights and fundamental freedoms, as set forth in the Charter. It requires as well a deeper understanding and respect for the rights of minorities and respect for the needs of the more vulnerable groups of society, especially women and children. This is not only a political matter. The social stability needed for productive growth is nurtured by conditions in which people can readily express their will. For this, strong domestic institutions of participation are essential. Promoting such institutions means promoting the empowerment of the unorganized, the poor, the marginalized. To this end, the focus of the United Nations should be on the "field," the locations where economic, social and political decisions take effect . . . (46).

Just as it is vital that each of the organs of the United Nations employ its capabilities in the balanced and harmonious fashion envisioned in the Charter, peace in the largest sense cannot be accomplished by the United Nations system or by governments alone. Non-governmental organizations, academic institutions, parliamentarians, business and professional communities, the media and the public at large must all be involved. The New Peacekeeping Partnership must continue to grow.

MAKING IT WORK

In analyzing *An Agenda for Peace* in the Winter 1993 issue of *Washington Quarterly*, Thomas G. Weiss considers a number of recommendations that he believes if implemented will allow the international community to effectively grasp the opportunity presented to it in the basic strategy outlined above. These suggestions are as pertinent now as they were four years ago.

The first of these, Weiss says, is negative: to set aside the unrealistic expectations about the short-term contributions of regional organizations to international peace and security. These organizations can play a helpful role in diplomatic arm-twisting, as shown by the Association of Southeast Asian Nations (ASEAN) in Cambodia and by the Contadora Group in Central America. But with the exceptions of NATO and the OSCE, which together possess advanced cooperative procedures, they are and will remain poor sources for supplying international military forces to help quell interstate and local conflict over the short term (see Haglund and Pentland, this volume). Therefore it is important that regional capacity be developed where it is most needed. The Organization of African Unity and the Organization of American States are two prime candidates.

Weiss's second recommendation, which is best served through UN financial restructuring, is that top priority be given to placing UN military operations on a solid financial base. This would create, for starters, a fifty-million-dollar revolving fund to help the UN move into action more swiftly in the event of a crisis. Most importantly, though, Weiss believes that switching the budgeting of UN military operations to defense ministries and away from foreign affairs would in itself go a long way toward the implementation of better fact-finding, preventive diplomacy, and peacekeeping.

A third recommendation Weiss makes is that the role of the World Court be emphasized, for the rise in internecine cultural conflict has generated new questions of how to define sovereignty, command and control, human rights and humanitarian intervention. There have been significant inroads in addressing war crimes issues in Bosnia, though lack of enforcement has led to problems. Granted, UN resolutions are often vague in order to secure intergovernmental assent, but Weiss warns that objective standards that dictate action increasingly will be necessary. In his opinion, these deserve substantial attention and political backing and should stir debate not just among legal experts but also within interested governments.

Another recommendation Weiss makes is to focus on the need for military humanitarian support forces, for he charges that in spite of the UN's mixed efforts in Bosnia-Herzegovina and Somalia, as well as the allied coalition's efforts in 1991 in Kurdistan, it is remarkably unsure about ensuring that truly opprobrious behavior against civilians by governments or insurgents will no longer be tolerated (Weiss 1993).

And last, Mr. Weiss argues that the UN must give "pride of place" to the new thinking about peace-enforcement units, for this is the crossover point after traditional peacekeeping. To this end, the Canadian government released a 1995 report on rapid reaction capability. The report notes that it is incumbent upon national governments to consider through greater research, education, and training the issues mentioned above if the international community is to respond decisively, quickly, and appropriately to an array of circumstances along the crisis continuum.

TOWARD A NEW PHILOSOPHY OF TRAINING AND PREPARATION

The NPP is based on the premise that with the continuing challenges of dealing with a bilingual and multiethnic society, Canada provides an excellent setting for leadership in peacekeeping. Canada also enjoys contacts and cooperative relationships with a wide range of both developing and multiethnic states. More specifically the demands of contemporary requirements mean that participants must be highly trained by experts in the know. The two common approaches to peacekeeping are professional and "off-the-street." The first is the one espoused by Canada. It holds that the best training for peacekeeping is training for general purpose combat. Quite simply, professional career soldiers are the best peacekeepers. Other "full-fledged peacekeepers," particularly in Europe and Australia, also have adopted this approach of maintaining a strong combat capability in their armed forces, who they will provide with mission-specific training as the nature of an operation becomes known. Denmark, on the other hand, has earmarked a particular formation as its reaction brigade and includes extensive "peacekeeping" training in its regular training schedule (Nishihara 1993). To an extent, "peace enforcer" countries such as the United States have also reiterated their support for multinational training and field exercises, as exemplified by former US President Bush's September 1992 speech to the UN General Assembly, during which he suggested the facilities of Fort Dix, New Jersey, be opened for just such a purpose (Nishihara 1993). However, in their case, the apparent preference is to simultaneously strengthen the combat function of UN peacekeeping operations, allowing the US to continue to play the role of police chief as it heads up an international coalition.

The second approach, or "off-the-street," is typically practiced by countries without professional armed forces. Personnel may or may not have reserve military force experience and may be recruited directly from among the civilian population. They are given basic training in a particular skill and then are dispatched to be part of a UN peacekeeping mission. The weakness of this approach, however, is that when these soldiers are faced with unexpected situations, there is no reservoir of experience and expertise from which to draw. It is thus acknowledged, at least in private, that the professional approach to peacekeeping is by far the more preferred.

"Self-restrained peacekeepers" such as Germany and Japan, however, respond to the call from the UN to contribute peacekeeping troops in a manner that falls under neither approach. Wanting to play a greater role in world affairs but still facing some constitutional and popular immobility, and to a significant degree the negative legacy of having had strong combat capabilities at one time, Germany and Japan have typically responded to the call for "peacekeepers" on an ad hoc basis, giving a limited amount of training and then dispatching peacekeeping units to a theater of operations to perform specific tasks. The internal debate has not been one of *do we want to contribute troops?* Rather it has been one of *how do we justify what their role will be?* For instance, in Germany the crux of the issue has not been whether Germany could send its forces overseas to play the role of "traditional peacekeepers" under the UN. There is broad consensus among the two major ruling parties and the opposition Social Democratic Party (SDP) on this point. The issue is whether Germany could participate in "combat missions" such as UN-sanctioned enforcement actions outside the NATO area without amending their national constitution. Likewise, Japan seems determined to find ways to strengthen its "non-combatant" contribution to UN-sanctioned missions (Nishihara 1993).

Recognizing that the best preparation for peacekeeping is general purpose combat training, there is a need to provide generic and scenario-specific education and training. There are certain characteristics, standard operating procedures, and interoperability mechanisms common to all peacekeeping operations that ought to be imparted to those who wish to be participants. It would also be of benefit to units and individuals if they could receive education and training appropriate to the particular mission on which they are about to embark.

It is no longer possible for a few countries to be peacekeepers to the world, or for military and humanitarian organizations to be isolated one from one another. The number of missions has increased at such a rate as to require the widest possible participation by a greater number of countries and the closest possible cooperation and coordination between the military and the other peacekeeping partners. It is thus in the interests of the countries and agencies with the most knowledge to pass it on to others willing to participate. In the post–Cold War world there is simply too much conflict for a few member states to manage without broad assistance.

This has made the training of special forces in the nuances of peacekeeping in the context of multilateral operations very attractive. Faced with fiscal constraints and the pressure to do more with less, governments are getting choosier about the conflicts in which they become involved. Coordination of effort and resources is the best solution, providing a way to pursue international peace, security, and stability without jeopardizing domestic demands. Moreover, coordinated effort or multilateralism offers a role to those state and nonstate actors that want one, regardless of the size or nature of their contribution. The whole cannot function effectively without the strength and diversity of its parts.

Multilateral operations also have the distinct advantage of exemplifying the cooperative behavior that is desired among disputing parties. As outlined above, the nature of conflict has changed to the extent that UN peacekeepers now are intervening in intrastate conflicts, often between deeply rooted cultural interests that strike at the core of perceptions of "self" and "nation." In order to be effective—that is, in order to initiate a process or dialogue—peacekeepers must be sensitive to the local environment. Working within the context of a multilateral operation may help to avoid the appearance of "imposition from the outside," instead demonstrating the ability of people of different cultures and vocations to cooperate.

There is, therefore, a need for a program that assists in the education and training of participants, at different levels and in different activities, in peacekeeping and development activities. The question of how peacekeeping training ought to be conducted is currently being debated within UN circles.

There are those who hold that it is a national responsibility, while others insist that there ought to be some sort of UN involvement to ensure a certain common level of competence. Many experienced peacekeepers are disappointed that the UN Secretariat officials and peacekeeping mission commanders are not more stringent when it comes to reprimanding those who are not able to carry out their assigned tasks. There appears to be too much of a concern for the feelings of the individual and for the possible reaction of national governments rather than a recognition that the Security Council mandate must be carried out in the most professional manner possible.

In addition to the share-the-load advantage to be gained by widening participation, there is the added advantage of the benefits that peacekeeping brings to the individuals who are members of the national contingents. The international awareness education, together with the citizenship duties performed, pay great dividends to the contributing country when the peacekeepers return home.

The UN was founded to prevent a third world war. Now we need to broaden our horizons and intensify our efforts to deal with the entire spectrum of contemporary and future challenges. We must make full use of the expertise of all the peacekeeping partners.

CONCLUSIONS

This chapter has proposed a new definition of, and a new partnership approach to, peacekeeping. Both are based on the concept of inclusion. It is clear that the changing face of peacekeeping reflects a changing international environment in which conflicts, particularly ethnic conflicts, are increasingly complex and in which the use of nontraditional peacekeeping methods is required to bring about the cessation of violence and a process that will enable disputing parties to consider the underlying source of their hostility. These methods may not always have the consent of the parties involved, but they will have the consensual support of the international community, for as conflicts proliferate among and, more importantly, between states, they jeopardize the future stability of the world order. The fact is that in the twenty-first century, as technology and the movement of people outpace our ability to redefine state boundaries, when conflict festers in one region it is likely to affect other regions too. This will most certainly be the case in "wartorn" countries pulled by competing and diverse demands.

Therefore out of necessity the great divide that once existed between the military and humanitarian aid agencies and between traditional peacekeepers of different states has been bridged. While objectivity, consistency, and impartiality remain standards for potential peacekeepers, there is also a requirement to balance national interest with the need to guarantee an acceptable measure of international peace, security, and stability. Though "conflict" in some form will remain a natural part of all relationships, it will be possible to dilute tension and to arrive at a "resolution." However, to achieve a measure of success will require greater integration of military and nonmilitary activities and actors, a division of labor, and a standardization of competence and skills—all premised on the continuing importance of the combat capability. For policy-makers this will mean a radical rethinking of the way governments prepare and deploy their troops for peacekeeping missions and a reevaluation of how best to balance national interest with the overriding purpose of contributing to global peace and the need for general combat capability with the need for mission-specific training. Also, it will mean concerted effort to translate to their domestic constituencies just what is the New Peacekeeping Partnership and how it falls within the realistic and multilateral framework of the post–Cold War environment.

For the United Nations the convergence of needs and actors of the New Peacekeeping Partnership will require the organization's infrastructure to "catch up" with global expectations and the pronouncements of the secretary-general. While the consensus is emerging that the United Nations is the forum of choice to deal with rapidly proliferating post–Cold War conflicts, that enthusiasm has not been matched by commensurate financial commitment. In fact, many member states are in arrears.

NOTES

1. For other definitions see Boutros-Ghali 1992, Berdal 1993, and the introductory chapter in this volume. Also see the work of Wiseman 1983.

2. For the full text of Mr. Pearson's speech see the *Toronto Daily Star,* 11 December 1957.

REFERENCES

Amer, R. 1994. "The United Nations Reactions to Foreign Military Interventions." *Journal of Peace Research* 31: 4.

Berdal, Mats R. 1993. *Whither UN Peacekeeping?* Adelphi Paper, no. 281.

Boutros-Ghali, Boutros. 1992. *An Agenda for Peace: Preventive Diplomacy, Peacemaking and Peacekeeping.* New York: DPI Press.

"Canada's Agenda for International Peace and Security." 1993. Seminar convened by the Hon. Barbara McDougall, secretary of state for external affairs, Ottawa, 8–9 February.

Capstick, Lt. Col. M. D., and Maj. D. M. Capstick. 1994. "Last Negotiation Training for Peace Operations: One Unit's Experience of Translating Theory to Practice." Paper presented for peace operation workshop held at the University of Maryland, 15–17 February.

Carment, David. 1994. "The Ethnic Dimension in World Politics: Theory, Policy and Early Warning." *Third World Quarterly* 15: 4.

Eide, Asbjorn. 1987. "Outlawing the Use of Force: The Efforts by the United Nations." In *The United Nations and the Maintenance of International Peace and Security.* Dordrecht, The Netherlands: Martinus Nijhoff Publishers, 99–145.

"Humanitarian Emergencies and Armed Conflict: The Possible Contribution of Outside Military Forces." Report to the International Peace Academy Workshop, New York, and the Ministry of Foreign Affairs, Helsinki, Finland, 24–26 October 1989.

Huntington, Samuel P. 1993. "The Clash of Civilizations." *Foreign Affairs* 72, no. 3: 22–49.

Laubich, Lori M. 1987. *Neutrality vs. Fairness: Can the Mediator's Conflict Be Resolved.* Working Paper Series 87–2. Cambridge, Mass.: Harvard Law School Program on Negotiation.

Lewis, Paul. 1993. "Reluctant Warriors: UN Member States Retreat from Peacekeeping Roles." *New York Times* [international edition], 12 December: 22.

"Life, Death and Aid: The Mèdecins Sans Frontières Report on World Crisis Intervention," edited by François Jean. Routledge, London (1993).

Morrison, Alex. 1992. *A Standing UN Military Force: Future Prospects.*

Paper presented at "Peacekeeping and the Challenge of Civil Conflict Resolution," University of New Brunswick, 25–26 September.

Moynihan, Daniel Patrick. 1993. *Pandemonium: Ethnicity in International Politics.* Toronto: Oxford University Press.

Mulroney, Brian. 1991. Address given at the Centennial Anniversary Convocation, Stanford University, Stanford, Cal., 29 September.

Nishihara, Masashi. 1993. "Trilateral Country Roles: Challenges and Opportunities." In *Keeping the Peace in the Post-Cold War Era: Strengthening Multilateral Peacekeeping.* Draft report prepared for the Trilateral Commission.

Pearson, Lester B. 1957. "Man Conquering Outer Space, but Not Himself—Close Gulf between Material and Moral Progress, Is Advice," *Toronto Daily Star,* 11 December: 17.

Waltz, Kenneth. 1959. *Man, the State and War: A Theoretical Analysis.* New York: Columbia University Press.

Weiss, Thomas G. 1990. *Humanitarian Emergencies and Military Help in Africa.* International Peace Academy, New York.

———. 1993. "New Challenges for UN Military Operations: Implementing an Agenda for Peace." *Washington Quarterly* 16, no. 1: 51–66.

Wiseman, Henry. 1983. *Peacekeeping: Appraisals and Proposals.* New York: Pergamon.

10

Ethnic Conflict at the International Level

An Appraisal of Conflict Prevention and Peacekeeping

DAVID CARMENT AND PATRICK JAMES

INTRODUCTION

Emerging ethnic identities present a fundamental challenge to the international community in the post–Cold War era. Much remains to be learned about the prevention of destructive ethnic conflict and peacekeeping for cases in which violence already is at hand. The contributions of this volume, which this chapter summarizes, are intended to provide both basic knowledge and insights about policy. With respect to basic knowledge, three objectives exist. The first is to identify domestic and international conditions associated with the onset of violent ethnic strife. A second goal is to relate this knowledge to preventive strategies for third-party interventions that promote early and rapid deescalation in tensions. Third, and perhaps most challenging, is the search for conditions under which proactive, conventional, and aggravated peacekeeping operations are likely to succeed. With respect to policy, the volume's approach is to provide a theoretical context for study of the potential for violent ethnic conflicts and existing mechanisms to deal with them, evaluate regional and global instruments for conflict prevention, and suggest a set of measures for the improvement of peacekeeping and conflict prevention policies.

Why are insights about both basic processes and policies related to ethnic conflict so urgently needed? Even a brief, four-point review of contemporary global politics is sufficient to answer that question. First, technological change sustains the trend toward more rapid escalation of international crises. Decision makers are pressured to make critical decisions in progressively shorter time intervals, and that is especially problematic when underlying conflicts concern explosive issues connected to ethnic identity. Second, international organizations and individual states experience a great deal of pressure to manage and even resolve ethnic conflicts. This perceived responsibility for action to preserve human rights and political stability is unlikely to go away. Third, a possible long-term decline in the utility of coercive diplomacy creates the need to coordinate military actions with diplomatic communications. This kind of cooperation is made difficult by a limited ability to demonstrate clear resolve and identify limited objectives, especially when the number of actors involved expands beyond a very few. Fourth, and finally, the size and diversity of the modern world creates problems for civilian control over military forces stationed abroad. These complications may even outpace improvements in communications and transportation, which makes peacekeeping a more risky and potentially unattractive venture with the passing of time.

Previous chapters make it clear that the UN, the world's leading international organization, is not equal to the challenges created by the preceding four factors. The pace of events is faster than ever before, pressure exists for help in multiple regions, coordination of diplomatic and military strategies is crucial, and ethnic conflict occurs in a larger and more diverse international system. The demands on the UN's abilities to manage and resolve ethnic conflict seem overwhelming when juxtaposed with the difficulties that the organization currently faces. Debates occur within the ranks of the UN over division of labor and burden sharing. The UN is still recovering financially from a recent phase of activity and must deal with the problem of unpaid dues from its members. Perhaps most important of all is the intense conflict with the US, by far the most important member of the organization, over a wide range of important issues. Collectively, the findings from this volume indicate that:

1. as the number of fatalities increase, the likelihood that third-party intervention will be successful is reduced (Harvey, Haglund & Pentland, Kaufman);

2. disputes involving interstate territorial or conventional security issues are far more amenable to successful third-party intervention than are intrastate ethnic issues (Ryan, James, Kaufman);

3. third-party intervention is most successful when the parties to a conflict possess a "legal" personality (states as opposed to nonstate actors) (Kriesberg, Morrison, Ryan);

4. multigroup conflicts are less amenable to deescalation due to agency and constituency problems (Kaufman, James);

5. strategic barriers to conflict reduction, such as intransigence, are due to a weak response from the international community and the gains expected from continued fighting (Harvey, Martin, Fortmann and Rousell).

Taken together, these problems mean that the UN, at least for now, is not equipped to manage or resolve ethnic conflict across the board. Thus the preceding chapters take seriously the idea that both theory and practical insight are needed if the UN and other international organizations are to achieve more in the areas of prevention and peacekeeping as related to ethnic conflict.

With these points in mind, this chapter summarizes the volume's contributions to understanding international politics as related to prevention and management of ethnic conflict. It proceeds in three sections. First, the management of ethnic conflict through peacekeeping is assessed. The second section focuses on prevention of ethnic conflict. Third, and finally, recommendations are offered about future efforts toward peacekeeping and prevention with respect to intrastate conflict.

MANAGING ETHNIC CONFLICT THROUGH PEACEKEEPING:
PROBLEMS AND PROSPECTS

Erosion of the Westphalian foundations of world politics coincides with the end of the international system shaped by the Cold War.[1] The increasing articulation of cultural and regional differences among indigenous populations, the growing incidence and scale of transnational migration and refugee flows, and heightened levels of ethnically based persecution, discrimination, and involuntary assimilation have rendered most societies multiethnic and assured the continuing significance of such differences. While not all of the disagreements between ethnic groups can be expected to escalate into violence, more than a few have produced intractable and destructive conflicts and one or more of these conflicts ultimately could reach a level that overwhelms international resources and capabilities. Not surprisingly, the explosion of ethnic strife around the world brings into question the capacity and commitment of international and regional organizations to prevent and manage ethnic strife.[2]

Peacekeeping is the nonviolent use of third-party armed forces to maintain peace among belligerents.[3] Peacekeepers act as impartial referees, working to keep the peace primarily through negotiations, persuasion, and reassurance. Given the nature of their task, peacekeepers can succeed only if all major parties to a conflict agree to their mission and cooperate in carrying it out. The responsibility of the international community is to provide skilled peacekeepers and support—material and diplomatic—for their operation. The conventional viewpoint is that peacekeeping is unlikely to be valuable if it goes beyond the traditionally cooperative basis and into assertiveness vis-à-vis one or more of the combatants.

Conventional peacekeeping is most effective in managing disputes between member states of the international system. Peacekeeping, in these conflicts, is essentially observation: the belligerents are separated and the peacekeepers are not vulnerable to attack. This type of peacekeeping most often occurs after a cease-fire is obtained and when force and interposition are deemed unnecessary. Thus, impartiality seems to work best where intervention is needed least: when the belligerents already have learned through bitter experience and sheer exhaustion that they are ready for the negotiating table.

A general perception now prevails that the fundamental nature of third-party intervention has changed. For example, the controversial tasks performed by at least some recent interstate coalitions might be regarded as incompatible with traditional peacekeeping. This view is reinforced by negative results from recent operations that outwardly adhered to traditional principles of belligerent consent, impartiality, and the use of force only in self-defense. It can become virtually impossible for third parties to refrain from using force beyond self-defense when operating in areas of ongoing hostilities.

Recent peacekeeping missions have taken place either in the midst of internal wars or prior to the outbreak of violence. Unlike those of the Cold War, which primarily concerned the resolution of interstate disputes after military engagements, newer peacekeeping missions focus on complex, intrastate, identity-based disputes. The most extreme example of this type, represented best perhaps by Somalia, is when an armed group operates outside the control of recognized political authorities and resists peacekeeping efforts.

According to James, a peacekeeping mission can in theory assist in guaranteeing agreements between ethnic disputants.[4] The task is made easier if the ethnic groups have reached a self-imposed "hurting stalemate."[5] Then the purpose of the intervention is exclusively to separate the forces and keep the peace. At this stage a viable peacekeeping mission may require territorial demarcation as well as some minimal agreement between enemies, which represents an intrastate equivalent to the traditional interstate peacekeeping efforts of the UN.

Third parties usually become involved in an intrastate ethnic conflict after other options appear to be exhausted. When vital interests are at stake in a conflict, intermediaries are unlikely to be very effective in bringing about a peaceful settlement. Disunity and lack of cohesion within the ranks of the adversaries can make it difficult for the third party to engage in meaningful conflict resolution because respective leaders lack the power or authority to make decisions or concessions. If peacekeeping is to succeed, leaders must consider either conflict management (a "kept peace") or resolution preferable to continued fighting *and* be able to convince their followers to accept that alternative and comply with it. States that support the peacekeepers' mission can help by using diplomatic pressure or coercive threats to persuade the parties to cooperate. Governments typically agree to the deployment of peacekeeping troops primarily to stop intervention by another international actor whom they fear more. In some cases, however, such as before the 1991–92 war in Croatia, the parties are so intent on violence that no credible coercive threat is likely to prevent war.[6]

This argument about peacekeeping is based on both theory and evidence. At the level of theory, Kaufman and James identify why peacekeeping intervention in an ongoing ethnic conflict is likely to give rise to considerable problems. Chiefly, it is suggested, this is connected to the depth of conflict and associated urgency of the need to come out on top. In consequence, peacekeepers are likely to be viewed instrumentally rather than as independent actors.

Assertive peacekeeping can turn peacekeepers, in the eyes of the adversaries, into participants in the conflict (Kaufman, James). The parties then will treat them accordingly. This development is entirely compatible with the peacekeepers' best efforts to behave impartially. Peacekeepers rarely succeed if they must use force. The UN Congo operation in the early 1960s is a rare example of forceful action by peacekeepers that succeeded, primarily because the opponent was weak and isolated. The Multinational Force in Beirut in 1982–83 illustrates the more common fate of peacekeepers who try to use force: they come to be perceived as belligerent and end up as targets of the side they appear to oppose.

Mandates also are more likely to change during the life of a peacekeeping operation. When other increasingly common problems, such as the absence of full consent from adversaries, the lack of an effective government in host countries, and the need for more robust rules of engagement are considered, the challenge to preventive peacekeeping can be appreciated.

Two recent and well-known operations, Bosnia (UNPROFOR) and Somalia (UNOSOM II), represent a transition in peacekeeping. These "assertive" or "second-generation" peacekeeping operations are characterized by refugees on a massive scale, more comprehensive peace plans, a basic recognition of the concept of peacebuilding, a generally broader application of military capabilities and expertise, and an emphasis on humanitarian aspects. Basic operational differences from traditional peacekeeping include a greater number and variety of contributors, the need for contact and cooperation with a much wider segment of the local population and authorities, and more complex coordination (see Morrison, this volume).

Peacekeeping is potentially useful for two kinds of tasks in ethnic disputes: preventing an internal conflict from becoming violent or spreading into an adjacent territory (Kaufman). However, given the nature of what peacekeepers do—the work normally includes persuasion, negotiation, and reassurance—they can be effective only if both sides to a conflict agree to and cooperate with their mission. Success is more likely if adversaries also recognize the limitations in using violence to resolve differences and are open to the conditions for peace presented to them. Lacking such acceptance and commitments, enforcement operations are likely to be ineffective at best and destructive at worst. Soldiers asked to operate under such conditions are exposed to a variety of potentially conflicting demands.

Morrison's analysis identifies several possible ways to make peacekeeping more effective. First, the more complex an operation is, the greater the need for operational clarity at the outset. The increasing number and variety of contributors and the need for cooperation with divided local populations and authorities adds uncertainty to a mission. Add the increasingly common need for higher intensity operations to the complications posed by the lack of effective government in host countries, and it becomes clear why an ambiguous mandate is to be avoided at all costs.[7] If leaders of NGOs, governments, and international organizations are uncertain about how a mission is to accomplish its goals (or, more significantly, the nature of those goals), potential for abuse of the procedures is greater.

Second, ethnic conflicts are multifaceted phenomena that demand a multifunctional response. Table 10.1 identifies current peacekeeping tasks. The list begins with more traditional purposes, such as military disengagement, and ends with preventive measures, like arms control and disarmament. The range of tasks that may face the UN and other organizations with respect to peacekeeping is truly daunting. Only in recent years are policy-makers beginning to understand the importance of proper peacekeeping. The costs of failure—material, political, and human—have led to sober second thoughts about the efficacy of ad hoc conventional peacekeeping and to something of a chill in the activity altogether.

Missions that involve goals clearly beyond those of traditional peacekeeping, such as neutralizing local forces and pushing belligerent parties towards the negotiating table, require different strategies and tactics (Harvey). Filling this doctrinal void requires research, education, and training. It also means recognizing those situations for which conventional peacekeeping is appropriate. Thus, the United Nations needs to improve the definition of missions, peacekeeping mandates, force levels, and budgets. Poorly implemented and ambiguous mandates are derived from a basic misinterpretation of adversarial will, oversimplification of disputes, and underestimation of mission complexity. Bosnia, for example, is less a failure of humanitarian principles than forethought and planning.

Table 10.1

Current Peacekeeping Tasks

Military	traditional peacekeeping functions such as separation of forces, observation, disarmament, and de-mining; military support for a range of political and humanitarian operations; and, if required, application of coercive military measures including a measured and appropriate use of force.
Political	the continuing need for negotiations by diplomatic and civil affairs personnel at strategic, operational and local levels.
Repatriation	the return and/or settlement of displaced persons and refugees.
Human Rights	the monitoring and enforcement of human rights guarantees.
Humanitarian Assistance	the provision of food, fuel, shelter and medical care in order to save lives and alleviate suffering.
Law and Order	the development of essential law and order structures such as civil and border police.
Reconstruction/ Rehabilitation	the rebuilding of infrastructure and the re-establishment of essential social functions including education, job-creation, justice, health and welfare.
Elections	the arrangements for, and implementation of, post-conflict democratic elections.
Arms Control/ Disarmament	development of such measures as the Conventional Forces in Europe treaty for the affected state(s) to enhance the prospects for longer term stability.

While the United Nations continues to be the dispute resolution mechanism of choice within the international community, the amount of conflict in today's world is simply too much for the military forces of a few states to effectively manage. Demand for peacekeeping services, in particular, is outpacing the UN's ability to supply. This imbalance is complicated further by the continuing reluctance of member states to provide commensurate financial resources. Thus an approach is needed that seeks to bring together all aspects and actors of post–Cold War peacekeeping, operating from the premise of general combat capability, yet recognizing the need for mission-specific training. States will have to be more discriminating about the sites and types of peacekeeping they choose. Furthermore, success should be defined not as resolution of conflict per se but instead as the cessation of violence and initiation of a process whereby adversaries can address underlying sources of hostility (Ryan).

PREVENTING ETHNIC CONFLICT

Conflict prevention encompasses a variety of strategies, including reassurance, acts of inducement (either deterrence or compellence) from a third party, and preemption. Preventive action can include positive (promises and rewards) and negative (coercion and punishments) strategies.[8] The contributors to this volume agree that third parties to a conflict should employ as many different preventive approaches as possible, including economic, political, and military initiatives. More generally, the crisis-management dimension of conflict prevention focuses on immediate control and reduction of violence (Harvey; Pentland and Haglund; Fortmann, Martin and Roussel; Kriesberg), while the long-term dimension pertains to development and political processes (Ryan, Morrison, Kriesberg). These categories are not mutually exclusive; the primary distinction depends on the utility of force as an instrument of conflict prevention.

For example, ethnic conflicts leading to crises call for superior leverage and leadership that are capable of directing, containing, and reducing the level of violence and spillover. Conceptualizing third-party intervention as a tool that the international community can use during bargaining with hostile militias is an important theoretical insight. Three military strategies are possible: peace enforcement, efforts at mediation coupled with low-intensity conventional peacekeeping, and withdrawal (Harvey). Each strategy involves risk. Inaction may precipitate undesirable outcomes, but forceful intervention can lead to further escalation and unnecessary costs for the intervener.[9] Finally, low-intensity missions may produce not only undesirable results for the third party but also lead to further gains for the aggressor (assuming that one side or the other can be identified in that role). Multilateral force, if applied at an ideal level, should be just sufficient to guarantee access to refugees, protect aid workers, and shield ordinary citizens.

Another immediate priority is commitment to a full range of political, diplomatic, and military instruments in managing a conflict. While such a comprehensive list is beyond the scope of any single state (let alone a group of states), with the appropriate major power backing and organizational support, violence can be reduced and conflict ameliorated. When the possibility of uncontrolled escalation is sufficiently clear, the great powers are compelled to support preventive action. Essential tasks include the containing of spillover effects and resolving specific humanitarian dilemmas within a regional context.[10]

Working alongside this basic reality has been a decided shift in conflict management approaches away from sponsoring proxy wars and toward accommodation of contending interests. A continuing military presence will be needed in some cases to deter regional aggression and guarantee assistance to hard-pressed minorities. Other occasions may call for rapid deployment of a coalition of forces to respond to state failure or imminent political collapse and possibly insurgency. The Bosnian crisis reveals that regional organizations (specifically NATO and the OSCE) have an emerging capacity to carry out these and other tasks in an effective and consistent manner. Over the long term, third parties have an important role to play in restructuring a state's security institutions and supporting specific civilianization tasks (Haglund and Pentland).

NATO peacekeeping operations represent a form of conflict prevention. Peacekeeping serves as means to a political end in two ways. First, commitments to support joint peacekeeping operations constitute a basic deterrent against undesirable regional adventurism. For example, the NATO Charter specifically defines the organization's responsibility for peacekeeping in article 5: members agree that an armed attack against one or more of them constitutes an attack against them all (Haglund and Pentland). Joint peacekeeping efforts also have a stabilizing influence through the integration of states into multilateral structures.

It is essential to recognize that the international community's most central preventive contributions will occur over the long term. Confidence-building measures and conversion of professionalized defense forces (which includes their de-ethnification and broadening commitments to collective security) are essential to lasting stability (Ryan). These are identified in table 10.2. Key factors that facilitate prevention of violent conflict include mutual restraint arising from identification with the adversary and availability of nonviolent avenues for expression and resolution of differences. States, international organizations, and NGOs might foster these conditions through early recognition of identity-based politics, unconditional dialogue, and acknowledgment of grievances through open and democratic processes (Kriesberg; Ryan). Although the right of secession should not be automatically ruled out, limits on self-determination and the rights of minorities remain essential to viable government (James). These limits are accepted broadly in international law, which gives the benefit of a doubt to states rather than insurgent minorities. States, however, lose both domestic and international legitimacy to the extent that they violate human rights and the collective aspirations of identity groups.

Ryan argues that the OSCE is a "trailblazer" in the area of conflict prevention. The OSCE institutionalized weekly meetings of the Permanent Committee and created a high commissioner for national minorities. Together, the Permanent Committee and the high commissioner are directed to contain and deescalate ethnic tensions. Thus the OSCE acts as a conduit for ethnic grievances. In the event that international efforts are successful in reducing overt tensions, long-term strategies become necessary. For new states this process includes the facilitation of transparency in national defense planning and enduring democratic control of the armed forces. The expression "democratic control of the military" generally is understood to mean subordination of the armed forces to democratically elected political authorities; however, less agreement exists on how to achieve it, what structures are necessary and what role should be played by parliaments (Martin, Fortmann and Roussel).

Table 10.2

Prevention of Ethnic Conflict:
A Summary of Techniques

1.	using preventive deployment, which due to changing circumstances and complexity of the situation requires a force that is highly mobile and has reliable, protected communications.
2.	establishment of enclaves that separate ethnic groups.
3.	guaranteeing and denying movement (which requires large and well-protected forces (ground and air) cargo aircraft, and increasing use of armor).
4.	providing guidelines for the international community to follow regarding the recognition of secessionist minorities and irredentist struggles and sanctioning states that do not follow these guidelines.
5.	including all participants in a conflict in the negotiation process.
6.	providing an internationally organized peacekeeping rapid reaction force as a legitimate deterrent for the reduction of violent interstate ethnic conflict.
7.	assisting the interim civil community which requires effort to establish containment sites and for the military to secure and supervise the handing over of weapons.
8.	ensuring the safe return of displaced populations and training local cadres to clear the war zone.
9.	continuing protection of humanitarian relief.
10.	using resolution techniques operating outside external state interference (assuming that the conflict has not resulted in the destruction of one or more groups) that allow the main antagonists to derive solutions at their own pace.

Conflict prevention is a political act with political ramifications (Ryan). Except for when a mediator is appointed for purposes of fact-finding or good offices—referring to preventive diplomacy—the very act of preventing conflict requires that sides be taken, rights wronged, imbalances addressed, and victims protected.

Redefining success forces actors to think creatively about measures and, in particular, the kinds of political arrangements that not only will contain and reverse the spread of ethnic unrest but prevent it in the long run. Beyond using traditional diplomacy and providing mediation, conflict prevention also means developing mechanisms that give representatives of communal groups incentives to enter into internationally brokered negotiations and arrangements. Above all, it means finding creative political solutions to the problems of disaffected groups. Foundations properly laid by efforts to create, among other things, fair systems of rules and distribution of scarce resources to meet basic human needs for survival and dignity will head off or at least control many problems.

Regional organizations offer several advantages in pursuit of conflict prevention, most notably, familiarity with the history of the locale and parties to an impending dispute. These organizations often have the most at stake and therefore generally are more willing to get involved. By their proximity to a conflict, regional organizations almost inevitably are involved, because their members must deal with refugee-related problems and other consequences. Finally, states that hesitate to refer a local dispute to the United Nations—for fear that it will no longer be under their control—may be more willing to see the matter addressed at a regional level (Haglund and Pentland; Fortmann, Martin and Rousell).

Regional approaches, of course, also entail some difficulties. To begin, regional organizations, almost by definition, cannot constrain actors from outside of their boundaries. Another shortcoming is that disciplinary measures such as sanctions, embargoes, and blockades are difficult if not impossible to impose. Regional organizations also tend to be reluctant to deploy military force abroad. Members states in regional organizations also tend to differ, sometimes in important ways, on procedures and norms; Germany versus France on NATO involvement is the classic example of this problem. For all of these reasons and others, peacekeeping by regional organizations is better when restricted to low-intensity activities. Anything more demanding than that will tend to bring out divisions among members and produce disappointing results.

Technical approaches to conflict prevention are likely to prove insufficient (Ryan). It is important that international organizations improve existing mechanisms for conflict prevention and resolution; the peacekeeping mission sent to Macedonia by the UN, for example, is a step in the right direction. However, a serious international response to the need for ethnic conflict prevention must go deeper in at least four areas.

One of the most urgent needs in every conflict-prone, multiethnic state is for creation of a civil society and denationalization of institutions. Such measures help to counter the claims by nationalists that the state is (and should be) the instrument of the dominant cultural group. In particular, norms and mechanisms for minority protection need to be developed. International monitoring may even be needed to ensure compliance with these norms. The UN and regional organizations are well placed to supply such support, but the resolve is not always there.

A second basic problem for conflict prevention is dealing with the international aspects of insecurity. Differences between regional actors who might want to intervene in ethnic conflicts for strategic, economic, or affective reasons need to be resolved. Alternatively, an attempt can be made to insulate a multiethnic state from destructive regional pressures, which also means settling the "territorial destiny" of disputed regions in a way that can satisfy the interests of all parties.

Third among the priorities is appropriate economic development. It is especially important for development projects to recognize the interests and needs of different cultural groups. International agencies such as the IMF and the World Bank would have to link aid distribution to the records of states in distributing wealth in a way compatible with the principles of ethnic development.

A fourth way to enhance conflict prevention would be through contingency planning, which allows policy-makers to prepare in advance for necessary actions and envision their proper timing. Contingency planning assesses the likelihood of each scenario and is constantly updated to reflect relevant changes in the environment. Such planning allows for integration of different programs of action that call for coordination among a wide range of actors at the national and international level. Like firefighters trained to treat every alarm as a genuine emergency, contingency planning must create the possibility for an effective response when each situation is viewed as a potential "worst case" scenario.

CONCLUSIONS

While the threat of violence by one country against another has not disappeared, the sources and the manifestations of conflict are changing. Struggles within states involving civil wars, local insurrections, or ethnic violence far outnumber those stemming from external aggression or conflict between states, especially in recent years.[11] Most recent interventions by the UN are motivated less by direct threats to international peace and security than images of violence that is fierce and costly in human terms.

Conflict prevention and peacekeeping entail concerted attention to specific problems in which the causes of strife are proximate and visible. Conflict prevention is not just a blanket scheme designed to address underlying tensions between groups. To act solely to prevent latent or underlying conflict is a misguided premise for designing any policy. When effectively channeled, intergroup tensions serve an important and functional role in all societies. Indeed, it would be extremely dangerous to assume that conflict prevention is automatically a neutral activity under such circumstances (Kriesberg).

For at least two reasons, there still remains a significant gap between identifying conditions associated with violent ethnic conflict and development of effective preventive measures. First, armed conflict is often an acceptable choice to leaders of ethnic groups if the alternative is loss of power, assimilation of the group, or, at worst, genocide. Early intervention is crucial, but rarely is there a collective political will to act prior to the outbreak of violence. Second, states need to better utilize the UN Charter Laws that are relevant to operations generally defined within the spectrum of peace support operations and examine how these can be strengthened. Current peacekeeping operations are ad hoc. Each mandate is defined for a particular case. How, under such circumstances, can international law on peacekeeping and peace-enforcement operations be strengthened? What status under international law should be accorded to individuals engaged in the types of operations above? Should the UN pursue a codified approach to clearly define the basic legal parameters and regulations for peacekeeping operations? These and other important questions remain unanswered.

Recent missions such as those in Somalia and Bosnia do not represent a failure of humanitarian principles. Instead, these missions lacked forethought, mandate, analysis, and planning. Matching an appropriate response to an escalating ethnic conflict is a complex task. If policy planners are uncertain of what they wish to accomplish, the greater the chance that the policy will fail. The ambiguous and poorly implemented mandates in Bosnia and Somalia derived from a basic misinterpretation of adversarial will, oversimplification of the disputes, and underestimation of mission complexity. Furthermore, results from preventive action should be amenable to assessment and follow-up: Did the conflict de-escalate? Did hostilities abate? Have refugees been reincorporated into state structures? Did a disruption in arms transfers or the removal of land mines reduce levels of violence? These and other specific questions must be answered if conflict prevention is to improve.

Final reflections on conflict prevention and peacekeeping focus on four points. First, conflict analysis must examine not only the triggers and root sources of conflicts but also the tools necessary for conflict reduction over the lifetime of a conflict. Assessments of various strategies in this volume (Kaufman, Ryan, James and Kriesberg), as well as by Lund (1996), Dixon (1996), and Diehl (1993), suggest that particular third-party strategies are suited to relatively narrow time frames within the phases of a conflict.[12]

Second, major powers are not likely to become heavily involved in preventing ethnic conflicts until it is clear that substantial political, military, or humanitarian benefits will be gained from the intervention. This finding is consistent with Alexander George's argument that the essence of statecraft is to develop and manage relationships with other states in ways that will protect and enhance one's own security and welfare. Lund has argued that a state will act in a way that favors its own particular interests and often a state may be unable to act until has secured the support of its public and/or political elite (Lund 1996). State interests may not always coincide expeditiously nor may they be self-evident in every instance. Therefore it is important to illuminate linkages, identify common ground, and locate associated opportunity structures.

Finally, rare is the direct proof that preventive efforts are responsible for accomplishing anything significant. Even if they have, leaders are confronted with a particularly difficult task when trying to mount large-scale preventive efforts. Thus, proposals on conflict prevention are often more farsighted than current circumstances permit. This is because the thinking of interested governments has yet to move sufficiently far to reshape their approach to the many ways in which peace is sustained. In other words, to effectively anticipate and address impending conflicts, the international community needs not only to consider revising the existing provisions and mechanisms for maintaining peace but changing the attitudes of its users and publics.

NOTES

1. See Ferguson and Mansbach, *Polities.*

2. Useful treatments of procedures for conflict prevention include Chigas et al., "Preventive Diplomacy and the OSCE," and Guillmette, "Beyond Emergency Assistance." See also Carment, "NATO and the International Politics of Ethnic Conflict: Perspectives on Theory and Policy"; institutional perspectives are identified in Bauwens and Reychler, *The Art of Conflict Prevention,* 1–21.

3. While the UN remains the principal organization with responsibility for peacekeeping, others with such responsibilities include the North Atlantic Treaty Organization (NATO), the Organization for Security and Cooperation in Europe (OSCE), the Multinational Force (MNF) in Lebanon, and the Unified Task Force (UNITAF) in Somalia.

4. Citations without year of publication refer to chapters in this volume.

5. See Zartman, "Alternative Attempts at Crisis Management."

6. Article 3 common to the 1949 Geneva Conventions expresses fundamental rules that are binding for everyone in all circumstances, whether the conflict is internal or external. Thus international humanitarian law protects people against abuse of power and sets limits on the conduct of military or police operations, which in turn provides the foundation for governments to exert pressure on combatants to refrain from the most egregious behavior.

7. For example, the mandate of UNOSOM II, covering the whole territory of Somalia, would include the following military tasks: (a) monitoring that all factions continue to respect the cessation of hostilities and other agreements to which they had consented; (b) preventing the resumption of violence and, if necessary, taking appropriate action against any faction that violated or threatened to violate the cessation of hostilities; (c) maintaining control of the heavy weapons of the organized factions which would have been brought under international control pending their eventual destruction or transfer to a newly constituted national army; (d) seizing the small arms of all unauthorized armed elements and assisting in the registration and security of such arms; (e) securing or maintaining security at all ports, airports, and lines of communications required for

the delivery of humanitarian assistance; (f) protecting the personnel, installations, and equipment of the United Nations and its agencies, ICRC as well as NGOs, and taking such forceful action as might be required to neutralize armed elements that attacked or threatened to attack such facilities and personnel, pending the establishment of a new Somali police force that could assume this responsibility; (g) continuing the program for mine-clearing in the most afflicted areas; (h) assisting in the repatriation of refugees and displaced persons within Somalia; and (i) carrying out such other functions as might be authorized by the Security Council. For more detailed treatments see "Peacekeeping Missions Current and Past" and Moreno and Vega, "Lessons from Somalia."

8. For example, John Ruggie (1993) developed a theory to clarify the strategic dimensions of third-party military intervention. Addressing the issue within the context of UN activity, Ruggie argues that there is a need to fill the "doctrinal void" between peacekeeping and peace enforcement. Peacekeeping, according to Ruggie, is an attempt to overcome a coordination problem between belligerents by enhancing transparency and establishing clearly defined rules of the game. Highly intense operations are compared to a game of chicken: an escalatory ladder of means up to and including war is used to "force an aggressor off its track" (29). Missions that involve goals clearly beyond those of traditional peacekeeping, such as seeking to neutralize local forces and to push belligerent parties toward the negotiating table, require different strategies. Ruggie proposes that international forces be given the means and mandate to "deter, dissuade and deny" (D^3) the use of force by local protagonists. If deterrence of violence fails, Ruggie argues, deployed forces attempt to dissuade parties from continuing military activities. Failure on this level necessitates the use of force to deny any one side military victory in a conflict.

9. The probability of successful third-party intervention without resorting to force depends on the ability of the third party to satisfy all four prerequisites for successful deterrence: communication, commitment, capability, and resolve. States are more capable than international organizations of satisfying more of these prerequisites, more often (Harvey).

10. Decision-makers need to determine whether rules of engagement should be changed for intrastate conflicts where there are refugees, unprotected citizens, and zones of turmoil and peace. A narrow reading of the peacekeeper's current "use of force in self-defense" does not extend to the protection of civilian populations in the UN area of responsibility. At least two questions become obvious: (1) Should changes to the rules of engagement that do not affect (i.e., broaden the authority of) the mandate of a mission remain the responsibility of the commander in the field?; and (2) How can methods be defined for individuals to engage in self-defense

in a way that includes authority to provide emergency help to the civilian population in the UN area of responsibility?

11. See Wallensteen and Sollenberg, "After the Cold War."

12. Howard Adelman (1996) argues that humanitarian realism is the appropriate frame of reference for developing and enhancing conflict prevention. Presumably, this perspective means that equal weighting be given to both state values and state interests in the formation of preventive policies.

REFERENCES

Adelman, Howard. 1996. "Responding to Failed States." Paper prepared for a conference on Canada and global issues. Ottawa, September, 1996.

Arend, Anthony Clark, and Robert J. Beck. 1993. *International Law and the Use of Force*. London: Routledge.

Bauwens, Werner, and Luc Reychler, eds. 1994. *The Art of Conflict Prevention*. London: Brassey's.

Betts, Richard K. 1994. "The Delusion of Impartial Intervention." *Foreign Affairs* 73, no. 6 (November/December): 20–33.

Carment, David. 1993. "The International Dimensions of Ethnic Conflict: Concepts, Indicators and Theory." *Journal of Peace Research* 30: 137–50.

———. 1995. "NATO and the International Politics of Ethnic Conflict: Perspectives on Theory and Policy." *Contemporary Security Policy* 16, no. 3: 347–79.

Carment and Patrick James, eds. 1997. *Wars in the Midst of Peace: The International Politics of Ethnic Conflict*. Pittsburgh: University of Pittsburgh Press.

Chigas, Diane, et al. 1996. "Preventive Diplomacy and the OSCE." In *Preventing Conflict in the Post-Communist World: Mobilizing International and Regional Organizations,* edited by Abram Chayes and Antonia Handler Chayes. Washington, D.C.: Brookings Institution, 25–97.

Diehl, Paul F. 1993. *International Peacekeeping*. Baltimore: John Hopkins University Press.

Dixon, W. J. 1996. "Third-Party Techniques for Preventing Conflict Escalation and Promoting Peaceful Settlement." *International Organization* 50, no.4: 653–81.

Druke, Luise. 1994. "The United Nations in Conflict Prevention." In *The Art of Conflict Prevention,* edited by Werner Bauwens and Luc Reychler. London: Brassey's Atlantic Commentarie.

Durch, William J. 1993. *The Evolution of UN Peacekeeping: Case Studies and Comparative Analysis*. New York: St. Martin's.

Ferguson, Yale H., and Richard W. Mansbach. 1996. *Polities*. Columbia: University of South Carolina Press.

Gurr, Ted, Robert. 1990. "Ethnic Warfare and the Changing Priorities of Global Security." *Mediterranean Quarterly* 1 (winter): 82–98.

———. 1992. "The Internationalization of Protracted Communal Conflicts since 1945: Which Groups, Where and How." In *The Internationalization of Communal Strife,* edited by Manus Midlarsky. London: Routledge, 4–24

———. 1991. "Minorities at Risk: The Dynamics of Ethnopolitical Mobilization and Conflict, 1945–1990." International Studies Association Annual Meeting, Vancouver.

———. 1994. "Peoples against States: Ethnopolitical Conflict and the Changing World System." *International Studies Quarterly* 38: 347–77.

Horowitz, Donald. 1985. *Ethnic Groups in Conflict*. Berkeley, Cal.: University of California Press.

Lund, M. S. 1996. *Preventing Violent Conflict: A Strategy for Preventive Diplomacy.* Washington, D.C.: U.S. Institute of Peace Press.

Mackinlay, John. 1993. "Defining a Role beyond Peacekeeping." In *Military Implications of United Nations Peacekeeping Operations,* edited by William H. Lewis. McNair Paper, no. 17. Washington, D.C.: Institute for National Strategic Studies.

———. 1993. "Problems for U.S. Forces in Operations beyond Peacekeeping." In *Peacekeeping: The Way Ahead,* edited by William H. Lewis. McNair Paper, no. 25. Washington, D.C.: Institute for National Strategic Studies.

Moreno, Rafael, and Juan Jose Vega. 1994. "Lessons from Somalia." *Peacekeeping and International Relations* (May/June): 11–12.

Moynihan, Daniel Patrick. 1993. *Pandemonium: Ethnicity in International Politics*. Toronto: Oxford University Press.

"Peacekeeping Missions Current and Past." UN Home Page (http://www.un.org).

Picco, Giandomenico. 1994. "The UN and the Use of Force: Leave the Secretary-General Out of It." *Foreign Affairs* (September/October): 14–18.

Roberts, Adam. 1996. "The Crisis in UN Peacekeeping." *In Managing Global Chaos,* edited by C. Crocker, F. Hampson, and P. Aaal. Washington, D.C.: U.S. Institute of Peace Press.

Ruggie, John Gerard. 1994. "The New U.S. Peacekeeping Doctrine." *Washington Quarterly.* 17: 4.

———. 1993. "The United Nations: Stuck in a Fog between Peacekeeping and Enforcement." In *Peacekeeping: The Way Ahead,* edited by William H. Lewis. McNair Paper, no. 25. Washington, D.C.: Institute for National Strategic Studies.

————. 1993. "Wandering in the Void: Charting the UN's New Strategic Role." *Foreign Affairs* (November/December): 26–31.

Sewall, Sarah. 1994. "Peace Enforcement and the United Nations." *Peace Support Operations and the U.S. Military*, edited by Dennis J. Quinn. Washington, D.C.: National Defence University Press.

Towards a Rapid Reaction Capability for the United Nations. 1995. Ottawa: Department of Foreign Affairs and International Trade.

Urquhart, Brian. 1993. "For a UN Volunteer Military Force." *New York Review of Books* 40, no. 11 (June 10): 3–4.

Wallensteen, Peter, and Margareta Sollenberg. 1995. "After the Cold War: Emerging Patterns of Armed Conflict 1989–94." *Journal of Peace Research* 32: 345–60.

Weiss, Thomas G. 1994. "Intervention: Whither the United Nations." *Washington Quarterly* 17: 109–28.

Wendt, D. 1994. "The Peacemakers: Lesson of Conflict Resolution for the Post-Cold War Era." *Washington Quarterly* 17: 3.

Whitman, Jim, and Ian Bartholomew. 1994. "Collective Control of UN Peace Support Operations." *Security Dialogue* 25: 77–92.

Wurmser, David, and Nancy Bearg Dyke. 1994. *The Professionalization of Peacekeeping: A Study Group Report*. Washington, D.C.: U.S. Institute of Peace Press, 1–67.

Zartman, William. 1988. "Alternative Attempts at Crisis Management." In *New Issues in International Crisis Management*, edited by G. Winham. Boulder, Colo.: Westview.

CONTRIBUTORS

David Carment is assistant professor of international affairs at the Norman Paterson School of International Affairs, Carleton University. His publications include articles in the *Journal of Conflict Resolution, Journal of Peace Research,* and *Third World Quarterly.* He is coeditor along with Patrick James of *Wars in the Midst of Peace: The International Politics of Ethnic Conflict* (1997).

Michel Fortmann is associate professor of political science and chair of military and strategic studies at the University of Montreal. His publications include *Diplomacy of Hope: Canada and Disarmament, 1945–1988* (1992) and *Proliferation et non-proliferation nucleaires: strategie et control* (1993).

David G. Haglund is professor of political science and director of the Center for International Relations at Queen's University. His publications include *From Euphoria to Hysteria: European Security after the Cold War* (1993) and *Can America Remain Committed? US Security Horizons in the 1990's* (1992).

Frank Harvey is associate professor of political science at Dalhousie University. His publications include articles in the *Canadian Journal of Political Science* and *Journal of Politics.* He is the author of *The Future's Back: Nuclear Rivalry, Deterrence Theory and Crisis Stability after the Cold War* (1996).

Alan James is research professor of international relations at Keele University. His publications include *Sovereign Statehood: The Basis of International Society* (1986) and *Peacekeeping in International Politics* (1990).

Patrick James is professor and chair of political science at Iowa State University. His publications include *Crisis and War* (1988) and *Politics and Rationality* (coedited with William James Booth and Hudson Meadwell, 1993).

Stuart Kaufman is associate professor of political science at the University of Kentucky. His publications include articles in *World*

Politics and *Journal of Slavic Military Studies.*

Louis Kriesberg is professor of sociology and director of the Program on the Analysis and Resolution of Conflicts at Syracuse University. His publications include *Intractable Conflicts and Their Resolution* (with Terrel A. Northrup and Stuart J. Thorson, 1989) and *International Conflict Resolution* (1992).

Pierre Martin is associate professor of political science at the University of Montreal. His publications include articles in the *Canadian Journal of Political Science* and *Comparative Politics.*

Alex Morrison is executive director of both the Canadian Institute of Strategic Studies and the Pearson Peacekeeping Centre. His publications include *The Voice of Defence* (1982) published by DND Canada, and *Nuclear Strategy in the 90s: Deterrence, Defence, and Disarmament,"* (1989).

Charles C. Pentland is professor of political science and scholar in residence at the Center for International Relations at Queen's University. His publications include *Issues in Global Politics* (1983) and *International Theory and European Integration* (1973).

Stéphane Roussel is a doctoral candidate in political science at the University of Montreal. His publications include articles in *Etudes Internationales* and *Canadian Defence Review.*

Stephen Ryan is professor of peace and conflict studies at Magee College, University of Ulster. His publications include *Ethnic Conflict and International Relations* (1991) and articles in *Ethnic and Racial Studies* and *Review of International Studies.*

Index

DAVID CARMENT is an assistant professor of international affairs in the Norman Paterson School of International Affairs at Carleton University in Ottawa. In addition to teaching courses on conflict analysis, mediation, and resolution, Carment is a North Atlantic Treaty Organization Research Fellow and former Military and Strategic Studies of the Department of National Defence of Canada Doctoral Fellow. In 1993–94 he held a Social Sciences and Humanities Research Council of Canada Post-Doctoral Fellowship at the Hoover Institution on War, Revolution and Peace. He has published articles on third-party intervention, ethnic conflict, NATO, and early warning in several journals, including *Journal of Conflict Resolution, Etudes Internationales, Third World Quarterly, Journal of Peace Research,* and *Contemporary Security Policy.*

PATRICK JAMES is a professor and chair of the Department of Political Science at Iowa State University. His publications include five books and sixty articles and book chapters, of which the book *War in the Midst of Peace* was also edited with David Carment. James has held the Milton R. Merrill Chair of the Department of Political Science at Utah State University and the Peace Fellowship at the Hoover Institution, Stanford University.